ADMINISTRATIVE
LAW

DELMAR CENGAGE Learning

Options.

Over 300 products in every area of the law: textbooks, online courses, CD-ROMs, reference books, companion websites, and more – helping you succeed in the classroom and on the job.

Support.

We offer unparalleled, practical support: robust instructor and student supplements to ensure the best learning experience, custom publishing to meet your unique needs, and other benefits such as Delmar Cengage Learning's Student Achievement Award. And our sales representatives are always ready to provide you with dependable service.

Feedback.

As always, we want to hear from you! Your feedback is our best resource for improving the quality of our products. Contact your sales representative or write us at the address below if you have any comments about our materials or if you have a product proposal.

Accounting and Financials for the Law Office • Administrative Law • Alternative Dispute Resolution • Bankruptcy Business Organizations/Corporations • Careers and Employment • Civil Litigation and Procedure • CLA Exam Preparation • Computer Applications in the Law Office • Constitutional Law • Contract Law • Court Reporting Criminal Law and Procedure • Document Preparation • Elder Law • Employment Law • Environmental Law • Ethics Evidence Law • Family Law • Health Care Law • Immigration Law • Intellectual Property • Internships Interviewing and Investigation • Introduction to Law • Introduction to Paralegalism • Juvenile Law • Law Office Management • Law Office Procedures • Legal Nurse Consulting • Legal Research, Writing, and Analysis • Legal Terminology • Legal Transcription • Media and Entertainment Law • Medical Malpractice Law Product Liability • Real Estate Law • Reference Materials • Social Security • Sports Law • Torts and Personal Injury Law • Wills, Trusts, and Estate Administration • Workers' Compensation Law

---

DELMAR CENGAGE Learning
Executive Woods
5 Maxwell Drive
Clifton Park, New York 12065-2919

For additional information, find us online at:
www.cengagebrain.com/delmar

ADMINISTRATIVE LAW

John D. DeLeo, Jr.

DELMAR
CENGAGE Learning™

Australia • Brazil • Japan • Korea • Mexico • Singapore • Spain • United Kingdom • United States

Administrative Law

John D. DeLeo

Vice President, Career Education Strategic Business Unit: Dawn Gerrain

Director of Learning Solutions: John Fedor

Managing Editor: Robert Serenka

Acquisitions Editor: Shelley Esposito

Product Manager: Melissa Riveglia

Director of Production: Wendy Troeger

Production Manager: Mark Bernard

Content Project Manager: Mark Bernard

Technology Project Manager: Sandy Charette

Director of Marketing: Wendy Mapstone

Channel Manager: Gerard McAvey

Cover Images: Getty Images

Cover Design: Bernadette Skok

Test Design: Judy Orozco

For product information and technology assistance, contact us at
Cengage Learning Customer & Sales Support, 1-800-354-9706

For permission to use material from this text or product,
submit all requests online at **www.cengage.com/permissions**
Further permissions questions can be emailed to
permissionrequest@cengage.com

Library of Congress Control Number: 2007943967

ISBN-13: 978-1-4018-5877-3

ISBN-10: 1-4018-5877-5

Delmar
Executive Woods
5 Maxwell Drive
Clifton Park, NY 12065
USA

Cengage Learning is a leading provider of customized learning solutions with office locations around the globe, including Singapore, the United Kingdom, Australia, Mexico, Brazil, and Japan. Locate your local office at **www.cengage.com/global**

Cengage Learning products are represented in Canada by Nelson Education, Ltd.

To learn more about Delmar, visit **www.cengage.com/delmar**

Purchase any of our products at your local bookstore or at our preferred online store **www.cengagebrain.com**

Notice to the Reader

Publisher does not warrant or guarantee any of the products described herein or perform any independent analysis in connection with any of the product information contained herein. Publisher does not assume, and expressly disclaims, any obligation to obtain and include information other than that provided to it by the manufacturer. The reader is expressly warned to consider and adopt all safety precautions that might be indicated by the activities described herein and to avoid all potential hazards. By following the instructions contained herein, the reader willingly assumes all risks in connection with such instructions. The publisher makes no representations or warranties of any kind, including but not limited to, the warranties of fitness for particular purpose or merchantability, nor are any such representations implied with respect to the material set forth herein, and the publisher takes no responsibility with respect to such material. The publisher shall not be liable for any special, consequential, or exemplary damages resulting, in whole or part, from the readers' use of, or reliance upon, this material.

Printed in the United States of America
2 3 4 5 6 15 14 13 12 11

To my son, Ben DeLeo

Contents

PART I
History and Creation of Administration Agencies   1

CHAPTER 1
Introduction to Administrative Law   2

CHAPTER 4
Adjudication—Judicial Power of Agencies
104

CHAPTER 5
Overview of Agency Activities
138

Cases by Chapter

Preface

INTRODUCTION

The text is written for college students who are taking an introductory course in administrative law. The text is also written for paralegals and for students in such courses as political science, government, and business that cover the agency regulation of businesses. The goal of the text is to take the mystery out of the study of administrative law by presenting a practical easy to read guide.

APPROACH

Administrative law is a unique field that can be difficult for students to grasp and to keep interested in the material. Teaching administrative law is likewise a challenge. This is so because administrative law is this strange conglomeration of learning the workings of thousands of agencies at the federal, state, and local levels. Agencies have been created by a variety of federal and state statutes over the nation's history, and as a result, each agency does things differently. Few subject areas are so varied. The federal Administrative Procedure Act (APA) is a unifying statute and provides a good framework (it does not include the underlying policy or substance of an area of law) that students should know. But the APA is limited in its scope and does not apply to state agencies, which have their own way of doing things in accordance with their laws. Further, state agencies (just like federal agencies) all function a little bit differently, thus hindering understanding by further splintering the subject matter. Fortunately for students and instructors as well, most students have had some kind of experience with administrative agencies. The approach of the text is to give a variety of practical examples of what agencies do and how they are controlled so students can relate their personal experiences and base of knowledge to how agencies function.

Many of the exhibits give practical information on what agencies do in society. For example, Exhibit 1-1 gives a list of events that can occur in the real world (such as a hurricane or plane crash) and then gives the agency that would respond. Exhibit 1-6 lists the agencies that might be involved in a business start-up. To meet the unique challenges of administrative law, the text does not attempt to cover substantive areas of administrative law but instead focuses on how agencies function procedurally. Substantive areas such as environmental, labor, securities regulation, tax, Social Security, workers compensation, consumer, worker safety, and banking law are at the core of administrative law and deserve separate texts of their own. However, it is hoped that this text will lay the foundation so that students will be prepared to take courses in these substantive fields.

ORGANIZATION

The text is divided into three parts. Part I covers the creation, history, and scope of administrative law; Part II covers the power of agencies; and Part III covers control of agency power. Chapter 1 explains how agencies fit into the constitutional structure of separation of powers and checks and balances. The creation of agencies through the enabling act is covered, and as an example, Exhibit 1-7 shows how the Department of Homeland Security was established. For context, a brief historical overview of the history of agencies is provided. Part II begins with Chapter 2 and covers the quasi-legislative power of rulemaking. Chapter 3 continues the coverage of agency power with executive power, followed in Chapter 4 with the agency power of adjudication. Chapter 5 surveys the multitude of agency activities including processing claims, licensing, inspections, recalls, and seizures of products. The various methods of Alternative Dispute Resolution (ADR) are covered as well as the Freedom of Information Act (FOIA) and the Privacy Act. Part III consists of Chapter 6 Judicial Control of Administrative Agencies, Chapter 7 Legislative Control of Administrative Agencies, and Chapter 8 Executive Control of Administrative Agencies.

FEATURES

- Chapter Objectives
- Chapter Outlines
- Sidebars
- Exhibits
- Case Law
- Chapter Summaries
- Key Terms

- Review Questions
- More Information
- Practical Applications
- Learn About the Agencies
- Web Sites to Access More Information
- Putting It All Together
- Administrative Law Summary
- Glossary

Chapter Objectives are included to give students a sense of what should be learned. The exhibits and sidebars aid in grasping the complex concepts. The More Information feature exposes students to the wealth of information on administrative agencies available on the Internet. The Practical Applications feature gets students involved by having the students apply the concepts learned in the chapter either through directed Internet exercises or through analysis of exhibits in the chapter. The Learn About the Agencies feature further exposes students to administrative law by having students access the agency Web sites and describe the function of selected agencies. The Appendices contain the Constitution of the United States, selected sections of the Administrative Procedure Act, Executive Order 12,866, a Putting It All Together feature, and an Administrative Law Summary. The Putting It All Together feature consists of the complete opinion of the global warming case from the United States Supreme Court, *Massachusetts v. EPA,* 127 S. Ct. 1438 (2007). As students read the case and work through the corresponding questions, they will see firsthand how the Supreme Court addresses many of the key concepts that are at the core of administrative law. The Administrative Law Summary allows students to quickly access key concepts of administrative law including the powers and controls of administrative agencies. Also included is a Glossary of key terms.

SUPPLEMENTAL TEACHING MATERIALS

- The **Instructor's Manual with Test Bank** is available on-line at www.paralegal.delmar.cengage.com in the Instructor's Lounge under Resource. Written by the author of the text the *Instructor's Manual* contains teaching suggestions and teaching tips for lectures, answers to review questions, chapter outlines, Internet exercises, and test bank.

- **On-line Companion**™—The Online Companion™ Web site can be found at www.paralegal.delmar.cengage.com in the Resource section of the Web site. The On-line Companion™ contains the following:
  - Study tips
  - Chapter outlines
  - Quizzes
  - Internet exercises
- **Web page**—Come visit our Web site at www.paralegal.delmar.cengage.com, where you will find valuable information specific to this book such as hot links and sample materials to download, as well as other Cengage Learning products.

Please note the Internet resources are of a time-sensitive nature and URL addresses may often change or be deleted.

Contact us at paralegal.delmar.cengage.com

Acknowledgments

I would like to thank Melissa Riveglia for all her help. Many thanks go to Shelley Esposito. Thanks also go to Pam Fuller. I appreciate the help of Naomi Atkins who offered valuable comments.

I would like to acknowledge the use of *Oran's Dictionary of Law,* 3rd edition by Daniel Oran, in preparing many of the Key Terms and the Glossary.

I wish to thank the following reviewers:

Ruth Astle
San Francisco State University
Oakland, CA

Bernard Behrend
Duquesne University
Pittsburgh, PA

Constance Herinkova
South College
Knoxville, TN

Linda Wilke Heil
Central Community College
Grand Island, NE

Scott Myers
Marist College
Poughkeepsie, NY

Daniel O'Shea
Suffolk University
Boston, MA

Beth R. Pless
Northeast Wisconsin Technical College
Green Bay, WI

Debra Wicks
Evans City, PA

PART I

History and Creation of
Administration Agencies

CHAPTER 1

Introduction to Administrative Law

CHAPTER OBJECTIVES

After reading this chapter, you should be able to:

- Demonstrate a basic understanding of the role that administrative agencies play in American society.

- Understand how and why agencies are created.

- Explain where administrative agencies function within the federal and state systems.

- Trace the historical background that shaped the development of administrative agencies.

- Categorize the types of administrative agencies.

- Examine the areas of law that come within the scope of administrative law.

CHAPTER OUTLINE

INTRODUCTION TO ADMINISTRATIVE LAW

Chances are that if a news matter has caught your eye or you are dealing with something in your personal life, administrative law is involved. This is so because an agency of the government, whether it is federal, state, or local, has a say in deciding many of the issues in our daily lives. Agencies are created by a legislature to deal with social problems. For example, take a look at Exhibit 1-1, which lists some issues and the corresponding agencies that have been charged with handling the issue.

As you look at this list, you may readily see that studying administrative law is challenging and will present a unique chance to examine a variety of relevant and interesting issues in an area of law that is critical to how society functions. Despite the variety that encompasses administrative law, there are common threads and basic principles that can be studied and understood. For instance, the basic principle of separation of powers, so familiar in constitutional law, is manifest in administrative law. The following sections will explain where administrative agencies fit within the constitutional structure that includes both federal and state authority.

Administrative Law and the Constitution

The United States Constitution is the supreme law of the land. All federal, state, and local agency officials must abide by the Constitution. The following sections will discuss the constitutional principles of separation of powers and federalism as those principles relate to administrative law. As you look at Exhibit 1-2, which sets out the structure of the federal government, note how the Constitution is listed at the top of the government. Then note the three branches of government which form the separation of powers. Next, examine the various departments of the executive branch of government, and lastly, observe a list of some of the agencies of the federal government.

Administrative Law and Separation of Powers

The Constitution created three branches of government. Article I created the Congress as the legislative branch, Article II created the executive branch headed by the president, and Article III created the judicial branch to interpret the law and resolve disputes. This separation of powers was designed to avoid the concentration of power in any one branch and to create a system of checks and balances within the federal government. For example, Congress passes bills, but the president can

Exhibit 1-1

Agencies and Their Functions

ISSUE	AGENCY
Hurricane	Federal Emergency Management Agency (FEMA)
Plane crash	National Transportation Safety Board (NTSB), Transportation Security Authority (TSA), Federal Bureau of Investigation (FBI)
Flu shot shortage	Centers for Disease Control (CDC), Department of Health and Human Services (DHHS)
Terrorism	Department of Homeland Security (DHS), FBI
Sexually explicit material on television	Federal Communications Commission (FCC)
The warning siren goes off at a nuclear power plant	Nuclear Regulatory Commission (NRC)
Irregularities in the stock market	Securities and Exchange Commission (SEC)
Sexual harassment	Equal Employment Opportunity Commission (EEOC)
The space shuttle explodes	National Aeronautics and Space Administration (NASA)
Two giant companies announce that they plan to merge	Federal Trade Commission (FTC) and Department of Justice
Injury on the job	State workers' compensation agency
Renewal of a driver's license	Motor vehicle agency
You lose your job	State unemployment agency
Permit to remodel your house	Local building, zoning, or other agency

either sign into law or veto the bill. The president negotiates treaties, but the Senate must ratify a treaty by a two-thirds (2/3) vote. The president appoints federal judges, including justices of the Supreme Court, but the Senate must approve the nomination. With respect to

Exhibit 1-2

The Government of the United States

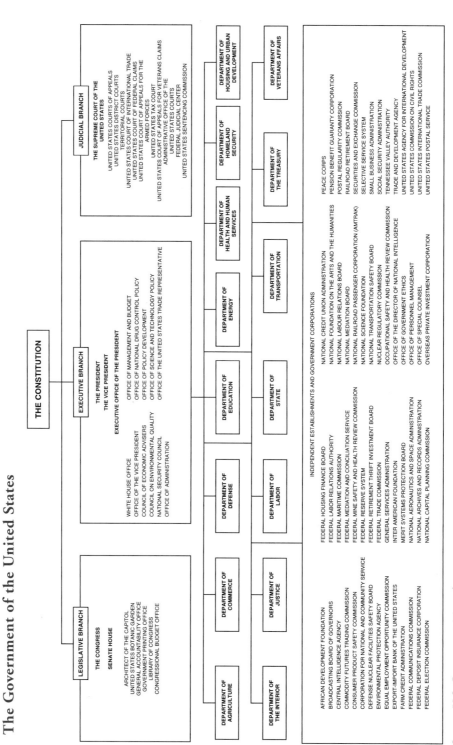

Source: U.S. Government Manual

administrative law, Congress can pass a bill creating an agency, but the president can veto the bill so that the agency will not come into existence. See Chapter 7 for some of the key Supreme Court cases on separation of powers and the role played by the president and Congress. Critical to separation of powers and checks and balances is the power of the courts to declare laws passed by Congress and the president to be unconstitutional. This power, stemming from the case of *Marbury v. Madison*, 5 U.S. 137 (1803), is called the power of *judicial review*. Under the power of judicial review, even if the Congress and president agree and pass a law, the Supreme Court can check the power of the other branches by declaring the law unconstitutional.

> **Like the federal system, all states have constitutions involving separation of powers and checks and balances.**

Administrative Law and Federalism

To further avoid concentrations of power, the Constitution divides power again between the federal and state governments under the principle of *federalism*. The framers of the Constitution felt that federalism provided a double layer of security to protect the rights of the people. The *Tenth Amendment* states that all powers not delegated to the federal government are reserved to the states and the people; hence, states retain their *sovereignty* alongside the federal government in the system of federalism. States are free to pass any laws (including administrative laws and the creation of administrative agencies) as long as those laws do not conflict with the Constitution or federal law. If a state law conflicted with the Constitution or federal law, the state law would be nullified or *preempted* under the *Supremacy Clause* of the Constitution. Article VI, Clause 2 states that the Constitution and federal law is the supreme law of the land. For example, if a state passed a law creating an agency to regulate nuclear power, that law would be preempted by federal law because Congress has preempted or taken over the entire field of nuclear power.

When states exert sovereignty by establishing agencies in such areas as marriage, traffic control, or worker safety, the states are exercising what is called *police power*. Police power is the power not delegated to the federal government and which is retained by the states to pass laws to protect the health, safety, and welfare of its citizens. The federal government does not possess police power. When Congress

judicial review
the power to declare acts of Congress, actions of the president and acts of the states unconstitutional when those acts conflict with the Constitution

federalism
the division of power into one federal government and the governments of the 50 states

Tenth Amendment
the amendment that states that all powers not given to the federal government are reserved to the states and the people

sovereignty
the supreme, absolute and uncontrollable power by which an independent state is governed

preempted
when Congress takes over an entire field of law by passing laws under the Supremacy Clause with the effect of nullifying conflicting state law

Supremacy Clause
Article VI, Clause 2 of the Constitution, which makes the Constitution and federal laws superior to conflicting state law

police power
power of the states to pass laws to protect the health, safety, and welfare of citizens

enumerated powers

the powers granted to Congress and listed specifically in Article I of the Constitution

Necessary and Proper Clause

the provision of the Constitution (Article I, Section 8, Clause 18) that gives Congress the power to pass all laws appropriate to carry out its functions; also called the elastic clause

interstate commerce

things, people, and commercial activities that cross state lines

commerce clause

the provision of the Constitution (Article I, Section 8, Clause 3) that gives Congress power to control interstate commerce; also known as *commerce power*

concurrent power

power that is possessed by both the federal and state governments

acts, it must base the law on one of the *enumerated powers* contained within the Constitution. The enumerated powers are listed in Article I and include the power to tax and spend, coin money, declare war, and regulate interstate commerce. By enumerating or delegating these powers, the Constitution limits Congress to these specified areas. However, Congress can also make all laws that are "necessary and proper" for carrying into execution the enumerated powers. The *Necessary and Proper Clause* is also called the elastic clause because it has the effect of stretching the reach of the enumerated powers. When the Necessary and Proper Clause is coupled with the enumerated powers, the scope of what Congress can do (including the area of administrative law) far exceeds the enumerated powers listed in Article I. For example, Congress passed the 1964 Civil Rights Act outlawing discrimination based on its power over *interstate commerce* (known as the *commerce clause* or commerce power) and the Necessary and Proper Clause. The Equal Employment Opportunity Commission (EEOC) is the federal agency created under the Civil Rights Act to enforce its provisions. Similarly, Congress has used its commerce power to pass legislation in administrative law in such fields as the environment (creating the Environmental Protection Agency [EPA]), worker safety (creating the Occupational Safety and Health Administration [OSHA]), and consumer protection (creating the Consumer Product Safety Commission [CPSC]).

It must also be noted that in many areas the federal and state governments have the same powers. This shared authority, or *concurrent power*, accounts for the fact that often federal and states agencies operate within the same field of administrative law. For example, both the federal government and the states have agencies that deal with taxes, consumer protection, and worker safety. See Exhibit 1-3 for an overview of federal and state power.

> The states also have constitutions, which establish the office of governor, the state legislature, and the state court system. State legislatures in turn create and delegate power to state agencies.

Although there is no constitutional provision which establishes administrative agencies, the emergence of administrative law in the modern system of government has spurred many to call agencies the unofficial

Exhibit 1-3

Federal versus State Power

FEDERAL POWER	STATE POWER	SHARED POWER
Interstate commerce	Intrastate commerce	Certain criminal laws
Immigration and naturalization	General health and welfare laws (police power)	Taxes
Foreign affairs		Worker safety laws
Treaties		Consumer laws
Declaring war	Real estate laws	Housing
Coining money	Family laws	Banking
	Inheritance and laws on wills	Employment laws
	Licensing of most professions	

"fourth branch of government." Agencies, as the "unofficial fourth branch," possess legislative power and issue *regulations* similar to statutes passed by Congress or a state legislature. Moreover, agencies possess *executive power* (see Chapter 3) similar to that of the president or a governor as they investigate and enforce their regulations. Lastly, agencies possess a form of judicial power in that they often have authority to *adjudicate* disputes (see Chapter 4) by holding hearings, like courts of law, to determine if their regulations have been violated. For example, the EPA issues regulations (legislative power) to implement Congress' desire to protect the environment; the EPA enforces the regulations it issues (executive power) and then holds a hearing (judicial power) to determine if a business is in violation of its regulation. See Exhibit 1-4.

The *delegation* of legislative, executive, and judicial powers to the EPA by Congress at first glance might appear to violate the fundamental principles of separation of powers and of checks and balances so crucial to our constitutional structure. The framers of the Constitution were very worried that concentration of power was a threat to freedom and so created the three branches with defined powers. However, as we shall see in more detail in this chapter, the Supreme Court has ruled that if done properly, delegation of power to an agency is constitutional. The supreme courts of many states have made similar rulings.

rule or regulation
a statement by an agency that sets policy and has the force of law

executive power
power to investigate and carry out rules and regulations

adjudicate
power of courts to hold hearings and settle disputes

delegation
the transfer of power from Congress to an executive agency

Exhibit 1-4

Separation of Powers and Powers of Agencies

CONSTITUTIONAL ARTICLE	BRANCH	POWER
Article I, Section 1 Legislative Power	Congress	To enact laws
"All legislative Powers herein granted shall be vested in a Congress of the United States, which shall consist of a Senate and a House of Representatives. . ."		
Article II, Section 1 Executive Power	President	To enforce and execute the laws
"Executive Power shall be vested in a President of the United States. . ."		
Article III, Section 1 Judicial Power	Judiciary	To interpret the law and settle disputes
"The judicial Power of the United States, shall be vested in one supreme Court, and in such inferior Courts as the Congress may from time to time ordain and establish. . ."		

POWER POSSESSED BY MANY AGENCIES

Legislative—agencies issue regulations which have the force of law.

Executive—agencies investigate and enforce their regulations.

Judicial—agencies hold hearings and determine if their regulations have been violated.

Many times in administrative law, the Latin term "quasi" is placed before the three powers possessed by agencies to demonstrate the distinct role that agencies play. For example, agencies are said to possess quasi-executive power, quasi-legislative power, and quasi-judicial power. Quasi merely means "sort of" or "as if."

Administrative Law and Administrative Agency Defined

The definition of an agency reinforces the preceding principles. An *administrative agency* is a subbranch of the government set up by a legislature to carry out laws by wielding legislative, executive, and judicial power. *Administrative law* is the study of how agencies are created, how agencies do their work in exercising their delegated powers, and how agencies are controlled. The core functions of agencies are to address economic and social issues. See Exhibit 1-5.

administrative agency

a subbranch of the government set up by a legislature to carry out laws by wielding legislative, executive, and judicial power

administrative law

the study of how agencies are created, how agencies do their work in exercising their delegated powers, and how agencies are controlled

Exhibit 1-5	
Function and Role of Agencies	
Address economic values	Regulation of economic markets, through enforcement of antitrust, antimonopoly, and restraint of trade laws
Address social values	Regulation of environment, protection of public health, protection of workers, enforcement of antidiscrimination laws, and delivery of social services

This chapter will cover how agencies are created, the constitutional issues involved in their creation, and the different kinds of agencies. Legislatures create agencies to accomplish the goals that they set, whether that goal is to clean up the environment or to improve worker safety. Agencies offer numerous advantages in meeting the identified goals. These advantages include:

- flexibility—to resolve disputes with a minimum of formal procedures
- efficiency—to resolve disputes in a timely manner
- expertise—to employ experts to assist in meeting legislative goals

Agencies are sometimes created as a reaction to some kind of triggering event that occurs in society. For example, the United States Department of Homeland Security was created in response to the terrorist attacks of September 11. Some branch of the government must be tasked with addressing these problems, and Congress or a state legislature has decided that an agency is better equipped to handle the matter. Congress makes a judgment when it passes a statute creating the agency that an agency is better suited to do the job. In addition to flexibility, efficiency, and expertise, Congress may not want to be politically accountable on certain hot topics. For example, with an issue such as Social Security reform or closure of military bases, Congress creates a commission to make recommendations. These recommendations may anger or be unpopular with important constituencies, so Congress may wish to step back from the issue. Congress has ultimate responsibility, but Senators and members of the House of Representatives can often deflect political pressure by pointing to the commission, which was responsible for the unpopular action (such as raising Social Security taxes).

To look at administrative law in a practical manner, imagine a person starting a restaurant. How does administrative law impact the restaurant industry? Look at Exhibit 1-6 and the agencies involved in starting and maintaining a restaurant.

To round out this introduction to administrative law, it must be noted that as powerful as agencies are, controls are in place to check that power. For example, if an agency issues a regulation or adjudication with respect to the issues contained in Exhibit 1-1, that decision can be challenged in the courts. Part III of the text examines in detail the various checks on the power of administrative agencies. We turn now to a more detailed discussion of the creation of administrative agencies, delegation of power, and separation of powers issues.

Creation of Agencies, Issues of Separation of Powers, and Delegation

enabling act

a statute which creates and empowers an administrative agency

Agencies are created when Congress or a state legislature passes a statute known as an *enabling act*. The enabling act not only creates the agency, but it also empowers the agency with legislative power (power to issue rules or regulations), executive power (power to investigate and enforce its rules), and judicial power (power to hold hearings and determine if its regulations have been violated). The legislature transfers power and delegates its authority to the administrative agency by enactment of the enabling act. The legislature is in effect saying "agency go forth and work on the problem." See Exhibit 1-7 to trace the path of a Congressional bill, as that bill becomes a law creating the Department of Homeland Security.

Amendments to an agency's powers and termination of an agency must go through the same process as that indicated in Exhibit 1-7. Once created, the agency can get on with the mission that was laid out in the enabling act. See Exhibit 1-8, Organizational Chart for Department of Homeland Security. To read a history of the Department of

Exhibit 1-6

Agencies and Businesses

ISSUE	AGENCY
Taxes	Internal Revenue Service (IRS) and state and local tax agencies
Obtain a liquor license	State licensing authority
Cover employees for Social Security	Social Security Administration (SSA)
Cover employees for workers' compensation and unemployment compensation	State agencies
Sexual harassment, gender, racial, or religious discrimination	Equal Employment Opportunity Commission (EEOC) and state agency
Safety on the job	Occupational Safety and Health Administration (OSHA)
Health inspections	State and local agencies
Quality control on food	Department of Agriculture (DOA)
	State agencies and Centers for Disease Control (CDC)
	Food and Drug Administration (FDA)
Advertising	Federal Trade Commission (FTC) and state agencies
Legal status of employees	United States Citizenship and Immigration Service (USCIS) and Immigration and Customs Enforcement (ICE)

Homeland Security and to see which agencies became a part of the department, go to http://www.dhs.gov/xabout/history/editorial_0133.shtm.

The delegation of power by Congress to agencies has raised constitutional concerns over the years. These concerns are reflected in the Supreme Court's establishment of what has been called the nondelegation doctrine. The Supreme Court has at times referred to the transfer of power to agencies as the *delegation doctrine* and sometimes as the *nondelegation doctrine*, because the Court struggled to find a consistent approach to the constitutional status of agencies.

delegation doctrine

when Congress creates an agency by passing a law (an enabling act) and transferring power to the agency. The transfer of legislative, executive, and judicial power is delegation that gives life to the agency and enables the agency to do its work.

nondelegation doctrine

the limits and requirements for a constitutionally valid transfer of power to an agency as established by the Supreme Court

Exhibit 1-7

How an Agency Is Created

Congress—Article I

House   Senate

CREATION OF DEPARTMENT OF HOMELAND SECURITY

PATH OF A BILL

Events of September 11 trigger a need for improved security

V

Bill H.R. 5005 to establish the Department of Homeland Security is introduced on June 24, 2002

Assigned to various Committees

V

Committees hold Hearings

V

Committee Report issued

V

H.R. 5005 is discharged from all Committees and is ready for a vote

V

Debate and Passage

V

Final Vote in House 295 – 132 on July 26, 2002

V

Senate
Considered by Senate from September 4 until September 22, 2002

V

Senate votes 94 – 0 with amendments

V

House agrees to Senate amendments

V

Signed into law by the President on November 25, 2002

V

Becomes Public Law No: 107-296 (which is the Enabling Act)

Exhibit 1-8

Organizational Chart for Department of Homeland Security

U.S. DEPARTMENT OF HOMELAND SECURITY

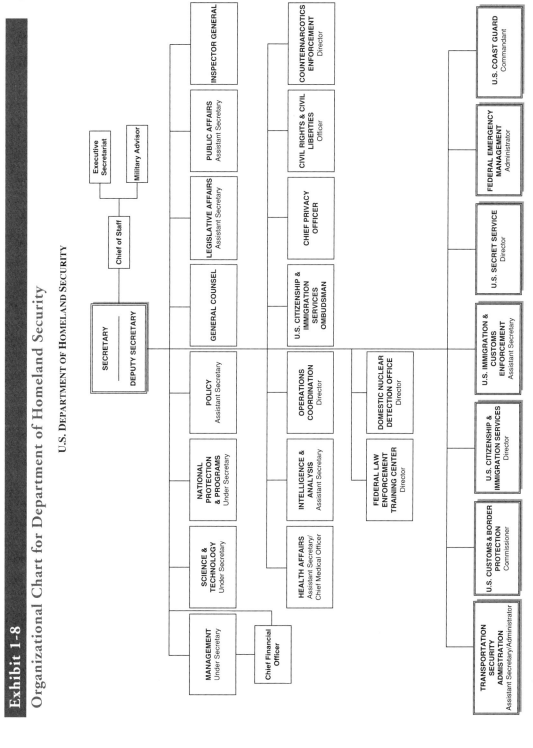

Source: http://www.dhs.gov

Exhibit 1-9

Delegation Doctrine and Nondelegation Doctrine

Delegation Doctrine—Congress creates an agency by passing a law (an enabling act) and transferring power to the agency. The transfer of legislative, executive, and judicial power is delegation that gives life to the agency and enables the agency to do its work.

Nondelegation Doctrine—The limits and requirements for a constitutionally valid transfer of power to an agency as established by the Supreme Court.

For the current discussion, think of the delegation doctrine and the nondelegation doctrine as representing two sides of the same constitutional principle. The delegation doctrine can be defined as the transfer of power to the agency, while the nondelegation doctrine sets the limits and requirements for a constitutionally valid transfer of power. See Exhibit 1-9 for an overview of delegation and nondelegation.

In support of the nondelegation doctrine, the Court stated in *Field v. Clark*, 143 U.S. 649, 692 (1892), "[t]hat Congress cannot delegate legislative power to the president is a principle universally recognized as vital to the integrity and maintenance of the system of government." The Court in a number of such cases reflected that the framers of the Constitution were so concerned about separating power to avoid concentrations of power that they created the system of separation of powers and check and balances. Therefore, creating an administrative agency and giving the agency legislative, executive, and judicial power seems to violate the constitutional structure represented in the nondelegation doctrine. As the following quote indicates, the Supreme Court has found value in the nondelegation doctrine and has identified three functions that the nondelgation doctrine performs.

> As formulated and enforced by this Court, the nondelegation doctrine serves three important functions. First, and most abstractly, it ensures to the extent consistent with orderly governmental administration that important choices of social policy are made by Congress, the branch of our Government most responsive to the popular will. Second, the doctrine guarantees that, to the extent Congress finds it necessary to delegate authority, it provides the recipient of that authority with an "intelligible principle" to guide the exercise of the delegated discretion. Third, and derivative of the second, the doctrine ensures that courts charged with reviewing the exercise of delegated legislative discretion will be able to

test that exercise against ascertainable standards, *Industrial Union Department v. American Petroleum Institution,* 448 U.S. 607, 685 (1980) (Rehnquist, J., concurring).

The issue can be laid out as follows: Article I of the Constitution clearly states that all legislative power shall be vested in the Congress, so it could be argued that Congress cannot delegate power to an agency. The logical extension of this reasoning would leave no room for administrative agencies. To keep the valuable aspects of the nondelgation doctrine with its adherence to separation of powers while at the same time realizing the practical necessity of administrative agencies, the Court had developed another doctrine called an *intelligible principle.* If Congress expresses an intelligible principle to which the agency is directed to conform, then the delegation is legal.

An intelligible principle sets standards to which an agency must adhere but still allows the flexibility for the agency to act while implementing the will of Congress. "It is not necessary that Congress supply administrative officials with a specific formula for their guidance in a field where flexibility and adaptation of the congressional policy to infinitely variable conditions constitute the essence of the program," *Lichtner v. United States,* 334 U.S. 742, 786 (1948). Using the intelligible principle standard to judge delegation, the Supreme Court has ruled only twice that the Congress delegated power to the president or an agency in an unconstitutional manner. Both cases struck down key parts of President Franklin Roosevelt's New Deal legislation, which was designed to get the country out of the Great Depression in the 1930s. In *A.L.A. Schechter Poultry Corp. v. United States,* 295 U.S. 495 (1935), Congress delegated broad power to the president for him to set codes of fair competition in the poultry industry. In what has been labeled the "sick chicken" case, the Court ruled that Congress never transferred an intelligible principle for the president to govern the writing of the codes. In other words, the delegation of authority from Congress to the president was considered too broad and therefore was invalid. In *Panama Refining Co. v. Ryan,* 293 U.S. 388 (1935), known as the "hot oil" case, the Supreme Court invalidated a delegation of power that allowed the president to prohibit the transportation of oil in interstate commerce. One other case from the 1930s should also be noted. In *Carter v. Carter Coal Co.,* 298 U.S. 238 (1936), the Court struck down a delegation of power to private groups. The Court stated that delegations to private groups were the "most obnoxious form of delegation."

These cases reflect the Supreme Court's concern about the proper delegation of authority from Congress to the executive branch. However, since the 1930s and in recognition of the critical importance that

intelligible principle
the principle that when Congress delegates power to an agency, the delegation includes enough guidelines and standards for the agency to exercise that power in a constitutional manner

agencies have come to play in modern society, the Court has invariably allowed delegations of power to the president and agencies. The case of *Yakus v. United States,* 321 U.S. 414 (1944), is illustrative of this modern approach. In *Yakus,* Congress delegated power to an agency to set maximum prices for certain products. The Court upheld the delegation even though the agency had little guidance from Congress on the prices to be set.

In *Amalgamated Meat Cutters and Butcher Workmen v. Connally,* 337 F. Supp. 737 (D.D.C. 1971) (see excerpt in Case Law at the end of the chapter), a federal law delegated to the president the power to freeze prices, rents, wages, and salaries. The Court upheld the delegation of this power to the president. The Court found that the law supplied sufficient standards because it did not permit the president to set prices and wages below their level on May 25, 1970. In addition, the law precluded the president from singling out a particular sector of the economy in which to impose controls, absent a finding that wages or prices in that sector had increased disproportionately.

In 2001, the Supreme Court again looked at the nondelegation doctrine in *Whitman v. American Trucking Association,* 531 U.S. 457 (2001), and reaffirmed the power of agencies. In *Whitman,* the Supreme Court upheld the power of the EPA to establish uniform standards of certain pollutants at levels that protect public health.

See Exhibit 1-10 for a listing of key cases on delegation. Note that when the delegation is upheld, the Court has found an intelligible principle to measure whether the agency has properly used the power delegated to it by Congress. When an issue of delegation is raised, the focus is not on the delegation itself but on the *agency's use* of the power delegated to it by Congress. For example, the Secretary of Labor and the Occupational Safety and Health Administration were authorized by Congress in the Occupational Safety and Health Act of 1970, 29 U.S.C.A. Section 655(b)(5), to set standards "which most adequately assures, to the extent feasible, on the basis of the best available evidence that no employee shall suffer impairment of health . . ." In both *Industrial Union Dept., AFL-CIO v. American Petroleum Institute,* 448 U.S. 607 (1980), (see excerpt in Case Law at the end of the chapter) and *American Textile Mfgs. Institute v. Donovan,* 452 U.S. 490 (1981), the Court upheld the *delegation* of power. However, in *Industrial Union,* the Court struck down the benzene standards set by OSHA because OSHA had not made the findings of significant risk to health required under the statute. In *American Textile,* however, the Court upheld a rule that set cotton dust standards because OSHA had made a finding that cotton dust was a significant

Exhibit 1-10

Delegation of Power—Key Cases

CASE	DELEGATION OF POWER FROM CONGRESS TO PRESIDENT OR AGENCY	RESULT
Schechter Poultry Corp. v. United States (1935) (sick chicken case)	President authorized to issue a code of fair competition in the poultry industry	Unconstitutional delegation of power
Panama Refining Co. v. Ryan (1935) (hot oil case)	President authorized to prohibit interstate shipment for oil	Unconstitutional delegation of power
Carter v. Carter Coal Co. (1936)	Private groups authorized to issue a code of conduct in the coal industry	Unconstitutional delegation of power
National Broadcasting Co. v. United States (1943)	FCC authorized to regulate public airwaves in the public interest	Delegation of power upheld
Yakus v. United States (1941)	Agency given power to set prices of commodities at a level that will be fair and equitable	Delegation of power upheld
Kent v. Dulles (1958)	Secretary of State given power to issue passports	Delegation of power upheld
Arizona v. California (1963)	Secretary of the Interior authorized to allocate water rights	Delegation of power upheld
Industrial Union Dept., AFL-CIO v. American Petroleum Institute (1980) (striking down benzene standards); *American Textile Mfgs. Institute v. Donovan* (1981) (upholding cotton dust standards)	OSHA and Secretary of Labor authorized to set the standards which most adequately assures, to the extent feasible, on the basis of the best available evidence, that no employee shall suffer impairment of health	Delegation of power upheld

(Continued)

Exhibit 1-10 (Continued)

Touby v. United States (1991)	Attorney General authorized to designate a drug as a controlled substance for the purposes of criminal drug enforcement if doing so was necessary to avoid an imminent hazard to the public safety	Delegation of power upheld
Whitman v. American Trucking Association (2001)	EPA authorized to establish uniform national standards of certain pollutants at levels that protect public health	Delegation of power upheld

> All states have state constitutions that delegate power to state legislatures who in turn create and delegate power to state agencies.

risk to health. Once OSHA made the finding of significant risk, the statute required the regulation to protect workers' health. In summary, the Supreme Court has held that Congress has (since the 1930s) appropriately delegated its power and authority to administrative agencies. It is another question as to whether a particular agency used the delegated power in the manner instructed by Congress. The use of the power by the agency rather than the delegation of power in the first instance remains an ongoing issue.

Agency Discretion

discretion
the ability of an agency to make choices concerning how the agency will do its work

Discretion is the ability to choose among different alternatives. We all exercise *discretion.* As you read this, you are exercising your discretion because you are choosing among different alternatives. You could be watching television or reading another book right now. Agencies have discretion in that they have the ability to choose among different alternatives. Congress delegates power to the agency, and then the delegation of power gives the agency the discretion to choose how it will do its work. For example, Congress may pass a statute that says: "The air is polluted. EPA, clean it up." The EPA then uses its discretion and issues a rule that bans lead in gasoline. Congress did not say one way or the other if banning lead in gas was appropriate, but the agency needs the flexibility based on its expertise to use its discretion to solve the problem. When the EPA issues the rule that bans lead in gasoline, it is using its discretion.

The proper level of discretion is crucial to an agency functioning properly. If too little discretion is delegated, then the agency will lack the flexibility it needs to solve the problem. On the other hand, if too much discretion is given, the agency has little guidance on how to properly implement the intent of the legislature when it charged the agency to solve the problem. See Chapter 6 for a discussion of agency discretion and how the courts analyze issues when they are called upon to review agency decisions. See Chapter 7 for a discussion on how the legislature uses discretion to control administrative agencies. Generally, a court will not disturb a decision of an agency when that decision is based on agency discretion.

Procedural Law and Substantive Law

Substantive law establishes rights, responsibilities, and duties; procedural law sets out the manner and method one must go through to secure substantive rights. *Procedural law* sets out the rules that must be followed to secure substantive rights, as opposed to substantive law, which encompasses the rights and duties themselves. For example, the law of negligence establishes substantive rights. Other examples of substantive law are the law of contacts, criminal law, and the law of wills and estates. Under negligence law, we have a duty not to injure others, and if an individual is injured by another's negligence, the injured party has a right to sue for money damages. Procedural law sets out the methods used to get the money damages. Procedural law fixes the timing of the phases of the lawsuit, the kinds of documents that must be filed, and deadlines for filing. These steps make up procedural law that must be adhered to during the course of a lawsuit.

It is useful to divide administrative law into substantive law and procedural law. The steps required to file a claim for Social Security disability or retirement benefits represent procedural law. The regulations that define the requirements for an award of Social Security disability benefits represent substantive law. As another example, procedural law would include the steps to obtain a nuclear power plant license; whereas

substantive law
the area of law that establishes rights, responsibilities, and duties

procedural law
the area of law that must be followed to secure substantive rights

the regulations that set safety issues and radiation levels would involve substantive law. Additionally, the steps an alien must go through to file for a permanent visa are procedural, whereas the whole area of immigration law would be considered substantive. This text will focus more on procedural law rather than substantive law so that you can acquire a practical overview of how agencies operate. The reason is obvious in that no one text can cover the substantive law of Social Security, immigration, environmental, labor, banking, antitrust, and other substantive areas of agency jurisdiction. However, the procedural law concepts are applicable to all agencies. Keeping in mind the two divisions of substantive law and procedural law will be of benefit as you progress through the text.

Sources of Administrative Law

Sources of administrative law include the Constitution, statutes, common law, executive orders, and rules or regulations.

The Constitution

Because the United States Constitution is the supreme law of the land, all federal, state, and local agencies must operate within its bounds. The Constitution consists of seven articles that comprise the original text, in addition to the Bill of Rights (first ten amendments) and seventeen other amendments. The Constitution is the source of many rights such as freedom of speech, due process, and equal protection. As agencies go about their day-to-day activities, they must not infringe on constitutional rights. For example, the Supreme Court has ruled in *Goldberg v. Kelly,* 397 U.S. 254 (1970), that if a state were to terminate the benefits of an individual welfare recipient without notice and a hearing, that action would violate due process. See Chapter 6 for a discussion of the *Goldberg* case and the impact of the Constitution on administrative law.

Statutes

statutes

laws enacted by a legislature

Federal and state governments pass *statutes* which add to rights found in the Constitution. Statutes are laws enacted by a legislature. We have already encountered one type of statute, the enabling act, which creates an administrative agency. See the following excerpts of the enabling acts that created the Department of Commerce and the Department of Education.

There shall be at the seat of government an executive department to be known as the Department of Commerce, and a Secretary of Commerce . . . 15 U.S.C. § 1501.

There is established an executive department to be known as the Department of Education, 20 U.S.C. § 3411.

Many of the enabling acts are enforced through federal and state agencies. Federal agencies are governed to a great extent by the *Administrative Procedure Act (APA)*. States have also passed similar administrative procedure acts.

After the passage of the enabling act, Congress can pass subsequent statutes that further define the authority of an agency's power. For example, Congress passed the following statute to limit the power of the Consumer Product Safety Commission to regulate firearms.

The Consumer Product Safety Commission shall make no ruling or order that restricts the manufacture or sale of firearms, firearms ammunition, or components of firearms ammunition, including black powder or gunpowder for firearms. Pub.L. 94-284, § 3(e).

Administrative Procedure Act (APA)

a federal law that describes how federal agencies must do business (such as rulemaking, holding hearings, and other procedures) and how disputes go from the federal agencies into a court. Some states also have administrative procedure acts.

Common Law

In the absence of a statute on point, courts have developed a body of *common law*. For example, the law of negligence has been developed by judges and for the most part is common law. Common law plays a lesser role in administrative law because of the proliferation of so many statutes and regulations, but judges may turn to common law where the Constitution, statutes, and regulations are not on point.

common law

legal principles created by judges in the absence of a statute

Executive Orders

An executive order is an order issued by the president or governor directing an agency to follow a certain policy. For example, presidents and governors have issued executive orders banning discrimination by administrative agencies. See Chapter 8 for a discussion of executive orders in the context of presidential control of executive agencies.

Rules or Regulations

Agencies issue regulations which are statements of policy and which implement and enforce a statute. As the role of agencies has grown, so have the number of regulations, to the point where federal and state regulations literally take up thousands of pages of text. Reading and analyzing the vast sea of regulations remains a challenge for all those involved in administrative law. See Chapter 2 for a discussion of agency regulations.

Brief Historical Overview

See Exhibit 1-11 for a brief overview of the history of agencies in the United States. Note the dates and the key developments in each era. Exhibit 1-11 supplies some of the historical background on the evolution and the role agencies have played in American history.

Early Years of the Country—1789–1870s

During this time, the role of the government was very limited. Neither Congress nor the states utilized agencies to any great extent. The little regulation that existed involved steamships and internal improvements, such as the building of bridges and canals. Compare this era of little or no administrative agencies to the eras that follow as the role of administrative law grows with the expansion of the United States.

Exhibit 1-11

Administrative Law Historical Timeline

ERA	MAJOR FEATURE
Early Years of the Country—1789–1870s	Very little regulation by the federal government or the states.
Populist Era—1870s–1890s	States attempt to regulate business, especially the railroads.
Progressive Era—1890s–1920s	Federal government attempts to regulate corporations and monopolies.
Depression and New Deal—1920s–1930s	New Deal legislation creates numerous agencies.
Post New Deal and Adoption of APA—1946	Congress passes the Administrative Procedure Act (APA) to institute uniformity in agency functions.
Modern Era—1960s–Present	Creation of numerous agencies in areas of environmental protection, worker safety, consumerism, and antidiscrimination.

Populist Era—1870s–1890s

The Populist Era was a time when various groups such as farmers and small businesses banded together to counteract the growing power of big business and especially the all-powerful railroads. Organizations such as the Grange and the Farmer's Alliance exerted influence over state governments for regulations to control the railroads and rates for storage in grain elevators. Although agencies did not exert the influence that we experience today, the Populist movement nevertheless enjoyed some success, and in *Munn v. Illinois*, 94 U.S. 113 (1876), the United States Supreme Court upheld state laws that set maximum rates for storage in grain elevators.

Progressive Era—1890s–1920s

The Progressive Era was also marked by groups who attempted to organize to counter big corporations, business monopolies, and the railroads. The Progressives were successful in electing many persons to political office. Their national agenda included worker rights and safety, consumer protection, and control of big business. During this era many states established agencies such as workers' compensation and unemployment compensation boards, and the federal government responded as well by establishing what is known today as the Food and Drug Administration and the Federal Trade Commission.

Depression and New Deal—1920s–1930s

To get the country out of the Great Depression, President Franklin Roosevelt launched the New Deal. As a result, a number of new agencies were established including the Works Progress Administration, Civilian Conservation Corps, and National Recovery Administration, all of which were designed to stimulate national economic recovery. See the previous discussion in this chapter on coverage of the Supreme Court, where the Supreme Court held unconstitutional much of the New Deal legislation because of issues of illegal delegation of power to agencies. However, note that many agencies created in the New Deal survive today and greatly influence society. Those agencies include the Securities and Exchange Commission, National Labor Relations Board, Social Security Administration, and Federal Communications Commission.

Post New Deal and Adoption of Administrative Procedure Act (APA)—1946

After the dramatic growth in the number of agencies, Congress realized that there was not a uniform set of procedures to govern the operations of the agencies. Most agencies used their own set of procedures and rules, and confusion reigned. Congress' solution was to pass the Administrative Procedure Act. The APA sets out uniform procedures to be followed by most federal agencies, and given its importance, we will be dealing with this law throughout this book. Many states have also passed similar laws establishing uniform procedures for agencies in their jurisdictions.

Modern Era—1960–Present

The Modern Era brought a new wave of agencies spurred on by the Civil Rights movement and the consumer and environmental movements. Agencies created include:

> Equal Employment Opportunity Commission
>
> Department of Energy
>
> Department of Health Education and Welfare
>
> Department of Education—carved out of Health Education and Welfare
>
> Environmental Protection Agency
>
> Occupational Safety and Health Administration
>
> Consumer Product Safety Commission
>
> Department of Housing and Urban Development

Types of Agencies

Another challenge in understanding administrative law is to grasp the many types of agencies, their functions, and even their names. Do not let the name of a given agency be confusing. For instance, federal, state, or local agencies can be called "commissions," "boards," "agencies," "administrations," or other names, but for the purposes of study, they all are governmental administrative agencies.

Executive Department or Cabinet Level

In what is known as the President's Cabinet, executive departments include the Department of Defense, Department of Treasury,

Department of State, Department of Health and Human Services, Department of Justice, and the newest *department*, the Department of Homeland Security. The heads of these departments are called Secretaries, except for the head of the Department of Justice, who is called the Attorney General of the United States. See Exhibit 1-12 for a listing of the President's Cabinet. Exhibit 1-12 also contains many of the agencies within the various cabinet offices. See Exhibit 1-13 for the organizational chart of the Department of Justice.

The heads of the cabinet are nominated by the president and must be approved by the Senate. They are known as *political appointees*. The president can remove them at his pleasure. Once confirmed, Congress can only remove these appointees by the impeachment process. Generally, the president will select the cabinet members from his own political party who share the views of the president. Once in office, the cabinet members will carry out the policies within their department as directed by the president. For example, if the president's policy is for tax cuts, then the Secretary of the Treasury will no doubt implement policy aimed at cutting taxes. We will discuss in detail the role that the president plays in controlling the executive agencies of the government in Chapter 8. Note Exhibit 1-14, which is a listing of major departments and agencies of the state government of Pennsylvania. The governor, like the president, has power to appoint the heads of most state agencies. A governor's power to appoint the heads of the agencies varies, depending on the state's constitution and statutes. For example, in Pennsylvania, the governor appoints the head of the Department of Agriculture (which must be approved by the state Senate), but the Attorney General is elected directly by the people.

Subcabinet

Within a cabinet department there is a subcabinet, which is responsible for a prescribed area of responsibility. Review Exhibit 1-12, which contains many of the *subcabinet* agencies. For example, in Exhibit 1-12, note the breakdown of the Under Secretary of Homeland Security for Customs & Border Protection. Also note in Exhibit 1-12 that the FBI is a subagency within the Department of Justice. The heads of the subcabinet agencies generally are nominated by the Senate and must be approved by the Senate.

Independent-Agency Type or Commission/Board Type

Congress has attempted to remove political considerations in administrative law by creating agencies that are independent of both the

department
the major administrative division headed by an officer of cabinet rank who is known as a secretary

political appointees
heads of the cabinet who serve at the pleasure of the president and who can be removed by the president at any time and for any reason

subcabinet
an agency that is located inside a cabinet department; for example, the Centers for Disease Control (CDC) is located inside the Department of Health and Human Services.

Exhibit 1-12

President's Cabinet

Department of Agriculture (USDA)

- · Agricultural Research Service
- · Animal & Plant Health Inspection Service
- · Cooperative State Research, Education, and Extension Service
- · Economic Research Service
- · Farm Service Agency
- · Forest Service
- · National Agricultural Library
- · Natural Resources Conservation Service
- · Research, Economics & Education
- · Rural Development

Department of Commerce (DOC)

- · Bureau of the Census
- · Bureau of Economic Analysis (BEA)
  ·STAT-USA Database (password may be required)
- · Bureau of Export Administration
- · FEDWorld
- · International Trade Administration (ITA)
- · National Institute of Standards & Technology (NIST)
- · National Marine Fisheries Service (NMFS)
- · National Oceanic & Atmospheric Administration (NOAA)
- · National Ocean Service
- · National Technical Information Service (NTIS)
- · National Telecommunications & Information Administration
- · National Weather Service
- · Patent and Trademark Office Database

Department of Defense (DOD)

- · American Forces Press Service
- · Air Force (USAF)
  ·Air Force Research Laboratory (AFRL)
- · Army (USA)
  ·Army Field Manuals (full text)
  ·Training and Doctrine Command (TRADOC)
- · BosniaLINK
  ·TaLon archive (a newsletter for the soldiers of Task Force Eagle)
- · DIOR Reports (full text) including "Top 100 Contractors" and "100 Contractors Receiving the Largest Dollar Volume"

Exhibit 1-12 (Continued)

- Defense Contract and Audit Agency (DCAA)
- Defense Finance and Accounting Service (DFAS)
- Defense Information Systems Agency (DISA)
- Defense Intelligence Agency (DIA)
- Defense Logistics Agency (DLA)
- Defense Technical Information Center (DTIC)
- DTIC Web Links
- DefenseLINK Locator (GILS)
- Joint Chiefs of Staff (JCS)
- Marine Corps (USMC)
- National Guard
- National Security Agency (NSA)
- Navy (USN)
- DON CIO (Naval Information Systems Management)

Department of Education

- Educational Resources Information Center (ERIC) and Other Clearinghouses
- National Library of Education (NLE)
- Other Federal Government Internet Educational Resources

Department of Energy

- Environment, Safety and Health (ES&H)
- Federal Energy Regulatory Commission
- Los Alamos National Laboratory
- Office of Science
- Southwestern Power Administration

Department of Health and Human Services (HHS)

- Administration for Children and Families
- Agency for Healthcare Research and Quality (AHCRQ)
- Centers for Disease Control and Prevention (CDC)
- Food and Drug Administration (FDA)
- National Institutes of Health (NIH)
- National Library of Medicine (NLM)

Department of Homeland Security (DHS)

- Bureau of Citizenship and Immigration Services
- Customs & Border Protection
- Coast Guard
- Federal Emergency Management Agency (FEMA)

(Continued)

Exhibit 1-12 (Continued)

- Federal Law Enforcement Training Center
- Secret Service
- U.S. Intelligence Community (Jobs)

Department of Housing and Urban Development (HUD)

- Government National Mortgage Association (Ginnie Mae)
- Housing and Urban Development Reading Room
- Office of Healthy Homes and Lead Hazard Control
- Public and Indian Housing Agencies

Department of the Interior (DOI)

- Bureau of Indian Affairs
- Bureau of Land Management
- Bureau of Reclamation
- Fish and Wildlife Service
- Geological Survey
- Minerals Management Service
- National Park Service
- Office of Surface Mining

Department of Justice (DOJ)

- Bureau of Alcohol, Tobacco, Firearms and Explosives (ATF)
- Drug Enforcement Agency (DEA)
- Federal Bureau of Investigation (FBI)
- Federal Bureau of Prisons
- Office of Justice Programs (OJP)
- United States Marshals Service (USMS)

Department of Labor (DOL)

- Bureau of Labor Statistics (BLS)
- Mine Safety and Health Administration
- Occupational Safety & Health Administration (OSHA)

Department of State (DOS)

- Department of State Library

Department of Transportation (DOT)

- Bureau of Transportation Statistics
- Federal Aviation Administration (FAA)
- National Transportation Library (a digital library)

Exhibit 1-12 (Continued)

Department of the Treasury
- Alcohol and Tobacco Tax and Trade Bureau (TTB)
- Bureau of Engraving and Printing
- Bureau of Public Debt
- Executive Office for Asset Forfeiture
- Financial Crimes Enforcement Network
- Financial Management Service (FMS)
- Internal Revenue Service (IRS)
- Office of the Comptroller of the Currency
- Office of Thrift Supervision (OTS)
- U.S. Mint

Department of Veterans Affairs

Source: http://www.loc.gov/rr/news/fedgov.htm

president and Congress. These independent agencies can be divided into agencies that are headed by one person and agencies that are run by a board or commission. An agency that is run by one person is usually called an "agency" or "administration." For example, the EPA is headed by one person. The Central Intelligence Agency (CIA) is headed by one person. The other type of *independent agency* is the commission/board type. The president still nominates, and the Senate must approve, but in this type, the members of the commission serve fixed terms in office and cannot be removed by the president except for cause. For example, the Consumer Product Safety Commission consists of members who are appointed by the president and must be approved by the Senate. Members of the commission cannot be removed by anyone, including the president, except for cause. Convictions of crimes or serious ethical lapses short of breaking the law are reasons for discharge for cause. By setting up the commission/board type in this manner, Congress expects that the agency can be independent and go about protecting the public interest in a better way.

independent agency
an agency not under the direct control of the president which can be headed by a single person or be composed of multiple members in the form of a board or commission

Regulatory, Social Welfare, Ratemaking

An agency can also be grouped by the function it performs. For example, the EPA is a *regulatory agency* because it issues rules and regulations to protect the environment. On the other hand, Social Security is a

regulatory agency
an agency that issues rules and regulations which must be obeyed by individuals and businesses; for example, the Environmental Protection Agency is a regulatory agency

Exhibit 1-13

Organizational Chart for United States Department of Justice

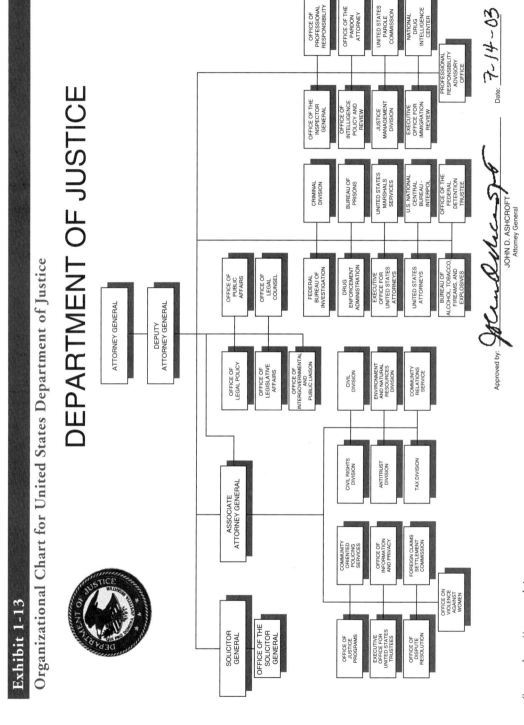

DEPARTMENT OF JUSTICE

ATTORNEY GENERAL

DEPUTY ATTORNEY GENERAL

ASSOCIATE ATTORNEY GENERAL

SOLICITOR GENERAL

OFFICE OF THE SOLICITOR GENERAL

OFFICE OF LEGAL POLICY

OFFICE OF LEGISLATIVE AFFAIRS

OFFICE OF INTERGOVERNMENTAL AND PUBLIC LIAISON

OFFICE OF PUBLIC AFFAIRS

OFFICE OF LEGAL COUNSEL

OFFICE OF JUSTICE PROGRAMS

EXECUTIVE OFFICE FOR UNITED STATES TRUSTEES

OFFICE OF DISPUTE RESOLUTION

COMMUNITY ORIENTED POLICING SERVICES

OFFICE OF INFORMATION AND PRIVACY

FOREIGN CLAIMS SETTLEMENT COMMISSION

OFFICE ON VIOLENCE AGAINST WOMEN

CIVIL RIGHTS DIVISION

ANTITRUST DIVISION

TAX DIVISION

CIVIL DIVISION

ENVIRONMENT AND NATURAL RESOURCES DIVISION

COMMUNITY RELATIONS SERVICE

FEDERAL BUREAU OF INVESTIGATION

DRUG ENFORCEMENT ADMINISTRATION

EXECUTIVE OFFICE FOR UNITED STATES ATTORNEYS

UNITED STATES ATTORNEYS

BUREAU OF ALCOHOL, TOBACCO, FIREARMS, AND EXPLOSIVES

CRIMINAL DIVISION

BUREAU OF PRISONS

UNITED STATES MARSHALS SERVICES

U.S. NATIONAL CENTRAL BUREAU - INTERPOL

OFFICE OF THE FEDERAL DETENTION TRUSTEE

OFFICE OF THE INSPECTOR GENERAL

OFFICE OF INTELLIGENCE POLICY AND REVIEW

JUSTICE MANAGEMENT DIVISION

EXECUTIVE OFFICE FOR IMMIGRATION REVIEW

OFFICE OF PROFESSIONAL RESPONSIBILITY

OFFICE OF THE PARDON ATTORNEY

UNITED STATES PAROLE COMMISSION

NATIONAL DRUG INTELLIGENCE CENTER

PROFESSIONAL RESPONSIBILITY ADVISORY OFFICE

Approved by: _____   Date: _7-14-03_

JOHN D. ASHCROFT
Attorney General

Source: http://www.usdoj.gov

Exhibit 1-14

State Government in Pennsylvania

Governor of Pennsylvania

Governor's Offices

- Office of Lieutenant Governor
- Office of First Lady

Agencies, Authorities, Boards, Commissions, Councils, Departments, and Offices

- Administration
- Aging
- Agriculture
- Attorney General
- Banking
- Board of Claims
- Board of Pardons
- Budget
- Bureau of Liquor Control Enforcement
- Bureau of State Employment
- Capital Police
- Civil Service Commission
- Commission on Crime and Delinquency
- Community and Economic Development
- Conservation and Natural Resources
- Consumer Advocate
- Corrections
- Education
- Environmental Protection
- Fish and Boat Commission
- Game Commission
- General Counsel
- General Services
- Governor's Advisory Commission on African American Affairs
- Governor's Advisory Commission on Asian American Affairs
- Governor's Advisory Commission on Latino Affairs
- Governor's Green Government Council
- Governor's Sportsmen's Advisory Council
- Health
- Historical and Museum Commission
- Independent Regulatory Review Commission
- Insurance

(Continued)

Exhibit 1-14 (Continued)

- Juvenile Court Judges' Commission
- Labor and Industry
- Liquor Control Board
- Medical Care Availability and Reduction of Error Fund (Mcare)
- Military and Veterans Affairs
- Milk Marketing Board
- Office of Administrative Law Judge
- Office of Health Care Reform
- Office of Inspector General
- Office of Management and Productivity
- Office of Public Liaison
- Office of the State Fire Commissioner
- Office of the Victim Advocate
- Office of PA Open for Business
- Patient Safety Authority
- Pennsylvania Commission for Women
- Pennsylvania Council on the Arts
- Pennsylvania Emergency Management Agency
- Pennsylvania Health Care Cost Containment Council (PHCCCC)
- Pennsylvania Higher Education Assistance Agency (PHEAA)
- Pennsylvania Higher Educational Facilities Authority (PHEFA)
- Pennsylvania Housing Finance Agency (PHFA)
- Pennsylvania Human Relations Commission
- Pennsylvania Infrastructure Investment Authority (PENNVEST)
- Pennsylvania Lottery
- Pennsylvania Municipal Retirement System
- Pennsylvania Public School Employees' Retirement System (PSERS)
- Pennsylvania Rural Development Council
- Probation and Parole

Source: *The Pennsylvania Manual,* Volume 117

social welfare agency

an agency that dispenses social services such as Social Security

social welfare agency because its mission is to ensure that retirees and disabled individuals get financial and medical benefits to which they are entitled under the Social Security laws. The Federal Energy Regulatory Commission serves as a ratemaking agency by establishing appropriate energy prices. See Exhibit 1-15 for examples of the various types of agencies. Note that many agencies can serve multiple functions, meaning that an agency can be both regulatory and independent. A regulatory agency or social welfare agency can be at the subcabinet level or be

---

Exhibit 1-15

Examples of Types of Agencies

EXECUTIVE DEPARTMENTS

Cabinet level—political appointments by president and must be approved by senate

DEPARTMENT OF HEALTH AND HUMAN SERVICES (HHS) (Cabinet)

Centers for Disease Control (CDC) (subcabinet)

Food and Drug Administration (FDA) (subcabinet and regulatory)

DEPARTMENT OF THE INTERIOR (Cabinet)

National Park Service (subcabinet)

DEPARTMENT OF JUSTICE (DOJ) (Cabinet)

Drug Enforcement Agency (DEA) (subcabinet)

Federal Bureau of Investigation (FBI) (subcabinet)

DEPARTMENT OF TREASURY (Cabinet)

Bureau of Alcohol, Tobacco, Firearms and Explosives (ATF) (regulatory)

Internal Revenue Service (IRS) (regulatory)

DEPARTMENT OF LABOR (Cabinet)

Occupational Safety and Health Administration (OSHA) (subcabinet and regulatory)

INDEPENDENT—TWO TYPES

1. Commission or Board

Consumer Product Safety Commission (regulatory)

Equal Employment Opportunity Commission (regulatory)

2. Agency headed by one person, called an administrator

Environmental Protection Agency (EPA) (regulatory)

Generally, members of independent agencies serve fixed terms and cannot be removed except for cause.

---

a commission type. See Exhibit 1-16 for a listing of some of names that an "agency" can be called.

What Agencies Do Not Do

After reading this chapter, one can see some of the many things that agencies do inside this area known as administrative law. Administrative

Exhibit 1-16	
Multitude of Names of an Agency	
NAME	EXAMPLE
Agency	Central Intelligence Agency (CIA)
Bureau	Federal Bureau of Investigation (FBI)
Commission	Equal Employment Opportunity Commission (EEOC)
Board	National Transportation Safety Board (NTSB)
Department	Department of Labor (DOL)
Center	Centers for Disease Control (CDC)
Office	Office of Independent Counsel (OIS)
Authority	Local sewer or water authority

What is in a name? Sometimes the functions of a federal and state agency are easy to discern. For example, the federal Department of Agriculture and a state Department of Agriculture work on very similar issues regarding agriculture. However, the federal Department of State is involved with foreign affairs and diplomacy with other countries while most state Departments of State are charged with monitoring and certifying elections and have nothing to do with foreign affairs.

law involves some kind of issue between a private individual, business or corporation, and the government. When the EPA attempts to fine a business because of violations of pollution standards, that is administrative law in action. The government is involved. Conversely, when homeowners sue the same company for money damages and allege that the pollution emissions damaged their health, that is not a function of administrative law, but a private dispute. Administrative law and regulations may be relevant in the private lawsuit, but administrative law, as that term is used, is not involved in the case. Actions involving private parties involved in automobile accidents, medical malpractice, and breach of contract cases are also examples of private disputes that are not included in the area of administrative law.

The other key area of law *not* included in the field of administrative law is criminal law. The EPA or the IRS cannot put individuals or corporations on trial, but they can refer the case to the proper federal or state law enforcement authorities. Thereafter, the case would proceed in the criminal justice system, not through an administrative agency. Most agencies have no role in the criminal justice system because of the guarantees in the Constitution. When an individual or corporation faces charges in the criminal justice system, the Constitution guarantees the right to a lawyer, right to a jury trial, right to a grand jury indictment, and other rights specific to criminal justice. Generally, administrative law is not focused on criminal matters, but rather on civil issues between the government and the individuals or corporations involved. See Exhibit 1-17 for a comparison of administrative law, private disputes, and criminal law.

Exhibit 1-17

Scope of Administrative Law

AREA OF LAW	ISSUES PRESENTED	FORUM FOR RESOLUTON	PRESIDING OFFICER
Administrative law	An issue between a private individual and a government agency concerning the interpretation and enforcement of regulations	Resolved inside the agency with an appeal to a court of law; no right to a jury trial	Administrative Law Judge (ALJ) or Hearing Officer
Private disputes	A dispute between private individuals, usually in the form of a lawsuit for money damages	Resolved in a court of law with the right to a jury trial in most cases	Judge
Criminal law	Criminal charges brought by the state or federal authorities for violations of criminal law where a person's life or liberty could be taken away	Resolved in a court of law with the full measure of constitutional rights, including the right to a jury trial and the right to a lawyer	Judge

As you grapple with the legal concepts of administrative law, keep in mind the constant tension in society between regulation to protect the public and the burden that regulation places on industry, business, and the public that pays higher prices for products and services that are regulated. Government regulators spend taxpayer dollars measuring the flow rate of ketchup and the length of pickle stems. Two rat hairs may not make your Wheaties contaminated, but three rat hairs might. Look at a container of yogurt or a bag of potato chips to see the nutritional information required by regulation. The Food and Drug Administration defended a rule through more than seven years of litigation with the heart of the dispute being whether should peanut butter be 87% or 90% peanuts. On the other hand, if an underground mine explodes and miners are trapped or a hotel fire kills hundreds of people, the national reaction is "What happened?" Congressional hearings are held, agency heads are called to testify, and the question turns to whether these tragedies are the result of failures of an administrative agency to do its job. This issue of how much regulation and its costs permeates all of administrative law.

CASE LAW

AMALGAMATED MEAT CUTTERS AND BUTCHER WORKMEN v. CONNALLY
337 F.Supp. 737 (D.D.C.1971).

[The Economic Stabilization Act of 1970 (Act) empowered the President "to issue such orders and regulations as he may deem appropriate to stabilize prices, rents, wages, and salaries." To restrain inflation during the Vietnam war, President Nixon used that authority to freeze prices, rents, wages, and salaries for ninety days. He adopted rules imposing wage and price controls after the freeze expired. Violators were subject to criminal fines. Plaintiff Union argued that the Act "vests unbridled legislative power in the President."]

The Government cites numerous authorities but relies most heavily on *Yakus* . . . [which] carries forward the doctrine [of *J. W. Hampton*] . . . that there is no forbidden delegation of legislative power "if Congress shall lay down by legislative act an intelligible principle" to which the official or agency must conform.

Concepts of control and accountability define the constitutional requirement. The principle permitting a delegation of legislative power, if there has been a sufficient demarcation of the field to permit a judgment whether the agency has kept within the legislative will, establishes a principle of accountability under which compatibility with the legislative design may be ascertained not only by Congress but by the courts and the public. That principle was conjoined in *Yakus* with a recognition that the burden is on the party who assails the legislature's choice of means for effecting its purpose, a burden that is met "only if we could say that there is an absence of standards for the guidance of the Administrator's action, so that it would be impossible in a proper proceeding to ascertain whether the will of Congress has been obeyed . . . ."

[The Act supplied sufficient standards. It did not permit the President to set prices and wages below their level on May 25, 1970. It precluded the President from singling out a particular sector of the economy in which to impose controls, absent a finding that wages or prices in that sector had increased disproportionately. Moreover, the legislative history set forth Congress' purpose—the same purpose as the 1942 act sustained in *Yakus*. Standards can be articulated in legislative history rather than in express statutory language.]

We see no merit in the contention that the Act is constitutionally defective because the timing of the imposition of controls was delegated to the President . . . . Viewing the President as a physician in charge, Congress could advise but not mandate his diagnosis. It sought in the national interest to have the right remedy available on a standby basis, if the President should wish to adopt that prescription, following his further reflection and taking into account future developments and experience . . . .

[The court emphasized the connection between domestic inflation and international trade.] The consequence for international trade, liquidity and monetary relationships enhances the range of power Congress can permissibly delegate to the President.

It is also material, though not dispositive, to note the limited time frame established by Congress for the stabilization authority delegated to the President. [The 1970 Act had a six month lifespan.] Two subsequent extensions provided even shorter durations.

(Continued)

[The court concluded that Congress had provided sufficient standards for wage-price controls after the freeze expired—broad fairness and the removal of "gross inequities."] Another feature that blunts the "blank check" rhetoric is the requirement that any action taken by the Executive under the law, subsequent to the freeze, must be in accordance with further standards as developed by the Executive. This requirement, inherent in the Rule of Law and implicit in the Act, means that however broad the discretion of the Executive at the outset, the standards once developed limit the latitude of subsequent executive action . . . . [T]here is an on-going requirement of intelligible administrative policy that is corollary to and implementing of the legislature's ultimate standard and objective . . . .

The safeguarding of meaningful judicial review is one of the primary functions of the doctrine prohibiting undue delegation of legislative powers . . . . The Government concedes and we agree that the Executive's actions under the 1970 Act are not immune from judicial review . . . . Challenges may be made under the provisions for judicial review in the [APA].

By the same token actions under this 1970 Act are subject to the administrative procedure provisions of the APA. [However, neither the rulemaking nor adjudication sections of the APA would be applicable, since the President could utilize the good-cause exemptions from rulemaking and no statute required the agency to provide adjudicatory hearings. The court suggested that the ongoing administration of the program could be challenged for failure to provide meaningful opportunity for interested persons to present objections or for courts to discharge their judicial review function.]

We end this section of the opinion with broad closing references to precedent . . . . We do not understand *Yakus* to rest in a crucial sense on the exercise of the war power . . . . [T]here have not been any Supreme Court rulings holding statutes unconstitutional for excessive delegation of legislative power since *Panama Refining* and *Schechter* . . . . These cases express a principle that has validity—reserved for the extreme instance . . . . Both cited cases dealt with delegation of a power to make federal crimes of acts that never had been such before and to devise novel rules of law in a field in which there had been no settled law or custom. They are without vigor in a case like [this] where the delegation is in a context of historical experience with anti-inflation legislation . . . .

CASE LAW

INDUSTRIAL UNION DEPARTMENT, AFL – CIO v. AMERICAN PETROLEUM INSTITUTE
448 U.S. 607 (1980)

[The Occupational Safety and Health Act delegates authority to the Secretary of Labor to adopt safety and health standards for the workplace. Under § 3(8), the standards must be "reasonably necessary or appropriate to provide safe or healthful . . . places of employment." In setting standards for toxic materials, § 6(b)(5) of the Act directs the Secretary "to set the standard which most adequately assures, to the extent feasible . . . that no employee will suffer material impairment of health . . . ."

The Occupational Safety and Health Administration (OSHA), which discharges the Secretary's responsibilities under this Act, construed the statute to require it to set standards at the safest possible level which is technologically feasible and which would not cause material economic impairment of the industry.

This case involves the standard for benzene, an industrial chemical which in high concentration causes leukemia and other illnesses. OSHA set the standard for benzene at 1 part per million, although OSHA did not find, and research did not establish, that there is danger to the health of workers at levels of concentration below 10 parts per million.

In the enabling act Congress never specified whether it wanted OSHA to balance costs to industry against benefits to workers or whether it wanted OSHA to set standards at the safest possible level without consideration of costs. A four-justice plurality, in an opinion written by STEVENS, J., overturned the benzene standard. Interpreting § 6(b)(5), the plurality held that OSHA must find, before promulgating a standard, that it is necessary and appropriate to remedy a *significant risk* of material health impairment:]

In the absence of a clear mandate in the Act, it is unreasonable to assume that Congress intended to give the Secretary the unprecedented power over American industry that would result from the Government's view of §§ 3(8) and 6(b)(5), coupled with OSHA's cancer policy. Expert testimony that a substance is probably a human carcinogen—either because it has caused cancer in animals or because individuals have contracted cancer following extremely high exposures—would justify the conclusion that the substance poses

(Continued)

some risk of serious harm no matter how minute the exposure and no matter how many experts testified that they regarded the risk as insignificant. That conclusion would in turn justify pervasive regulation limited only by the constraint of feasibility. In light of the fact that there are literally thousands of substances used in the workplace that have been identified as carcinogens or suspect carcinogens, the Government's theory would give OSHA power to impose enormous costs that might produce little, if any, discernible benefit.

If the Government was correct in arguing that neither § 3(8) nor § 6(b)(5) requires that the risk from a toxic substance be quantified sufficiently to enable the Secretary to characterize it as significant in an understandable way, the statute would make such a "sweeping delegation of legislative power" that it might be unconstitutional under the Court's reasoning in *Schechter Poultry* and *Panama Refining*. A construction of the statute that avoids this kind of open-ended grant should certainly be favored.

[REHNQUIST, J., concurred in the judgment, arguing that § 6(b)(5) was invalid under the delegation doctrine:]

[I]n my opinion decisions such as *Panama Refining* suffer from none of the excesses of judicial policymaking that plagued some of the other decisions of that era. The many later decisions that have upheld congressional delegations of authority to the Executive Branch have done so largely on the theory that Congress may wish to exercise its authority in a particular field, but because the field is sufficiently technical, the ground to be covered sufficiently large, and the Members of Congress themselves not necessarily expert in the area in which they choose to legislate, the most that may be asked under the separation-of-powers doctrine is that Congress lay down the general policy and standards that animate the law, leaving the agency to refine those standards, "fill in the blanks," or apply the standards to particular cases. These decisions, to my mind, simply illustrate the above-quoted principle stated more than 50 years ago by Mr. Chief Justice Taft that delegations of legislative authority must be judged "according to common sense and the inherent necessities of the governmental co-ordination."

Viewing the legislation at issue here in light of these principles, I believe that it fails to pass muster. Read literally, the relevant portion of § 6(b)(5) is completely precatory, admonishing the Secretary to adopt the most protective standard if he can, but excusing him from that duty if he cannot. In the case of a hazardous substance for which a "safe" level is either unknown or impractical, the language of § 6(b)(5) gives the Secretary absolutely no indication where on the continuum of relative safety he should draw his line. Especially in light of the importance of the interests at stake, I have no doubt that the provision at issue, standing alone, would violate the doctrine against uncanalized delegations of legislative power. For me the remaining question, then, is whether additional standards are ascertainable from the legislative history or statutory context of § 6(b)(5) or, if not, whether such a standardless delegation was justifiable in light of the "inherent necessities" of the situation.

One of the primary sources looked to by this Court in adding gloss to an otherwise broad grant of legislative authority is the legislative history of the statute in question . . . . I believe that the legislative history demonstrates that the feasibility requirement, as employed in § 6(b)(5), is a legislative mirage, appearing to some Members but not to others, and assuming any form desired by the beholder . . . . [and] there is little or nothing in the remaining provisions of the Occupational Safety and Health Act to provide specificity to the feasibility criterion in § 6(b)(5) . . . .

In some cases where broad delegations of power have been examined, this Court has upheld those delegations because of the delegatee's residual authority over particular subjects of regulation. In *United States v. Curtiss–Wright Export Corp.*, 299 U.S. 304, 307 (1936), this Court upheld a statute authorizing the President to prohibit the sale of arms to certain countries if he found that such a prohibition would "contribute to the reestablishment of peace." This Court reasoned that, in the area of foreign affairs, Congress "must often accord to the President a degree of discretion and freedom from statutory restriction which would not be admissible were domestic affairs alone involved . . . ." In the present cases, however, neither the Executive Branch in general nor the Secretary in particular enjoys any independent authority over the subject matter at issue.

Finally, as indicated earlier, in some cases this Court has abided by a rule of necessity, upholding broad delegations of authority where it would be "unreasonable and impracticable to compel Congress to prescribe detailed rules" regarding a particular policy or situation. But no need for such an evasive standard as "feasibility" is apparent in the present cases. In drafting § 6(b)(5), Congress was faced with a clear, if difficult, choice between balancing statistical lives and industrial resources or authorizing the Secretary to elevate human life above all concerns save massive dislocation in an affected industry . . . . That Congress chose, intentionally or unintentionally,

(*Continued*)

to pass this difficult choice on to the Secretary is evident from the spectral quality of the standard it selected. . . .

As formulated and enforced by this Court, the nondelegation doctrine serves three important functions. First, and most abstractly, it ensures to the extent consistent with orderly governmental administration that important choices of social policy are made by Congress, the branch of our Government most responsive to the popular will . . . . Second, the doctrine guarantees that, to the extent Congress finds it necessary to delegate authority, it provides the recipient of that authority with an "intelligible principle" to guide the exercise of the delegated discretion . . . . Third, and derivative of the second, the doctrine ensures that courts charged with reviewing the exercise of delegated legislative discretion will be able to test that exercise against ascertainable standards.

I believe the legislation at issue here fails on all three counts. The decision whether the law of diminishing returns should have any place in the regulation of toxic substances is quintessentially one of legislative policy. For Congress to pass that decision on to the Secretary in the manner it did violates, in my mind, John Locke's caveat—reflected in the cases cited earlier in this opinion—that legislatures are to make laws. Nor, as I think the prior discussion amply demonstrates, do the provisions at issue or their legislative history provide the Secretary with any guidance that might lead him to his somewhat tentative conclusion that he must eliminate exposure to benzene as far as technologically and economically possible. Finally, I would suggest that the standard of "feasibility" renders meaningful judicial review impossible.

We ought not to shy away from our judicial duty to invalidate unconstitutional delegations of legislative authority solely out of concern that we should thereby reinvigorate discredited constitutional doctrines of the pre-New Deal era. If the nondelegation doctrine has fallen into the same desuetude as have substantive due process and restrictive interpretations of the Commerce Clause, it is, as one writer has phrased it, "a case of death by association." J.H. Ely, Democracy and Distrust: A Theory of Judicial Review 133 (1980) . . . .

If we are ever to reshoulder the burden of ensuring that Congress itself make the critical policy decisions, these are surely the cases in which to do it. It is difficult to imagine a more obvious example of Congress simply avoiding a choice which was both fundamental for purposes of the statute and yet politically so divisive that the necessary decision or compromise was difficult, if not impossible, to hammer out in the legislative forge. Far from detracting from the substantive authority of Congress, a declaration that the first sentence of § 6(b)(5) of the Occupational Safety and Health Act constitutes an invalid delegation to the Secretary of Labor would preserve the authority of Congress. If Congress wishes to legislate in an area which it has not previously sought to enter, it will in today's political world undoubtedly run into opposition no matter how the legislation is formulated. But that is the very essence of legislative authority under our system. It is the hard choices, and not the filling in of the blanks, which must be made by the elected representatives of the people. When fundamental policy decisions underlying important legislation about to be enacted are to be made, the buck stops with Congress and the President insofar as he exercises his constitutional role in the legislative process.

[The concurring opinion of POWELL, J., argued that a cost-benefit balancing was required before OSHA could set a standard. MARSHALL, J., dissented (joined by BRENNAN, WHITE, and BLACKMUN, JJ.). Marshall argued that Congress had intended precisely what OSHA had done. As to delegation, he wrote:]

. . . While my brother Rehnquist eloquently argues that there remains a place for [the delegation] doctrine in our jurisprudence, I am frankly puzzled as to why the issue is thought to be of any relevance here. The non-delegation doctrine is designed to assure that the most fundamental decisions will be made by Congress, the elected representatives of the people, rather than by administrators. Some minimal definiteness is therefore required in order for Congress to delegate its authority to administrative agencies. Congress has been sufficiently definite here. The word "feasible" has a reasonably plain meaning, and its interpretation can be informed by other contexts in which Congress has used it. . . . In short Congress has made the "critical policy decision" in this case . . . .

The plurality's apparent suggestion . . . that the nondelegation doctrine might be violated if the Secretary were permitted to regulate definite but nonquantifiable risks is plainly wrong. Such a statute would be quite definite and would thus raise no constitutional question under *Schechter Poultry* . . . .

CHAPTER SUMMARY

Administrative law permeates every aspect of society. Administrative law is the study of how agencies are created, how agencies do their work, and how agencies are controlled. An agency is a subbranch of the government set up by a legislature to carry out laws by the use of legislative, executive, and judicial power. Congress and state legislatures create agencies to address economic issues (regulation of industries) and to protect social interests (regulation of the environment, protection of public health, and delivery of social services). Agencies are created by a law called an enabling act wherein legislative, executive, and judicial power is transferred or delegated to the agency because agencies can deliver flexibility, efficiency, and expertise and can deflect political pressure. Agencies issue rules that have the force of law to fill in the gaps of broadly worded statutes to implement the will of the legislature in the area assigned to the agency. Agencies enforce their regulations and hold hearings to determine if their regulations have been violated. The president or governor of a state, Congress or a state legislature, and the federal and state courts can exercise control over the agencies to hold them accountable for their actions.

Federal agencies function inside a federal system of separation of powers and checks and balances. Through the principle of federalism, which divides power between the federal government and the governments of the 50 states, state agencies function to provide for the health, welfare, and safety of their citizens. Administrative law does not generally involve criminal law and private disputes.

KEY TERMS

adjudicate

administrative agency

administrative law

Administrative Procedure Act (APA)

commerce clause

common law

concurrent power

delegation

delegation doctrine

department

discretion

enabling act

enumerated powers

executive power

federalism

independent agency

intelligible principle

interstate commerce

judicial review

Necessary and Proper Clause

nondelegation doctrine	social welfare agency
police power	sovereignty
political appointees	statutes
preempted	subcabinet
procedural law	substantive law
regulatory agency	Supremacy Clause
rule or regulation	Tenth Amendment

REVIEW QUESTIONS

1. Give some reasons for the importance of administrative law.
2. List and briefly describe the powers possessed by agencies.
3. How are agencies created?
4. Discuss the delegation and nondelegation doctrines.
5. What is agency discretion?
6. State the historical eras that have characterized the development of administrative law.
7. What are some of the various types of agencies?
8. Describe the scope of administrative law.

MORE INFORMATION

1. Go to http://thomas.loc.gov. Scroll down to Government resources and click. Then click on Executive Branch. You can then click on the various agencies and subagencies of the federal government.
2. While on http://thomas.loc.gov, click on Legislative Process to see a detailed account of how a bill becomes a law.

PRACTICAL APPLICATIONS

1. Go to your state's Web site and do the following:
   A. Note the agencies of the government and their functions.
   B. List all the agencies that are considered part of the governor's cabinet.
   C. Make a list of the various independent agencies.
2. Go to the Web site for the Department of the Interior at http://www.doi.gov. Name five subagencies that are included in the Department of Interior.

3. Go to the Web site of the Department of Commerce at http://www.commerce.gov. Name five subagencies that are included in the Department of Commerce.
4. In 2004, Congress established a new agency called the Office of the Director of National Intelligence. To obtain the enabling act which created this agency and other information, go to http://thomas.loc.gov.
   Select the 108th Congress.
   Do a bill search for S. 2845.
   A.   Who was the main sponsor of this bill?
   B.   What was the last major action on the bill?

@

L E A R N   A B O U T   T H E   A G E N C I E S

Go to the Web sites of the following agencies and state their function.

1. NLRB—National Labor Relations Board—http://www.nlrb.gov
2. NASA—National Aeronautics and Space Administration—http://www.nasa.gov
3. NTSB—National Transportation Safety Board—http://www.ntsb.gov
4. EEOC—Equal Employment Opportunity Commission—http://www.eeoc.gov
5. IRS—Internal Revenue Service—http://www.irs.gov

PART II

What Do Agencies Do?

CHAPTER 2

Rulemaking—Legislative Power of Agencies

CHAPTER OBJECTIVES

After reading this chapter, you should be able to:

- Assess the role that agency rulemaking plays in regulating society.
- Outline the steps in formal rulemaking.
- Outline the steps in informal rulemaking.
- Define and describe exempted rules.

CHAPTER OUTLINE

INTRODUCTION TO RULES AND RULEMAKING

As examined in Chapter 1, agencies implement the laws passed by a legislature by issuing rules. Once an agency receives delegated power from either Congress or a state legislature, it can issue rules to fill in the gaps left in the legislation. A *rule or regulation* is a statement of policy issued by the agency that implements the will of Congress. A rule or regulation is the gap-filler that supplies specific direction on how persons are to act under the law. Section 551(4) of the Administrative Procedure Act (APA) states that a rule:

> "means the whole or a part of an agency statement of general or particular applicability and future effect designed to implement, interpret, or prescribe law or policy . . ."

Section 551(5) of the APA states that "rulemaking means agency process for formulating, amending, or repealing a rule."

Rules or regulations mean exactly the same in this context, and the terms are used interchangeably. For instance, Congress may pass a statute which declares in effect that "we must clean up the air." The Environmental Protection Agency (EPA) will then issue a regulation to the effect that "all lead must be out of gasoline." Congress's policy to "clean up the air" is general in nature but provides an intelligible principle from which to act. Therefore, because the EPA has been delegated authority to "fill in the gaps" and has to clean up the air, the agency uses its expertise to devise a regulation eliminating lead from gasoline.

As another example, Congress may say "cotton dust in factories is a health hazard." The Occupational Safety and Health Administration (OSHA) may then issue regulations to fill in the gaps of this law by specifying the acceptable level of cotton dust in cotton factories. Agency rules or regulation are the reasons why we see a construction worker wearing a hardhat, why there is no lead in gasoline, why there is fluoride in drinking water, and why we can read the ingredients in a bag of potato chips. The source of this power is found in the enabling act which created the agencies and endowed the agency with this rulemaking power. Regulations give us direction as to how to proceed and what is acceptable behavior. Regulations allow for those in industry or people in private lives to be on notice of what is expected and give everyone a chance to conform to the standards.

Rules or regulations are like statutes. They apply generally to everyone and bind society to conform to them from the time they are officially in place. When properly enacted, regulations have the full force of law and can alter and affect legal rights. See Chapter 4 and

rule or regulation

a statement of policy issued by an agency to implement a statute and which has the force of law. Rules and regulations represent the legislative power of agencies.

specifically Exhibit 4-3 for a comparison of agency rulemaking (legislative power) and agency adjudication (judicial power).

The following sections will examine the kind of rules and processes by which rules are made. The preceding examples, such as the requirement of ingredients on food or warnings on medicines, are called *legislative rules*. Legislative rules are the rules we are so familiar with and which we are confronted with on a daily basis.

A useful way to think of legislative rules is to group them (as does the APA) into two categories, informal and formal. The following sections will cover informal and formal rules, followed by a set of rules that are exempted from the requirements of both informal and formal rulemaking.

Informal Rulemaking

Reflect back on the various rules and regulations that have been mentioned so far. Most of these rules were enacted informally by *informal rulemaking*. Informal rulemaking on the federal level (known as "notice and comment") is authorized by section 553 of the APA. Most states have statutes that also allow for notice and comment procedure for rulemaking.

Informal rulemaking is known as "notice and comment" because all that is required is notice to the public of a proposed rule, a chance for the public to participate by submitting comments to the agency, and publication of the final rule which takes into consideration the public comments. For example, if a federal agency issues a new safety standard for cars, the agency will first publish a proposed rule in the *Federal Register*, have a comment period, usually 60 days to take into account the comments received, and then issue a final rule—that is it. The publication of the final rule must occur 30 days before the rule becomes effective. The *Federal Register* is a daily government publication that keeps the public informed of actions of the federal government. The *Federal Register* provides legal notice to the public of proposed regulations, final regulations, and other information concerning the actions of the executive branch.

With informal rulemaking, there is no requirement that a hearing on the rule be held. This process is very simple. But keep in mind that agency staff may have labored for many months to be in a position to issue a proposed rule. For example, to come up with new safety standards for cars would require much planning, testing by engineers, and consultation with safety experts inside and outside government. Consequently, the bulk of the work has taken place prior to notice, so the

legislative rule
rules that have the force of law and carry out the intent of the statute, the most familiar of which are formal and informal

informal rulemaking
rulemaking done with the notice and comment procedure

Federal Register
the government publication that publishes proposed and final rules of the federal agencies

purpose of informal rulemaking is to provide public notice of an impending regulation while providing an opportunity for input before the rule is final.

To summarize, the informal rulemaking process requires the agency to:

1. PROVIDE NOTICE. Notice of the proposed rule by the agency issuing the rule, including the proposed authority under which the rule is proposed.

2. ALLOW COMMENT. After notice, the agency must give interested parties an opportunity to participate in the rulemaking through submission of written comments. The comment period is usually 30 to 60 days.

3. PUBLISH FINAL REGULATON IN THE *FEDERAL REGISTER*. After considering the submitted comments, the agency must submit a concise general statement of the basis and purpose of the final rule. The final rule does not become effective until 30 days after its publication in the *Federal Register*. This gives interested parties a chance to ask the agency to amend or repeal the rule.

Code of Federal Regulations

the compilation of all the rules and regulations issued by federal agencies. It is updated each year and divided into 50 titles.

Once a rule is final, the rule will be published in the **Code of Federal Regulations** (C.F.R.). The C.F.R is published by the Government Printing Office as the official compilation of federal regulations and is a codification of the regulations issued by the federal agencies. Codification is the process of grouping and organizing the various regulations into topics. The C.F.R. is divided into 50 titles that represent broad areas subject to federal regulation. For example, Title 42 of the C.F.R. groups all the regulations dealing with public health, whereas Title 49 contains regulations on transportation. Each volume of the C.F.R. is updated once each calendar year and is issued on a quarterly basis.

See Exhibit 2-1 for an excerpt from the *Federal Register* concerning a proposed rule.

See Exhibit 2-2 for an excerpt from the *Federal Register* concerning a final rule.

See Exhibit 2-3 for an excerpt from the *Code of Federal Regulations*.

Formal Rulemaking

Formal rulemaking is very rare because an agency is required to do so only when directed by a statute, usually the enabling act. Another reason that formal rulemaking is rare is the decision of the Supreme Court in *United States v. Florida East Cost Railway Co.* 410 U.S. 224 (1973),

Exhibit 2-1

Federal Register

Monday,
September 20, 2004

Part III

Securities and Exchange Commission

17 CFR Part 248
Disposal of Consumer Report
Information; Proposed Rule

(Continued)

Exhibit 2-1 (Continued)

56304   Federal Register/Vol. 69, No. 181/Monday, September 20, 2004/Proposed Rules

SECURITIES AND EXCHANGE
COMMISSION

17 CFR Part 248

[Release Nos. 34–50361, IA–2293, IC–26596;
File No. S7–33–04]

RIN 3235–AJ24

Disposal of Consumer Report Information

AGENCY: Securities and Exchange Commission.
ACTION: Proposed rule.

SUMMARY: The Securities and Exchange Commission ("Commission") is publishing for comment amendments to the rule under Regulation S–P requiring financial institutions to adopt policies and procedures to safeguard customer information ("safeguard rule"). The proposed amendments would implement the provision in section 216 of the Fair and Accurate Credit Transactions Act of 2003 requiring proper disposal of consumer report information and records. Section 216 directs the Commission and other federal agencies to adopt regulations requiring that any person who maintains or possesses a consumer report or consumer information derived from a consumer report for a business purpose must properly dispose of the information. The proposed amendments also would require the policies and procedures adopted under the safeguard rule to be in writing.
DATES: Comments should be received on or before October 20, 2004.
ADDRESSES: Comments may be submitted by any of the following methods:
Electronic Comments
  • Use the Commission's Internet comment form (*http://www.sec.gov/ rules/proposed.shtml*); or
  • Send an e-mail to *rule-comments@sec.gov.* Please include File Number S7–33–04 on the subject line; or
  • Use the Federal eRulemaking Portal (*http://www.regulations.gov*). Follow the instructions for submitting comments.
  Paper Comments
  • Send paper comments in triplicate to Jonathan G. Katz, Secretary, Securities and Exchange Commission, 450 Fifth Street, NW., Washington, DC 20549–0609.
All submissions should refer to File Number S7–33–04. This file number should be included on the subject line if e-mail is used. To help us process and review your comments more efficiently, please use only one method. The Commission will post all comments on the Commission's Internet Web site

(*http://www.sec.gov/rules/ proposed/shtml*). Comments will also be available for public inspection and copying in the Commission's Public Reference Room, 450 Fifth Street, NW., Washington, DC 20549. All comments received will be posted without change; we do not edit personal identifying information from submissions. You should submit only information that you wish to make available publicly.
FOR FURTHER INFORMATION CONTACT: For information regarding the proposed rule amendments as they relate to brokers or dealers, contact Catherine McGuire, Chief Counsel, Brian Bussey, Assistant Chief Counsel, or Tara Prigge, Attorney, Office of Chief Counsel, at the Division of Market Regulation, (202) 942–0073; as they relate to transfer agents registered with the Commission, contact Jerry Carpenter, Assistant Director, or David Karasik, Special Counsel, Office of Clearance and Settlement, at the Division of Market Regulation, (202) 942–4187; or as they relate to investment companies or to investment advisers registered with the Commission, contact Penelope W. Saltzman, Branch Chief, or Vincent M. Meehan, Attorney, Office of Regulatory Policy, at the Division of Investment Management, (202) 942–0690, Securities and Exchange Commission, 450 Fifth Street, NW., Washington, DC 20549.
SUPPLEMENTARY INFORMATION: The Commission is requesting public comment on proposed amendments to Regulation S–P under section 501(b) of the Gramm-Leach Bliley Act ("GLBA") [15 U.S.C. 6801(b)], section 216 of the Fair and Accurate Credit Transactions Act of 2003 ("FACT Act" or "Act") [15 U.S.C. 1681w], the Securities Exchange Act of 1934 (the "Exchange Act") [15 U.S.C. 78], the Investment Company Act of 1940 (the "Investment Company Act") [15 U.S.C. 80a], and the Investment Advisers Act of 1940 (the "Investment Advisers Act") [15 U.S.C. 80b].

Table of Contents

Text of Proposed Rules

I. Background

  Section 216 of the FACT Act adds a new section 628 to the Fair Credit Reporting Act ("FCRA").[1] The section is intended to prevent unauthorized disclosure of information contained in a consumer report and to reduce the risk of fraud or related crimes, including identity theft, by ensuring that records containing sensitive financial or personal information are appropriately redacted or destroyed before being discarded.[2] Section 216 of the FACT Act requires the Office of the Comptroller of the Currency, the Board of Governors of the Federal Reserve System, the Federal Deposit Insurance Corporation, the Office of Thrift Supervision (collectively, the "Banking Agencies"), the National Credit Union Administration, the Federal Trade Commission ("FTC") (collectively with the Banking Agencies, the "Agencies"), and the Commission to issue regulations requiring "any person that maintains or otherwise possesses consumer information, or any compilation of consumer information, derived from consumer reports for a business purpose, to properly dispose of any such information or compilation."[3] The Agencies and the Commission are required to consult and coordinate with each other so that, to the extent possible, regulations implementing this section are consistent and comparable. In addition, section 216 requires that the regulations must be consistent with the GLBA and other provisions of Federal law. The Commission staff has coordinated with the Agencies to develop a proposal regarding the disposal of consumer report information, and the Commission is now requesting public comment on that proposal.[4]

---

[1] 15 U.S.C. 1681. The FACT Act was signed into law on December 4, 2003. Pub. L. No. 108–159, 117 Stat. 1952 (2003). Section 628 is codified at 15 U.S.C. 1681w.
[2] *See* 108 Cong. Rec. S13,889 (Nov. 4, 2003) (statement of Sen. Nelson).
[3] The regulations must be issued in final form by December 4, 2004.
[4] The Banking Agencies have proposed to implement section 216 of the FACT Act by amending their existing guidelines on safeguarding customer information. *See* Proper Disposal of Consumer Information Under the Fair and Accurate Credit Transactions Act of 2003. 69 FR 31913 (June 8, 2004). The National Credit Union Administration has published a similar proposal. *See* Fair Credit Reporting—Proper Disposal of Consumer Information Under the Fair and Accurate Credit Transactions Act of 2003. 69 FR 30601 (May 28, 2004). The FTC has proposed a separate rule to implement section 216 of the Act. *See* Disposal of Consumer Report Information and Records, 69 FR 21388 (April 20, 2004) ("FTC Proposal").

Exhibit 2-2

National Archives and Records Administration
Littera Scripta Manet
1985

Federal Register

Tuesday,
April 19, 2005

Part II

Securities and Exchange Commission

17 CFR Part 275
Certain Broker-Dealers Deemed Not To Be Investment Advisers; Final Rule

(Continued)

Exhibit 2-2 (Continued)

20424   Federal Register/Vol. 7, No. 74/Tuesday, April 19, 2005/Rules and Regulations

SECURITIES AND EXCHANGE
COMMISSION

17   CFR Part 275

[Release Nos. 34–51523; IA–2376; File No.
S7–25–99]

RIN 3235-AH78

Certain Broker-Dealers Deemed Not To Be
Investment Advisers

AGENCY: Securities and Exchange Commission.
ACTION: Final rule.

SUMMARY: The Securities and Exchange
Commission is adopting a rule addressing the
application of the Investment Advisers Act of 1940
to broker-dealers offering certain types of
brokerage programs. Under the rule, a broker-
dealer providing advice that is solely incidental to
its brokerage services is excepted from the
Advisers Act if it charges an asset-based or fixed
fee (rather than a commission, mark-up, or mark-
down) for its services, provided it makes certain
disclosures about the nature of its services. The
rule states that exercising investment discretion is
not "solely incidental to" the business of a broker
or dealer within the meaning of the Advisers Act
or to brokerage services within the meaning of the
rule. The rule also states that a broker or dealer
provides investment advice that is not solely
incidental to the conduct of its business as a
broker or dealer or to its brokerage services if the
broker or dealer charges a separate fee or
separately contracts for advisory services. In
addition, the rule states that when a broker-dealer
provides advice as part of a financial plan or in
connection with providing planning services, a
broker-dealer provides advice that is not solely
incidental if it: holds itself out to the public as a
financial planner or as providing financial planning
services; or delivers to its customer a financial
plan; or represents to the customer that the advice
is provided as part of a financial plan or financial
planning services. Finally, under the rule, broker-
dealers are not subject to the Advisers Act solely
because they offer full-service brokerage and
discount brokerage services (including electronic
brokerage) for reduced commission rates.
DATES: *Effective date:* April 15, 2005, except that 17
CFR 275.202(a)(11)– 1(a)(1)(ii) is effective May 23, 2005.
Compliance dates: see Section IV of this Release.
FOR FURTHER INFORMATION CONTACT:
Robert L. Tuleya, Senior Counsel, or Nancy M.
Morris, Attorney-Fellow, at 202–551–6787,
larules@sec.gov, Office of Investment Adviser

Regulation, Division of Investment Management,
Securities and Exchange Commission, 450 Fifth
Street, NW, Washington, DC 20549–0506.
SUPPLEMENTARY INFORMATION: The Securities and
Exchange Commission ("Commission" or "SEC") is
adopting new rule 202(a)(11)–1[1] under the Investment
Advisers Act of 1940 ("Advisers Act" or "Act").[2]

Table of Contents

I.   Introduction

This rulemaking addresses the question of when the
investment advisory activities of a broker-dealer
subject it to the Advisers Act. The activities of broker-
dealers are regulated primarily under the Securities
Exchange Act of 1934[3] and by the self-regulatory
organizations ("SROs"). The activities of investment
advisers are regulated primarily under the Advisers Act.

---
[1] 17 CFR 275.202(a)(11)–1. When we refer to rule 202(a)(11)–1
or any paragraph in that rule, we are referring to 17 CFR
275.202(a)(11)–1 where it is published in the Code of Federal
Regulations.
[2] 15 U.S.C. 80b–1. When we refer to the Advisers Act, or
any paragraph of the Act, we are referring to 15 U.S.C. 80b
of the United States Code in which the Act is published.
[3] 15 U.S.C. 78a ("Exchange Act").

The Advisers Act and the Exchange Act are not
exclusive in their application to advisers and
broker-dealers, respectively. Many broker-dealers
are also registered with us as advisers because of
the nature of the services they provide or the
form of compensation they receive. Until recently,
the division between broker-dealers and
investment advisers was fairly clear, and the
regulatory obligations of each fairly distinct. Of
late, however, the distinctions have begun to blur,
raising difficult questions regarding the application
of statutory provisions written by Congress more
than half a century ago.

Our efforts to address this question, which
began in 1999, have prompted substantial interest
from advisers and broker-dealers as well as
groups representing the interests of investors. We
very much appreciate the efforts of these groups
in commenting on our proposal, meeting with us
and our staff, and offering their many suggestions.
The evolution of our thinking about these
questions, and the important contribution these
commenters have made to that evolution, is
demonstrated in the rule we are today adopting.
Although many commenters urge that all who
render investment advice must be regulated as
advisers, Congress created a different scheme of
regulation—one that excepted many who provide
investment advice, including many broker-dealers
registered under the Exchange Act, from the
Advisers Act. As a consequence, many of the
concerns about broker-dealer conduct voiced in
the course of this rulemaking may be more
appropriately addressed under the Exchange Act.
Although we share the concern that there is
confusion about the differences between broker-
dealers and investment advisers, and although we
believe that some of that confusion may be a
result of broker-dealer marketing (including the
titles broker-dealers use), we do not believe that
this confusion arises as a result of this rulemaking
or that it is confined to the new programs
addressed by this rulemaking. Indeed, to a large
extent, this rulemaking does address confusion in
the context of the brokerage programs addressed
here. Again, however, we believe that many of
these concerns may more appropriately fall under
broker-dealer regulation and, as stated below, the
Chairman has directed our staff to determine and
report to us within 90 days the options for most
effectively responding to these issues and a
recommended course of action. This schedule
reflects both our appreciation of the significance
of these concerns and our determination to
pursue an appropriate and effective solution.

Exhibit 2-3

Excerpt from *Code of Federal Regulations*

Code of Federal Regulations]

[Title 21, Volume 2]

[Revised as of April 1, 2005]

[CITE: 21CFR101.22]

TITLE 21–FOOD AND DRUGS

CHAPTER I–FOOD AND DRUG ADMINISTRATION

DEPARTMENT OF HEALTH AND HUMAN SERVICES

SUBCHAPTER B–FOOD FOR HUMAN CONSUMPTION

PART 101 – FOOD LABELING

Subpart B–Specific Food Labeling Requirements

Sec. 101.22 Foods; labeling of spices, flavorings, colorings and chemical preservatives.

(a)(1) The term *artificial flavor* or *artificial flavoring* means any substance, the function of which is to impart flavor, which is not derived from a spice, fruit or fruit juice, vegetable or vegetable juice, edible yeast, herb, bark, bud, root, leaf or similar plant material, meat, fish, poultry, eggs, dairy products, or fermentation products thereof. Artificial flavor includes the substances listed in 172.515(b) and 182.60 of this chapter except where these are derived from natural sources.

(2) The term *spice* means any aromatic vegetable substance in the whole, broken, or ground form, except for those substances which have been traditionally regarded as foods, such as onions, garlic and celery; whose significant function in food is seasoning rather than nutritional; that is true to name; and from which no portion of any volatile oil or other flavoring principle has been removed. Spices include the spices listed in 182.10 and part 184 of this chapter, such as the following:

Allspice, Anise, Basil, Bay leaves, Caraway seed, Cardamon, Celery seed, Chervil, Cinnamon, Cloves, Coriander, Cumin seed, Dill seed, Fennel seed, Fenugreek, Ginger, Horseradish, Mace, Marjoram, Mustard flour, Nutmeg, Oregano, Paprika, Parsley, Pepper, black; Pepper, white; Pepper, red; Rosemary, Saffron, Sage, Savory, Star aniseed, Tarragon, Thyme, Turmeric.

Paprika, turmeric, and saffron or other spices which are also colors, shall be declared as "spice and coloring" unless declared by their common or usual name.

(Continued)

Exhibit 2-3 (Continued)

(3) The term *natural flavor* or *natural flavoring* means the essential oil, oleoresin, essence or extractive, protein hydrolysate, distillate, or any product of roasting, heating or enzymolysis, which contains the flavoring constituents derived from a spice, fruit or fruit juice, vegetable or vegetable juice, edible yeast, herb, bark, bud, root, leaf or similar plant material, meat, seafood, poultry, eggs, dairy products, or fermentation products thereof, whose significant function in food is flavoring rather than nutritional. Natural flavors include the natural essence or extractives obtained from plants listed in 182.10, 182.20, 182.40, and 182.50 and part 184 of this chapter, and the substances listed in 172.510 of this chapter.

(4) The term *artificial color* or *artificial coloring* means any "color additive" as defined in 70.3(f) of this chapter.

(5) The term *chemical preservative* means any chemical that, when added to food, tends to prevent or retard deterioration thereof, but does not include common salt, sugars, vinegars, spices, or oils extracted from spices, substances added to food by direct exposure thereof to wood smoke, or chemicals applied for their insecticidal or herbicidal properties.

(b) A food which is subject to the requirements of section 403(k) of the act shall bear labeling, even though such food is not in package form.

(c) A statement of artificial flavoring, artificial coloring, or chemical preservative shall be placed on the food or on its container or wrapper, or on any two or all three of these, as may be necessary to render such statement likely to be read by the ordinary person under customary conditions of purchase and use of such food. The specific artificial color used in a food shall be identified on the labeling when so required by regulation in part 74 of this chapter to assure safe conditions of use for the color additive.

(d) A food shall be exempt from compliance with the requirements of section 403(k) of the act if it is not in package form and the units thereof are so small that a statement of artificial flavoring, artificial coloring, or chemical preservative, as the case may be, cannot be placed on such units with such conspicuousness as to render it likely to be read by the ordinary individual under customary conditions of purchase and use.

(e) A food shall be exempt while held for sale from the requirements of section 403(k) of the act (requiring label statement of any artificial flavoring, artificial coloring, or chemical preservatives) if said food, having been received in bulk containers at a retail establishment, is displayed to the purchaser with either (1) the labeling of the bulk container plainly in view or (2) a counter card,

Exhibit 2-3 (Continued)

sign, or other appropriate device bearing prominently and conspicuously the information required to be stated on the label pursuant to section 403(k).

(f) A fruit or vegetable shall be exempt from compliance with the requirements of section 403(k) of the act with respect to a chemical preservative applied to the fruit or vegetable as a pesticide chemical prior to harvest.

(g) A flavor shall be labeled in the following way when shipped to a food manufacturer or processor (but not a consumer) for use in the manufacture of a fabricated food, unless it is a flavor for which a standard of identity has been promulgated, in which case it shall be labeled as provided in the standard:

(1) If the flavor consists of one ingredient, it shall be declared by its common or usual name.

(2) If the flavor consists of two or more ingredients, the label either may declare each ingredient by its common or usual name or may state "All flavor ingredients contained in this product are approved for use in a regulation of the Food and Drug Administration." Any flavor ingredient not contained in one of these regulations, and any nonflavor ingredient, shall be separately listed on the label.

(3) In cases where the flavor contains a solely natural flavor(s), the flavor shall be so labeled, e.g., "strawberry flavor", "banana flavor", or "natural strawberry flavor". In cases where the flavor contains both a natural flavor and an artificial flavor, the flavor shall be so labeled, e.g., "natural and artificial strawberry flavor". In cases where the flavor contains a solely artificial flavor(s), the flavor shall be so labeled, e.g., "artificial strawberry flavor".

which created a presumption *against* formal rulemaking. In this case, the court ruled that a statute authorizing an agency to act "after a hearing" did not trigger formal rulemaking. What is needed to trigger formal rulemaking is a phrase that includes the words "after a hearing on the record." Few statutes have these words or its equivalent; thus, formal rulemaking remains a rare event. The Food and Drug Administration (FDA) is an example of an agency that uses formal rulemaking because the statute under which it operates requires it. See the following excerpt from the federal statutes that require the FDA to engage in formal rulemaking.

As soon as practicable after such request for a public hearing, the Secretary, after due notice, shall hold such a public hearing for the purpose of receiving evidence relevant and material to the issues raised by such objections. At the hearing, any interested person may be heard in person or by representative. As soon as practicable after completion of the hearing, the Secretary shall by order act upon such objections and make such order public. Such order shall be based only on substantial evidence of record at such hearing and shall set forth, as part of the order, detailed findings of fact on which the order is based. The Secretary shall specify in the order the date on which it shall take effect, except that it shall not be made to take effect prior to the ninetieth day after its publication unless the Secretary finds that emergency conditions exist necessitating an earlier effective date, in which event the Secretary shall specify in the order his findings as to such conditions. 21 U.S.C. § 371(c)(3).

Note the words "substantial evidence of record at such hearing," which trigger formal rulemaking.

formal rulemaking

when an agency uses a hearing on the record to establish a rule

Formal rulemaking follows generally the procedures of informal rulemaking except that a hearing on the record is required. Sections 556 and 557 of the APA set out the requirements of formal rulemaking. First, the agency publishes notice of the hearing date in the *Federal Register*. Next, the hearing is conducted by a hearing officer, which is like a trial and can include opening statements and testimony of witnesses who can be cross-examined. Written material can also be submitted. The parties are entitled to submit proposed findings and conclusions or exceptions to the rule. The record of the hearing must show the ruling on each finding conclusion or exception. After the hearing, the hearing officer will submit findings and conclusions with the reasons for implementing the rule. The rule will then be published in the *Federal Register*. The final rule is published 30 days before it becomes effective. With these added layers of procedure that come with a formal hearing, we can see that formal rulemaking can be very time-consuming and costly, hence the presumption against formal rulemaking.

See Exhibit 2-4 which lists some characteristics of rules.

Hybrid Rulemaking

hybrid rule

a rule with some characteristics of both formal and informal rulemaking

Sometimes a statute requires more than informal but less than formal rulemaking. The result is a *hybrid rule*. For example, a hybrid rule would be created by adding to informal rulemaking a limited right to cross-examine and to present rebuttal evidence. Congress, not the courts, can create hybrid rules. The Supreme Court ruled in *Vermont Yankee Nuclear Power Corp. v. Natural Resources Defense Council*, 435

Exhibit 2-4
Characteristics of Rules or Regulations

The terms rules and regulations have exactly the same meaning.	Rules and regulations are issued by agencies to fill in gaps left by statutes.	Rules and regulations alter and affect legal rights.
Rules and regulations have the force of law and must be obeyed.	Rules and regulations represent power delegated to an agency by Congress.	Rules and regulations are akin to statutes and reflect legislative power of agencies.
Rules and regulations apply across the board to all, not just to single individuals or businesses.	Most rules are made through an informal process which is called "notice and comment."	Very few rules are made formally which requires a hearing on the record.

U.S. 519 (1978), that courts are not permitted to take an informal rule and turn it into a hybrid. (See excerpt in Case Law later in the chapter.) In *Vermont Yankee,* the lower court required input (including the requirement of a trial-like hearing) above and beyond what was statutorily required in assessing the environmental effects from nuclear waste. The Supreme Court made it clear that as long as the agency met the minimum requirements for informal rulemaking and there were no constitutional requirements, the court cannot require more. To do so would be an interference with the administrative process that Congress has instituted.

Congress creates hybrid rules when a statute does not require formal rulemaking but includes such phrases as "public hearing is required" or "an opportunity for the oral presentation of evidence must be afforded." The Federal Trade Commission (FTC) and OSHA are agencies that use hybrid rulemaking.

Here is an example of a statute creating a hybrid rulemaking process for the FTC.

> Prior to the publication of any notice of proposed rulemaking pursuant to paragraph (1)(A), the Commission shall publish an advance notice of proposed rulemaking in the *Federal Register.* 15 U.S.C. § 57(a)(2)(A).

Note that the FTC is required to issue an advanced notice of proposed rulemaking. The advance notice is not required by the APA, but Congress has added this requirement and thus has created a hybrid rulemaking process. If a court were to add this provision, it would run afoul of *Vermont Yankee.*

Exempted Rulemaking

Section 553 of the APA exempts agencies from formal and informal rulemaking procedures if the rule falls into specific categories. Some of the more common examples of *exempted rulemaking* under section 553 of the APA are:

exempted rules
rules that are not implemented by informal or informal methods

- Good cause exception—when an agency determines that notice and comment would be impracticable, unnecessary, or contrary to the public interest. For example, measures to protect the public from adulterated food or safety risks would fall under the good cause exception. As another example, the Federal Aviation Administration (FAA) issued a valid rule under this exception when it required helicopters used in air tours be equipped with emergency flotation devices and prohibited flying below minimum altitudes, *Hawaii Helicopter Operators Assoc. v. FAA,* 51 F.3d 212 (9th Cir. 1995).
- Rulemaking in the area of military or foreign affairs.
- Rules concerning agency management of personnel.
- Procedural rules—rules that establish how an agency functions.
- Rules concerning public property, loans, grants, benefits and contracts.
- Interpretive rules—rules that explain an agency's rules and provide guidelines to the meaning of regulations.
- Policy statements—(not really rules) but policy statements explain the objectives of an agency and announce the agency's future intentions but do not establish legal rights and obligations.

nonlegislative rules
when an agency issues a statement of clarification to advise the public on the agency's interpretation of the statutes and rules it administers. Nonlegislative rules, such as interpretive rules and policy statements, are advisory only and do not have the force of law.

Interpretive rules and policy statements are known as *nonlegislative rules.* Unlike legislative rules, nonlegislative rules are issued to advise the public and affected industries of how the agency interprets and construes its regulations. For example, the Equal Employment Opportunity Commission (EEOC) issues guidelines that interpret the Civil Rights Act of 1964. Because EEOC does not have the power to issue legislative rules, the guidelines are nonlegislative and not binding.

Sometimes agencies that have the power to issue legislative rules issue policy statements and interpretive rules to clarify existing regulations. The line between a policy statement and interpretive rule, on the one hand, and a legislative rule, on the other, is not always clear. *Hoctor v. USDC*, 82 F.3d 165 (7th Cir. 1996), is an example of the difficulty in distinguishing a legislative rule and an interpretive rule. (See excerpt in Case Law later in the chapter.) The Animal Welfare Act authorizes the Department of Agriculture (USDA) to adopt rules "to govern the humane handling, care, treatment, and transportation of animals by dealers." A regulation required that a facility housing animals "must be constructed of such material and such strength as appropriate for the animals involved." An internal memorandum (which was issued without notice and comment) said that all dangerous animals must be inside a fence at least 8 feet high. When a dealer in exotic animals was penalized for having only a 6 foot high fence, the court had to decide if the 8 foot fence requirement was a valid interpretive rule. The court stated that the 8 foot requirement was based on an arbitrary choice, similar to the statute of limitations. When agencies base rules on arbitrary choices, they are legislating, and so these rules require notice and comment. Because the 8 foot standard was not issued by the notice and comment procedure and its effect was to change and not interpret the existing rule, the penalty against the dealer could not stand.

Negotiated Rulemaking

Negotiated rulemaking (5 U.S.C. §§ 561–570) allows the agency and interested parties to work together and draft a rule that is acceptable to everyone affected by the rule. Typically, an agency will form a committee composed of members of the industry affected and public interest groups in an attempt to reach a consensus on a rule. Once the proposed rule has been tentatively agreed upon, the agency will follow notice and comment procedures of informal rulemaking. Congress made findings which expressed the hope that negotiated rulemaking could be a useful tool in administrative law and noted that formal and informal rulemaking can:

> "discourage the affected parties from meeting and communicating with each other, and may cause parties with different interests to assume conflicting and antagonistic positions and to engage in expensive and time-consuming litigation over agency rules..." and can "deprive[s] the affected parties and the public of the benefits of face-to-face negotiations and cooperation in developing and reaching agreement on a rule. It also deprives them of the benefits

of shared information, knowledge, expertise, and technical abilities possessed by the affected parties. . ." Negotiated rulemaking, on the other hand, "can increase the acceptability and improve the substance of rules, making it less likely that the affected parties will resist enforcement or challenge such rules in court. It may also shorten the amount of time needed to issue final rules." 5 U.S.C. § 561.

The number of rules implemented by negotiated rulemaking remains small; however, Congress's findings offer hope that negotiated rulemaking can be used to improve this aspect of administrative law.

RULEMAKING IN PERSPECTIVE

Agencies can only issue legislative rules after receiving power delegated to them by Congress or a state legislature. Legislative rules are the ones we are most familiar with, have the force of law, and are binding "laws." Nonlegislative rules are not based on delegated powers and therefore do not have the force of law. Legislative rulemaking gives the agencies tremendous power over our lives; however, agencies must follow the Constitution and may only make legislative rules when Congress has granted them that power. For example, the FDA issued legislative rules regulating tobacco products, including cigarettes. The Supreme Court held that Congress never delegated such power to the FDA and struck down the regulations because the FDA exceeded its powers, *FDA v. Brown and Williamson,* 529 U.S. 120 (2000). Agency power can be controlled in a number of ways including the challenging of a rule in a court. Control of rulemaking by the courts is covered in Chapter 6.

CASE LAW

VERMONT YANKEE NUCLEAR POWER CORP. v. NATURAL RESOURCES DEFENSE COUNCIL, INC.
435 U.S. 519, 98 S.Ct. 1197, 55 L.Ed.2d 460 (1978).

REHNQUIST, JUSTICE:
[The Natural Resources Defense Council (NRDC) challenged a rule promulgated by the Atomic Energy Commission (AEC). The NRDC contended that the absence of discovery or cross-examination denied it a meaningful opportunity to participate in the rulemaking proceedings. The District of Columbia Circuit Court of Appeals remanded the rule to the AEC. According to the Supreme Court, the

---

"ineluctable mandate" of the circuit court's decision was that "the procedures followed during the hearings were inadequate." The Court stated that "[a]gencies are free to grant additional procedural rights in the exercise of their discretion, but reviewing courts are generally not free to impose them if the agencies have not chosen to grant them." Thus, "[a]bsent constitutional constraints or extremely compelling circumstances," administrative agencies "'should be free to fashion their own rules of procedure and to pursue methods of inquiry capable of permitting them to discharge their multitudinous duties.'" The Court cited several "compelling" reasons for its holding:]

In the first place, if courts continually review agency proceedings to determine whether the agency employed procedures which were, in the court's opinion, perfectly tailored to reach what the court perceives to be the "best" or "correct" result, judicial review would be totally unpredictable. And the agencies, operating under this vague injunction to employ the "best" procedures and facing the threat of reversal if they did not, would undoubtedly adopt full adjudicatory procedures in every instance. Not only would this totally disrupt the statutory scheme, through which Congress enacted "a formula upon which opposing social and political forces have come to rest," but all the inherent advantages of informal rulemaking would be totally lost.

Secondly, it is obvious that the court in these cases reviewed the agency's choice of procedures on the basis of the record actually produced at the hearing, and not on the basis of the information available to the agency when it made the decision to structure the proceedings in a certain way. This sort of Monday morning quarterbacking not only encourages but almost compels the agency to conduct all rulemaking proceedings with the full panoply of procedural devices normally associated only with adjudicatory hearings.

Finally, and perhaps most importantly, this sort of review fundamentally misconceives the nature of the standard for judicial review of an agency rule. The court below uncritically assumed that additional procedures will automatically result in a more adequate record because it will give interested parties more of an opportunity to participate in and contribute to the proceedings. But informal rulemaking need not be based solely on the transcript of a hearing held before an agency. Indeed, the agency need not even hold a formal hearing. Thus, the adequacy of the "record" in this type of proceeding is not correlated directly to the type of procedural devices employed, but rather turns on whether the agency has followed the statutory

(*Continued*)

mandate of the Administrative Procedure Act or other relevant statutes. If the agency is compelled to support the rule which it ultimately adopts with the type of record produced only after a full adjudicatory hearing, it simply will have no choice but to conduct a full adjudicatory hearing prior to promulgating every rule. In sum, this sort of unwarranted judicial examination of perceived procedural shortcomings of a rulemaking proceeding can do nothing but seriously interfere with that process prescribed by Congress.

CASE LAW

HOCTOR v. UNITED STATES DEPARTMENT OF AGRICULTURE
82 F.3d 165 (7th Cir.1996).

POSNER, C.J.:

[The Animal Welfare Act authorizes the Department of Agriculture (USDA) to adopt rules "to govern the humane handling, care, treatment, and transportation of animals by dealers." Using notice and comment procedure, USDA adopted a rule entitled "Structural Strength" requiring that the facility housing animals "must be constructed of such material and of such strength as appropriate for the animals involved." 9 C.F.R. § 3.125(a). USDA later adopted an internal memorandum addressed to its inspectors, in which it said that all dangerous animals must be inside a perimeter fence at least 8 feet high.

Hoctor dealt in exotic cats, including three lions, two tigers, and seven ligers (a liger is a cross between a male lion and a female tiger), six cougars, and two snow leopards (but no tigons). The pens were surrounded by a "containment fence" and the entire property by a "perimeter fence" 6 feet high. Hoctor was penalized by USDA because the perimeter fence was only 6 rather than 8 feet high. It would cost him many thousands of dollars to replace the fence. The issue is whether the internal memorandum is a valid interpretive rule.]

A rule promulgated by an agency that is subject to the APA is invalid unless the agency first issues a public notice of proposed rulemaking, describing the substance of the proposed rule, and gives the public an opportunity to submit written comments; and if after receiving the comments it decides to promulgate the rule it must set forth the basis and purpose of the rule in a public statement. These procedural requirements do not apply, however, to "interpretative rules, general statements of policy, or rules of agency organization, procedure, or practice." § 553(b)(A).

Distinguishing between a "legislative" rule, to which the notice and comment provisions of the Act apply, and an interpretive rule, to which these provisions do not apply, is often very difficult—and often very important to regulated firms, the public, and the agency. Notice and comment rulemaking is time-consuming, facilitates the marshaling of opposition to a proposed rule, and may result in the creation of a very long record that may in turn provide a basis for a judicial challenge to the rule if the agency decides to promulgate it. There are no formalities attendant upon the promulgation of an interpretive rule, but this is tolerable because such a rule is "only" an interpretation. Every governmental agency that enforces a less than crystalline statute must interpret the statute, and it does the public a favor if it announces the interpretation in advance of enforcement, whether the announcement takes the form of a rule or of a policy statement, which the Administrative Procedure Act assimilates to an interpretive rule. It would be no favor to the public to discourage the announcement of agencies' interpretations by burdening the interpretive process with cumbersome formalities. . . .

We may assume, though we need not decide, that USDA has the statutory authority to require dealers in dangerous animals to enclose their compounds with eight foot-high fences. . . .

The only ground on which the Department defends sanctioning Hoctor for not having a high enough fence is that requiring an eight-foot-high perimeter fence for dangerous animals is an interpretation of the Department's own structural-strength regulation, and "provided an agency's interpretation of its own regulations does not violate the Constitution or a federal statute, it must be given 'controlling weight unless it is plainly erroneous or inconsistent with the regulation.'" The "provided" clause does not announce a demanding standard of judicial review, although the absence of any reference in the housing regulation to fences or height must give us pause. The regulation appears only to require that pens and other animal housing be sturdy enough in design and construction, and sufficiently well maintained, to prevent the animals from breaking through the enclosure—not that any enclosure, whether a pen or a

(*Continued*)

perimeter fence, be high enough to prevent the animals from escaping by jumping over the enclosure. . . .

Our doubts about the scope of the regulation that the eight-foot rule is said to be "interpreting" might seem irrelevant, since even if a rule requiring an eight-foot perimeter fence could not be based on the regulation, it could be based on the statute itself, which in requiring the Department to establish minimum standards for the housing of animals presumably authorizes it to promulgate standards for secure containment. But if the eight-foot rule were deemed one of those minimum standards that the Department is required by statute to create, it could not possibly be thought an interpretive rule. For what would it be interpreting? When Congress authorizes an agency to create standards, it is delegating legislative authority, rather than itself setting forth a standard which the agency might then particularize through interpretation. Put differently, when a statute does not impose a duty on the persons subject to it but instead authorizes (or requires—it makes no difference) an agency to impose a duty, the formulation of that duty becomes a legislative task entrusted to the agency. Provided that a rule promulgated pursuant to such a delegation is intended to bind, and not merely to be a tentative statement of the agency's view, which would make it just a policy statement, and not a rule at all, the rule would be the clearest possible example of a legislative rule, as to which the notice and comment procedure not here followed is mandatory, as distinct from an interpretive rule; for there would be nothing to interpret. . . . That is why the Department must argue that its eight-foot rule is an interpretation of the structural-strength regulation—itself a standard, and therefore interpretable—in order to avoid reversal.

Even if, despite the doubts that we expressed earlier, the eight-foot rule is consistent with, even in some sense authorized by, the structural-strength regulation, it would not necessarily follow that it is an interpretive rule. It is that only if it can be derived from the regulation by a process reasonably described as interpretation. Supposing that the regulation imposes a general duty of secure containment, the question is, then, Can a requirement that the duty be implemented by erecting an eight-foot-high perimeter fence be thought an interpretation of that general duty?

"Interpretation" in the narrow sense is the ascertainment of meaning. It is obvious that eight feet is not part of the meaning of secure containment. But "interpretation" is often used in a much broader sense. A process of "interpretation" has transformed the Constitution into a body of law undreamt of by the framers. To skeptics the Miranda rule is as remote from the text of the Fifth Amendment as the eight-foot rule is from the text of 9 C.F.R. § 3.125(a). But our task in this case is not to plumb the mysteries of legal theory; it is merely to give effect to a distinction that the Administrative Procedure Act makes, and we can do this by referring to the purpose of the distinction. The purpose is to separate the cases in which notice and comment rulemaking is required from the cases in which it is not required. As we noted at the outset, unless a statute or regulation is of crystalline transparency, the agency enforcing it cannot avoid interpreting it, and the agency would be stymied in its enforcement duties if every time it brought a case on a new theory it had to pause for a bout, possible lasting several years, of notice and comment rulemaking. Besides being unavoidably continuous, statutory interpretation normally proceeds without the aid of elaborate factual inquiries. When it is an executive or administrative agency that is doing the interpreting it brings to the task a greater knowledge of the regulated activity than the judicial or legislative branches have, and this knowledge is to some extent a substitute for formal fact-gathering.

At the other extreme from what might be called normal or routine interpretation is the making of reasonable but arbitrary (not in the "arbitrary or capricious" sense) rules that are consistent with the statute or regulation under which the rules are promulgated but not derived from it, because they represent an arbitrary choice among methods of implementation. A rule that turns on a number is likely to be arbitrary in this sense. There is no way to reason to an eight-foot perimeter-fence rule as opposed to a seven-and-a-half foot fence or a nine-foot fence or a ten-foot fence. None of these candidates for a rule is uniquely appropriate to, and in that sense derivable from, the duty of secure containment. This point becomes even clearer if we note that the eight-foot rule actually has another component—the fence must be at least three feet from any animal's pen. Why three feet? Why not four? Or two?

The reason courts refuse to create statutes of limitations is precisely the difficulty of reasoning to a number by the methods of reasoning used by courts. One cannot extract from the concept of a tort that a tort suit should be barred unless brought within one, or two, or three, or five years. The choice is arbitrary and courts are uncomfortable with making arbitrary choices. They see this as a legislative function. Legislators have the democratic legitimacy to make choices among value judgments, choices based on hunch or guesswork or even

(Continued)

the toss of a coin, and other arbitrary choices. When agencies base rules on arbitrary choices they are legislating, and so these rules are legislative or substantive and require notice and comment rulemaking, a procedure that is analogous to the procedure employed by legislatures in making statutes. The notice of proposed rulemaking corresponds to the bill and the reception of written comments to the hearing on the bill.

The common sense of requiring notice and comment rulemaking for legislative rules is well illustrated by the facts of this case. There is no process of cloistered, appellate-court type reasoning by which the Department of Agriculture could have excogitated the eight-foot rule from the structural-strength regulation. The rule is arbitrary in the sense that it could well be different without significant impairment of any regulatory purpose. But this does not make the rule a matter of indifference to the people subject to it. There are thousands of animal dealers, and some unknown fraction of these face the prospect of having to tear down their existing fences and build new, higher ones at great cost. The concerns of these dealers are legitimate and since, as we are stressing, the rule could well be otherwise, the agency was obliged to listen to them before settling on a final rule and to provide some justification for that rule, though not so tight or logical a justification as a court would be expected to offer for a new judge-made rule. Notice and comment is the procedure by which the persons affected by legislative rules are enabled to communicate their concerns in a comprehensive and systematic fashion to the legislating agency. The Department's lawyer speculated that if the notice and comment route had been followed in this case the Department would have received thousands of comments. The greater the public interest in a rule, the greater reason to allow the public to participate in its formation.

We are not saying that an interpretive rule can never have a numerical component. *See, e.g., American Mining Congress v. Mine Safety & Health Administration,* [1108, 995 F.2d 1106, 1113 (D.C.Cir. 1993)]. There is merely an empirical relation between interpretation and generality on the one hand, and legislation and specificity on the other. Especially in scientific and other technical areas, where quantitative criteria are common, a rule that translates a general norm into a number may be justifiable as interpretation. . . . Even in a nontechnical area the use of a number as a rule of thumb to guide the application of a general norm will often be legitimately interpretive. Had the Department of Agriculture said in the internal memorandum that it could not imagine a case in which a perimeter fence for dangerous animals that was lower than eight feet would provide secure containment, and would therefore presume, subject to rebuttal, that a lower fence was insecure, it would have been on stronger ground. For it would have been tying the rule to the animating standard, that of secure containment, rather than making it stand free of the standard, self-contained, unbending, arbitrary. To switch metaphors, the "flatter" a rule is, the harder it is to conceive of it as merely spelling out what is in some sense latent in a statute or regulation, and the eight-foot rule in its present form is as flat as they come. At argument the Department's lawyer tried to loosen up the rule, implying that the Department might have bent it if Hoctor proposed to dig a moat or to electrify his six-foot fence. But an agency's lawyer is not authorized to amend its rules in order to make them more palatable to the reviewing court.

The Department's position might seem further undermined by the fact that it has used the notice and comment procedure to promulgate rules prescribing perimeter fences for dogs and monkeys. Why it proceeded differently for dangerous animals is unexplained. But we attach no weight to the Department's inconsistency, not only because it would be unwise to penalize the Department for having at least partially complied with the requirements of the APA, but also because there is nothing in the Act to forbid an agency to use the notice and comment procedure in cases in which it is not required to do so. We are mindful that the court in *United States v. Picciotto*, 875 F.2d 345, 348 (D.C.Cir. 1989), thought that the fact that an agency had used notice and comment rulemaking in a setting similar to the case before the court was evidence that the agency "intended" to promulgate a legislative rule in that case, only without bothering with notice and comment. The inference is strained, and in any event we think the agency's "intent," though a frequently cited factor, is rather a makeweight. What the agency intends is to promulgate a rule. It is for the courts to say whether it is the kind of rule that is valid only if promulgated after notice and comment. It is that kind of rule if, as in the present case, it cannot be derived by interpretation. The order under review, based as it was on a rule that is invalid because not promulgated in accordance with the required procedure, is therefore
VACATED.

Reprinted from Asimow, M.; Bonfield, A.; and Levin, R. State and Federal Administrative Law, 2nd ed. ©1998, with permission of Thomson West.

CHAPTER SUMMARY

Rules (also referred to as regulations) represent the legislative power of agencies. Rules and regulations are issued by agencies to implement the intent of statutes. They are called gap-fillers because they provide the details to the policies that are left out of broadly worded statutes. Legislative rules have the force of law and affect and alter legal rights. Nonlegislative rules such as interpretive rules and policy statements clarify existing rules and statutes and are not binding because they are not based on delegated power. The most common kind of rule or regulation is created in a process designated informal rulemaking, also called "notice and comment." Formal rulemaking is rare and requires a hearing on the record. Rules are first published in the *Federal Register* and then permanently placed and organized by title in the *Code of Federal Regulations*. Exempted rules do not have to be implemented by notice and comment, nor do they have to be established formally.

KEY TERMS

Code of Federal Regulations
exempted rules
Federal Register
formal rulemaking
hybrid rule

informal rulemaking
legislative rule
nonlegislative rules
rule or regulation

REVIEW QUESTIONS

1. Discuss the importance of agency rules, also known as regulations, in administrative law.
2. Distinguish between formal and informal rulemaking.
3. List some examples of exempted rules.
4. In what publication are proposed and final rules published?
5. In what publication are agencies' rules arranged by subject matter and codified?

MORE INFORMATION

1. Go to http://www.regulations.gov to see how to comment on pending federal regulations.
2. Stay on http://www.regulations.gov to view the comments of others.

PRACTICAL APPLICATIONS

1. Go to the *Federal Register's* main page at http://www.gpoaccess.gov/fr/index.html.
   See 1994 Volume 59 through 2007 Volume 71.
   Select simple search 1994 forward.
   Select Volume 61.
   Put in a search "page 44396."
   Click on hit 2 and answer the following:
   A. What is the name of the agency that issued the regulations?
   B. What is the subject of the regulations?
   C. Is this a proposed or a final rule?
   Scroll down to a heading called "A Purpose and Overview of Rule."
   D. What law does the agency cite as the authority for its jurisdiction over this subject?
   Scroll down to a heading called "Background."
   As of the date of these regulations, answer the following:
   E. How many Americans smoked cigarettes?
   F. How many used smokeless tobacco?
   G. How many people die each year from tobacco-related illnesses?
2. Go to the Web site of the Food and Drug Administration (FDA) at http://www.fda.gov.
   Click on "about FDA."
   A. State what the FDA regulates.
   B. State what the FDA does not regulate.
3. Review Exhibit 2-2, which is an excerpt from the *Federal Register* concerning a proposed rule.
   A. State the name of the agency which issued this rule.
   B. What law does this rule implement?
   C. What is the last day to send a comment to the agency about this proposed rule?
   D. What is the subject matter of the proposed rule?
4. Review Exhibit 2-4, which is an excerpt from the *Code of Federal Regulations*.
   A. State the name of the agency which issued this rule.
   B. What is the topic of this regulation?
   C. How does the rule define the term "spice"?
   D. Give three examples of a spice.

@

L E A R N   A B O U T   T H E   A G E N C I E S

Go to the Web sites of the following agencies and state their function.

1. SEC—Securities and Exchange Commission—http://www.sec.gov
2. DHHS—Department of Health and Human Services—http://www.os.dhhs.gov
3. TSA—Transportation Security Agency—http://www.tsa.gov/public
4. FEMA—Federal Emergency Management Agency—http://www.fema.gov
5. NTSB—National Transportation Safety Board—http://www.ntsb.gov

Agency Enforcement of Regulations

CHAPTER OBJECTIVES

After reading this chapter, you should be able to:

- Demonstrate an understanding of how agencies enforce their regulations.

- Compare and contrast an agency's enforcement of its regulations with the criminal law.

- Examine the enforcement power of agencies within the scope of the Fourth Amendment.

- Examine the enforcement power of agencies within the scope of the Fifth Amendment.

CHAPTER OUTLINE

INTRODUCTION TO ENFORCEMENT OF REGULATIONS

executive power

of an agency—power to carry out and enforce the rules and regulation issued by that agency

Chapter 1 laid out the basic framework of agency powers and explained that agencies possess forms of legislative, executive, and judicial power. Review Exhibit 1-4, Separation of Powers and Powers of Agencies. Chapter 2 covered agencies' legislative power, which is known as the power to issue rules and regulations. Chapter 4 will cover judicial power. This chapter covers the power of agencies to enforce their regulations, sometimes called *executive power.* To effectively enforce their regulations, agencies need information. Many agencies are empowered to enforce their regulations by requiring those they regulate to first collect information and then disclose that information when the agency requests it. For example, the Nuclear Regulatory Commission (NRC) requires nuclear power plants to report any accident involving a nuclear reactor or any lost or damaged radioactive materials. Similarly, the Mine Safety and Health Administration requires reports on mine safety.

In addition to collecting information, agencies often perform investigations to ensure that the regulated industry is in compliance with agency regulations. The scope of agency power concerning record-keeping and investigations is very broad because agencies on the federal and state level have been delegated this authority by the legislature. For example, look at Exhibit 3-1, which sets out the power of the Federal Trade Commission (FTC), and note that the FTC can prosecute "any inquiry necessary to its duties," may "gather and compile information," and can investigate most businesses in the United States. Other agencies have similar grants of power. This delegation of power to agencies at the federal level is mandated by section 555(c) of the Administrative Procedure Act (APA) which states that investigations by agencies must be . . . "authorized by law." In other words, the investigation must be within the agency's jurisdiction. For example, note in Exhibit 3-1 that the FTC has no power to investigate banks, savings and loans, federal credit unions, and common carriers because Congress did not delegate such power to it.

Another reason why the scope of agency power concerning record-keeping and investigations is so broad is the rulings from the courts. For example, in *United States v. Morton Salt,* 338 U.S. 632, 642–643 (1950), the United States Supreme Court in ruling that businesses must comply with agency requests for information stated:

> The only power that is involved here is the power to get information from those who best can give it and who are most interested in not doing so. Because judicial power is reluctant if not unable to summon evidence until it is shown to be relevant to issues in lit-

igation, it does not follow that an administrative agency charged with seeing that the laws are enforced may not have and exercise powers of original inquiry. It has a power of inquisition, if one chooses to call it that, which is not derived from the judicial function. It is more analogous to the Grand Jury, which does not depend on a case or controversy for power to get evidence but can investigate merely on suspicion that the law is being violated, or even just because it wants assurance that it is not. When investigative and accusatory duties are delegated by statute to an administrative body, it, too, may take steps to inform itself as to whether there is probable violation of the law.

The Court in *Morton Salt* noted that an agency has the power to investigate as long as the demand is not too indefinite and the information sought is reasonably relevant. This is a standard which most agencies can meet, and therefore agencies get what they want in most instances.

A limitation on agencies' power in this area is that of privilege. A *privilege* is a right of an individual not to disclose information. A privilege we are most familiar with, the Fifth Amendment privilege not to incriminate oneself (know as "taking the Fifth"), will be covered later in the chapter. Other privileges that can come into play in the administrative law setting include: attorney-client privilege, physician-patient privilege, and spousal privilege.

privilege
the right to prevent disclosure, or duty to refrain from disclosing, information communicated within a specially recognized confidential relationship

Before we continue with agency executive power, it is useful to compare and contrast enforcement in the criminal context to that in administrative law.

Comparison to Enforcement of Criminal Law

The coverage of investigations in this text is limited to those conducted by administrative agencies in their job of enforcing their own regulations. Issues in criminal enforcement such as obtaining search warrants and the rights of the criminal suspects are subjects of the criminal law and criminal procedure and are not within the realm of administrative law. This is so because when a person's life or liberty is at stake, important constitutional rights are triggered, such as the right to a jury trial, the right to remain silent, and the right to an attorney. Investigations by agencies can lead to possible criminal violations wherein the agency can make a recommendation to law enforcement officials that criminal violations may have occurred. For example, the Internal Revenue Service (IRS), after conducting an investigation into an individual's taxes, may make a recommendation to the federal prosecutor that the individual should be prosecuted for violations of federal criminal tax law. An agency such as the IRS or Occupational Safety and Health Administration (OSHA) can impose civil fines, but the agency only recommends criminal prosecutions. The person or corporation is not prosecuted for criminal violations inside the system of administrative law. When an agency recommends criminal charges, the focus will shift from an administrative law system (where civil fines and other penalties may be imposed) to a criminal justice system (where a person can be sent to prison). Once inside the criminal justice system, a defendant enjoys the full measure of constitutional rights, whereas persons subjected to enforcement actions by agencies will have more limited constitutional protections.

> The Attorney General of the United States is the chief law enforcement officer of federal law. The Attorney Generals of the states are chief law enforcement officers in their jurisdictions.

Recordkeeping and Reporting

As stated in the introduction, agencies have broad authority to require recordkeeping and reporting. Numerous statutes require recordkeeping. For example, OSHA requires that businesses keep records on work-related illnesses and injuries. The IRS requires businesses to keep records of its employees. The FTC requires businesses to keep records to ensure that they have not been engaging in unfair trade practices. An unfair trade or deceptive practice means those practices that cause or are likely to cause substantial injury to consumers which is not reasonably avoidable by consumers themselves and not outweighed by countervailing benefits to consumers or to competition. 15 U.S.C. § 45(n). The Environmental Protection Agency (EPA) requires companies to keep lists of hazardous wastes and make reports of discharge of pollutants into the environment. State health agencies require hospitals to keep records of the injuries and illnesses they treat.

Fighting a recordkeeping requirement as too costly generally does not work, as illustrated in *Appeal of FTC Line Business Report Litigation,* 595 F.2d 685 (D.C. Cir. 1978). In this case, companies unsuccessfully challenged a requirement by the FTC that detailed financial information be broken down by product category or "line of business." The companies argued that the cost to assemble the records was excessive because they did not have the data in the form that was required. The Court stated that a request for recordkeeping is not excessive "absent a showing that compliance threatens to disrupt or unduly hinder the normal operations of a business." The record demonstrated that "assuming the accuracy of the most extravagant cost estimates, the costs of compliance were de minimis [too small to have an impact] relative to the overall corporate operating budgets." *Appeal of FTC Line Business Report Litigation,* 595 F.2d at 703–704. As far as the reporting requirements are concerned, companies sometimes object to reporting matters that have the potential of revealing confidential data or trade secrets to their competitors. In *Appeal of FTC Line Business Report Litigation,* the companies also raised these issues. The Court stated that even if the information potentially revealed confidential data or trade secrets, this would not necessarily relieve companies of their reporting requirements. The Court noted that the agency can take measures to ensure that data are not improperly revealed to competitors and to the public. Consequently, reporting can be required even if expensive and where adequate measures are taken to protect trade secrets.

Investigations/Inspections

In addition to collecting information, agencies may perform investigations. Investigations can take the form of routine inspections, such as a health inspection of a restaurant, or of a complex inquiry, such as whether Microsoft should be considered a monopoly. Many businesses and individuals cooperate with the investigation. For example, businesses supply answers to agency questionnaires or meet informally with agency officials to exchange information. However, if an agreement cannot be reached on what information should be released, a subpoena or search warrant may be used by the agency. This in turn can lead into issues involving the Fourth and Fifth Amendments to the Constitution, which will be covered in the following sections.

Local health officials many times will publish in the local newspaper the score a certain restaurant received on the health inspection. Check your local newspaper to see if a restaurant you frequent has receive a passing health score.

Search Warrants and the Fourth Amendment

Although both administrative and criminal law search warrants are covered under the Fourth Amendment, administrative search warrants are judged under a less stringent standard when compared to the criminal law search warrant. The Fourth Amendment states that:

> The right of the people to be secure in their persons, houses, papers, and effects, against unreasonable searches and seizures, shall not be violated, and no Warrants shall issue, but upon probable cause, supported by Oath or affirmation, and particularly describing the place to be searched, and the persons or things to be seized.

search warrant

a court order directing that a search and seizure can occur; in criminal law it is issued on a showing of probable cause.

To obtain a *search warrant*, officials must present an affidavit to a judge. The judge will issue the warrant in a criminal case if probable cause exists. Probable cause is not a mere suspicion that a law has been broken but requires a reasonable suspicion that there is a fair probability that evidence of crime will be found in a particular place. In contrast, the Supreme Court has ruled that an agency *does not* have to meet the probable cause standard required in the criminal law context to secure a search warrant. *Camara v. Municipal Court,* 387 U.S. 523 (1967). (See excerpt in Case Law at the end of the chapter.) Probable cause to conduct an administrative search exists if:

> reasonable legislative or administrative standards for conducting an area inspection are satisfied with respect to a particular dwelling. Such standards, which will vary with the municipal program being enforced, may be based upon the passage of time, the nature of the building (e.g., a multifamily apartment house), or the condition of the entire area, but they will not necessarily depend upon specific knowledge of the condition of the particular dwelling. *Camara,* 387 U.S. at 538.

The Court further explained why administrative law searches and searches under the criminal law should be treated differently:

> The warrant procedure is designed to guarantee that a decision to search private property is justified by a reasonable governmental interest. But reasonableness is still the ultimate standard. If a valid public interest justifies the intrusion contemplated, then there is probable cause to issue a suitably restricted search warrant. Such an approach neither endangers time-honored doctrines applicable to criminal investigations nor makes a nullity of the probable cause requirement in this area. It merely gives full recognition to the competing public and private interests here at stake and, in so

doing, best fulfills the historic purpose behind the constitutional right to be free from unreasonable government invasions of privacy. *Camara,* 387 U.S. at 539.

Generally, the courts prefer that searches be conducted after issuance of a search warrant. The Supreme Court has developed numerous exceptions to the search warrant requirement. Administrative searches do not require a search warrant if:

- The subject of the search is a pervasively regulated industry such as alcohol, firearms, mining, and junkyards.
- There is a statute that authorizes the search.
- The agency is looking for a violation of a regulation rather than searching for violations of criminal law.

In addition, a firefighter can seize, without a warrant, evidence of arson which is in *plain view* when the evidence is discovered in the course of fighting the fire. *Michigan v. Tyler,* 436 U.S. 499 (1978). Under the plain view exception to the search warrant requirement, when the firefighter is on the premises lawfully to fight the fire, he or she can seize items that come into his or her view. Similarly, if a firefighter or police officer is executing a search warrant for X but in the course of the search discovers Y, the firefighter or police officer can seize Y under the plain view exception. In noting that both firefighters and police officers are governed by the Fourth Amendment, the Court in *Tyler* stated that:

plain view
the rule that if police officers or firefighters see or come across something while acting lawfully, that item may be used as evidence in a trial even if the police did not have a search warrant

> there is no diminution in a person's reasonable expectation of privacy nor in the protection of the Fourth Amendment simply because the official conducting the search wears the uniform of a firefighter rather than a policeman, or because his purpose is to ascertain the cause of a fire rather than to look for evidence of a crime, or because the fire might have been started deliberately. Searches for administrative purposes, like searches for evidence of crime, are encompassed by the Fourth Amendment. And under that Amendment, one governing principle, justified by history and by current experience, has consistently been followed: except in certain carefully defined classes of cases, a search of private property without proper consent is unreasonable unless it has been authorized by a valid search warrant. The showing of probable cause necessary to secure a warrant may vary with the object and intrusiveness of the search, but the necessity for the warrant persists. *Michigan v. Tyler,* 436 U. S. at 506.

The Court then set out the parameters of what firefighters can do under the Fourth Amendment:

In summation, we hold that an entry to fight a fire requires no warrant, and that once in the building, officials may remain there for a reasonable time to investigate the cause of the blaze. Thereafter, additional entries to investigate the cause of the fire must be made pursuant to the warrant procedures governing administrative searches. Evidence of arson discovered in the course of such investigations is admissible at trial, but if the investigating officials find probable cause to believe that arson has occurred and require further access to gather evidence for a possible prosecution, they may obtain a warrant only upon a traditional showing of probable cause applicable to searches for evidence of crime. *Michigan v. Tyler,* 436 U.S. at 511–512.

open fields doctrine

the principle that a search warrant is not usually required for search of an open area far from an occupied building

When conducting administrative searches, inspectors sometimes also gather evidence that is in "plain view" from public areas. In doing so the inspection is justified under the ***open fields doctrine***. For example, in *Air Pollution Variance Bd. of Colorado v. Western Alfalfa Corp.,* 416 U.S. 861 (1974), a state inspector entered the premises of a business in the day without consent to inspect smoke coming from smokestacks. The inspector never entered any of the buildings and viewed what anyone in the city near the plant could have seen. The Court held that the inspection was conducted under the open fields exception and was not a search for the purposes of the Fourth Amendment, and therefore no warrant was required.

In another example, the EPA conducted a search of a large industrial complex by aerial photography. The Court stated that an industrial complex is:

> comparable to an open field and as such it is open to the view and observation of persons in aircraft lawfully in the public airspace immediately above or sufficiently near the area for the reach of cameras. . . . [therefore] . . . the taking of aerial photographs of an industrial plant complex from navigable airspace is not a search prohibited by the Fourth Amendment. *Dow Chemical Co. v. United States,* 476 U.S. 227, 239 (1986).

In the area of employment, the Supreme Court has ruled agency regulations that allow for random, warrantless drug testing of customs service employees and railroad employees do not violate the Fourth Amendment. *National Treasury Employees Union v. Von Raab,* 489 U.S. 656 (1989) and *Skinner v. Railway Labor Executives' Assn.,* 489 U.S. 602 (1989). Here the Court weighs the privacy interests of the individuals against the legitimate interests of the government. Because of the highly regulated nature of their jobs, customs agents and railroad employees have a lesser expectation of privacy than the general public. Given the lesser expectation of privacy coupled with the serious need of the government to combat illicit drugs and protect the safety of the public, the Court strikes the balance in favor of allowing the testing. In *Von Raab* (customs service employees), the Court stated that:

> the Government's need to conduct the suspicionless searches required by the Customs program outweighs the privacy interests of employees engaged directly in drug interdiction, and of those who otherwise are required to carry firearms. . . .

> We think Customs employees who are directly involved in the interdiction of illegal drugs or who are required to carry firearms in the line of duty likewise have a diminished expectation of privacy in respect to the intrusions occasioned by a urine test. *National Treasury Employees Union v. Von Raab,* 489 U.S. at 668, 672.

Reaching the same conclusion in *Skinner* (railroad employees), the Court explained:

> In sum, imposing a warrant requirement in the present context would add little to the assurances of certainty and regularity already afforded by the regulations, while significantly hindering, and in many cases frustrating, the objectives of the Government's testing program. We do not believe that a warrant is essential to render the intrusions here at issue reasonable under the Fourth Amendment... In limited circumstances, where the privacy interests implicated by the search are minimal, and where an important governmental interest furthered by the intrusion would be placed in jeopardy by a requirement of individualized suspicion, a search may be reasonable despite the absence of such suspicion. We believe this is true of the intrusions in question here. *Skinner v. Railway Labor Executives' Assn.,* 489 U.S. at 624.

Fourth Amendment issues are also raised in public schools. For example, the Supreme Court held in *New Jersey v. T.L.O.,* 469 U.S. 325 (1985), that although the Fourth Amendment does apply to searches conducted in a public schools, school officials are not required to obtain a search warrant because the probable cause standard of the criminal law does not apply. In *T.L.O.,* a school official searched a student's purse after the student was caught smoking in the lavatory. The purse contained marijuana. The Court ruled that the marijuana can be admitted as evidence in the student's disciplinary proceeding. The Court reached its decision by balancing the privacy interests of the students against the need for the school to maintain order and discipline. The Court acknowledged the legitimate expectation of privacy of the students but nevertheless held that:

> Under ordinary circumstances, a search of a student by a teacher or other school official will be justified at its inception when there are reasonable grounds for suspecting that the search will turn up evidence that the student has violated or is violating either the law or the rules of the school. Such a search will be permissible in its scope when the measures adopted are reasonably related to the objectives of the search and not excessively intrusive in light of the age and sex of the student and the nature of the infraction. *New Jersey v. T.L.O.,* 469 U.S. at 341–342.

Furthermore, random drug testing of student athletes in the public schools is permitted under the Fourth Amendment. *Vernonia School Dist. 47J v. Acton,* 515 U.S. 646 (1995). The Court noted that student athletes participate voluntarily in athletics and have a reduced expectation of privacy by going out for the team. In balancing the student's diminished expectation of privacy with the school's legitimate need to reduce drug use, the Court upheld the drug testing policy against a Fourth Amendment challenge. Based on the principles established in *T.L.O.* and *Vernonia,* the Court extended the use of random drug testing in public schools to extracurricular activities such as band, pom-pom, and cheerleading and participation in such organizations as Future Farmers of America and Future Homemakers of America. *Board of Education of Independent School District No. 92 of Pottawatomie County v. Earls,* 536 U.S. 822 (2002).

Subpoenas and the Fourth Amendment

subpoena

a court's order to a person that he or she appears in court to testify in a case; some administrative agencies may also issue subpoenas.

subpoena duces tecum

a subpoena by which a person is commanded to bring documents to court or to an administrative agency

Many agencies are authorized to issue *subpoenas* to obtain information. Agencies also issue subpoenas that command a person to bring specified documents to the administrative agency. This type of subpoena is called a *subpoena duces tecum.*

Although agencies have the power to issue subpoenas, most do not have enforcement power. If the recipient does not honor the subpoena, the agency must go to a judge and request the court to enforce the subpoena. At that point, if the recipient still failed to comply, he or she would be held in contempt of court and possibly be sentenced to jail. A subpoena issued by an agency can involve search and seizure issues related to the Fourth Amendment. As with search warrants, a less demanding standard applies to administrative subpoenas and for similar reasons (see previous section). An agency can issue a subpoena and investigate merely on the "suspicion that the law is being violated, or even just because it wants assurance that it is not." *United States, v. Morton Salt Co.,* 338 U.S. 632, 642-643 (1950). The court's function in administrative law is to protect against abuses of the agency. For example, in *Freese v. FDIC,* 837 F. Supp. 22 (D.N.H. 1993) (see excerpt in Case Law at the end of the chapter), the Court found that an agency issued a subpoena for the improper purpose of obtaining personal financial records. However, the scope of issues which may be raised in the enforcement of a subpoena is narrow because of the important governmental interest in the expeditious investigation of possible unlawful activity in order to protect the public. In sum, a court will enforce a subpoena if it does not transcend the agency's investigatory power, the demand is not unduly burdensome or too indefinite, and the information sought is reasonably relevant. *FTC v. Texaco,* 555 F.2d 862, 872 (D.C. Cir. 1977). Most agency subpoenas meet this standard, and therefore the agency generally gets the materials it seeks.

> The U.S. Supreme Court ruled that there is no constitutional right of privacy with respect to a person's bank records in that the Fourth Amendment does not prevent an agency from subpoenaing a depositor's checks or deposit slips. *United States v. Miller,* 425 U.S. 435 (1976).

Agency Enforcement by Filing a Complaint

Armed with the information collected either by visual inspection, review of records obtained by subpoena, or collection of evidence via a physical search (either with or without a search warrant), an agency can enforce its regulations by filing a complaint against an individual or business that may have violated a regulation. For example, in 2003, the FTC filed a complaint against a business alleging unfair trade practice. The complaint alleged improper billing of customer accounts and failure to deliver promised services with respect to the national telemarketers "no call" list. See FTC Press Release at http://www.ftc.gov/opa/ 2003/05/kenchase.htm.

Another example of an FTC enforcement procedure involved the famous mouthwash, Listerine. The makers of Listerine ran advertisements in print and on radio and television essentially claiming that Listerine could prevent the common cold. The FTC filed a complaint against Warner-Lambert, charging the company with misrepresenting

Listerine's healing powers. Hearings were held before an Administrative Law Judge (ALJ) which took more than four months and produced more than 4,000 pages of testimony and exhibits. The ALJ concluded and the full FDA essentially agreed that the medical claims were not supported by the scientific evidence. The FDA ordered Warner-Lambert to:

(1) cease and desist from representing that Listerine will cure colds or sore throats, prevent colds or sore throats, or that users of Listerine will have fewer colds than non-users;

(2) cease and desist from representing that Listerine is a treatment for, or will lessen the severity of, colds or sore throats; that it will have any significant beneficial effect on the symptoms of sore throats or any beneficial effect on symptoms of colds; or that the ability of Listerine to kill germs is of medical significance in the treatment of colds or sore throats or their symptoms;

(3) cease and desist from disseminating any advertisement for Listerine unless it is clearly and conspicuously disclosed in each such advertisement, in the exact language below, that: "Contrary to prior advertising, Listerine will not help prevent colds or sore throats or lessen their severity." *Warner-Lambert v. FTC,* 562 F.2d 749, 753 (D.C. Cir. 1977).

Warner-Lambert appealed this order to the federal appeals court which upheld the order but removed the exact language requirement as unwarranted.

Chapter 6 will discuss what happens before, during, and after a hearing. See Exhibit 3-1 for an overview of the FTC investigative procedures. For another example of an agency's complaint procedures, see Exhibit 3-2 regarding the EEOC.

As a final note, the decision to initiate an investigation and enforcement proceeding is left to the discretion of the agency and is a decision with which the courts generally do not interfere.

Fifth Amendment Rights

Issues in agency investigations involving the Fifth Amendment generally revolve around the right not to incriminate oneself, which is also known as the privilege against self-incrimination. The Fifth Amendment states in part that no person "shall be compelled in any criminal case to be a witness against himself." Any person can invoke the Fifth Amendment right to refuse to give testimony at trial, at a grand jury, at Congressional investigations, and at another person's civil or criminal trial if such testimony might be incriminating.

Exhibit 3-1

FTC Enforcement Procedures

A. In General

The Commission may "prosecute any inquiry necessary to its duties in any part of the United States" (FTC Act Sec. 3, 15 U.S.C. Sec. 43) and may "gather and compile information concerning, and . . . investigate from time to time the organization, business, conduct, practices, and management of any person, partnership, or corporation engaged in or whose business affects commerce, excepting banks, savings and loan institutions . . . federal credit unions . . . and common carriers . . ." [FTC Act Sec. 6(a), 15 U.S.C. Sec. 46(a)]. Pre-complaint investigations are generally non-public, and thus are not identified on this site. On occasion the existence of an investigation may be identified in a press release.

B. Specific Investigative Powers

The Commission's specific investigative powers are defined in Sections 6, 9, and 20 of the FTC Act, 15 U.S.C. Secs. 46, 49, and 57b-1, which authorize investigations and various forms of compulsory process.

1. *Sections 9 and 20 of the FTC Act*

Section 9 of the FTC Act authorizes the Commission to "require by subpoena the attendance and testimony of witnesses and the production of all such documentary evidence relating to any matter under investigation" (15 U.S.C. Sec. 49). Any member of the Commission may sign a subpoena, and both members and "examiners" (employees) of the agency may administer oaths, examine witnesses, and receive evidence.

Under Commission Rule 2.7 (16 C.F.R. Sec. 2.7), a party may raise objections to a subpoena by filing a petition to quash. Such petitions are resolved by a designated Commissioner, and the designated Commissioner's ruling may thereafter be appealed to the full Commission.

If a party fails to comply with a subpoena (either without filing a petition to quash, or after a duly filed petition is denied), the Commission may seek enforcement of the subpoena in "[a]ny of the district courts of the United States within the jurisdiction of which such inquiry is carried on" (15 U.S.C. Sec. 49). After the Commission files its petition to enforce a subpoena, and following receipt of any response from the subpoena recipient, the court may enter an order requiring compliance. Refusal to comply with a court enforcement order is subject to penalties for contempt of court. . . .

(Continued)

Exhibit 3-1 (Continued)

2. Section 6(b) of the FTC Act

Another investigative tool, this one available in both competition and consumer protection matters, appears in Section 6 of the FTC Act, 15 U.S.C. Sec. 46. Section 6(b) empowers the Commission to require the filing of "annual or special" reports or answers in writing to specific questions for the purpose of obtaining information about "the organization, business, conduct, practices, management, and relation to other corporations, partnerships, and individuals" of the entities to whom the inquiry is addressed. As with subpoenas and CIDs, the recipient of a 6(b) order may file a petition to quash, and the Commission may seek a court order requiring compliance. In addition, the Commission may commence suit in Federal court under Section 10 of the FTC Act, 15 U.S.C. Sec. 50, against any party who fails to comply with a 6(b) order after receiving a notice of default from the Commission. After expiration of a thirty-day grace period, the defaulting party is liable to a penalty of $110 for each day of noncompliance.

The Commission's 6(b) authority enables it to conduct wide-ranging economic studies that do not have a specific law enforcement purpose. (An example is the "Line-of-Business" study conducted in the 1970s, which required corporations to report line of business profitability and other data on a yearly basis.) Section 6(b) also enables the Commission to obtain to specific questions as part of an antitrust law enforcement investigation, where such information would not be available through subpoena because there is no document that contains the desired answers. Section 6 also authorizes the Commission to "make public from time to time" portions of the information that it obtains, where disclosure would serve the public interest [15 U.S.C. Sec. 46(f)].

Source: http://ftc.gov

Exhibit 3-2

EEOC Enforcement Procedures

The employer is notified that the charge has been filed. From this point there are a number of ways a charge may be handled:

· A charge may be assigned for priority investigation if the initial facts appear to support a violation of law. When the evidence is less strong, the charge may be assigned for follow-up investigation to determine whether it is likely that a violation has occurred.

Exhibit 3-2 (Continued)

- EEOC can seek to settle a charge at any stage of the investigation if the charging party and the employer express an interest in doing so. If settlement efforts are not successful, the investigation continues.
- In investigating a charge, EEOC may make written requests for information, interview people, review documents, and, as needed, visit the facility where the alleged discrimination occurred. When the investigation is complete, EEOC will discuss the evidence with the charging party or employer, as appropriate.
- The charge may be selected for EEOC's mediation program if both the charging party and the employer express an interest in this option. Mediation is offered as an alternative to a lengthy investigation. Participation in the mediation program is confidential, is voluntary, and requires consent from both charging party and employer. If mediation is unsuccessful, the charge is returned for investigation.
- A charge may be dismissed at any point if, in the agency's best judgment, further investigation will not establish a violation of the law. A charge may be dismissed at the time it is filed, if an initial in-depth interview does not produce evidence to support the claim. When a charge is dismissed, a notice is issued in accordance with the law which gives the charging party 90 days in which to file a lawsuit on his or her own behalf.
- If the evidence obtained in an investigation does not establish that discrimination occurred, this will be explained to the charging party. A required notice is then issued, closing the case and giving the charging party 90 days in which to file a lawsuit on his or her own behalf.
- If the evidence establishes that discrimination has occurred, the employer and the charging party will be informed of this in a letter of determination that explains the finding. EEOC will then attempt conciliation with the employer to develop a remedy for the discrimination.
- If the case is successfully conciliated, or if a case has earlier been successfully mediated or settled, neither EEOC nor the charging party may go to court unless the conciliation, mediation, or settlement agreement is not honored.
- If EEOC is unable to successfully conciliate the case, the agency will decide whether to bring suit in federal court. If EEOC decides not to sue, it will issue a notice closing the case and giving the charging party 90 days in which to file a lawsuit on his or her own behalf. In Title VII and ADA cases against state or local governments, the Department of Justice takes these actions.

Source: http://eeoc.gov

In order to be able to invoke the right to remain silent and refuse to testify, it must be likely that the testimony given will be used in a criminal prosecution. For example, if a person is found not guilty in a criminal case and then is sued in a civil case for the same event, that person cannot invoke the Fifth Amendment at the civil trial. There is no Fifth Amendment right because the person cannot incriminate himself, as double jeopardy prevents a second prosecution. Note also that the Fifth Amendment cannot be used by a defendant to refuse to give a blood sample, DNA sample, writing sample, or fingerprints. Also, physical items such as guns or bloody clothes are not testimony covered in the Fifth Amendment right not to incriminate oneself because these are objects and not testimony.

When agencies issue subpoenas to an individual or obtain a search warrant, that individual may have concerns that turning over the documents would expose him or her to criminal sanctions. However, it is extremely difficult to raise a Fifth Amendment challenge where the records sought are part of an administrative investigation that is enforcing administrative rules and the law requires the records to be kept in the public interest. For example, if a state or federal taxing authority (IRS or state tax department) issues a subpoena to an individual, then the tax records of that individual must be produced. The attorney or accountant of that individual must also honor the subpoena and produce such records in his or her possession. One has a better chance of successfully raising the Fifth Amendment when a rule singles out a group and requires an individual in that group to report to the government if he or she is engaging in criminal activities. For example, in *Marchetti v. United States,* 390 U.S. 39 (1968), a statute in essence required a person to report to the IRS if he or she were engaged in illegal gambling. This kind of requirement was found in *Marchetti* to violate the Fifth Amendment.

With respect to personal papers, the Supreme Court has made a distinction between documents that are requested by subpoena and those sought via a search warrant. The very same materials sought could be obtained by search warrant but not by subpoena. The Supreme Court explained this distinction in *Andresen v. Maryland,* 427 U.S. 463 (1976), as follows:

> the protection afforded by the Self-Incrimination Clause of the Fifth Amendment adheres basically to the person, not to information that may incriminate him. Thus, although the Fifth Amendment may protect an individual from complying with a subpoena for the production of his personal records in his possession because the very act of production may constitute a compulsory authentication of

incriminating information, a seizure of the same materials by law enforcement officers differs in a crucial respect, the individual against whom the search is directed is not required in the discovery, production, or authentication of incriminating evidence. *Andresen,* 427 U.S. at 473–474.

Note also that only *individuals* and not corporations or partnerships can assert the Fifth Amendment.

Fifth Amendment and State Agencies

The Fifth Amendment issue has arisen in unemployment compensation cases which are resolved by state agencies. In a typical fact pattern, a claimant seeking unemployment compensation has a right to a hearing on his or her eligibility for benefits. Unlike a criminal case, however, if the claimant refuses to testify at the hearing, the claimant's silence creates an inference that the claimant's testimony would be damaging to the case.

In *Caloric Corp. v. Com., Unemployment Compensation Bd. of Review,* 452 A.2d 907 (1982), the court stated:

> The Fifth Amendment not only protects the individual against being involuntarily called as a witness against himself in a criminal prosecution but also privileges him not to answer official questions put to him in any other proceeding, civil or criminal, formal or informal, where the answers might incriminate him in future criminal proceedings. . . However, as distinguished from the situation in criminal cases, the Fifth Amendment does not forbid adverse inferences against parties to civil actions [including unemployment case] where they refuse to testify . . . . *Caloric Corp.,* 452 A.2d at 909.

Issues of Immunity

Even if the Fifth Amendment applies, that right can be supplanted by a grant of immunity. *Immunity* is the freedom from prosecution based on anything a witness says that is given by the government to a witness who is forced to testify.

The government can force a witness to testify when immunity is granted. In an unemployment case, such as the one discussed in the previous section, the state can limit the invocation of the Fifth Amendment at a claimant's hearing by extending a grant of immunity from prosecution based on the testimony given at the hearing. *Vann v. Unemployment Compensation Board,* 494 A.2d 1081 (1985), citing the

immunity
the freedom from prosecution based on anything the witnesses says that is given by the government to a witness who is forced to testify

Pennsylvania statute that grants immunity (43 P.S. § 828). To illustrate, even if a claimant admits in his or her hearing to theft on the job, his testimony cannot be used against him or her in any criminal prosecution.

CASE LAW

CAMARA v. MUNICIPAL COURT
387 U.S. 523, 87 S.Ct. 1727, 18 L.Ed.2d 930 (1967).

MR. JUSTICE WHITE delivered the opinion of the Court.
[City building inspectors sought to inspect Camara's apartment under a San Francisco ordinance that authorized them to enter buildings "to perform any duty imposed upon them by the Municipal Code." When Camara refused to allow the inspectors to enter his apartment without a warrant, he was charged with violating the municipal code which made it illegal to refuse to permit a lawful inspection.]

[The Fourth Amendment was designed] to safeguard the privacy and security of individuals against arbitrary invasions by governmental officials. The Fourth Amendment thus gives concrete expression to a right of the people which "is basic to a free society." As such, the Fourth Amendment is enforceable against the States through the Fourteenth Amendment;

. . .[E] in certain carefully defined classes of cases, a search of private property without proper consent is "unreasonable" unless it has been authorized by a valid search warrant. . . .

. . .[W]e hold that administrative searches of the kind at issue here are significant intrusions upon the interests protected by the Fourth Amendment, that such searches when authorized and conducted without a warrant procedure lack the traditional safeguards which the Fourth Amendment guarantees to the individual. [Because] of the nature of the municipal programs under consideration, however, these conclusions must be the beginning, not the end, of our inquiry . . .

[In] cases in which the Fourth Amendment requires that a warrant to search be obtained, "probable cause" is the standard by which a particular decision to search is tested against the constitutional mandate of reasonableness . . .

[T]he only effective way to seek universal compliance with the minimum standards required by municipal codes is through routine periodic inspections of all structures. It is here that the probable cause debate is focused, for the agency's decision to conduct an area inspection is unavoidably based on its appraisal of conditions in the area as a whole, not on its knowledge of conditions in each particular building . . .

[Unfortunately,] there can be no ready test for determining reasonableness other than by balancing the need to search against the invasion which the search entails. But we think that a number of persuasive factors combine to support the reasonableness of area code-enforcement inspections. First, such programs have a long history of judicial and public acceptance. Second, the public interest demands that all dangerous conditions be prevented or abated, yet it is doubtful that any other canvassing technique would achieve acceptable results. Many such conditions—faulty wiring is an obvious example—are not observable from outside the building and indeed may not be apparent to the inexpert occupant himself. Finally, because the inspections are neither personal in nature nor aimed at the discovery of evidence of crime, they involve a relatively limited invasion of the urban citizen's privacy. . . .

Having concluded that the area inspection is a "reasonable" search of private property within the meaning of the Fourth Amendment, it is obvious that "probable cause" to issue a warrant to inspect must exist if reasonable legislative or administrative standards for conducting an area inspection are satisfied with respect to a particular dwelling. Such standards, which will vary with the municipal program being enforced, may be based upon the passage of time, the nature of the building (*e.g.*, a multifamily apartment house), or the condition of the entire area, but they will not necessarily depend upon specific knowledge of the condition of the particular dwelling. . . .

Since our holding emphasizes the controlling standard of reasonableness, nothing we say today is intended to foreclose prompt inspections, even without a warrant, that the law has traditionally upheld in emergency situations. *See North American Cold Storage Co. v. City of Chicago*, 211 U.S. 306 (seizure of unwholesome food); *Jacobson v. Commonwealth of Massachusetts*, 197 U.S. 11 (compulsory smallpox vaccination); *Compagnie Francaise De Navigation a Vapeur v. Louisiana State Board of Health*, 186 U.S. 380 (health quarantine); *Kroplin v. Truax*, 119 Ohio St. 610, 165 N.E. 498 (summary destruction of tubercular cattle). On the other hand, in the case of most routine area inspections, there is no compelling urgency to inspect at a particular time or on a particular day. Moreover, most citizens allow inspections of their property without a warrant. Thus, as a practical matter and in light of the Fourth Amendment's requirement that a

(*Continued*)

warrant specify the property to be searched, it seems likely that warrants should normally be sought only after entry is refused unless there has been a citizen complaint or there is other satisfactory reason for securing immediate entry. Similarly, the requirement of a warrant procedure does not suggest any change in what seems to be the prevailing local policy, in most situations, of authorizing entry, but not entry by force, to inspect.

In this case, appellant has been charged with a crime for his refusal to permit housing inspectors to enter his leasehold without a warrant. There was no emergency demanding immediate access; in fact, the inspectors made three trips to the building in an attempt to obtain appellant's consent to search. Yet no warrant was obtained and thus appellant was unable to verify either the need for or the appropriate limits of the inspection. [W]e therefore conclude that appellant had a constitutional right to insist that the inspectors obtain a warrant to search and that appellant may not constitutionally be convicted for refusing to consent to the inspection. . . .

Reprinted from Funk, W., Shapiro. S., and Weaver. R. Administiative Procedure and Practice: Problems and Cases. © 2006, with permission of Thomson West.

CASE LAW

FREESE v. FEDERAL DEPOSIT INSURANCE CORP.
837 F.Supp. 22 (D.N.H.1993).

LOUGHLIN, SENIOR DISTRICT JUDGE. . . .
On October 10, 1991, the Federal Deposit Insurance Corporation ("FDIC") was appointed receiver and liquidating agent for New Hampshire Savings Bank. On September 18, 1992, the FDIC issued an Order of Investigation. The purpose of the investigation was to determine whether any valid claims existed against the Bank's former officers and directors; whether sufficient assets existed to pursue any potential claims against them; and whether the FDIC should seek to freeze or attach any of their assets.

In connection with the investigation, the FDIC issued administrative subpoenas *duces tecum* on June 3, 1993, to [several persons who] were former officers and directors of the New Hampshire Savings Bank. The subpoenas were identical and sought extensive personal financial information in relation to the plaintiffs and their families for the five years preceding the date of the subpoenas. . . .

It is well settled that an agency subpoena is enforceable if the subpoena is issued for a proper purpose authorized by Congress, if the information sought is relevant to that purpose and is adequately described within the subpoena, and the statutory procedures have been followed in the subpoena's issuance. . . . An affidavit from a government official is sufficient to establish a prima facie showing that the requirements have been met.

The plaintiffs have not alleged that the subpoenas in this case were issued in violation of statutory procedure. Instead, the plaintiffs claim that the subpoenas were sought for improper purposes, that even if the court determined that the purposes were proper the information sought was not relevant to those purposes and that the subpoenas were issued in violation of the Fourth Amendment.

In the Order of Investigation, the FDIC has stated four purposes for which the subpoenas were issued. The FDIC seeks to determine whether (1) the former officers and directors of the New Hampshire Savings Bank may be liable as a result of any action or failure to act; (2) the pursuit of litigation against the plaintiffs would be cost effective; (3) the FDIC should seek to avoid any transfers made by the plaintiffs; and (4) the FDIC should seek an attachment of the plaintiffs' assets.

A determination of whether the pursuit of a civil suit against the plaintiffs would be cost effective is not a proper purpose to issue a subpoena. The FDIC may not freely peruse personal financial records in order to determine the party's financial ability to satisfy a judgment. Courts have routinely denied access to personal financial records in civil discovery reasoning that a party's ability to satisfy a judgment is irrelevant to the subject matter of the action. While the rules of civil discovery do not control an administrative subpoena, even the broad powers of the FDIC do not extend to an invasion of privacy.

The FDIC urges that even if determining the cost effectiveness of the litigation is not a proper purpose, the remaining articulated purposes are sufficient to justify the issuance of the subpoena. The FDIC asserts that subpoenas were necessary to determine whether the plaintiffs may be liable for any action or inaction as officers and directors of New Hampshire Savings Bank or whether the FDIC should freeze or avoid any transfer of the plaintiffs' assets. However, the FDIC fails to assert that there was even a suspicion of wrongdoing on the part of the plaintiffs.

In her affidavit, Emily E. Sommers, Senior Attorney in the Professional Liability Section of the FDIC, simply states that the

(*Continued*)

information sought is relevant to the purposes for which the subpoenas were issued. On the basis of this bald statement the FDIC urges that there is a *prima facie* showing that the requirements necessary to the issuance of the subpoena were met. The FDIC claims that a review of all of the plaintiffs' and their spouses' financial documents for the past five years is necessary to determine if there were any "suspicious accretions to wealth."

The FDIC has not offered a basis on which to assert that the plaintiffs may have been liable for any wrongdoing in their capacities as directors or officers of New Hampshire Savings Bank.

. . . The court does not intend to imply that the FDIC was required to establish a showing of probable or reasonable cause in order to support the enforcement of the subpoena. However, to allow the FDIC to conduct a fishing expedition through the plaintiffs' private papers in the hope that some evidence of wrongdoing will surface flies in the face of the spirit, if not the letter, of the Fourth Amendment.

Commenting further, this shotgun approach to the use of the subpoena powers in a hubristic manner infringes upon fundamental constitutional rights we are all entitled to, even losers. There has been some mitigation of the untoward situation presented by the facts in this case as most documents have been sealed. Albeit, individuals subject to the subpoena powers have incurred legal expenses, anxiety and trepidation in facing the shotgun method the defendant has used to expose putative violations of the law. . . .

Reprinted from Funk, W., Shapiro. S., and Weaver. R. Administiative Procedure and Practice: Problems and Cases. © 2006, with permission of Thomson West.

CHAPTER SUMMARY

Agencies exert a kind of executive power when they enforce their regulations. Many agencies require individuals and businesses to disclose information and make reports on a regular basis. Sometimes agencies employ the use of subpoenas and search warrants in the course of their investigations, which can raise concerns under the Fourth and Fifth Amendments. Administrative searches raise Fourth Amendment issues but are judged under a less stringent standard as compared to the criminal law. Warrantless administrative law searches do not violate the Fourth Amendment when there is a statute that authorizes the search of an individual or business in a highly regulated area. Generally, the Fifth Amendment right not to incriminate oneself will not prevent the required production of such documents as tax records. The Fifth Amendment may protect against production of subpoenaed personal records but will not stop an execution of a valid search warrant. The Fifth Amendment right against self-incrimination applies to individuals but not to corporations.

KEY TERMS

executive power (of an agency)   privilege
immunity   search warrant
open fields doctrine   subpoena
plain view   subpoena duces tecum

REVIEW QUESTIONS

1. What are the sources of agency power to enforce its regulations?
2. What are the limitations of agency power to enforce its regulations?
3. Discuss the role that the Fourth Amendment plays concerning agency investigations. Include in your answer the guidelines that agencies must follow with respect to subpoenas and search warrants.
4. Discuss the role that the Fifth Amendment plays concerning agency investigations. Include in your answer the distinction that the United States Supreme Court has made between documents obtained by a subpoena and a search warrant.

MORE INFORMATION

1. To learn about the Occupational Safety and Health Administration reporting requirements, go to http://www.osha.gov.
2. To learn about inspection and reporting requirements of the Nuclear Regulatory Commission, go to http://www.nrc.gov.

PRACTICAL APPLICATIONS

1. Go to the Web site of the Mine Safety and Health Administration at http://www.msha.gov and answer the following:

    A. What statute created the Mine Safety and Health Administration?

    B. How many coal miner fatalities occurred in 2005?

2. Review Exhibit 3-1 and answer the following:

    A. What kinds of business entities does the FTC have the power to investigate?

    B. What kinds of business entities are exempted from the FTC's power to investigate?

    C. What can the FTC do if a person does not comply with a subpoena?

3. Review Exhibit 3-2 and answer the following:

    A. What steps can the EEOC take when investigating a charge of discrimination?

    B. What happens if the EEOC decides not to sue and not bring a case into federal court?

4. Go to the Web site of the U.S. Department of Labor at http://www.dol.gov and state five laws that are enforced by the Department of Labor.

LEARN ABOUT THE AGENCIES

Go to the Web sites of the following agencies and state their functions.

1. GAO—General Accountability Office—http://www.gao.gov
2. GPO—Government Printing Office—http://www.access.gpo.gov
3. SSA—Social Security Administration—http://www.ssa.gov
4. OMB—Office of Management and Budget—http://www.whitehouse.gov/omb
5. FTC—Federal Trade Commission—http://www.ftc.gov

Adjudication—Judicial Power of Agencies

C H A P T E R   O B J E C T I V E S

After reading this chapter, you should be able to:

- Understand the role agencies play in the adjudication of issues.
- Distinguish formal and informal adjudication.
- Distinguish rulemaking and adjudication.
- Identify and assess the various stages of agency adjudication.

CHAPTER OUTLINE

INTRODUCTION TO ADJUDICATION

This chapter concludes the coverage of the three powers possessed by agencies. Chapter 2 covered legislative-type power (rulemaking); Chapter 3 covered enforcement of agency regulations (executive power). The third agency power is judicial power which is known as *adjudication.* Adjudication is similar to the process a court of law goes through when deciding cases. Adjudication is the process that an agency goes through to reach a decision on the matter before it. If settlement cannot be reached, adjudication will continue until the matter is resolved.

FORMAL AND INFORMAL ADJUDICATION

As with formal rulemaking, the federal Administrative Procedure Act (APA) divides adjudication into informal and formal. As with formal rulemaking, formal adjudication is rare. See Exhibit 4-1, which compares formal and informal rulemaking and formal and informal adjudication. *Formal agency action,* for the most part, is composed of formal rulemaking (on the record formulation of rules), covered in Chapter 2, and formal adjudication (on the record resolution of a dispute). "On the record" connotes a trial-like hearing including the right to an attorney (an attorney will not be appointed as in a criminal case; however, individuals have the right to hire an attorney to represent them at the∞hearing), the right to present evidence, and the right of cross-examination where a presiding officer hears the evidence and issues an order. Section 554(a) of the federal APA states that formal rulemaking and formal adjudication come into play only when required by statute. Therefore, in order to determine whether an agency is required to proceed formally, when making a rule or adjudicating a dispute, one would have to review the agency's enabling act. The following quote from the case of *Crestview Parke Care Center v. Thompson*, 373 F.3d 743, 748 (6th Cir. 2004), is a succinct explanation of the formal/informal distinction.

> The starting point is the Administrative Procedure Act ("APA"), which establishes a detailed set of procedures for formal agency adjudications. These procedures mirror the elements of a judicial trial and establish the proper method of conducting an oral evidentiary hearing. *See* 5 U.S.C. §§ 554(a), 556(d), 557. Agencies need only employ this set of formal adjudication procedures if there is an "adjudication required by statute to be determined on the record after opportunity for an agency hearing. 5 U.S.C. § 554(a). Lower courts have explicitly held that a formal adjudica-

adjudication

the process that an agency goes through to reach a decision on the matter before it

formal agency action

actions taken by an agency with a formal hearing that is on the record

informal agency action

actions taken by an agency that are not on the record and without a formal hearing

hearing on the record

an enabling act provision which requires an agency to perform formal rulemaking and formal adjudication

tion featuring an oral evidentiary hearing is required by the APA only when a statute explicitly calls for a hearing "on the record. The Supreme Court has also implied that formal adjudication procedures are only necessary when a statute uses the magic words "on the record." *Cf. United States v. Fla. E. Coast Ry.*, 410 U.S. 224, 237–38, 93 S. Ct. 810, 35 L. Ed. 2d 223 (1973) (holding that formal rulemaking procedures prescribed by 5 U.S.C. §§ 556, 557 are required only when a statute mandates that rules be made "on the record"); *Vt. Yankee Nuclear Power Corp. v. Natural Res. Def. Council, Inc.*, 435 U.S. 519, 548, 98 S. Ct. 1197, 55 L. Ed. 2d 460 (1978) (ruling that courts cannot require an agency to use more formal rulemaking procedures than those required by statute); *PBGC v. LTV Corp.*, 496 U.S. 633, 654–55, 110 S. Ct. 2668, 110 L. Ed. 2d 579 (1990) (upholding an informal agency adjudication without an oral hearing when the statute did not require a hearing to be on the record).

> Be aware that many states do not divide their agency activities into formal and informal in the same manner as federal agencies are required to do under the APA. States may refer to their proceeding as "formal" or "informal," but these labels have no reference to the federal APA. See Sidebars 4-2 and 4-3 for further comparisons of formal and informal adjudication.

Even when an agency's adjudication is informal, there still will likely be internal procedures that must be followed. These internal procedures can be rules on various time frames to act, discovery (exchange of information), prehearing conferences, and rules for settlement negotiations. Obviously, the best way to determine an agency's procedures is to review the rules, regulations, or published information from that agency.

GENERAL CATEGORIES OF AGENCY ADJUDICATION

Agency adjudications can be placed into two categories. In the first category, the agency adjudicates a claim for a benefit. For example, the Social Security Administration (SSA) can make an adjudication that a claimant is entitled to benefits. In the second category of adjudication, the agency

Exhibit 4-1	
Formal versus Informal Actions under the Federal APA	
Formal rulemaking Formal adjudication	To identify formal actions, look for the words "hearing on the record."
Informal rulemaking Informal adjudication	Most of what agencies do is informal. If the words "hearing on the record" are not there, it is informal.

order

the final disposition of an administrative adjudication; the order can compel an action or provide a penalty for violation of a regulation.

hearing

also called an adjudication, the process in which facts and evidence are presented before an agency official for a decision

makes a determination as to whether an individual or business has violated a regulation, which can lead to an order to compel action or the imposition of a fine. For example, the Environmental Protection Agency (EPA) can make an adjudication that a factory has violated a regulation by emitting excessive pollutants into the air, order the company to stop polluting, and impose a monetary fine. See Exhibit 4-2.

The final result of an administrative adjudication is an *order*, which is the determination whether the claimant is entitled to a benefit or if the company is in compliance with the regulation.

Adjudications are also referred to as *hearings*. A hearing can be defined as the process in which facts and evidence are presented before an agency official for a decision. When Social Security benefits are denied to a claimant, that claimant has the right to a hearing. Most parties who deal with agencies have the right to some kind of hearing to resolve their issue. The extent to which a hearing is required and the timing of the hearing involve due process rights, which will be covered in Chapter 6. For now, the focus in the next sections will be the comparison of adjudication to rulemaking, the role played by the decision-maker who presides over many hearings or agency adjudications, and some common characteristics of agency adjudications.

Exhibit 4-2	
Categories of Administrative Adjudications	
ADJUDICATION	**EXAMPLE**
An individual makes claim for a benefit, and the agency denies the claim.	A hearing is conducted by an ALJ to determine if a claimant is entitled to Social Security benefits.
An agency alleges a violation of a regulation.	A hearing is held before an ALJ to determine if a business has violated an environmental regulation.

ADJUDICATION AND RULEMAKING COMPARED

Adjudication is a judicial function that involves specifically named parties such as claimant John Smith v. the Social Security Administration or Environmental Protection Agency v. ABC Company. Adjudication looks backward and judges events that have already transpired and resolves conflicts. Adjudication resolves issues such as: Is John Smith entitled to Social Security benefits? Did ABC Company violate a regulation and pollute the environment? In contrast, rulemaking, as you recall from Chapter 2, is a legislative function that implements laws (fills gaps) that apply to large groups and which sets a standard for future application. For example, Congress passes a law that allows for a disabled individual to claim Social Security disability benefits. The SSA then issues a regulation defining a disability as "the inability to engage in any substantial gainful activity by reason of any . . . impairment . . . expected to result in death or . . . to last 12 months." 42 U.S.C. § 423 (d)(1)(A). Through the process of adjudication, the SSA implements this rule and determines if an individual is disabled. See Exhibit 4-3 which compares adjudication and rulemaking.

COMMON CHARACTERISTICS OF AGENCY ADJUDICATIONS

An adjudication can be as simple as a police officer writing out a parking ticket or a fire marshal telling you to put out a cigarette. An adjudication can be as complex as the Food and Drug Administration (FDA) holding a hearing on whether to license a new drug. Recall that the federal APA divides adjudications into formal and informal. Recall also that formal adjudications are only required when the enabling act states that a hearing "on the record" is required. The APA sets out detailed requirements for formal adjudications but very little guidance on informal adjudications, which are by far much more common. Even if a statute does not require formal adjudication, many agencies institute their set of procedures that add to the "formality" of the adjudication. More importantly, a particular matter may require a hearing because of constitutional requirements of due process. For example, Social Security is not designated as one of the adjudications that are required to be "formal," but the Supreme Court has ruled that a person who is denied Social Security disability benefits must be afforded a hearing because due process requires it. See Chapter 6 for a discussion of due process.

Exhibit 4-3

Adjudication and Rulemaking Compared

Adjudication	Judicial function	Involves specified individuals	Looks backward	Resolves conflicts	An administrative law judge can issue an order granting Social Security benefits.
Rulemaking	Legislative function	Involves large groups	Looks forward	Implements law by filling gaps	SSA issues a rule defining disability and the criteria to be met to obtain benefits.

With so many agencies, federal, state, and local, and with such variety of procedure from agency to agency, generalization is impossible. Further, many states, unlike the APA, do not divide adjudications into formal and informal. And last, agency adjudications will vary depending on a variety of factors which include:

- Subject of the matter at issue
- Policies and practices of the agency
- Applicable statutes
- Regulations
- Court-imposed rules
- Constitutional considerations

As noted, many states do not have the rigid dividing line of formal and informal adjudications as such. Instead, many states define what an adjudication is, which in turn resolves whether the matter must be resolved by the "formal" procedures or resolved "informally." For example, Pennsylvania defines adjudication as ". . . any final order, decision, determination or ruling by an agency affecting personal or property rights . . ." If a person's rights are affected, then that person gets the protection of the state APA because the agency rendered an adjudication. For example, when a person is denied unemployment compensation benefits, that is adjudication because person or property rights are affected. However, a letter of reprimand to police officers by a city council is not an adjudication. In the letter the officers were merely warned of their abusive conduct. Because the letter did not discharge, demote, or suspend the officers, there was no concrete alteration of their legal status, and thus there was no adjudication. *Guthrie v. Borough of Wilkinsburg*, 478 A.2d 1279 (1984).

The use of the terms formal and informal can be quite confusing. On the one hand, the APA divides adjudications into formal and informal. On the other hand, when the word formal is used generally in administrative law, it means a hearing which has the characteristics of a court trial (right to an attorney, testimony of witnesses, cross-examination, opening and closing statements, introduction of exhibits, disclosure of information to the opponents, and a statement of reasons for the determination with an indication of the evidence relied on). As the number of these characteristics of a court trial increases, the more the adjudication resembles what can be called a formal adjudication.

With the understanding of this extreme diversity of administrative law adjudications, some common threads are as follows:

- **Parties:** The parties are the agency involved and an individual or business who is either seeking a benefit or is contesting an adverse ruling regarding a violation of an agency regulation.

- **Notice to Parties:** Adequate notice to the parties of the proceedings must be given. Many agencies require, as does the APA [Section 554(b)], that persons entitled to notice of an agency hearing be informed of the time and place of the hearing, the legal authority that the agency is relying on, and the matters of fact and law asserted. An interested party may intervene or come into the proceedings after it starts.

- **Stages of the Adjudication: When an individual seeks a benefit:** A claimant files a claim for Social Security benefits. If denied, the claimant can request a hearing before an administrative law judge. Finally, if denied again, the claimant can appeal, first inside the agency and then to a federal court. Refer to Exhibit 4-4 to view the process of Social Security adjudication. See Exhibit 4-5 to view the process of a state worker's compensation adjudication.

- **Stages of the Adjudication: When an agency brings an action to enforce a regulation or law:** An agency may investigate a consumer complaint of unfair trade practices by a business. The agency and the company can enter into a *consent decree* that will end the adjudication, or the agency can issue an administrative complaint and the issues will be resolved before an administrative law judge. If the business is dissatisfied with the decision, it can take an appeal into a court. Refer to Exhibit 4-6 to view the process of a typical agency adjudication to enforce a regulation.

- *Administrative Law Judge:* The administrative law judge (ALJ) presides at agency hearings. ALJs must be unbiased and are generally independent from the agency. To assure independence, federal ALJs, like many state administrative law judges, have their salaries set by a separate agency, receive cases on a random basis, can only be removed for cause, and are selected from a list of qualified candidates.

- **Prehearing:** Prehearing proceedings include discovery (exchange of information between the parties) and a pretrial conference where the ALJ and the parties can exchange information, identify issues, and, if possible, reach a settlement of the case.

consent decree
the settlement of an administrative adjudication in which a person or business agrees to take certain actions without admitting fault

administrative law judge
the official who is the presiding officer at administrative hearings; depending on the applicable agency, this person can also be called a hearings examiner, hearings officer, referee, or claims examiner.

> The person who presides at an administrative hearing can be titled an administrative law judge, hearings officer, hearings examiner, referee, or claims examiner.

- **The Hearing Itself:** The hearing is less formal than a trial in court. Most rules of evidence do not apply. The ALJ presides, makes rulings on motions and evidence, and makes the decision at the end of the hearing. Witnesses testify and can be cross-examined. Experts such as doctors can also testify. Judges in courts of law can take judicial notice of matters that are common knowledge and not reasonably subjected to dispute. These matters can include recognition of historical, geographic, or scientific matters. When judicial notice is invoked, the matters are taken as facts without the necessity of any party actually proving them, which can save time and expense. In administrative law, a similar concept is referred to as *official notice* and can be a great time-saver in administrative cases. Parties have the right to contest a fact that has been admitted through official notice. To prevail at the hearing, a party must prove its case by a *preponderance of the evidence.* This is the same standard that a plaintiff must establish in a civil case. The parties have a right to be represented by an attorney at the hearing. Many federal and state agencies allow nonattorney representation. See Exhibit 4-7 for a list of some of the agencies that allow nonattorney representation at administrative hearings. See Exhibit 4-8, which is the form used by the SSA for appointment of a representative. See Exhibit 4-9, which is a request for a hearing by an administrative law judge.

- **Decision of the ALJ or Other Decisionmaker:** The ALJ makes a decision after review of the facts and the law. Parties are allowed to submit in writing proposed findings of fact and conclusions of law which are what a party hopes the ALJ will adopt. The ALJ will review the evidence and write in the decision his or her findings of fact and the conclusions reached which explains why the adjudication came out as it did. Most federal APA formal adjudications result in an initial decision by the ALJ, which will be the final decision, unless appealed. If the initial decision is appealed, the agency will review it, after which it can be appealed into a court. (See Section 557 of the APA.) The adjudication will

official notice

when an agency decisionmaker recognizes the existence of certain facts without proof

preponderance of the evidence

the standard of proof required in most administrative hearings, just enough evidence to make it more likely than not that the claimant should win, or being convinced by about 51 percent

There are more than 1,300 Administrative Law Judges assigned to 31 federal agencies. The agency employing the largest number of Administrative Law Judges, more than 1,184, is the SSA. Two other agencies with large numbers of Administrative Law Judges include the U.S. Department of Labor, with 50, and the National Labor Relations Board, with 60. The remaining Administrative Law Judges are employed in agencies with 1 to 19 judges. Although all Administrative Law Judges are assigned to specific agencies, under a program administered by the Office of Personnel Management, judges from one agency can be assigned to hear cases for another agency when case loads warrant such action.
Source: http://www.faljc.org/

There is no right to a jury trial in administrative adjudications as there is in a civil or criminal trial.

the record
the information the agency actually uses in reaching its decisions

result in an order, either granting or denying benefits or ordering compliance with a regulation. Even if not a formal adjudication under the APA, the decisionmaker must state the reasons for the decision and state the evidence relied on in reaching the decision. In most states, the decisionmaker is required to explain his or her decision and demonstrate the connection between the facts and conclusion and the evidence in *the record.* Federal and state agency decisionmakers must base their decision only on the evidence properly admitted in the hearing; if not, that decision might be overturned. For example, in *Wallace v. Bowen,* 869 F.2d 187 (3rd Cir. 1988) (see excerpt in Case Law at the end of the chapter), an ALJ's decision to deny Social Security disability benefits was reversed. The Court ruled that the ALJ improperly relied on the claimant's medical records which were obtained after the hearing and without the opportunity for cross-examination. It is also important for the decision to be written clearly, not only so that the parties know precisely the terms of the decision, but also to provide a court with an adequate record, which may be used in an appeal to review the decision. If the

Note that this discussion of adjudication happens inside the agency. A decision must normally be appealed inside the agency before it goes to a court of law. When a court reviews an agency adjudication, that is called judicial review, which will be covered in Chapter 6.

Exhibit 4-4

Adjudication of Social Security Disability Benefit

Claimant files with U.S. Supreme Court and is denied again.

↑

Claimant files appeal with U.S. Court of Appeals and is denied again.

↑

Claimant files with U.S. District Court and is denied again.

↑

Claimant files appeal with Appeals Council and is denied again.

↑

Claimant has hearing before ALJ and is denied again.

↑

Claimant is denied benefits.

↑

Claimant files claim for benefits.

Exhibit 4-5

Adjudication—Workers' Compensation

Appeal to PA Supreme Court

↑

Appeal to PA Commonwealth Court

↑

Appeal to Worker Compensation Appeal Board

↑

Hearing before worker compensation judge (WCJ)

↑

Compensation denied

↑

Petition for compensation is filed

↑

Worker is injured on the job

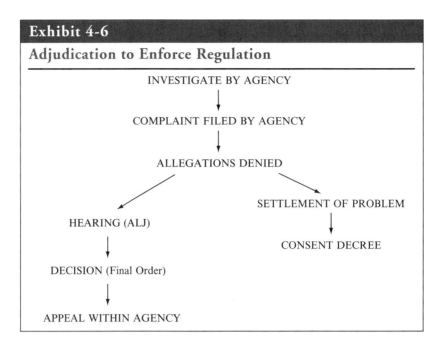

Exhibit 4-6

Adjudication to Enforce Regulation

INVESTIGATE BY AGENCY

↓

COMPLAINT FILED BY AGENCY

↓

ALLEGATIONS DENIED

HEARING (ALJ)   SETTLEMENT OF PROBLEM

↓   ↓

DECISION (Final Order)   CONSENT DECREE

↓

APPEAL WITHIN AGENCY

Exhibit 4-7

Some Federal Agencies That Permit Nonattorney Representation

Consumer Product Safety Commission—16 C.F.R. § 1025.61
Drug Enforcement Agency—21 C.F.R. § 1316.50
Federal Energy Regulatory Commission—18 C.F.R. § 385.2101
Federal Maritime Commission—46 C.F.R. § 502.30
Food and Drug Administration—21 C.F.R. § 12.40
National Credit Union Administration—12 C.F.R. § 747.2
Occupational Safety and Health Review Commission—29 C.F.R. § 2200.22
Social Security Administration—42 U. S. § 406

court is unclear on how the agency, reached its decision, the court would have to send the case back to the agency, which would be a waste of time and effort. When a court looks at a decision of an agency, the court is engaging in judicial review, which is covered in Chapter 6. See Exhibit 4-10 for an adjudication by an ALJ of the National Labor Relations Board (NLRB).

Exhibit 4-8

Social Security Form for Appointment of Representative

Social Security Administration
Please read the back of the last copy before you complete this form.

Form Approved
OMB No. 0960-0527

Name (Claimant) **(Print or Type)**	Social Security Number
Wage Earner (If Different)	Social Security Number

Part I   **APPOINTMENT OF REPRESENTATIVE**

I appoint this person, _____ ,
(Name and Address)

to act as my representative in connection with my claim(s) or asserted right(s) under:

☐ Title II   ☐ Title XVI   ☐ Title XVIII   ☐ Title VIII
(RSDI)   (SSI)   (Medicare Coverage)   (SVB)

This person may, entirely in my place, make any request or give any notice; give or draw out evidence or information; get information; and receive any notice in connection with my pending claim(s) or asserted right(s).

☐ I appoint, or I now have, more than one representative. My main representative is _____ .
(Name of Principal Representative)

Signature (Claimant)	Address
Telephone Number (with Area Code)	Fax Number (with Area Code)	Date

Part II   **ACCEPTANCE OF APPOINTMENT**

I, _____ , hereby accept the above appointment. I certify that I have not been suspended or prohibited from practice before the Social Security Administration; that I am not disqualified from representing the claimant as a current or former officer or employee of the United States; and that I will not charge or collect any fee for the representation, even if a third party will pay the fee, unless it has been approved in accordance with the laws and rules referred to on the reverse side of the representative's copy of this form. If I decide not to charge or collect a fee for the representation, I will notify the Social Security Administration. (Completion of Part III satisfies this requirement.)

Check one: ☐ I am an attorney.   ☐ I am a non-attorney who is eligible to receive direct fee payment.

☐ I am not an attorney and I am ineligible to receive direct fee payment.

I have been disbarred or suspended from a court or bar to which I was previously admitted to practice as an attorney.   ☐ YES   ☐ NO

I have been disqualified from participating in or appearing before a Federal program or agency.   ☐ YES   ☐ NO

I declare under penalty of perjury that I have examined all the information on this form, and on any accompanying statements or forms, and it is true and correct to the best of my knowledge.

Signature (Representative)	Address
Telephone Number (with Area Code)	Fax Number (with Area Code)	Date

Part III (Optional)   **WAIVER OF FEE**

I waive my right to charge and collect a fee under sections 206 and 1631(d)(2) of the Social Security Act. I release my client (the claimant) from any obligations, contractual or otherwise, which may be owed to me for services I have provided in connection with my client's claim(s) or asserted right(s).

Signature (Representative)	Date

Part IV (Optional)   **WAIVER OF DIRECT PAYMENT**

by Attorney or Non-Attorney Eligible to Receive Direct Payment

I waive only my right to direct payment of a fee from the withheld past-due retirement, survivors, disability insurance or supplemental security income benefits of my client (the claimant). I do not waive my right to request fee approval and to collect a fee directly from my client or a third party.

Signature (Attorney or Eligible Non-Attorney (for Direct Payment) Representative)	Date

Form **SSA-1696-U4** (1-2005) EF (1-2005)   **(See Important Information on Reverse)**   **FILE COPY**
Destroy Prior Editions

(Continued)

Exhibit 4-8 (Continued)

INFORMATION FOR CLAIMANTS

What a Representative May Do

We will work directly with your appointed representative unless he or she asks us to work directly with you. Your representative may:

o   get information from your claim(s) file;

o   give us evidence or information to support your claim;

o   come with you, or for you, to any interview, conference, or hearing you have with us;

o   request a reconsideration, hearing, or Appeals Council review; and

o   help you and your witnesses prepare for a hearing and question any witnesses.

Also, your representative will receive a copy of the decision(s) we make on your claim(s). We will rely on your representative to tell you about the status of your claim(s), but you still may call or visit us for information.

You and your representative(s) are responsible for giving Social Security accurate information. It is wrong to willingly furnish false information. Doing so may result in criminal prosecution.

We usually continue to work with your representative until (1) you tell us that he or she no longer represents you; or (2) your representative tells us that he or she is withdrawing or indicates that his or her services have ended (for example, by filing a fee petition or not pursuing an appeal). We do not continue to work with someone who is suspended or disqualified from representing claimants.

What Your Representative(s) May Charge

Each representative you appoint can ask for a fee. To charge you a fee for services, your representative must get our approval. (Even when someone else will pay the fee for you, for example, an insurance company, your representative usually must get our approval.) One way is to file a fee petition. The other way is to file a fee agreement with us. In either case, your representative cannot charge you more than the fee amount we approve. If he or she does, promptly report this to your Social Security office.

o   Filing a Fee Petition

Your representative may ask for approval of a fee by giving us a fee petition when his or her work on your claim(s) is complete. This written request describes in detail the amount of time he or she spent on each service provided you. The request also gives the amount of the fee the representative wants to charge for these services. Your representative must give you a copy of the fee petition and each attachment. If you disagree with the information shown in the fee petition, contact your Social Security office. Please do this within 20 days of receiving your copy of the petition.

We will review the petition and consider the reasonable value of the services provided. Then we will tell you in writing the amount of the fee we approve.

What Your Representative(s) May Charge, continued

o   Filing A Fee Agreement

If you and your representative have a written fee agreement, one of you must give it to us before we decide your claim(s). We usually will approve the agreement if you both signed it; the fee you agreed on is no more than 25 percent of past-due benefits, or $5,300 (or a higher amount we set and announced in the Federal Register), whichever is less; we approve your claim(s); and your claim results in past-due benefits. We will tell you in writing the amount of the fee your representative can charge based on the agreement.

If we do not approve the fee agreement, we will tell you and your representative in writing. Then your representative must file a fee petition to charge and collect a fee.

After we tell you the amount of the fee your representative can charge, you or your representative can ask us to look at it again if either or both of you disagree with the amount. (If we approved a fee agreement, the person who decided your claim(s) also may ask us to lower the amount.) Someone who did not decide the amount of the fee the first time will review and finally decide the amount of the fee.

How Much You Pay

You never owe more than the fee we approve, except for:

o   any fee a Federal court allows for your representative's services before it; and

o   out-of-pocket expenses your representative incurs or expects to incur, for example, the cost of getting your doctor's or hospital's records. Our approval is not needed for such expenses.

Your representative may accept money in advance as long as he or she holds it in a trust or escrow account. If an attorney or a non-attorney who is eligible to receive direct fee payment represents you, and if your retirement, survivors, disability insurance, and/or supplemental security income claim(s) results in past-due benefits, we usually withhold 25 percent of your past-due benefits to pay toward the fee for you.

You must pay your representative directly:

o   the rest of the fee you owe

     -   if the amount of the fee is more than any amount(s) your representative held for you in a trust or escrow account and we withheld and paid your representative for you.

o   all of the fee you owe

     -   if we did not withhold past-due benefits, for example, because your representative waived direct payment, or you discharged the representative, or the representative withdrew from representing you before we issued a favorable decision; or if we withheld, but later paid you the money because your representative did not eithe ask for our approval until after 60 days of the date of your notice of award or tell us on time that he or she planned to ask for a fee.

Exhibit 4-8 (Continued)

Social Security Administration

Form Approved

Please read the back of the last copy before you complete this form.

OMB No. 0960-0527

Name (Claimant) **(Print or Type)**	Social Security Number

Wage Earner (If Different)	Social Security Number

Part I   **APPOINTMENT OF REPRESENTATIVE**

I appoint this person, _____ ,

(Name and Address)

to act as my representative in connection with my claim(s) or asserted right(s) under:

☐ Title II   ☐ Title XVI   ☐ Title XVIII   ☐ Title VIII

   (RSDI)   (SSI)   (Medicare Coverage)   (SVB)

This person may, entirely in my place, make any request or give any notice; give or draw out evidence or information; get information; and receive any notice in connection with my pending claim(s) or asserted right(s).

☐   I appoint, or I now have, more than one representative. My main representative is _____ .

(Name of Principal Representative)

Signature (Claimant)	Address
Telephone Number (with Area Code)	Fax Number (with Area Code) Date

Part II   **ACCEPTANCE OF APPOINTMENT**

I, _____ , hereby accept the above appointment. I certify that I have not been suspended or prohibited from practice before the Social Security Administration; that I am not disqualified from representing the claimant as a current or former officer or employee of the United States; and that I will not charge or collect any fee for the representation, even if a third party will pay the fee, unless it has been approved in accordance with the laws and rules referred to on the reverse side of the representative's copy of this form. If I decide not to charge or collect a fee for the representation, I will notify the Social Security Administration. (Completion of Part III satisfies this requirement.)

Check one: ☐ I am an attorney.   ☐ I am a non-attorney who is eligible to receive direct fee payment.

☐ I am not an attorney and I am ineligible to receive direct fee payment.

I have been disbarred or suspended from a court or bar to which I was previously admitted to practice as an attorney. ☐ YES ☐ NO

I have been disqualified from participating in or appearing before a Federal program or agency. ☐ YES ☐ NO

I declare under penalty of perjury that I have examined all the information on this form, and on any accompanying statements or forms, and it is true and correct to the best of my knowledge.

Signature (Representative)	Address
Telephone Number (with Area Code)	Fax Number (with Area Code) Date

Part III (Optional)   **WAIVER OF FEE**

I waive my right to charge and collect a fee under sections 206 and 1631(d)(2) of the Social Security Act. I release my client (the claimant) from any obligations, contractual or otherwise, which may be owed to me for services I have provided in connection with my client's claim(s) or asserted right(s).

Signature (Representative)	Date

Part IV (Optional)   **WAIVER OF DIRECT PAYMENT**

by Attorney or Non-Attorney Eligible to Receive Direct Payment

I waive only my right to direct payment of a fee from the withheld past-due retirement, survivors, disability insurance or supplemental security income benefits of my client (the claimant). I do not waive my right to request fee approval and to collect a fee directly from my client or a third party.

Signature (Attorney or Eligible Non-Attorney (for Direct Payment) Representative)	Date

Form **SSA-1696-U4** (1-2005) EF (1-2005)   **(See Important Information on Reverse)**   **CLAIMANT'S COPY**

Destroy Prior Editions

(Continued)

Exhibit 4-8 (Continued)

INFORMATION FOR CLAIMANTS

What a Representative May Do

We will work directly with your appointed representative unless he or she asks us to work directly with you. Your representative may:

o   get information from your claim(s) file;

o   give us evidence or information to support your claim;

o   come with you, or for you, to any interview, conference, or hearing you have with us;

o   request a reconsideration, hearing, or Appeals Council review; and

o   help you and your witnesses prepare for a hearing and question any witnesses.

Also, your representative will receive a copy of the decision(s) we make on your claim(s). We will rely on your representative to tell you about the status of your claim(s), but you still may call or visit us for information.

You and your representative(s) are responsible for giving Social Security accurate information. It is wrong to willingly furnish false information. Doing so may result in criminal prosecution.

We usually continue to work with your representative until (1) you tell us that he or she no longer represents you; or (2) your representative tells us that he or she is withdrawing or indicates that his or her services have ended (for example, by filing a fee petition or not pursuing an appeal). We do not continue to work with someone who is suspended or disqualified from representing claimants.

What Your Representative(s) May Charge

Each representative you appoint can ask for a fee. To charge you a fee for services, your representative must get our approval. (Even when someone else will pay the fee for you, for example, an insurance company, your representative usually must get our approval.) One way is to file a fee petition. The other way is to file a fee agreement with us. In either case, your representative cannot charge you more than the fee amount we approve. If he or she does, promptly report this to your Social Security office.

o   Filing a Fee Petition

Your representative may ask for approval of a fee by giving us a fee petition when his or her work on your claim(s) is complete. This written request describes in detail the amount of time he or she spent on each service provided you. The request also gives the amount of the fee the representative wants to charge for these services. Your representative must give you a copy of the fee petition and each attachment. If you disagree with the information shown in the fee petition, contact your Social Security office. Please do this within 20 days of receiving your copy of the petition.

We will review the petition and consider the reasonable value of the services provided. Then we will tell you in writing the amount of the fee we approve.

What Your Representative(s) May Charge, continued

o   Filing A Fee Agreement

If you and your representative have a written fee agreement, one of you must give it to us before we decide your claim(s). We usually will approve the agreement if you both signed it; the fee you agreed on is no more than 25 percent of past-due benefits, or $5,300 (or a higher amount we set and announced in the Federal Register), whichever is less; we approve your claim(s); and your claim results in past-due benefits. We will tell you in writing the amount of the fee your representative can charge based on the agreement.

If we do not approve the fee agreement, we will tell you and your representative in writing. Then your representative must file a fee petition to charge and collect a fee.

After we tell you the amount of the fee your representative can charge, you or your representative can ask us to look at it again if either or both of you disagree with the amount. (If we approved a fee agreement, the person who decided your claim(s) also may ask us to lower the amount.) Someone who did not decide the amount of the fee the first time will review and finally decide the amount of the fee.

How Much You Pay

You never owe more than the fee we approve, except for:

o   any fee a Federal court allows for your representative's services before it; and

o   out-of-pocket expenses your representative incurs or expects to incur, for example, the cost of getting your doctor's or hospital's records. Our approval is not needed for such expenses.

Your representative may accept money in advance as long as he or she holds it in a trust or escrow account. If an attorney or a non-attorney who is eligible to receive direct fee payment represents you, and if your retirement, survivors, disability insurance, and/or supplemental security income claim(s) results in past-due benefits, we usually withhold 25 percent of your past-due benefits to pay toward the fee for you.

You must pay your representative directly:

o   the rest of the fee you owe

-      if the amount of the fee is more than any amount(s) your representative held for you in a trust or escrow account and we withheld and paid your representative for you.

o   all of the fee you owe

-      if we did not withhold past-due benefits, for example, because your representative waived direct payment, or you discharged the representative, or the representative withdrew from representing you before we issued a favorable decision; or if we withheld, but later paid you the money because your representative did not either ask for our approval until after 60 days of the date of your notice of award or tell us on time that he or she planned to ask for a fee.

Form **SSA-1696-U4** (1-2005) EF (1-2005)

Exhibit 4-8 (Continued)

Social Security Administration
Please read the back of the last copy before you complete this form.

Form Approved
OMB No. 0960-0527

Name (Claimant) **(Print or Type)**	Social Security Number

Wage Earner (If Different)	Social Security Number

Part I APPOINTMENT OF REPRESENTATIVE

I appoint this person, _____ ,

(Name and Address)

to act as my representative in connection with my claim(s) or asserted right(s) under:

☐ Title II (RSDI) ☐ Title XVI (SSI) ☐ Title XVIII (Medicare Coverage) ☐ Title VIII (SVB)

This person may, entirely in my place, make any request or give any notice; give or draw out evidence or information; get information; and receive any notice in connection with my pending claim(s) or asserted right(s).

☐ I appoint, or I now have, more than one representative. My main representative is _____ .

(Name of Principal Representative)

Signature (Claimant)	Address

Telephone Number (with Area Code)	Fax Number (with Area Code)	Date

Part II ACCEPTANCE OF APPOINTMENT

I, _____ , hereby accept the above appointment. I certify that I have not been suspended or prohibited from practice before the Social Security Administration; that I am not disqualified from representing the claimant as a current or former officer or employee of the United States; and that I will not charge or collect any fee for the representation, even if a third party will pay the fee, unless it has been approved in accordance with the laws and rules referred to on the reverse side of the representative's copy of this form. If I decide not to charge or collect a fee for the representation, I will notify the Social Security Administration. (Completion of Part III satisfies this requirement.)

Check one: ☐ I am an attorney. ☐ I am a non-attorney who is eligible to receive direct fee payment.

☐ I am not an attorney and I am ineligible to receive direct fee payment.

I have been disbarred or suspended from a court or bar to which I was previously admitted to practice as an attorney. ☐ YES ☐ NO
I have been disqualified from participating in or appearing before a Federal program or agency. ☐ YES ☐ NO

I declare under penalty of perjury that I have examined all the information on this form, and on any accompanying statements or forms, and it is true and correct to the best of my knowledge.

Signature (Representative)	Address

Telephone Number (with Area Code)	Fax Number (with Area Code)	Date

Part III (Optional) WAIVER OF FEE

I waive my right to charge and collect a fee under sections 206 and 1631(d)(2) of the Social Security Act. I release my client (the claimant) from any obligations, contractual or otherwise, which may be owed to me for services I have provided in connection with my client's claim(s) or asserted right(s).

Signature (Representative)	Date

Part IV (Optional) WAIVER OF DIRECT PAYMENT

by Attorney or Non-Attorney Eligible to Receive Direct Payment

I waive only my right to direct payment of a fee from the withheld past-due retirement, survivors, disability insurance or supplemental security income benefits of my client (the claimant). I do not waive my right to request fee approval and to collect a fee directly from my client or a third party.

Signature (Attorney or Eligible Non-Attorney (for Direct Payment) Representative)	Date

Form **SSA-1696-U4** (1-2005) EF (1-2005)   (See Important Information on Reverse)   REPRESENTATIVE COPY
Destroy Prior Editions

(Continued)

Exhibit 4-8 (Continued)

INFORMATION FOR REPRESENTATIVES

Fees for Representation

An attorney or other person who wants to charge or collect a fee for providing services in connection with a claim before the Social Security Administration must first obtain our approval of the fee for representation. The only exceptions are if the fee is for services provided:

o   when a nonprofit organization or government agency will pay the fee and any expenses from government funds and the claimant incurs no liability, directly or indirectly, for the cost(s);

o   in an official capacity such as legal guardian, committee, or similar court-appointed office and the court has approved the fee in question; or

o   in representing the claimant before a court of law. A representative who has provided services in a claim before both the Social Security Administration and a court of law may seek a fee from either or both, but neither tribunal has the authority to set a fee for the other.

Obtaining Approval of a Fee

To charge a fee for services, you must use one of two, mutually exclusive fee approval processes. You must file either a fee petition or a fee agreement with us. In either case, you cannot charge more than the fee amount we approve.

o   Fee Petition Process

You may ask for approval of a fee by giving us a fee petition when you have completed your services to the claimant. This written request must describe in detail the amount of time you spent on each service provided and the amount of the fee you are requesting.

You must give the claimant a copy of the fee petition and each attachment. The claimant may disagree with the information shown by contacting a Social Security office within 20 days of receiving his or her copy of the fee petition. We will consider the reasonable value of the services provided, and send you notice of the amount of the fee you can charge.

o   Fee Agreement Process

If you and the claimant have a written fee agreement, either of you must give it to us before we decide the claim(s). We usually will approve the agreement if you both signed it; the fee you agreed on is no more than 25 percent of past-due benefits, or $5,300 (or a higher amount we set and announce in the Federal Register), whichever is less; we approve the claim(s); and the claim results in past-due benefits. We will send you a copy of the notice we send the claimant telling him or her the amount of the fee you can charge based on the agreement.

If we do not approve the fee agreement, we will tell you in writing. We also will tell you and the claimant that you must file a fee petition if you wish to charge and collect a fee.

After we tell you the amount of the fee you can charge, you or the claimant may ask us in writing to review the approved fee. (If we approved a fee agreement, the person who decided the claim(s) also may ask us to lower the amount.) Someone who did not decide the amount of the fee the first time will review and finally decide the amount of the fee.

Form **SSA-1696-U4** (1-2005) EF (1-2005)

Collecting a Fee

You may accept money in advance, as long as you hold it in a trust or escrow account. The claimant never owes you more than the fee we approve, except for:

o   any fee a Federal court allows for your services before it; and

o   out-of-pocket expenses you incur or expect to incur, for example, the cost of getting evidence. Our approval is not needed for such expenses.

If you are not an attorney and you are ineligible to receive direct payment, you must collect the approved fee from the claimant. If you are interested in becoming eligible to receive direct payment, you can find information on the procedures for becoming eligible for direct payment on our "Representing Claimants" website: http://www.ssa.gov/representation/.

If you are an attorney or a non-attorney whom SSA has found eligible to receive direct payment, we usually withhold 25 percent of any past-due benefits that result from a favorably decided retirement, survivors, disability insurance, or supplemental security income claim. Once we approve a fee, we pay you all or part of the fee from the funds withheld. We will also charge you the assessment required by section 206(d) and 1631(d)(2)(C) of the Social Security Act. You cannot charge or collect this expense from the claimant. You must collect from the claimant:

o   the rest he or she owes

     -   if the amount of the fee is more than the amount of money we withheld and paid you for the claimant, and any amount you held for the claimant in a trust or escrow account.

o   all of the fee he or she owes

     -   if we did not withhold past-due benefits, for example, because there are no past-due benefits, or the claimant discharged you, or you withdrew from representing the claimant; or

     -   if we withheld, but later paid the money to the claimant because you did not either ask for our approval until after 60 days of the date of the notice of award or tell us on time that you planned to ask for a fee.

Conflict of Interest and Penalties

For improper acts, you can be suspended or disqualified from representing anyone before the Social Security Administration. You also can face criminal prosecution. Improper acts include:

o   If you are or were an officer or employee of the United States, providing services as a representative in certain claims against and other matters affecting the Federal government.

o   Knowingly and willingly furnishing false information.

o   Charging or collecting an unauthorized fee or too much for services provided in any claim, including services before a court that made a favorable decision.

References

o   18 U.S.C. §§ 203, 205, and 207; and 42 U.S.C. §§ 406(a), 1320a-6, and 1383(d)(2)

o   20 CFR §§ 404.1700 et. seq. and 416.1500 et. seq.

o   Social Security Rulings 88-10c, 85-3, 83-27, and 82-39

Exhibit 4-8 (Continued)

Social Security Administration
Please read the back of the last copy before you complete this form.

Form Approved
OMB No. 0960-0527

Name (Claimant) **(Print or Type)**	Social Security Number

Wage Earner (If Different)	Social Security Number

Part I   **APPOINTMENT OF REPRESENTATIVE**

I appoint this person, _____ ,
                                           (Name and Address)

to act as my representative in connection with my claim(s) or asserted right(s) under:

☐   Title II   ☐   Title XVI   ☐   Title XVIII   ☐   Title VIII
    (RSDI)   (SSI)   (Medicare Coverage)   (SVB)

This person may, entirely in my place, make any request or give any notice; give or draw out evidence or information; get information; and receive any notice in connection with my pending claim(s) or asserted right(s).

☐   I appoint, or I now have, more than one representative. My main representative
     is _____ .
                          (Name of Principal Representative)

Signature (Claimant)	Address

Telephone Number (with Area Code)	Fax Number (with Area Code)	Date

Part II   **ACCEPTANCE OF APPOINTMENT**

I, _____ , hereby accept the above appointment. I certify that I have not been suspended or prohibited from practice before the Social Security Administration; that I am not disqualified from representing the claimant as a current or former officer or employee of the United States; and that I will not charge or collect any fee for the representation, even if a third party will pay the fee, unless it has been approved in accordance with the laws and rules referred to on the reverse side of the representative's copy of this form. If I decide not to charge or collect a fee for the representation, I will notify the Social Security Administration. (Completion of Part III satisfies this requirement.)

Check one: ☐ I am an attorney.   ☐ I am a non-attorney who is eligible to receive direct fee payment.

           ☐ I am not an attorney and I am ineligible to receive direct fee payment.

I have been disbarred or suspended from a court or bar to which I was previously admitted to practice as an attorney. ☐ YES ☐ NO

I have been disqualified from participating in or appearing before a Federal program or agency. ☐ YES ☐ NO

I declare under penalty of perjury that I have examined all the information on this form, and on any accompanying statements or forms, and it is true and correct to the best of my knowledge.

Signature (Representative)	Address

Telephone Number (with Area Code)	Fax Number (with Area Code)	Date

Part III (Optional)   **WAIVER OF FEE**

I waive my right to charge and collect a fee under sections 206 and 1631(d)(2) of the Social Security Act. I release my client (the claimant) from any obligations, contractual or otherwise, which may be owed to me for services I have provided in connection with my client's claim(s) or asserted right(s).

Signature (Representative)	Date

Part IV (Optional)   **WAIVER OF DIRECT PAYMENT**
by Attorney or Non-Attorney Eligible to Receive Direct Payment

I waive only my right to direct payment of a fee from the withheld past-due retirement, survivors, disability insurance or supplemental security income benefits of my client (the claimant). I do not waive my right to request fee approval and to collect a fee directly from my client or a third party.

Signature (Attorney or Eligible Non-Attorney (for Direct Payment) Representative)	Date

Form **SSA-1696-U4** (1-2005) EF (1-2005)   **(See Important Information on Reverse)**   **OHA COPY**
Destroy Prior Editions

(Continued)

Exhibit 4-8 (Continued)

COMPLETING THIS FORM TO APPOINT A REPRESENTATIVE

Choosing to Be Represented

You can choose to have a representative help you when you do business with Social Security. We will work with your representative, just as we would with you. It is important that you select a qualified person because, once appointed, your representative may act for you in most Social Security matters. We give more information, and examples of what a representative may do, on the back of the "Claimant's Copy" of this form.

Paperwork and Privacy Act Notice

The Social Security Administration (SSA) will recognize someone else as your representative if you sign a written notice appointing that person and, if he or she is not an attorney, that person signs the notice agreeing to be your representative. (You can read more about this in our regulations: 20 CFR §§ 404.1707 and 416.1507.) Giving the information this form requests is voluntary. Without it though, we may not work with the person you choose to represent you.

How to Complete This Form

Please print or type. At the top, show your full name and your Social Security number. If your claim is based on another person's work and earnings, also show the ''wage earner's'' name and Social Security number. If you appoint more than one person, you may want to complete a form for each of them.

Part I Appointment of Representative

Give the name and address of the person(s) you are appointing. You may appoint an attorney or any other qualified person to represent you. You also may appoint more than one person, but see ''What Your Representative(s) May Charge'' on the back of the ''Claimant's Copy'' of this form. You can appoint one or more persons in a firm, corporation, or other organization as your representative(s), but you may not appoint a law firm, legal aid group, corporation, or organization itself.

Check the block(s) showing the program(s) under which you have a claim. You may check more than one block. Check:

o   Title Il (RSDI), if your claim concerns retirement, survivors, or disability insurance benefits.

o   Title XVI (SSI), if your claim concerns supplemental security income.

o   Title XVIII (Medicare Coverage), if your claim concerns entitlement to Medicare or enrollment in the Supplementary Medical Insurance (SMI) plan.

If you will have more than one representative, check the block and give the name of the person you want to be the main representative.

How To Complete This Form, continued

Sign your name, but print or type your address, your area code and telephone number, and the date.

Part II Acceptance of Appointment

Each person you appoint (named in part I) completes this part, preferably in all cases. If the person is not an attorney, he or she must give his or her name, state that he or she accepts the appointment, and sign the form.

Part III (Optional) Waiver of Fee

Your representative may complete this part if he or she will not charge any fee for the services provided in this claim. If you appoint a second representative or co-counsel who also will not charge a fee, he or she also should sign this part or give us a separate, written waiver statement.

Part IV (Optional) Waiver of Direct Payment by an Attorney or a Non-Attorney Eligible to Receive Direct Payment

Your representative may complete this part if he or she is an attorney or a non-attorney who does not want direct payment of all or part of the approved fee from past-due retirement, survivors, disability insurance, or supplemental security income benefits withheld.

Paperwork Reduction Act Statement - This information collection meets the requirements of 44 U.S.C. § 3507, as amended by Section 2 of the Paperwork Reduction Act of 1995. You do not need to answer these questions unless we display a valid Office of Management and Budget control number. We estimate that it will take about 10 minutes to read the instructions, gather the facts, and answer the questions. **SEND THE COMPLETED FORM TO YOUR LOCAL SOCIAL SECURITY OFFICE. The office is listed under U. S. Government agencies in your telephone directory or you may call Social Security at 1-800-772-1213.** *You may send comments on our time estimate above to: SSA, 1338 Annex Building, Baltimore, MD 21235-6401. **Send only comments relating to our time estimate to this address, not the completed form.***

References

o   18 U.S.C. §§ 203, 205, and 207; and 42 U.S.C. §§ 406(a), 1320a-6, and 1383(d)(2)

o   20 CFR §§ 404.1700 et. seq. and 416.1500 et. seq.

o   Social Security Rulings 88-10c, 85-3, 83-27, and 82-39

Form **SSA-1696-U4** (1-2005) EF (1-2005)

Exhibit 4-9

Request for a Hearing by ALJ

SOCIAL SECURITY ADMINISTRATION OFFICE OF DISABILITY ADJUDICATION AND REVIEW	Form Approved OMB No. 0960-0269

REQUEST FOR HEARING BY ADMINISTRATIVE LAW JUDGE

*(Take or mail the **signed original** to your local Social Security office, the Veterans Affairs*
Regional Office in Manila or any U.S. Foreign Service post and keep a copy for your records)

See
Privacy Act Notice

1. CLAIMANT NAME	CLAIMANT SSN – –	2. WAGE EARNER NAME, IF DIFFERENT
3. CLAIMANT CLAIM NUMBER, IF DIFFERENT – –	4. SPOUSE'S NAME, IF NOT WAGE EARNER	SPOUSE'S CLAIM NUMBER OR SSN – –

5. I REQUEST A HEARING BEFORE AN ADMINISTRATIVE LAW JUDGE. I disagree with the determination made on my claim because:

An Administrative Law Judge of the Social Security Administration's Office of Disability Adjudication and Review or the Health and Human Services will be appointed to conduct the hearing or other proceedings in your case. You will receive notice of the time and place of a hearing at least 20 days before the date set for a hearing.

6. I have additional evidence to submit. ☐ Yes ☐ No Name and address of source of additional evidence: _____ _____ (Please submit it to the hearing office within 10 days. Your servicing Social Security Office will provide the address. Attach an additional sheet if you need more space.)	7. Do not complete if the appeal is a Medicare issue. Check one of the blocks: ☐ I wish to appear at a hearing. ☐ I do not wish to appear at a hearing and I request that a decision be made based on the evidence in my case. (Complete Waiver Form HA-4608)

You have a right to be represented at the hearing. If you are not represented but would like to be, your Social Security office will give you a list of legal referral and service organizations. If you are represented and have not done so previously, complete and submit form SSA-1696 (Appointment of Representative) unless you are appealing a Medicare issue.
Regardless of the issue you are appealing, you should complete No. 8 and your representative (if any) should complete No. 9. If you are represented and your representative is not available to complete this form, you should also print his or her name, address, etc., in No. 9.
I declare under penalty of perjury that I have examined all the information on this form, and on any accompanying statements or forms, and it is true and correct to the best of my knowledge.

8. (CLAIMANT'S SIGNATURE) (DATE)	9. (REPRESENTATIVE'S SIGNATURE/NAME) (DATE)
ADDRESS	(ADDRESS) ☐ ATTORNEY; ☐ NON ATTORNEY;
CITY STATE ZIP CODE –	CITY STATE ZIP CODE –
TELEPHONE NUMBER FAX NUMBER ( ) – ( ) –	TELEPHONE NUMBER FAX NUMBER ( ) – ( ) –

TO BE COMPLETED BY SOCIAL SECURITY ADMINISTRATION-ACKNOWLEDGMENT OF REQUEST FOR HEARING

10. Request received for the Social Security Administration on _____   by: _____
(Date)   (Print Name)

_____   _____   _____   _____
(Title)   (Address)   (Servicing FO Code)   (PC Code)

11. Was the request for hearing received within 65 days of the reconsidered determination?   ☐ YES   ☐ NO
If no is checked, attach claimant's explanation for delay; and attach copy of appointment notice, letter, or other pertinent material or information in the Social Security office.

	15. Check all claim types that apply:	
12. Claimant is represented ☐ Yes ☐ No ☐ List of legal referral and service organizations provided		
13. Interpreter needed ☐ Yes ☐ No Language (including sign language): _____	☐ RSI only	(RSI)
	☐ Title II Disability-worker or child only	(DIWC)
	☐ Title II Disability-Widow(er) only	(DIWW)
14. Check one: ☐ Initial Entitlement Case ☐ Disability Cessation Case ☐ Other Postentitlement Case	☐ SSI Aged only	(SSIA)
	☐ SSI Blind only	(SSIB)
16. HO COPY SENT TO: _____ HO on _____	☐ SSI Disability only	(SSID)
	☐ SSI Aged/Title II	(SSAC)
☐ CF Attached: ☐ Title II; ☐ Title XVI; ☐ Title VIII; ☐ T XVIII; ☐ Title II CF held in FO ☐ Electronic Folder ☐ CF requested ☐ Title II; ☐ Title XVI; ☐ Title VIII; ☐ T XVIII (Copy of email or phone report attached)	☐ SSI Blind/Title II	(SSBC)
	☐ SSI Disability/Title II	(SSDC)
	☐ Title XVIII	(HI/SMI)
17. CF COPY SENT TO: _____ HO on _____	☐ Title VIII Only	(SVB)
	☐ Title VIII/Title XVI	(SVB/SSI)
☐ CF Attached: ☐ Title II; ☐ Title XVI; ☐ T XVIII ☐ Other Attached:	☐ Other - Specify: _____	

Form **HA-501-U5** (5-2007) ef (5-2007)   TAKE OR SEND ORIGINAL TO SSA AND RETAIN A COPY FOR YOUR RECORDS
Destroy Prior Editions

(Continued)

Exhibit 4-9 (Continued)

PAPERWORK/PRIVACY ACT NOTICE

The Social Security Act (sections 205(a), 702, 1631(e)(1)(a) and (b), and 1869(b) (1) and (c), and Public Law 106-169 (Section 809(a)(1) of Sections 251(a)) and Section 1839(i) of the Act (P.L. 108-173) as appropriate) authorizes the collection of information on this form. We need the information to continue processing your claim. You do not have to give it, but if you do not you may not receive benefits under the Social Security Act. We may give out the information on this form without your written consent if we need to get more information to decide if you are eligible for benefits or if a Federal law requires us to do so. Specifically, we may provide information to another Federal, State, or local government agency which is deciding your eligibility for a government benefit or program; to the President or a Congressman inquiring on your behalf; to an independent party who needs statistical information for a research paper or audit report on a Social Security program; or to the Department of Justice to represent the Federal Government in a court suit related to a program administered by the Social Security Administration. We explain, in the Federal Register, these and other reasons why we may use or give out information about you. If you would like more information, get in touch with any Social Security office, the Veterans Affairs Regional Office in Manila, or any U.S. Foreign Service post.

We may also use the information you give us when we match records by computer. Matching programs compare our records with those of other Federal, State, or local government agencies. Many agencies may use matching programs to find or prove that a person qualifies for benefits paid by the Federal government. The law allows us to do this even if you do not agree to it.

Explanations about these and other reasons why information about you may be used or given out are available in Social Security offices. If you want to learn more about this, contact any Social Security office, the Veterans Affairs Regional Office in Manila, or any U.S. Foreign Service post.

Paperwork Reduction Act Statement - This information collection meets the requirements of 44 U.S.C. § 3507, as amended by Section 2 of the Paperwork Reduction Act of 1995. You do not need to answer these questions unless we display a valid Office of Management and Budget control number. We estimate that it will take about 10 minutes to read the instructions, gather the facts, and answer the questions. *You may send comments on our time estimate above to*: *SSA, 6401 Security Blvd., Baltimore, MD 21235-6401.* **Send *only* comments relating to our time estimate to this address, not the completed form.**

Exhibit 4-10

Adjudication of ALJ

UNITED STATES OF AMERICA

BEFORE THE NATIONAL LABOR RELATIONS BOARD

DIVISION OF JUDGES

NEW YORK BRANCH OFFICE

FIELD HOTEL ASSOCIATES, LP d/b/a HOLIDAY INN-

JFK AIRPORT and FIELD HOTEL ASSOCIATES, LP d/b/a

HOLIDAY INN- JFK AIRPORT, Debtor-in-Possession

And Case No. 29-CA-27411

NEW YORK HOTEL & MOTEL TRADES COUNCIL, AFL-CIO

Sharon Chau, Esq., Counsel for the General Counsel.

DECISION

Statement of the Case

Joel P. Biblowitz, Administrative Law Judge: This case was heard by me on June 20, 2006 in Brooklyn, New York. The Complaint herein, which issued on May 8, 2006 and was based upon an unfair labor practice charge that was filed on February 2, 2006 by New York Hotel & Motel Trades Council, AFL-CIO, herein called the Union, alleges that Field Hotel Associates, LP d/b/a Holiday Inn- JFK Airport and Field Hotel Associates, LP d/b/a Holiday Inn- JFK Airport, Debtor-in-Possession, herein called the Respondent, in about November 2005, reduced the work hours of its employee Shuhab Ahmed, unilaterally and without notice to the Union and an opportunity for the Union to bargain about the subject, in violation of Section 8(a)(1)(5) of the Act. Respondent failed to file an Answer to the Complaint herein.

In the absence of an Answer to the Complaint, Counsel for the General Counsel made a Motion for Default Judgment at the hearing, which I granted. I therefore make the following findings of fact and conclusions of law:

1. The unfair labor practice charge herein was filed by the Union on February 2, 2006 and a copy was served by regular mail on Respondent on or about February 8, 2006.

2(a) At all material times, Field Hotel Associates, LP, a limited liability company registered under the laws of the State of New York, with its principal office and place of business located at 144-02 135th Avenue, Jamaica, New York, has operated a hotel under the trade name Holiday Inn- JFK Airport, herein called the Holiday Inn facility.

(Continued)

Exhibit 4-10 (Continued)

(b) On or about October 29, 2004, Respondent Holiday Inn filed a bankruptcy petition in the United States Bankruptcy Court for the Eastern District of Pennsylvania.

(c) Respondent Debtor has been a debtor-in-possession with full authority to continue operations and exercise all powers necessary to administer its business.

3. During the past twelve month period, which period is representative of its annual operations in general, Respondent Holiday Inn, in the course and conduct of its business operations described above in subparagraph 2, derived gross revenues in excess of $500,000, and purchased and received at the Holiday Inn facility, goods and materials valued in excess $5,000 directly from points located outside the State of New York.

4. At all material times, Respondent has been an employer engaged in commerce within the meaning of Section 2(2), (6) and (7) of the Act.

5. At all material times, the Union has been a labor organization within the meaning of Section 2(5) of the Act.

6. The following employees of Respondent, herein called the Unit, constitute a unit appropriate for the purposes of collective bargaining within the meaning of Section 9(b) of the Act:

All full-time and regular part-time housekeeping and laundry employees, bar, banquet, kitchen, restaurant employees and maintenance employees employed by Respondent at its Holiday Inn facility, but excluding all other employees, including Human Resources Department employees, sales employees, accounting, life-guards, front office employees, office clerical employees, guards, managers, and supervisors as defined in Section 2(11) of the Act.

7. On September 29, 2005, the Union was certified by the Board as the exclusive collective bargaining representative of the Unit.

8. At all material times, the Union, by virtue of Section 9(a) of the Act, has been the exclusive representative of the Unit, for the purposes of collective bargaining.

9. Since on or about dates presently unknown in November 2005, Respondent, unilaterally and without notice to the Union and an opportunity to bargain, reduced the work hours of its employee Shuhab Ahmed.

10. The subject set forth in paragraph 9 relates to terms and conditions of employment of the Unit and is a mandatory subject for the purpose of collective bargaining.

Exhibit 4-10 (Continued)

11. Respondent engaged in the conduct described above in paragraph 9 without prior notice to the Union, and without affording the Union an opportunity to bargain with Respondent with respect to such conduct and the effects of such conduct.

12. By the conduct described above in paragraphs 9 and 11, Respondent has been failing and refusing to bargain collectively and in good faith with the exclusive collective bargaining representative of its employees within the meaning of Section 8(d) of the Act, in violation of Section 8(a)(1)(5) of the Act.

13. The unfair labor practices described above affect commerce within the meaning of Section 2(6) and (7) of the Act.

The Remedy

Having found that the Respondent has engaged in certain unfair labor practices, I recommend that it be ordered to cease and desist from engaging in these activities and that it be ordered to take certain affirmative action designed to effectuate the policies of the Act. As the Respondent unilaterally reduced the working hours of Shuhab Ahmed, without notice to the Union, the collective bargaining representative of the Unit, and without giving the Union an opportunity to bargain, I recommend that the Respondent be ordered to return Ahmed to his JD(NY)–31-06 5 10 15 20 25 30 35 40 45 50 3 work schedule prior to the unlawful change, and reimburse him for any loss of earnings and other benefits that he suffered as a result of the change, plus interest as computed in *New Horizons for the Retarded*, 283 NLRB 1173 (1987).

On these findings of fact and conclusions of law and on the entire record, I issue the following recommendations:

Order

The Respondent, Field Hotel Associates, LP d/b/a Holiday Inn- JFK Airport and Field Hotel Associates, LP d/b/a Holiday Inn- JFK Airport, Debtor-in-Possession, its officers, agents and representatives, shall:

1. Cease and desist from

(a) Making changes to the terms and conditions of employment of its Unit employees without prior notice to, and negotiations with, the Union.

(b) In any like or related manner interfering with, restraining or coercing employees in the exercise of the rights guaranteed them by Section 7 of the Act.

(*Continued*)

Exhibit 4-10 (Continued)

2. Take the following affirmative action necessary to effectuate the policies of the Act:

(a) Make Ahmed whole for any loss of earnings and other benefits that he suffered as a result of the unilateral reduction in his working hours in about November 2005, in the manner set forth above in the Remedy section, and reinstate his work hours as they were prior to the unlawful change.

(b) Preserve and, within 14 days of a request, or such additional time as the Regional Director may allow for good cause shown, provide at a reasonable place designated by the Board or its agents, all payroll records, Social Security payment records, timecards, personnel records and reports, and all other records, including an electronic copy of such records if stored in electronic form, necessary to analyze the amount of backpay due under the terms of this Order.

(c) Within 14 days after service by the Region, post at its facility in Jamaica, New York, copies of the attached notice marked "Appendix." Two copies of the notice, on forms provided by the Regional Director for Region 29, after being signed by the Respondent's authorized representative, shall be posted by the Respondent and maintained for 60 consecutive days in conspicuous places including all places where notices to employees are customarily posted. Reasonable steps shall be taken by the Respondent to ensure that the notices are not altered,

1 If no exceptions are filed as provided by Sec. 102.46 of the Board's Rules and Regulations, the findings, conclusions, and recommended Order shall, as provided in Sec. 102.48 of the Rules, be adopted by the Board and all objections to them shall be deemed waived for all purposes.

2 If this Order is enforced by a judgment of a United States court of appeals, the words in the notice reading "Posted by Order of the National Labor Relations Board" shall read "Posted Pursuant to a Judgment of the United States Court of Appeals Enforcing an Order of the National Labor Relations Board."

APPENDIX

NOTICE TO EMPLOYEES
Posted by Order of the
National Labor Relations Board
An Agency of the United States Government

Exhibit 4-10 (Continued)

The National Labor Relations Board has found that we violated
Federal labor law and has ordered us to post and obey this Notice.

FEDERAL LAW GIVES YOU THE RIGHT TO

Form, join, or assist a union

Choose representatives to bargain with us on your behalf

Act together with other employees for your benefit and protection

Choose not to engage in any of these protected activities

http://www.nlrb.gov

CASE LAW

WALLACE v. BOWEN
869 F.2d 187 (3rd Cir.1989).

SLOVITER, CIRCUIT JUDGE.
The Secretary of the Department of Health and Human Services
(HHS), after a hearing before an administrative law judge (ALJ) and
review by the Appeals Council, found appellant John R. Wallace not
disabled and therefore not entitled to social security disability insur-
ance benefits or to supplemental security income benefits. . . .
Wallace sought review before the district court, which upheld the
Secretary's decision and granted his motion for summary judgment.

   Wallace appeals on two grounds. First, he argues that the ALJ's
reliance upon medical expert reports obtained after the hearing without an opportunity for cross-examination by Wallace denied him
both his statutory right to have a decision on his claim based on "evidence adduced at the hearing," and his due process rights under the
Constitution. Second, he maintains that the ALJ's decision is not
supported by substantial evidence.

   Because we agree with Wallace that the ALJ's reliance upon
post-hearing reports in the circumstances of this case without the
opportunity for cross-examination denied him his statutory right to
a decision based on "evidence adduced at the hearing," we will not
consider Wallace's contention that the Secretary's decision is not supported by substantial evidence.

(Continued)

II.

In February 1985, Wallace, while working as a steelworker, suffered a heart attack. One month later he suffered a stroke which may have caused a loss of vision in the right eye,. . . .

In May 1985, Wallace applied for disability insurance benefits and supplemental security income on the ground of his heart condition and visual impairments. After his claims were denied, Wallace was granted a hearing before an administrative law judge pursuant to 42 U.S.C. § 405(b)(1). At that hearing, Wallace testified and introduced reports from his examining physicians detailing his cardiological and visual impairments. . . .

After the hearing, the ALJ sent Wallace's medical records to two "consultative physicians," Dr. Oberhoff, a Board-certified ophthalmologist, and Dr. Shugoll, a Board-certified cardiologist, who were both under contract with the HHS to render their medical opinions when requested. Dr. Oberhoff was asked whether Wallace's "visual difficulties" met or equaled one of the Listings for visual impairments contained in 20 C.F.R. pt. 404, subpt. P, App. 1, §§ 2.03–.05. Dr. Shugoll was asked whether Wallace's "cardiovascular disease" met or equaled the Listing for "[h]ypertensive vascular disease" in section 4.03 of the Listings. Each physician concluded that the claimant's impairments did not meet the relevant listing. . . .

The ALJ then rendered his decision, finding Wallace not disabled under the terms of the Social Security Act. In reaching this conclusion, the ALJ first found that "claimant's impairments do not meet or equal the criteria of any . . . Listing." In so finding the ALJ relied, in the ALJ's own words, "in particular [on] the medical advisor's [consultative physician's] observations." . . .

III.

Wallace's argument begins with the Social Security Act's provision for a hearing and for a determination based on evidence adduced at the hearing. Section 205(b) of the Act provides in relevant part:

> Upon request by any such individual [who receives an unfavorable determination of his claim] . . . [the Secretary] shall give such applicant . . . reasonable notice and opportunity for a hearing with respect to such decision, and, if a hearing is held, shall, *on the basis of evidence adduced at the hearing*, affirm, modify, or reverse his findings of fact and such decision.

. . . We believe, however, that it is unmistakable under the statute that the Secretary may not rely on post-hearing reports without giving the claimant an opportunity to cross-examine the authors of such reports, when such cross-examination may be required for a full and true disclosure of the facts.

In *Richardson v. Perales*, 402 U.S. 389, (1971), the Supreme Court, in considering the hearing and review procedures under the Social Security Act, "accept[ed] the proposition [ ] . . . that procedural due process is applicable to the adjudicative administrative proceeding involving 'the differing rules of fair play, which through the years, have become associated with differing types of proceedings.'" The Court equated the Social Security Act procedures with those of the Administrative Procedure Act, which expressly entitles a party, *inter alia*, "to conduct such cross-examination as may be required for a full and true disclosure of the facts." 5 U.S.C. § 556(d)(1982), *quoted in Richardson*, 402 U.S. at 409.

Although the Court held that examining physician reports adverse to claimant supplied before the hearing could be used as "substantial evidence" even though the reports were hearsay and the physicians were not present at the hearing, the Court carefully qualified its holding by approving such admission "when the claimant has not exercised his right to subpoena the reporting physician and thereby provide himself with the opportunity for cross-examination of the physician." . . . We construe *Richardson* as holding that an opportunity for cross-examination is an element of fundamental fairness of the hearing to which a claimant is entitled under section 205(b) of the Social Security Act, 42 U.S.C. § 405(b).

The Secretary argues that it is sufficient under the statute to give a claimant an opportunity to comment on and present additional evidence in response to post-hearing reports. He maintains that cross-examination is not necessary in cases such as this where a medical opinion is obtained post-hearing, in that the issue is "wholly medical" and can be "addressed with great probity by a physician who has reviewed the medical record." In the Secretary's view, the opportunity to provide written comment is an adequate substitute for cross-examination since "the only real possible objection" is that it is not supported by the medical record, an objection which can be equally well-made by written comment.

We disagree with the Secretary's evaluation of the utility of cross-examination in such a situation. Effective cross-examination could reveal what evidence the physician considered or failed to consider in formulating his or her conclusions, how firmly the physician holds to those conclusions, and whether there are any qualifications to the physician's conclusions. . . .

(Continued)

We thus hold that when an administrative law judge chooses to go outside the testimony adduced at the hearing in making a determination on a social security claim, the ALJ must afford the claimant not only an opportunity to comment and present evidence but also an opportunity to cross-examine the authors of any post-hearing reports when such cross-examination is necessary to the full presentation of the case, and must reopen the hearing for that purpose if requested. The necessary consequence of our opinion requires modification of the form letter to give notice that the claimant may request a supplementary hearing at which the claimant may cross-examine the authors of any post-hearing reports submitted by the Secretary. . . .

IV.

Ordinarily, whether cross-examination of the author of a report is necessary for a full and true disclosure of the facts, is a question entrusted to the ALJ in the first instance. *See* 5 U.S.C. § 556(d); 20 C.F.R. § 404.950(d)(1)(subpoena to issue "[w]hen it is reasonably necessary for the full presentation of a case"). It may be that different considerations apply to cross-examination with respect to post-hearing evidence than pre-hearing evidence because the applicant may find it more difficult to respond effectively to post-hearing reports in the absence of an opportunity to present live rebuttal evidence. In any event, in this case, it is apparent that the requisite standard governing the need for cross-examination has been met.

The consultative physician reports were substantially relied on by the ALJ both in his determination that Wallace's impairments, particularly his visual impairments, did not meet or equal the Listings and for his determination that Wallace was not so impaired that he could not do sedentary work. Although one of Wallace's examining physicians, Dr. Barnett, had found Wallace's visual impairments to equal the Listing in section 2.05, the ALJ stated that he relied "in particular" upon the report of Dr. Oberhoff, the consultative physician, to find that this impairment did not meet the Listing. Similarly, Dr. Oberhoff's report was given "greater weight" than that of an examining physician in determining Wallace's capacity to do sedentary work. Under these circumstances, we conclude the reliance upon evidence adduced outside of a hearing without the opportunity for cross-examination could have unfairly affected the ultimate result.

> ### V.
> We will therefore vacate the judgment of the district court and remand with directions for it to remand the case to the Secretary who should afford Wallace, at a minimum, the right to cross-examine the physicians.

Reprinted from Funk, W.; Shapiro, S.; and Weaver, R. Administrative Procedure and Practice: Problems and Cases. © 2006, with permission of Thomson West.

CHAPTER SUMMARY

Agencies possess quasi-judicial power, which is known as the power of adjudication. Adjudication is the process that an agency goes through to reach a decision on the matter before it. Agencies are called upon to adjudicate matters in two categories. In the first category, the agency adjudicates a claim for a benefit. In the second category, the agency must determine if an individual or business has violated an agency regulation. Adjudication is a judicial function that involves specified individuals and looks backward to resolve conflicts. By contrast, rulemaking is a legislative function that involves large groups and looks forward to implement the laws passed by legislatures. Procedures for agency adjudications vary depending on such factors as the subject matter of the dispute, policies and practices of the agency, statutes, regulations, and constitutional considerations. Common characteristics of agency adjudications include: parties, notice, a decisionmaker commonly know as an administrative law judge, prehearing, hearing, and the decision of the agency which either grants or denies benefits or decides if a regulation has been violated. A decision of an agency can be appealed to a court of law for review.

KEY TERMS

adjudication
administrative law judge
consent decree
formal agency action
hearing
hearing on the record

informal agency action
official notice
order
preponderance of the evidence
the record

REVIEW QUESTIONS

1. What are the basic differences between adjudication and rulemaking?
2. What are the two general categories of agency adjudication?
3. State some of the characteristics that are common to agency adjudications.
4. What is the standard of proof required to win at an administrative hearing?
5. State the titles of the various officials who preside at administrative hearings.

MORE INFORMATION

1. To see the salaries of federal administrative law judges, go to http://www.opm.gov.
2. To access adjudications from the Securities and Exchange Commission, go to http://www.sec.gov.
3. To access adjudications involving state civil rights cases, go to http://www.phrc.state.pa.us.
4. To access information on federal administrative law judges, go to http://www.oalj.dol.gov.
5. For a wealth of information on Social Security retirement benefits, disability, prescription drug plan, and forms, go to http://www.socialsecurity.gov.

PRACTICAL APPLICATIONS

1. Go to the Web site of the National Labor Relations Board at http://www.nlrb.gov. Click on ALJ Decisions.
Do a search of ALJ decisions with the search term "Bayou Concrete."
Find Case No. 15 –CA-177734 and answer the following:
   A. Who was the Administrative Law Judge who decided the case?
   B. Who initiated the case?
   C. What was his occupation?
   D. What is the underlying basis for the complaint against Bayou Concrete?
   E. How did the ALJ rule?
2. Go to the Web site of the Occupational Safety and Health Review Commission (OSHRC), which is a federal agency that decides contests of citations or penalties resulting from OSHA inspections in the workplace, at http://www.oshrc.gov.
Put in a search term "Blue Ridge Erectors" and answer the following:
   A. Who was the Administrative Law Judge who decided the case?
   B. State the violations of worker safety as alleged in Citation 1.
   C. State the violations of worker safety as alleged in Citation 1, Item 3.
   D. How did the ALJ rule on the various violations?

3. Review Exhibit 4-10 and answer the following:
    A. What is the name of the ALJ who decided the case?
    B. What was the violation of labor law that the ALJ found?
    C. What was the specific section that was violated?
    D. Briefly describe the remedy as stated by the ALJ.

L E A R N   A B O U T   T H E   A G E N C I E S

Go to the Web site of the following agencies and state their function.

FBI—Federal Bureau of Prisons—http://www.bop.gov
CIA—Central Intelligence Agency—http://www.cia.gov
CPSC—Consumer Product Safety Commission—http://www.cpsc.gov
EPA—Environmental Protection Agency—http://www.epa.gov
FDA—Food and Drug Administration—http://www.fda.gov/default.htm

Overview of Agency Activities

CHAPTER OBJECTIVES

After reading this chapter, you should be able to:

- Understand the nature and extent of agency activities.
- Access information from the agency Web sites.
- Understand Alternative Dispute Resolution (ADR).
- Make a request under the Freedom of Information Act (FOIA).
- Make a request for information under the Privacy Act.

CHAPTER OUTLINE

INTRODUCTION

This chapter is an overview of the many things agencies do. The chapter is a bridge from what we have learned in the first four chapters (creation and power of the agencies) to what we will learn in the last three chapters (control of agencies by the judicial, legislative, and executive branches). You will see references in this chapter to concepts we have covered in previous chapters. Use these references and the references to future chapters as a way of synthesizing and organizing the material from the text. The chapter also contains many agency Web sites so that you can follow up for more information. A good starting point to see the varied activities of federal agencies is located at http://www.fedworld.gov. See Sidebar 5-1 for a quick listing of the chapters and their subject matter.

> **Sidebar 5-1 Organizer for Administrative Law**
> *Chapter 1 Creation and Purpose of Agency*
> *Chapter 2 Legislative Power*
> *Chapter 3 Executive Power*
> *Chapter 4 Judicial Power (Adjudication)*
> *Chapter 5 Overview of Agency Activities*
> *Chapter 6 Control by the Courts*
> *Chapter 7 Control by the Legislature*
> *Chapter 8 Control by the Executive*

Topics that you are very familiar with are covered in this chapter. These include some of the more routine agency activities such as the issuing of a driver's license or an agency warning us that it is time to get a flu shot. We will also learn how to access information from an agency. Look at Exhibit 5-1, which is a list of some of those familiar agency activities. These types of activities are the subject of this chapter.

APPLICATIONS AND CLAIMS

Most individuals have filed or will file for a claim with an agency during their lifetime. Responding to such activity is probably the most common activity that agencies perform. Agencies process claims for workers' compensation benefits, unemployment compensation, Social

---

Exhibit 5-1

Examples of Agency Activities

ACTIVITY	AGENCY
Applying for a driver's license	State agency
License to engage in professions such as doctor, lawyer, architect, and dentist	State agency
Application for college grant or loan	State agency and Department of Education
Application for Social Security benefits, workers' compensation and unemployment benefits	Social Security Administration and state agency
Application to operate television or radio station	Federal Communications Commission (FCC)
Business safety and health inspection	Occupational Safety and Health Administration (OSHA) and state and local agencies
License to operate a nuclear power plant	Nuclear Regulatory Commission (NRC)
Advice on taxes	Internal Revenue Service (IRS) and state taxing agency
Negotiation and settlement of disputes	All agencies
Disclosure of information	Federal agencies are required to disclose information by the Freedom of Information Act (FOIA). Individuals can obtain their records held by agencies under the Privacy Act. States disclosure laws require disclosure of information held by state agencies.

Security benefits, welfare benefits, and student loans. The goal for the agency is to process the claim in a fair, timely, and efficient manner, which is greatly enhanced by the informal nature of the process. If benefits are denied, then the process can get more involved, and the person claiming benefits may be able to ask the agency to reconsider its decision. The agency and claimant will then need to adjudicate the issue. Recall that adjudication was the subject of Chapter 4. After the agency has finished its review and the claimant is still denied the benefit, the claimant has the option of taking the case to a court of law, which is the subject of Chapter 6.

LICENSING

Another common form of agency activity is licensing by agencies. This can be the issuance of a driver's license or licensing of various professions such as dentistry, chiropractic, medicine, law, cosmetology, funeral directing, haircutting, and landscape architects. Such professions are generally licensed by the state agencies. The agency in charge of a given area, in accordance with relevant legislation, is responsible for setting the procedures for the issuance of the license.

To learn more about the requirements of professional licensure in Pennsylvania, go to http://www.dos.state.pa.us.

In most states, one can check the credentials and get a profile of the professionals who are licensed by that state. For example, to get a profile of a physician practicing in Connecticut, go to http://www.dph.state.ct.us/index.html.

The Federal Communications Commission (FCC) issues licenses for radio and television stations, cable, and satellite. To see the various licensing requirements, go to http://www.fcc.gov.

The Nuclear Regular Commission (NRC) issues licenses to operate nuclear power plants, and the licensing process takes many years. To see the complexity of the licensing of a nuclear power plant, go to http://www.nrc.gov.

The Food and Drug Administration (FDA) has a complex application process to gain approval for new drugs. To see this application process, go to http://www.fda.gov.

The Federal Aviation Administration (FAA) must certify new aircraft for flight. To see the process of aircraft certification, go to http://www.airweb.faa.gov. Click on Regulatory and Guidance Library.

NEGOTIATION, SETTLEMENT, AND ALTERNATIVE DISPUTE RESOLUTION (ADR)

In administrative law, as in criminal law and civil litigation, the object is to settle the dispute swiftly and in a way that is fair to all parties. In criminal law, many cases are plea-bargained. Plea bargaining is the result of a negotiation and resolution by a prosecutor and defense attorney in a criminal case. In civil litigation, especially those cases involving personal injury, the vast majority of cases are ended by settlement. A settlement is the agreement by both sides in a civil case to compromise and end the case. In administrative law, agencies are similarly encouraged to settle any disputes that an individual may have with the agency. For example, the Securities and Exchange Commission (SEC) settled a case with an accounting firm that had been charged with improper audits of Xerox that misled investors about the true value of Xerox stock. (See http://www.sec.gov.) Recall that Chapter 4 covered adjudication, the administrative process that is used when a resolution cannot be reached. Adjudications can be lengthy and costly to all parties. Without the ability to resolve a case by way of compromise, the criminal, civil, and administrative caseload would be overwhelming.

Agencies use *Alternative Dispute Resolution (ADR)* to efficiently resolve issues. ADR is a term that includes various methods to resolve disputes before an agency. Some of the major methods of ADR are as follows:

Alternative Dispute Resolution (ADR)
the term to describe the various methods to quickly and efficiently resolve matters before an agency

- Mediation—a neutral third party assists in helping the parties reach an agreement.
- Facilitation—a neutral party coordinates meetings and promotes communication between the parties.
- Arbitration—the parties make a presentation in a setting less formal than a courtroom. The presentation can include testimony of witnesses with cross-examination and introduction of exhibits. If the parties are required to abide by the decision of the arbitrators, that is binding arbitration; if there is no such duty, then the arbitration is known as nonbinding.
- Fact-finding—to help resolve disputes over complex technology or scientific data, parties present the data to a panel of neutral experts who make advisory findings.
- Minitrials—the parties make a presentation to senior officials of an agency who have the authority to settle the dispute.

Congress has amended the Administrative Procedure Act (APA) to add alternative dispute resolution methods, which encourages but does not require agencies to use ADR. States are also turning to ADR. The Commonwealth Court of Pennsylvania, which handles appeals from workers' compensation cases and unemployment cases, has an ADR program. As with the federal program, it is voluntary. For more information on ADR, go to:

http://www.adr.org
http://www.nh.gov/judiciary/adrp/index.htm
http://www.in.gov/judiciary
Click on Judges.

AGENCY ADVICE

Advice from agency officials is another one of the most common forms of agency activity. Advice can take the form of a telephone call about the procedures to get a building permit or a formal letter from the Internal Revenue Service (IRS) about an allowable deduction on income tax. For instance, a business can ask the Environmental Protection Agency (EPA) about a category of potentially toxic emissions. When an agency gives advice, the interest of the public is promoted because an individual or business can obtain guidance on the proper way to act. Agency advice serves the interest of the agency because it furthers compliance with agency policy.

Mainly, agencies stand by the advice they give. However, the Supreme Court has ruled that even when the advice given by the agency turns out to be erroneous and a person relies on that advice and thereafter loses a benefit, the agency is *not* bound by such advice. For example, in *Schweiker v. Hanson,* 450 U.S. 785 (1981), the Court ruled that the Social Security Administration (SSA) could still deny benefits to a claimant, even though an agency employee erroneously told a claimant that she was not eligible, which prevented her from filing a claim. *In Office of Personnel Management v. Richmond,* 496 U.S. 414 (1990), a Navy personnel officer advised a naval employee that his Navy pension would not be jeopardized by taking an extra job. The advice was wrong, and the benefits were terminated. In these cases, the plaintiffs urged the Court to invoke the doctrine of estoppel. *Estoppel* is a judge-created right invoked to avoid injustice in certain circumstances. The plaintiffs argued that the government should be estopped from denying the benefit because the bad advice caused them to lose a benefit. Here the Court explains why the pension will not be allowed and why the Court will not "estop" the Navy from denying the benefit.

> The Appropriations Clause of the Constitution, Art. I, § 9, cl. 7, provides that: "No Money shall be drawn from the Treasury, but in Consequence of Appropriations made by Law." For the particular type of claim at issue here, a claim for money from the Federal Treasury, the Clause provides an explicit rule of decision. Money may be paid out only through an appropriation made by

estoppel

an equitable doctrine invoked to avoid injustice when one person makes a misrepresentation of fact to another person and that other person reasonably relies on the misrepresentation to his or her detriment law; in other words, the payment of money from the Treasury must be authorized by a statute. All parties here agree that the award respondent seeks would be in direct contravention of the federal statute upon which his ultimate claim to the funds must rest, 5 U.S.C. § 8337. . . . It follows that Congress has appropriated no money for the payment of the benefits respondent seeks, and the Constitution prohibits that any money "be drawn from the Treasury" to pay them.

Explaining why estoppel will not normally be invoked and the unsatisfactory practical consequences that would occur if it were, the Court stated that:

> [J]udicial use of the equitable doctrine of estoppel cannot grant respondent a money remedy that Congress has not authorized. . . . To open the door to estoppel claims would only invite endless litigation over both real and imagined claims of misinformation by disgruntled citizens, imposing an unpredictable drain on the public fisc. Even if most claims were rejected in the end, the burden of defending such estoppel claims would itself be substantial. Also questionable is the suggestion that if the Government is not bound by its agents' statements, then citizens will not trust them and will instead seek private advice from lawyers, accountants, and others, creating wasteful expenses. Although mistakes occur, we may assume with confidence that Government agents attempt conscientious performance of their duties and in most cases provide free and valuable information to those who seek advice about Government programs. A rule of estoppel might create not more reliable advice, but less advice. The natural consequence of a rule that made the Government liable for the statements of its agents would be a decision to cut back and impose strict controls upon Government provision of information in order to limit liability. Not only would valuable informational programs be lost to the public, but the greatest impact of this loss would fall on those of limited means, who can least afford the alternative of private advice. The inevitable fact of occasional individual hardship cannot undermine the interest of the citizenry as a whole in the ready availability of Government information. The rationale of the Appropriations Clause is that if individual hardships are to be remedied by payment of Government funds, it must be at the instance of Congress. *In Office of Personnel Management v. Richmond,* 496 U.S at 424–434.

The Court explained that Congress can provide for the instance when erroneous information is given and has done so in Social Security cases by providing that:

In any case in which it is determined to the satisfaction of the Secretary that an individual failed as of any date to apply for monthly insurance benefits under this title by reason of misinformation provided to such individual by any officer or employee of the Social Security Administration relating to such individual's eligibility for benefits under this title, such individual shall be deemed to have applied for such benefits on the later of the date on which the misinformation was given or the date upon which the applicant became eligible for benefits apart from the application requirement, Pub. L. 101–239, § 10302, 103 Stat. 2481. *In Office of Personnel Management v. Richmond,* 496 U.S at 429.

TESTING AND INSPECTIONS

Other agency activities involve testing and inspections. Numerous government agencies perform tests to determine the effectiveness and safety of products. The FDA performs tests on all of the drugs it approves for use by the public. Examples of agency inspections would include the safety inspection of an 18-wheeler by a state police officer and the Occupational Safety and Health Administration (OSHA) inspection at a manufacturing plant. State and local health inspectors also regularly inspect restaurants, hospitals, nursing homes, and other institutions.

The Animal & Plant Health Inspection Service (APHIS), through inspections and monitoring, safeguards our food supply and seeks to control the spread of pests, such as the Mediterranean fruit fly, and the spread of animal diseases such as mad cow disease. You can visit the Web site of APHIS and learn more about their inspection procedures. (See http://www.aphis.usda.gov.) You can also find at that site a list of some of the health and safety inspection services throughout the county.

See Exhibit 5-2, which is a list of OSHA inspections in the year 2004.

Recall from Chapter 3 that when agencies conduct inspections, constitutional issues with respect to the Fourth and Fifth Amendments may arise.

RECALLS, SEIZURES, SUSPENSIONS, AND QUARANTINES

Agencies have the power to act informally to seize food that is unfit for human consumption and recall products that are defective. Agencies can quickly act in the public interest to stop the spread of sickness caused by bad food and defective products. The Food Safety and

Exhibit 5-2

OSHA Inspection Statistics Fiscal Year 2004: 39,167 Inspections

NUMBER	PERCENT	REASON FOR INSPECTION
9,176	(23.4%)	Complaint/accident related
21,576	(55.1%)	High hazard targeted
8,415	(21.5%)	Referrals, follow-ups, etc.

NUMBER	PERCENT	INDUSTRY SECTOR
22,360	(57.1%)	Construction
8,755	(22.4%)	Manufacturing
378	(1%)	Maritime
7,674	(19.6%)	Other industries

In the inspections categorized above, OSHA identified the following violations:

VIOLATIONS	PERCENT	TYPE	CURRENT PENALTIES
462	(0.5%)	Willful	$14,553,171
61,666	(71.1%)	Serious	54,526,440
2,360	(2.7%)	Repeat	9,755,960
301	(0.3%)	Failure to abate	1,611,943
21,705	(25%)	Other	1,960,084
214	(0.2%)	Unclassified	2,785,342
86,708		TOTAL	$85,192,940

Source: http://www.osha.gov

Inspection Service (FSIS) inspects and regulates meats, poultry, and processed egg products. A food recall is a voluntary action by a manufacturer or distributor to protect the public from products that may cause health problems. Recalls are initiated by the manufacturer or distributor of the product, sometimes at the request of FSIS. If a company refuses to recall its products, FSIS has the authority under numerous federal statutes to detain and seize those products.

The Consumer Product Safety Commission (CPSC) is the federal agency that initiates mandatory or voluntary recalls of products ranging from baby cribs to lawn mowers to all kinds of children's toys. See Exhibit 5-3, which is a list of toy-related deaths reported by the CPSC.

Exhibit 5-3

Toy-Related Deaths from Consumer Product Safety Commission (CPSC)

UNITED STATES
CONSUMER PRODUCT SAFETY COMMISSION
WASHINGTON, DC 20207

Memorandum

Date: October 5, 2006

TO   :   The File

THROUGH :   Russell Roegner, Ph.D., Associate Executive Director $\mathcal{TRC}$
                    Directorate for Epidemiology

FROM   :   Joyce McDonald, EPHA RC for JM.

SUBJECT :   Toy-Related Deaths and Injuries, Calendar Year 2005

This memorandum provides information on toy-related deaths and injuries reported to the U.S. Consumer Product Safety Commission (CPSC) that occurred during the January 1, 2005 through December 31, 2005 time period.[1]

TOY-RELATED DEATHS

CPSC has reports of 20 toy-related deaths involving children under age 15 that occurred in 2005.[2] The toys involved in these fatal incidents were as follows:

Reported Toy-Related Deaths to Children 0-14 Calendar Year 2005[3]

Type of Toy	Deaths
TOTAL	**20**
Balls (choking)	6
Tricycles (1 drowning, 2 motor vehicle involvement)	3
Balloon (aspiration)	1
Plastic dart (aspiration)	1
Toy chest (asphyxia)	1
Toy all terrain vehicle (drowning)	1
Bead from toy horse figurine (aspiration)	1
Non-motorized scooter (motor vehicle involvement)	1
Fish-shaped flotation ring (drowning)	1
Kite (electrocution)	1
Slinky and ribbon (strangulation)	1
Costume with a cape (hanging)	1
Magnets from a building set (intestinal blockage)	1

[1] This analysis was prepared by CPSC staff and has not been reviewed or approved by, and may not necessarily reflect the views of the Commission.

[2] The 20 fatal toy-related incidents do not represent a sample of known probability of selection, and they may not include all the toy-related deaths occurring during the 2005 time period, in part because reporting is not complete for some data sources. Data was extracted on 05/24/2006.

[3] These data are based on reports from the In-depth Investigation file, the Injury and Potential Injury Incident file, the Death Certificate file and the National Electronic Injury Surveillance System for 1/1/2005 to 12/31/2005.

CPSC Hotline: 1-800-638-CPSC (2772) CPSC's Web Site: http://www.cpsc.gov

The recall of cars for defects each year is a common occurrence and is done under the authority of the National Highway Traffic Safety Administration (NHTSA). To see a list of defective and recalled motor vehicles, go to http://www-odi.nhtsa.dot.gov.

Similarly, the FDA had federal marshals seize hospital beds because the bed entrapped patients and caused many injuries and seven deaths. (See http://www.fda.gov/bbs/topics/ANSWERS/2005/ANS01347.html.)

To protect the public, recalls, seizures, and suspensions of professional licenses are done, in many instances, prior to or without a hearing. In addition, agencies can suspend the occupational licenses of professionals who serve the public, such as doctors, lawyers, and others. Suspension of professional licenses may require a hearing because of due process requirements. See Chapter 6 for detailed coverage of agencies and due process rights.

> The U.S. Consumer Product Safety Commission has jurisdiction over 15,000 types of consumer products. You can check to see the products that have been recalled on their Web site at http://www.cpsc.gov.

The president is also authorized under the Public Health Service Act to place persons suffering from certain communicable diseases on a quarantine list, such as those suffering from cholera, diphtheria, infectious tuberculosis, plague, smallpox, SARS, yellow fever, and viral hemorrhagic fevers (Lassa, Marburg, Ebola, Crimean-Congo, South American). The Secretary of Health and Human Services and the Centers for Disease Control are the health agencies that enforce such quarantines.

> SARS was one of the most recent diseases to be put on the list of diseases that can require quarantine. You can check the CDC Web site to stay up to date on this issue at http://www.cdc.gov.

Agency Disclosure of Information

Agencies acquire a lot of information and data in serving the needs of society. This information would be of little use to the public, if the public were not aware of its existence. Agencies use numerous methods to get out the information. Some of these methods include press conferences, press releases to the media, interviews of agency heads, advertising on radio and television, and published information on the Internet. For press releases concerning food recalls, go to http://www.fsis.usda.gov.

Examples of critical information include health risks of medicines and drugs, warnings on defective products, information on severe weather approaching a locality, eligibility for a state-sponsored health insurance plan for children, and the looming deadline for filing of taxes. See Exhibit 5-4 for examples of information that is supplied by agencies to the public and made available on the Internet.

If you go to the Web site of an agency, you will find a variety of information ranging from the merely helpful to the absolutely necessary.

> Which state is the wealthiest and which state is the poorest in terms of per capita income? The agency that provides this information is the Bureau of Economic Analysis, which is a subagency in the U.S. Department of Commerce. Go to http://www.bea.gov.

leak
an unauthorized release of information by an anonymous agency employee

whistle-blower statute
a law that provides legal protection to a government employee when the employee releases information that exposes government wrongdoing

A source of *unofficial* disclosure of information occurs when the agency leaks information to the press. A *leak* can benefit the public when the information leads to an investigation that reveals corruption or abuse. For example, during the Watergate scandal, a secret source known as "Deep Throat" leaked information concerning criminal activity in the Nixon Administration to Bob Woodward of the *Washington Post.* The source, who was finally revealed to be FBI official Mark Felt, helped to bring about the resignation of President Nixon. On the other hand, leaks can be harmful and even illegal. Leaking the name of a Central Intelligence Agency (CIA) agent to the press is an example of an illegal leak that could compromise national security and endanger the life of the agent.

Congress and many states have passed *whistle-blower statutes* to give legal protections for employees who speak out to expose government wrongdoing. Employees of agencies who expose government cor-

Exhibit 5-4

Examples of Agency Information Disclosed on the Internet

AGENCY	WEB SITE	INFORMATION
Food and Drug Administration (FDA)	http://www.fda.gov	List of approved drugs Flu information Diet information Recall of defective pregnancy test Buying medicines online
Federal Trade Commission (FTC)	http://www.ftc.gov	How to get on the "no-call list"
Centers for Disease Control (CDC)	http://www.cdc.com	Bird flu and SARS information
Occupational Safety and Health Administration (OSHA)	http://www.osha.gov	Injuries, illnesses and deaths on the job A guide to scaffold use Fire protection in shipyard
Federal Emergency Management Agency (FEMA)	http://www.fema.gov	Bioterrorism
U.S. Department of Justice	http://www.nsopr.gov	List of sex offenders (national)
Pennsylvania Commission on Crime and Delinquency	http://www.ojp.usdoj.gov/ ovc/help/map/pa.htm	Victim's compensation
Pennsylvania State Police	http://www.pameganslaw. state.pa.us/Sex offenders	List of sex offenders (state)

ruption, such as overcharging of the government for equipment and materials, could find protection under a whistle-blower statute. Two federal laws that involve agency disclosure of information to the public are the Freedom of Information Act (FOIA) and the Privacy Act, which will be covered in the next sections.

FREEDOM OF INFORMATION ACT (FOIA)

Freedom of Information Act (FOIA)

a law that requires federal agencies to disclose records or information upon written request

The *Freedom of Information Act (FOIA)*, 5 U.S.C. § 552, provides that any person has the right to request access to federal agency records or information. (See Appendix B for the text of the FOIA.) Agencies covered under the FOIA are required to disclose records upon receiving a written request, except for those records that are protected from disclosure under a specific exception. No single office handles FOIA requests, but each agency responds to requests for its own records.

The FOIA does not apply to the offices of the president and vice president, Congress, the federal courts, or to state or local agencies, nor does it apply to private companies. State and local records would be governed by the public disclosure laws of each state. There are other federal and state laws that may permit access to documents held by organizations not covered by the FOIA.

Anyone may request production of a record held by a federal agency. A request may seek a printed or typed document, tape recording, map, photograph, computer printout, or computer tape or disk from existing files. In response to such requests, an agency is not required to create a new record or document but is only required to disclose existing records that are not exempt from disclosure. Sometimes issues arise as to whether requested data is even an "agency record." In *The Bureau of National Affairs, Inc. v. United States Dep't of Justice*, 742 F.2d 1484 (D.C. Cir. 1984) (see excerpt in Case Law at the end of the chapter), the Court ruled that telephone message slips and appointment calendars that are:

> created solely for an individual's convenience, that contain a mix of personal and business entries, and that may be disposed of at the individual's discretion are not "agency records" under FOIA. *The Bureau of National Affairs, Inc. v. United States Dep't of Justice*, 742 F.2d at 1486.

Daily agendas, on the other hand, were agency records because they were created for the express purpose of facilitating the work of the agency and were not created for the personal convenience of any individual but for the convenience of the staff and to conduct official agency business.

Examples of records that are exempt from disclosure include documents classified in the interest of national security, information that is exempt under other laws (such as a law prohibiting disclosure of tax returns), confidential business information such as trade secrets, and personal and private documents such as medical records and law enforcement records. See *National Parks and Conservation Association v. Morton*, 498 F.2d 765 (D.C. Cir. 1974) (excerpted in Case Law at the end of the chapter), for a discussion on when an FOIA request is exempted based on the documents being confidential business records. The Court stated that a business record is confidential when its disclosure would impair the government's ability to obtain the necessary information in the future or cause substantial harm to the competitive position of the person from whom the information is sought.

The agency has 20 business days to determine if it will respond. The actual disclosure must be done in a reasonable time. FOIA requesters may have to pay a fee, although there are some exemptions. For example, if you are a student requesting information for a school project, many agencies will not charge for the first two hours of search time and for the first 100 pages of documents. If the request is denied, a requester has right to appeal the decision, first to the head of the agency and then to federal court.

The National Security Archive is an organization that uses the FOIA to obtain and publish declassified information on very interesting topics. Go to http://www.gwu.edu/~nsarchiv. Note the topics on the site which include documents on many world events such as the Cold War, nuclear weapons history, and U.S. government interventions in countries in Latin America, Asia, and the Middle East. Documents related to the events of September 11, 2001 are also available. In some instances, organizations such as the National Security Archive must file suit to force the government to release documents. Click on the FOIA link on the National Security Archive Web site to learn more about FOIA.

See Exhibit 5-5 for a sample FOIA request letter.

PRIVACY ACT

While the goal of the FOIA is to assure that agency records are available to the public, the goal of the Privacy Act, 5 U.S.C. § 552a, is to restrict the release of records to protect an individual's privacy interests. (See Appendix B for the text of the Privacy Act.) To that end, the Privacy Act protects an individual from an agency's release of personal records and states:

Exhibit 5-5

Sample FOIA Request Letter

Agency Head [or Freedom of Information Act Officer]
Name of Agency
Address of Agency
City, State, Zip Code

Re: Freedom of Information Act Request

Dear :

This is a request under the Freedom of Information Act.

I request that a copy of the following documents [or documents containing the following information] be provided to me: [identify the documents or information as specifically as possible].

In order to help to determine my status for purposes of determining the applicability of any fees, you should know that I am (insert a suitable description of the requester and the purpose of the request).

> [Sample requester descriptions:
> a representative of the news media affiliated with the **XXXX** newspaper (magazine, television station, etc.), and this request is made as part of news gathering and not for a commercial use.
> affiliated with an educational or noncommercial scientific institution, and this request is made for a scholarly or scientific purpose and not for a commercial use.
> an individual seeking information for personal use and not for a commercial use.
> affiliated with a private corporation and am seeking information for use in the company's business.]

[Optional] I am willing to pay fees for this request up to a maximum of $**XX**. If you estimate that the fees will exceed this limit, please inform me first.

[Optional] I request a waiver of all fees for this request. Disclosure of the requested information to me is in the public interest because it is likely to contribute significantly to public understanding of the operations or activities of the government and is not primarily in my commercial interest. [Include specific details, including how the requested information will be disseminated by the requester for public benefit.]

Exhibit 5-5 (Continued)

[Optional] I request that the information I seek be provided in electronic format, and I would like to receive it on a personal computer disk [or a CD-ROM].

[Optional] I ask that my request receive expedited processing because **XXXX**. [Include specific details concerning your "compelling need," such as being someone "primarily engaged in disseminating information" and specifics concerning your "urgency to inform the public concerning actual or alleged Federal Government activity."]

[Optional] I also include a telephone number at which I can be contacted during the hours of **XXXX**, if necessary, to discuss any aspect of my request.

Thank you for your consideration of this request.

Sincerely,

Name

Address

City, State, Zip Code

Telephone number [Optional]

Source: http://thomas.loc.gov

> No agency shall disclose any record . . . except pursuant to a written request by, or with the prior written consent of, the individual to whom the record pertains, 5 U.S.C. § 552a(b).

The term record means:

> any item, collection, or grouping of information about an individual that is maintained by an agency, including, but not limited to, his education, financial transactions, medical history, and criminal or employment history and that contains his name, or the identifying number, symbol, or other identifying particular assigned to the individual, such as a finger or voice print or a photograph, 5 U.S.C. § 552a(a)(4).

Most personal information in an agency's files is subject to the *Privacy Act*. The Act does allow for disclosure of certain records without the permission of the person. Examples where an agency can release an individual's records without the permission of that individual include release to the Bureau of Census, National Archives, and Congress and upon a court order. Release can also be made for purposes of doing statistical research and for law enforcement purposes.

Privacy Act
federal statute that sets out agency procedures for maintaining records on individuals and which gives the right of an individual to have access to his or her records and correct any errors

The Privacy Act also allows individuals to see and copy most personal information about themselves maintained by federal agencies and to seek amendment of any inaccurate and incomplete information. There is no central index of federal government records. Requests must be made directly to an agency. For example, a person who receives veteran's benefits can direct the request to the Department of Veterans Affairs. Students seeking information on loans should send a request to the Department of Education. Tax records are maintained by the IRS, and Social Security records are maintained by the SSA. The Privacy Act provides damages and injunctive relief for unauthorized disclosure of an individual's records.

See Exhibit 5-6 for a sample Privacy Act letter.

For a more detailed discussion of FOIA and the Privacy Act, see "A Citizen's Guide on Using FOIA and the Privacy Act" by the House Committee on Government Reform, which can be accessed at http://thomas.loc.gov. Note that FOIA and the Privacy Act are both part of the federal APA.

FOIA and the Privacy Act have been used by researchers to obtain documents relating to the Kennedy Assassination. In 1992, Congress passed the JFK Records Act, which established a commission that was charged with gathering all documents related to the assassination and placing the documents in the National Archives.

Exhibit 5-6

Sample Privacy Act Request

Privacy Act or Freedom of Information Officer
Name of Agency
Address of Agency
City, State, Zip Code

Re: Privacy Act and Freedom of Information Act Request for Access

Dear :

Exhibit 5-6 (Continued)

This is a request under the Privacy Act of 1974 and the Freedom of Information Act. I request a copy of any records [or specifically named records] about me maintained at your agency.

[Optional] To help you to locate my records, I have had the following contacts with your agency: [mention job applications, periods of employment, loans or agency programs applied for, etc.].

[Optional] I am willing to pay fees for this request up to a maximum of $XX. If you estimate that the fees will exceed this limit, please inform me first.

[Optional] Enclosed is [a notarized signature or other identifying document] that will verify my identity.

[Optional] I also include a telephone number at which I can be contacted during the hours of XXX, if necessary, to discuss any aspect of my request.

Thank you for your consideration of this request.

Sincerely,

Name

Address

City, State, Zip Code

Telephone number [Optional]

Source: http://thomas.loc.gov/cgi-bin/cpquery/T?&report=hr172&dbname=cp108&

CASE LAW

THE BUREAU OF NATIONAL AFFAIRS, INC. v. UNITED STATES DEPARTMENT OF JUSTICE
742 F.2d 1484 (D.C.Cir.1984).

MIKVA, J.:

In these cases we are asked to decide a novel question concerning the scope of the Freedom of Information Act (FOIA or the Act): whether appointment calendars, phone logs and daily agendas of government officials are "agency records" subject to disclosure under FOIA. We conclude that appointment materials that are created solely for an individual's convenience, that contain a mix of personal and business

(*Continued*)

entries, and that may be disposed of at the individual's discretion are not "agency records" under FOIA. . . .

. . . In 1981, the Bureau of National Affairs (BNA) filed a FOIA request with the Department of Justice (DOJ or the Justice Department) for all records of appointments and meetings between William Baxter, then Assistant Attorney General for Antitrust, and all parties outside the Justice Department. DOJ denied BNA's request on the ground that the materials were not "agency records" subject to disclosure under FOIA. . . .

The Environmental Defense Fund (EDF) requested the Office of Management and Budget (OMB) to disclose several categories of documents relating to the Environmental Protection Agency's (EPA) implementation of federal hazardous waste laws, particularly the 1980 Superfund legislation. OMB denied the request in part. . . .

Among the records requested by EDF were the appointment calendars and telephone logs of six OMB officials. . . .

Both DOJ and OMB claim that appointment materials are not "agency records" within the meaning of section 552(a)(4)(B) of FOIA. . . . Unless the calendars, agendas, and logs sought by BNA and EDF are "agency records" the district court lacks jurisdiction over their claims.

Neither the language of the statute nor the legislative history provides much guidance in fleshing out the meaning of the term "agency records." "As has often been remarked, the Freedom of Information Act, for all its attention to the treatment of 'agency records,' never defines that crucial phrase." Moreover, "the legislative history yields insignificant insight into Congress' conception of the sorts of materials the Act covers."

Nor does the case law indicate whether the appointment materials in these cases are "agency records." Most opinions in this circuit and elsewhere that focus on the meaning of the term "agency records" involved records that were created originally by entities exempt from FOIA's coverage and that later were transferred to a FOIA agency. The issue in those cases is whether a FOIA agency has "obtained" a record concededly "created" elsewhere. The instant cases, however, present a totally different issue: under what circumstances can an individual's creation of a record be attributed to the agency, thereby making the material an "agency record" disclosable under FOIA, rather than personal material not covered by the Act?

We turn to the case law to find the principles that should guide us in our analysis.

1. Judicial interpretation of the term "agency records"

The Supreme Court has elaborated on the meaning of the term "agency records" . . . . Thus, in determining whether the documents were "agency records" under FOIA, the Court focused on several factors: whether the documents were (1) in the agency's control; (2) generated within the agency; (3) placed into the agency's files; and (4) used by the agency "for any purpose." . . .

The government argues that we rejected a use test for determining whether a document is an "agency record" in *McGehee v. Central Intelligence Agency.* In *McGehee,* a relative of three victims who died at "People's Temple" in Jonestown, Guyana, filed a FOIA request with the Central Intelligence Agency (CIA) for documents relating to various aspects of the community led by Jim Jones. One of the issues on appeal was whether the documents obtained by the CIA from the State Department and the Federal Bureau of Investigation were "agency records" of the CIA. We concluded that they were. In prior cases, this court and others had held that, where documents originate within the Congress, the judiciary, and FOIA-exempt executive agencies, sometimes "special policy considerations militate against a rule compelling disclosure of [such] records . . . merely because such documents happen to come into the possession of an agency." Where the originating agency, however, is also covered by FOIA—as was the case in McGehee—we held that transfer of such documents to another FOIA agency did not alter their status as "agency records." Otherwise, agencies could shield themselves from FOIA by transferring documents to a different government department. We therefore concluded that "all records in an agency's possession, whether created by the agency itself or by other bodies covered by the Act, constitute agency records."

Here, reliance solely on a possession or control test could be the more restrictive approach. An "agency" may choose not to assert any control over a particular document, but an employee who created that document for the express purpose of enabling him to perform his duties certainly retains possession and control over the document. The issue is not simply whether the agency as an institution has taken steps to "obtain" the document. Rather, the question presented by these cases is whether, when an employee creates a document, that creation can be attributed to the agency under FOIA.

(Continued)

Under the case law, it is clear that, at least in some circumstances, the agency's use of a document is relevant for determining its status as an "agency record." Where, as here, a document is created by an agency employee, consideration of whether and to what extent that employee used the document to conduct agency business is highly relevant for determining whether that document is an "agency record" within the meaning of FOIA. Use alone, however, is not dispositive; the other factors mentioned in *Kissinger* must also be considered: whether the document is in the agency's control, was generated within the agency, and has been placed into the agency's files. Our inquiry must therefore focus on the totality of the circumstances surrounding the creation, maintenance, and use of the document to determine whether the document is in fact an "agency record" and not an employee's record that happens to be located physically within an agency.

In particular, the statute cannot be extended to sweep into FOIA's reach personal papers that may "relate to" an employee's work—such as a personal diary containing an individual's private reflections on his or her work—but which the individual does not rely upon to perform his or her duties. In this regard, use of the documents by employees other than the author is an important consideration. An inquiry is therefore required into the purpose for which the document was created, the actual use of the document, and the extent to which the creator of the document and other employees acting within the scope of their employment relied upon the document to carry out the business of the agency.

In adopting this analysis, we reject the government's invitation to hold that the treatment of documents for disposal and retention purposes under the various federal records management statutes determines their status under FOIA. Those statutes prescribe how federal agencies are to create, dispose of, and otherwise manage documents and other material. See, e.g., Federal Records Act of 1950, 44 U.S.C. § 3301 et seq. However tempting such a "bright line" test may be, it cannot be used as the divining rod for the meaning of "agency records" under FOIA. . . .

The government would have us . . . rely solely on the agencies' treatment of the documents under their records disposal regulations and policies to determine the status of those documents under FOIA. Rigid adherence to the records disposal regulations to determine the status of a document under FOIA, however, would contradict the policy of disclosure underlying FOIA. Although an agency's treatment of documents for preservation purposes may provide some guidance to a court, an agency should not be able to alter its disposal regulations to avoid the requirements of FOIA. . . .

2. Appointment materials as "agency records"

Three categories of appointment materials are sought in these cases: yellow telephone message slips; appointment calendars; and daily agendas indicating Mr. Baxter's schedule that were distributed to staff within the Antitrust Division of the Justice Department. All of these materials share three common attributes that are relevant for our analysis. First, all of these materials were "generated" within the agencies. They were prepared on government time, at government expense and with government materials, including the blank appointment calendars themselves. In several cases, the officials' personal secretaries maintained the appointment records as part of their official agency duties. Second, the materials have not been placed into agency files. Third, both DOJ and OMB permit their employees to dispose of these "non-record materials" at their discretion. Thus, the agencies have not sought to exercise any institutional control over appointment documents, although they could do so under the applicable statute and regulations. The government argues that this indicates that the agencies have not "obtained" the documents from their individual employees. In the context of these cases, however, the question is whether the employee's creation of the documents can be attributed to the agency for the purposes of FOIA, regardless of whether the agency requires employees to retain the documents. The government is correct, however, in one respect. Because FOIA does not require an agency to create or obtain a record, so long as the records disposal regulations permit destruction of "non-record materials" at the discretion of an agency or agency employee, documents will be available under FOIA solely based on whether an individual has chosen to keep those documents.

We now turn to the three categories of documents to analyze, in particular, how the documents are used within the agency.

A. Telephone message slips

EDF requested the telephone logs of certain OMB officials. No such logs existed, but one OMB official kept his yellow telephone message slips for short periods of time and disposed of them intermittently on a haphazard basis. The official indicated that the slips "contain[ed] no substantive information." Presumably they indicated the name of the caller, the date and time of the call and, possibly, a

(Continued)

telephone number where the caller could be reached. The purpose of creating these documents was to inform the official of any calls he had received while he was away from his office. The slips do not indicate why the call was made and, most importantly, whether the call was personal or related to official agency business.

It is clear that these slips are not "agency records" within the meaning of FOIA. No substantive information is contained in them. No one but the official for whom the messages were taken used the telephone slips in any way. And, in many cases, there might be no way for the official to segregate personal from business calls.

B. DAILY AGENDAS

Mr. Baxter's secretary at DOJ created daily agendas indicating Mr. Baxter's schedule. She circulated these agendas to certain members of Mr. Baxter's staff. Although the staff threw out the agendas regularly, Mr. Baxter's secretary maintained copies in her desk, apparently in the absence of any instructions to the contrary. The purpose of the agendas was to inform the staff of Mr. Baxter's availability; they facilitated the day-to-day operations of the Antitrust Division.

Unlike the telephone slips, the daily agendas are "agency records" within the meaning of FOIA. They were created for the express purpose of facilitating the daily activities of the Antitrust Division. Even though the agendas reflected personal appointments, they were circulated to the staff for a business purpose. The agency can segregate out any notations that refer to purely personal matters. The daily agendas, unlike the appointment calendars, were not created for Mr. Baxter's personal convenience, but for the convenience of his staff in their conduct of official business.

C. APPOINTMENT CALENDARS

The appointment calendars are the most difficult to categorize. The purpose of the calendars was to facilitate the individuals' performance of their official duties and to organize both their business and personal activities. Unlike the telephone slips, the calendars often gave some indication of the topic of a particular meeting, as well as the location and identity of the participants. Furthermore, it would be much easier to segregate the personal appointments from the business appointments than it would be with the case of a telephone message. In the case of Mr. Baxter and at least one OMB official, immediate staff had access to the calendars to determine the officials' availability. In that sense, the calendars were similar to the daily agendas.

We conclude, however, that these particular appointment calendars are not "agency records." They are distinguishable from the daily agendas in two important respects. First, they were not distributed to other employees, but were retained solely for the convenience of the individual officials. Second, the daily agendas were created by Mr. Baxter's secretary for the express purpose of informing other staff of Mr. Baxter's whereabouts during the course of a business day so that they could determine Mr. Baxter's availability for meetings. Thus the daily agendas were created for the purpose of conducting agency business. In contrast, the appointment calendars were created for the personal convenience of individual officials so that they could organize both their personal and business appointments.

The inclusion of personal items in the appointment calendars buttresses the conclusion that the calendars were created for the personal convenience of the individual employees, not for an official agency purpose. The inclusion of personal information does not, by itself, take material outside the ambit of FOIA, for personal information can be redacted from the copies of documents disclosed to a FOIA requester. But the presence of such information may be relevant in determining the author's intended use of the documents at the time he or she created them. Here, the appointment calendars were created for the personal convenience of individual officials in organizing both their personal and business appointments. Neither OMB nor DOJ required its employees to maintain such calendars. FOIA's reach does not extend to such personalized documents absent some showing that the agency itself exercised control over or possession of the documents. In contrast, the daily agendas were created and distributed to staff solely for their use in determining Mr. Baxter's availability for meetings. The personal information contained in the agendas is identical to that found in Mr. Baxter's appointment calendars and may be redacted from the copies made available to BNA.

We hold that, with the exception of the daily agendas that were distributed within the Antitrust Division, the appointment materials requested by EDF and BNA are not "agency records" within the meaning of FOIA. Our conclusion might be different if the agencies had exercised any control over the materials or if the documents had been created solely for the purpose of conducting official agency business. On the facts presented here, however, these documents are not "agency records." . . .

CASE LAW

NATIONAL PARKS AND CONSERVATION ASSOCIATION v. MORTON
498 F.2d 765 (D.C.Cir.1974).

TAMM, J.:

Appellant brought this action under the Freedom of Information Act, seeking to enjoin officials of the Department of the Interior from refusing to permit inspection and copying of certain agency records concerning concessions operated in the national parks. The district court granted summary judgment for the defendant on the ground that the information sought is exempt from disclosure under section 552(b)(4) of the Act which states:

(b) This section does not apply to matters that are—

(4) trade secrets and commercial or financial information obtained from a person and privileged or confidential. . . .

In order to bring a matter (other than a trade secret) within this exemption, it must be shown that the information is (a) commercial or financial, (b) obtained from a person, and (c) privileged or confidential. Since the parties agree that the matter in question is financial information obtained from a person and that it is not privileged, the only issue on appeal is whether the information is 'confidential' within the meaning of the exemption.

Unfortunately, the statute contains no definition of the word "confidential." In the past, our decisions concerning this exemption have been guided by the following passage from the Senate Report, particularly the italicized portion:

> This exception is necessary to protect the confidentiality of information which is obtained by the Government through questionnaires or other inquiries, *but which would customarily not be released to the public by the person from whom it was obtained.*

We have made it clear, however, that the test for confidentiality is an objective one. Whether particular information would customarily be disclosed to the public by the person from whom it was obtained is not the only relevant inquiry in determining whether that information is 'confidential' for purposes of section 552(b)(4). A court must also be satisfied that non-disclosure is justified by the legislative purpose which underlies the exemption. Our first task, therefore, is to ascertain the ends which Congress sought to attain in enacting the exemption for 'commercial or financial' information.

In general, the various exemptions included in the statute serve two interests—that of the Government in efficient operation and that of persons supplying certain kinds of information in maintaining its secrecy. The exemption with which we are presently concerned has a dual purpose. It is intended to protect interests of both the Government and the individual.

The "financial information" exemption recognizes the need of government policymakers to have access to commercial and financial data. Unless persons having necessary information can be assured that it will remain confidential, they may decline to cooperate with officials and the ability of the Government to make intelligent, well informed decisions will be impaired. This concern finds expression in the legislative history as well as the case law. . . . As the Senate Report explains:

> This exception is necessary to protect the confidentiality of information which is obtained by the Government through questionnaires or other inquiries. . . . It would also include information which is given to an agency in confidence, since a citizen must be able to confide in his Government. Moreover, where the Government has obligated itself in good faith not to disclose documents or information which it receives, it should be able to honor such obligations.

. . . Apart from encouraging cooperation with the Government by persons having information useful to officials, section 552(b)(4) serves another distinct but equally important purpose. It protects persons who submit financial or commercial data to government agencies from the competitive disadvantages which would result from its publication. . . . [The legislative] history firmly supports the inference that section 552(b)(4) is intended for the benefit of persons who supply information as well as the agencies which gather it. . . .

To summarize, commercial or financial matter is 'confidential' for purposes of the exemption if disclosure of the information is likely to have either of the following effects: (1) to impair the Government's ability to obtain necessary information in the future; or (2) to cause substantial harm to the competitive position of the person from whom the information was obtained.

The financial information sought by appellant consists of audits conducted upon the books of companies operating concessions in

(Continued)

national parks, annual financial statements filed by the concessioners with the National Park Service and other financial information. The district court concluded that this information was of the kind 'that would not generally be made available for public perusal.' While we discern no error in this finding, we do not think that, by itself, it supports application of the financial information exemption. The district court must also inquire into the possibility that disclosure will harm legitimate private or governmental interests in secrecy.

On the record before us the Government has no apparent interest in preventing disclosure of the matter in question. Some, if not all, of the information is supplied to the Park Service pursuant to statute. Whether supplied pursuant to statute, regulation or some less formal mandate, however, it is clear that disclosure of this material to the Park Service is a mandatory condition of the concessioners' right to operate in national parks. Since the concessioners are *required* to provide this financial information to the government, there is presumably no danger that public disclosure will impair the ability of the Government to obtain this information in the future.

As we have already explained, however, section 552(b)(4) may be applicable even though the Government itself has no interest in keeping the information secret. The exemption may be invoked for the benefit of the person who has provided commercial or financial information if it can be shown that public disclosure is likely to cause substantial harm to his competitive position. Appellant argues that such a showing cannot be made in this case because the concessioners are monopolists, protected from competition during the term of their contracts and enjoying a statutory preference over other bidders at renewal time. In other words, appellant argues that disclosure cannot impair the concessioners' competitive position because they have no competition. While this argument is very compelling, we are reluctant to accept it without first providing appellee the opportunity to develop a fuller record in the district court. It might be shown, for example, that disclosure of information about concession activities will injure the concessioner's competitive position in a non-concession enterprise. In that case disclosure would be improper. This matter is therefore remanded to the district court for the purpose of determining whether public disclosure of the information in question poses the likelihood of substantial harm to the competitive positions of the parties from whom it has been obtained. . . .

Reprinted from Funk, W.; Shapiro. S.; and Weaver, R. Administrative Procedure and Practice: Problems and Cases. © 2006, with permission of Thomson West.

CHAPTER   SUMMARY

Agencies perform a wide variety of functions and services. Some examples include processing claims and applications for benefits, licensing, giving advice, and disclosing information to the public. The Freedom of Information Act (FOIA) and Privacy Act regulate the disclosure of information from federal agencies. Most states have similar laws in their jurisdiction.

KEY   TERMS

Alternative Dispute Resolution (ADR)   leak
estoppel   Privacy Act
Freedom of Information Act (FOIA)   whistle-blower statute

REVIEW   QUESTIONS

1. List and describe some of the activities that agencies do.
2. Define Alternative Dispute Resolution and give three examples.
3. Generally agencies do not have to stand behind the advice they give. Explain why.
4. State examples of information that agencies disseminate to the public.
5. What are the purposes of the Freedom of Information Act (FOIA) and the Privacy Act?

MORE   INFORMATION

1. To see what the current national debt is, go to http://www.publicdebt.treas.gov.
2. For information on the bird flu, including federal and state preparations, go to http://www.pandemicflu.gov.
3. To see listings of consumer products that have been recalled, go to http://www.cpsc.gov.
4. To see listings of food products that have been recalled, go to http://www.fda.gov and http://www.fsis.usda.gov.
5. For a list of principal FOIA contacts in the federal agencies, go to http://www.usdoj.gov/oip/foiacontacts.htm.

6. To access the U.S. Department of Justice's FOIA Reference Guide, go to http://www.usdoj.gov/oip/04_3.html.

7. For a brief description of recent FOIA cases, go to http://www.usdoj.gov/oip/attachmentedec98.htm.

8. To access the U.S. Department of Justice's Overview of the Privacy Act, go to http://www.usdoj.gov/oip/04_7_1.html.

PRACTICAL APPLICATIONS

1. Pick a federal agency and send an FOIA and Privacy Act request to that agency. Most federal agencies have a link to FOIA and the Privacy Act on their Web site.

2. Search your state Web site and find your state's equivalent to FOIA and send a request for information to a state agency.

3. Go to the Web site of the Consumer Product Safety Commission at http://www.cpsc.gov.
   A. State five products that have been recalled in the last year and give the manufacturer and reason for the recall.
   B. What was the Consumer Product Safety Commission budget request for the 2006?

4. Go to the Web site of the Nuclear Regulatory Commission at http://www.nrc.gov and access the following:
   A. State the statute that created the NRC.
   B. What was the name of the predecessor of the NRC?
   While at the Web site of the NRC, click on the Electronic Reading Room, read about the accident at Three Mile Island, and answer the following:
   C. What year did the accident take place?
   D. What was the cause of the accident?
   E. What was the average dose of radiation to which the public was exposed?
   F. How many deaths are attributable to the accident?

LEARN ABOUT THE AGENCIES

1. FHWA—Federal Highway Administration—http://www.fhwa.dot.gov
2. FNS—Food and Nutrition Service—http://www.fns.usda.gov/fns/default.htm
3. ITA—International Trade Administration—http://trade.gov/index.asp
4. NCHS—National Center for Health Statistics—http://www.cdc.gov/nchs/about.htm
5. NOAA—National Oceanic Atmospheric Administration—http://www.noaa.gov

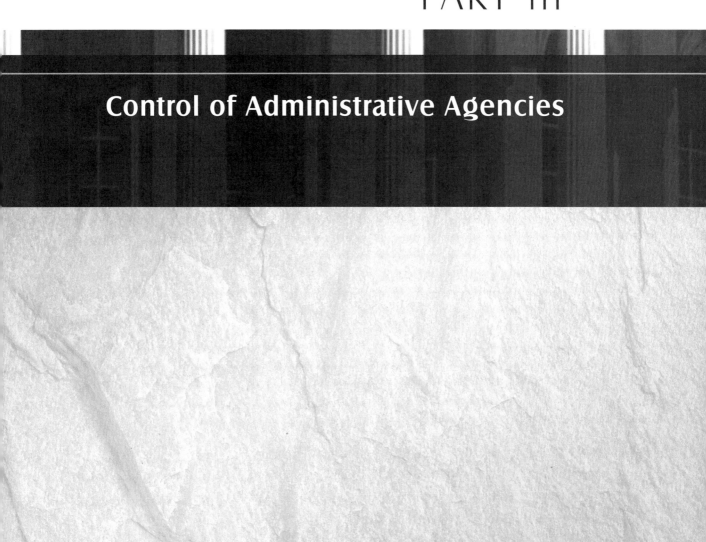

PART III

Control of Administrative Agencies

Judicial Control of Administrative Agencies

CHAPTER OBJECTIVES

After reading this chapter, you should be able to:

- Analyze how courts act as a control of administrative agencies.
- Distinguish judicial review generally and as it relates to administrative agencies.
- Categorize the interests that are and are not protected by due process.
- Distinguish procedural and substantive due process.
- Apply the constitutional tests of due process and equal protection to agency actions.
- Differentiate the various standards of review utilized by courts in reviewing agency actions.
- Explain the barriers to judicial review.

CHAPTER OUTLINE

INTRODUCTION TO JUDICIAL CONTROL

So far we have covered the tremendous power possessed by agencies. Chapter 2 covered the legislative power of rulemaking, Chapter 3 covered executive power, Chapter 4 covered the judicial power of adjudication, and Chapter 5 gave an overview of agency activities.

This chapter will cover how the judicial branch of government controls the power of agencies. Chapter 4 pointed out that an individual normally gets his or her case reviewed inside the agency in the process of adjudication. For example, recall that a decision adjudicating Social Security benefits goes through several layers of appeal *inside* the agency before the case is eligible to be reviewed by a court. See Exhibit 4-4. Now the focus shifts to an individual or business that has been adversely affected by a final decision of an agency to ask a *court of law* to review that decision. When a court reviews a decision of an agency, the court is engaging in *judicial review*.

judicial review

when a court looks at a decision of an administrative agency to see if the decision of the agency is in conformity with constitutional and statutory requirements; the decision reviewed by the court can be rulemaking or adjudication.

The term judicial review has two meanings. Judicial review in administrative law is when a court looks at a decision of an agency and reviews it to see if the agency made any errors. The term judicial review in a larger sense means the power of the courts (established in the case of *Marbury v. Madison*) to review acts of the Congress, the president, and the states and to strike down these acts if they are in conflict with the Constitution. In both instances, the court is acting as a check on the powers of the other branches of government.

Judicial review by the courts is designed to ensure that a person or business has been treated fairly in the administrative process. When the Social Security Administration (SSA) denies a claim, the claimant can take that decision of denial into a court and have a federal judge review it. If a state agency denies a claim for workers' compensation, the claimant in most states can take his or her case into a state court for review.

Judicial review also serves as an essential check on the power of agencies. As we saw in Chapter 1, agencies are creatures of the legislature that creates them and gives them power to act. Therefore, courts must be sure that the agency has acted within the powers delegated to it by the enabling act that created the agency and any others statutes which trans-

> The Administrative Procedure Act and many state statutes provide that a person suffering a legal wrong or who has been aggrieved by agency action shall have a right to appeal to a court of law.

ferred power and authority to the agency. For example, in *FDA v. Brown and Williamson*, 529 U.S.120 (2000), the Supreme Court ruled that the Food and Drug Administration (FDA) had exceeded its powers in issuing regulations that regulated tobacco products.

Finally, the courts act as a control on the power of agencies to make sure that the agency has acted within the Constitution. The constitutional issues are covered in the next section.

Exhibit 6-1

Reasons for Judicial Review

Judicial review ensures fairness to the public.	Judicial review ensures that an agency has treated an individual or business in a fair and reasonable manner by allowing a court of law to review a decision of the agency.
Judicial review ensures agencies are following the law.	Through judicial review, courts check to see that agency decisions do not conflict with the Constitution and are made within the powers delegated to the agency by the legislature.

CONSTITUTIONAL ISSUES AND JUDICIAL REVIEW

The Constitution embodies the framework of our government and describes the relationship individuals have with government at the federal, state, and local levels. The Constitution mandates what government can and cannot do; however, the Constitution does not regulate the behavior of private individuals. In this sense it can be said that only the government can violate an individual's constitutional rights. The phrase that has been adopted to describe the concept that only the federal, state, or local government can violate the Constitution is *state action.* For the Constitution to be violated, the "state," which includes the federal, state, or local government, must be the violator. The Constitution defines our relationship with our government and does not

state action
the principle that only the federal, state, or local governments can violate constitutional rights

regulate the relationships among individuals. Because agencies are part of the government, they are governed by the principle of state action. A main concern of the courts in the process of judicial review is making sure that due process has been satisfied by the agency in question. The due process clauses of the Fifth and Fourteenth Amendments to the United States Constitution require that no person be deprived of life, liberty, or property without due process of law. What constitutes due process of law varies from situation to situation, but the core of the idea is that a person should always have notice and a real chance to present his or her side in a legal dispute when the government attempts to take away life, liberty, or property. For example, when an agency fines a business for polluting the air, the agency is taking away "property," and it must do so in a way that satisfies due process. The landmark case of *Marbury v. Madison*, 5 U.S. 137 (1803), established the principle that the courts are the final arbiters of the meaning of the Constitution. Although the rise of the power of agencies was not contemplated by *Marbury v. Madison,* the principle is readily applicable to the actions of agencies in the twenty-first century. The courts, pursuant to *Marbury v. Madison,* perform their constitutional role to assess whether a federal, state, or local agency has violated the Constitution. The focus for agencies is generally the two due process clauses in the Constitution contained in the Fifth and Fourteenth Amendments.

The *due process clause of the Fourteenth Amendment* reads in part that no *state* shall "deprive any person of life, liberty or property, without due process of law." The *Fifth Amendment* also contains a due process clause which is directed toward the *federal* government. Accordingly, the courts in reviewing agency actions must be sure that the agency has not deprived an individual or business of due process. Courts must look to see that the agency has not violated procedural due process and also substantive due process. These two components of due process will be covered in the next sections.

Procedural Due Process

Due process includes a guarantee of fair procedure, sometimes referred to as *procedural due process*. Procedural due process requires that the government not:

> execute, imprison, or fine a defendant without giving him a fair trial, nor may it take property without providing appropriate procedural safeguards. . . . a State may have every right to discharge a teacher or punish a student—but the State may nevertheless violate the Constitution by failing to provide appropriate procedural safe-

due process clause of the Fourteenth Amendment

prohibits the states from depriving persons of life, liberty, or property without due process of law

due process clause of the Fifth Amendment

prohibits the federal government from depriving persons of life, liberty, or property without due process of law

procedural due process

requires the government to provide a fair procedure before life, liberty, or property can be taken away guards. The constitutional duty to provide fair procedures gives the citizen the opportunity to try to prevent the deprivation from happening, but the deprivation itself does not necessarily reflect any abuse of state power. Similarly, a deprivation may be the consequence of a mistake or a negligent act, and the State may violate the Constitution by failing to provide an appropriate procedural response. In a procedural due process claim, it is not the deprivation of property or liberty that is unconstitutional; it is the deprivation of property or liberty *without due process of law*—without adequate procedures. *Daniels v. Williams,* 474 U.S. 327, 338–339.

Determining which interests get protected as "property" or "liberty" is key because only if a given interest is labeled as a property or liberty interest is the government required to afford procedural due process. Once an interest has been identified as properly within the scope of liberty or property of the Fifth or Fourteenth Amendments, an agency must afford due process to those who appear before it. For example, the Supreme Court has found the following interests to be liberty or property interests under due process:

- Right to receive welfare benefits, *Goldberg v. Kelly,* 397 U.S. 254 (1970)
- Discharge of a tenured teacher from state university (or discharge of a nontenured teacher who can nevertheless establish some kind of contractual right), *Perry v. Sinderman,* 408 U.S. 593 (1972)
- Parole revocation, *Morrissey v. Brewer,* 408 U.S. 471 (1972)
- Transfer of an inmate from a prison to a mental institution, *Vitek v. Jones,* 445 U.S. 480 (1980)
- Termination of parental rights, *Santosky v. Kramer,* 455 U.S. 745 (1982)
- Involuntary commitment to a mental institution, *Addington v. Texas,* 441 U.S. 418 (1979)
- Corporal punishment in public school, *Ingraham v. Wright,* 430 U.S. 651 (1977)
- Suspension in public schools, *Goss v. Lopez,* 419 U.S. 565 (1975)
- Suspension of driver's license, *Bell v. Burson,* 402 U.S. 535 (1971)
- Suspension of professional license, *Willner v. Committee on Character and Fitness,* 373 U.S. 96 (1963)
- Cutting off utilities to customers, *Memphis Light, Gas and Water Division v. Craft,* 436 U.S. 1 (1978)

Courts have held that the following are *not* liberty or property interests under due process:

- Transfer of inmate from one prison to another, *Meachum v. Fano,* 427 U.S. 215 (1976)
- Denial of inmate visitation rights, *Kentucky Department of Corrections v. Thompson,* 490 U.S. 454 (1989)
- Injuries sustained by inmates caused by the negligence (as opposed to intentional harm) of prison officials, *Daniels v. Williams,* 474 U.S. 327 (1986)
- Right to one's reputation (a person whose name and photo appeared on fliers as "Active Shoplifter" distributed by police), *Paul v. Davis,* 424 U.S. 693 (1976)
- Discharge of a nontenured teacher from a state university, *Board of Regents v. Roth,* 408 U.S. 564 (1972)

The Court acknowledged in *Paul v. Davis* that there are a

> variety of interests which are difficult of definition but are nevertheless comprehended within the meaning of liberty or property as meant in the Due Process Clause. These interests attain constitutional status by virtue of the fact that they have been protected by state law, and we have repeatedly ruled that the procedural guarantees of the Fourteenth Amendment apply whenever the State seeks to remove or significantly alter that protected status. *Paul,* 424 U.S. at 710, 711.

Other factors which determine constitutional status are the severity of the loss suffered and whether the interest has been one protected in the nation's history and traditions. For example, liberty has been described in *Meyer v. Nebraska,* 262 U.S. 390, 399 (1923), as:

> not merely freedom from bodily restraint but also the right of the individual to contract, to engage in any of the common occupations of life, to acquire useful knowledge, to marry, establish a home and bring up children, to worship God according to the dictates of his own conscience. . .

As is representative of the preceding cases cited, when an agency attempts to deprive a person of liberty or property interests, procedural due process must be satisfied. For example, we learned in Chapter 4 that state agencies license medical professionals such as doctors. If a state licensing agency attempts to suspend a doctor from practicing medicine, that agency must afford the doctor due process of law. On the other hand, if a state department of corrections refuses to allow visitation rights to an inmate, that inmate is *not* entitled to the protections of procedural due process.

Once it is determined that a right is one contained within the meaning of due process, the question remains what process is due. The procedures that the agencies must afford will vary with the right at issue. More procedural safeguards are required for a felony trial than for suspension of a driver's license. For criminal trials, the maximum safeguards are required because a person's liberty and even life can be at stake. For a two-day suspension from school, a short opportunity to explain might be enough. In other contexts, when money or possessions are taken as opposed to liberty, perhaps a review after the fact is all that is required.

A leading case on procedural due process in administrative law is that of *Goldberg v. Kelly*, 397 U.S. 254 (1970). (See excerpt in Case Law at the end of the chapter.) *Goldberg* held that the right to receive welfare benefits was a property interest protected under due process and therefore the agency was required to afford due process before taking the right away. In so ruling, *Goldberg* established that welfare benefits which provide access to such essentials as food, clothing, and medical care are a form of government *entitlement*. It does not mean that welfare benefits (or any other form of property or liberty right) cannot be terminated; however, the agency must provide due process if liberty or property interests are threatened.

So the question we have to consider is: What process is due? The answer is found in examining the three basic components of procedural due process: notice, a hearing, and a fair judge.

entitlements
various forms of government benefits that cannot be taken away without due process

- Notice—Procedural due process requires timely and adequate notice of what the agency intends to do. The Supreme Court has stated that:

   An elementary and fundamental requirement of due process in any proceeding which is to be accorded finality is notice reasonably calculated, under all the circumstances, to apprise interested parties of the pendency of the action and afford them an opportunity to present their objections. The notice must be of such nature as reasonably to convey the required information and it must afford a reasonable time for those interested to make their appearance. *Mullane v. Central Hanover Bank & Trust Co.*, 339 U.S. 306, 314 (1950).

- A hearing—*Goldberg v. Kelly* held that a hearing was required to satisfy due process before welfare benefits could be terminated. However, a hearing is not always required *before* an interest is affected. According to *Mathews v. Eldridge,* 424 U.S. 319 (1976) (see excerpt in Case Law at the end of the chapter), courts must balance the private interest asserted, the risk of an erroneous deprivation of that interest, and the interest of the agency. Utilizing this balancing test, the Court held that termination of a person's Social Security disability benefits did not require a hearing *before* termination. A hearing must be held after the deprivation of the interest, but the Court did set a definite time. When the hearing must occur will vary, depending on the particular interest involved. A *termination* of a public employee requires a pretermination hearing. *Cleveland Bd. of Ed. v. Loudermill,* 470 U.S. 532 (1985). However, a *suspension* requires only a prompt postsuspension hearing. *Gilbert v. Homar,* 520 U.S. 924 (1997).

In the family law setting, if a social services agency takes a child from the home because of allegations of abuse, procedural due process requires a prompt and fair postdeprivation hearing. *Brokaw v. Mercer County,* 235 F.3d 1000 (7th Cir. 2000). Suspending a person's driver's license without *first* holding a hearing to protect safety on the roads satisfies due process. *Dixon v. Love,* 431 U.S. 105 (1977). In case of emergencies where public health and safety is at stake, an agency can seize property without a hearing. These cases include seizure of contaminated food and closing of a mine after a safety inspection revealed numerous risks to the employees and or to the environment.

- A fair judge—No matter when the hearing is held, due process requires a judge who is not biased against the parties, either on a personal level or because of monetary considerations. As we have seen, agencies not only adjudicate, but also investigate and prosecute violations. This commingling of functions has raised fairness concerns when the same person or body that investigates and prosecutes is also involved in the adjudication of the same matter. Section 554(d) of the Administrative Procedure Act (APA) (concerning formal adjudications) and many state statutes prohibit employees of agencies from prosecuting a case and then advising or participating in the adjudication of the same case, thus creating a wall of separation of the functions of prosecution and adjudication. However, the Supreme Court ruled that a combination of functions at the level of *agency heads* does not violate due process (the federal Constitution was not violated when a medical review board both investigated and brought charges against doctors, then ruled as to whether the doctors' licenses should be suspended) (*Withrow v. Larkin*, 421 U.S. 35 [1975]). Some state constitutions such as Pennsylvania's require a wall of separation even at the level of agency heads (state Constitution violated where medical board both prosecuted and adjudicated with respect to suspending doctors' licenses) (*Lyness v. Commonwealth, State Board of Medicine*, 605 A.2d 1204 [1992]). *Withrow* (interpreting the federal constitution) and *Lyness* (interpreting a state constitution) illustrate an important part of federalism discussed in Chapter 1. The key point is that states can add more rights than the federal Constitution requires, but can never afford less. See Exhibit 6-2, which sets out the basic framework of procedural due process.

Exhibit 6-2

Procedural Due Process

Fifth Amendment—governs federal agencies

Fourteenth Amendment—governs state agencies

No life, liberty, or property taken away without due process

Due process = right to:

1. Notice

2. A hearing

3. A fair judge

Substantive Due Process

In addition to satisfying procedural due process, agencies cannot infringe on substantive due process. If an interest involves substantive due process, then the agency cannot infringe on that interest *no matter* how fair the procedures are. The key to understanding substantive due process is to realize that only very few selected interests the United States Supreme Court has deemed fundamental will get the special protection of *substantive due process*. The kinds of rights that deserve special treatment under the *liberty* portion of the Fourteenth Amendment are those rights that have been seen by the Court to be fundamental. The most familiar of these *fundamental rights* are those contained in the Bill of Rights. These include freedom of speech, freedom of religion, and right to a jury trial. The Court has also recognized these are not the

substantive due process

the principle stemming from "liberty" of the due process clause which bars arbitrary government actions regardless of the fairness of the procedures used to implement them

liberty

a constitutional right; not only freedom from bodily restraint, but also the fundamental right of individuals to procreate, to use contraceptives, to have an abortion, to travel, to refuse medical attention, to live as a family, to marry (heterosexual), and to make decisions regarding childrearing

fundamental rights

basic or crucial rights that are most strongly protected by the Constitution only fundamental rights afforded constitutional protection. If these other rights are not written specifically in the text of the Constitution, how does a court find such rights? What are the outer limits of these rights? Probably the best explanation that the Supreme Court has given as to their methodology in establishing fundamental rights under substantive due process was written by Justice Harlan in a dissenting opinion in *Poe v. Ullman*, 367 U.S. 497 (1962). Justices who represent a wide range of judicial philosophies have cited this opinion throughout the years. Harlan noted that due process is not merely a *procedural* safeguard; rather it also has a substantive component that protects against arbitrary and tyrannical laws. Next, he noted that due process protections are not limited to those rights contained in the Bill of Rights but include interests deemed to be fundamental. As to discerning these fundamental rights, Harlan described the process as follows:

> Due process has not been reduced to any formula; its content cannot be determined by reference to any code. The best that can be said is that through the course of this Court's decisions it has represented the balance which our Nation built upon postulates of respect between that liberty and the demands of organized society. If the supplying of content to this Constitutional concept has of necessity been a rational process, it certainly has not been one where judges have felt free to roam where unguided speculation might take them. The balance of which I speak is the balance struck by this country, having regard for what history teaches are the traditions from which it developed as well as the traditions from which it broke. That tradition is a living thing. A decision of this Court which radically departs from it could not long survive, while a decision which builds on what has survived is likely to be sound. No formula could serve as a substitute, in this area, for judgment and restraint. *Poe*, 367 U.S. at 542.

Harlan emphasized that these constitutional rights must be discerned from the Constitution's larger context, which includes history and purpose, and that the establishment of these rights is not limited to the words contained in the Constitution. Harlan then stated that:

> inasmuch as this context is one not of words, but of history and purposes, the full scope of the liberty guaranteed by the Due Process Clause cannot be found in or limited by the precise terms of the specific guarantees elsewhere provided in the Constitution. This liberty is not a series of isolated points pricked out in terms of the taking of property; the freedom of speech, press, religion; the right to keep and bear arms; the freedom from unreasonable searches and seizures; and so on. It is a rational continuum which,

broadly speaking, includes freedom from all substantial arbitrary impositions and purposeless restraints and which also recognizes what a reasonable and sensitive judgment must, that certain interests require particularly careful scrutiny of the state needs asserted to justify their abridgment. . . Each new claim to Constitutional protection must be considered against a background of Constitutional purposes, as they have been rationally perceived and historically developed. Though we exercise limited and sharply restrained judgment, yet there is no mechanical yard-stick, no mechanical answer. The decision of an apparently novel claim must depend on grounds which follow closely on well-accepted principles and criteria. The new decision must take its place in relation to what went before and further cut a channel to what is to come. *Poe,* 367 U.S. at 543, 544.

When agencies make rulings that interfere with fundamental rights, it is the task of the courts to scrutinize and strike down these rulings if they invade liberty contrary to the interest of the individual or business. For example, the text of the Constitution is silent on the issue of marriage. But the Court, in using the substantive component of the "liberty" of the due process clause, found that marriage is an aspect of "liberty" protected from state interference and found unconstitutional a state law that banned interracial marriages. *Loving v. Virginia,* 388 U.S. 1 (1967). Using the previously referenced principles of Justice Harlan, the Court has also stated that: "These matters, involving the most intimate and personal choices a person may make in a lifetime, choices central to personal dignity and autonomy, are central to the liberty protected by the Fourteenth Amendment. At the heart of liberty is the right to define one's own concept of existence, of meaning, of the universe and of the mystery of human life." *Planned Parenthood of Southeastern PA. v. Casey,* 505 U.S. 833, 851 (1992).

In *Loving v. Virginia,* the Court ruled that a state agency cannot, pursuant to state law, refuse to grant a marriage license to a couple because they were not of the same race. That is so because marriage is a fundamental right stemming from liberty and is protected under substantive due process. Contrast that to the right of same-sex couples to be married. The Supreme Court has never ruled that sexual orientation is a fundamental right entitled to the constitutional protection of substantive due process. Therefore, state agencies *can* refuse to issue a license to a same-sex couple. Note again, that under the principles of federalism, states can add more rights than the federal Constitution requires and can pass laws that afford more rights to its citizens. A good example is Massachusetts, where same-sex marriages are legal based on the Massachusetts Constitution.

Other Fundamental Rights

The Supreme Court has over time established other constitutional rights that are seen as fundamental although not mentioned in the Constitution. The Supreme Court, more or less, followed the methodology set out by Justice Harlan in *Poe*. The Court has seen each of these rights as part of the nation's history, values, and traditions. When an agency makes a decision that infringes on these fundamental rights, a court can use judicial review to protect that interest. For example, in *Moore v. City of E. Cleveland*, 431 U.S. 497 (1977), a city ordinance defined a family to prohibit a grandmother from living with her two grandsons, who were first cousins rather than brothers. Because a government entity cannot intrude on the fundamental right to live as a family, the ordinance in question violated the substantive component of due process.

See Exhibit 6-3, which lists some of the fundamental rights that are not explicitly mentioned in the Constitution.

Exhibit 6-3

Examples of Fundamental Rights Derived from Liberty of the Due Process Clause of the Fourteenth Amendment

The Supreme Court has ruled in the cases cited that "liberty" of the due process clause includes rights that are fundamental because these rights are part of the nation's history, culture, and values.

Privacy (*Griswald v. Connecticut* [1965])

Use of contraceptives—married persons (*Griswald v. Connecticut* [1965])

Use of contraceptives— single persons (*Eisenstadt v. Baird* [1972])

Right to an abortion (*Roe v. Wade* [1973])

Procreation (*Skinner v. Okalahoma* [1942])

Parental decisions concerning child-rearing (*Meyer v. Nebraska* [1923] and *Pierce v. Society of Sisters* [1925])

Right to marry—heterosexual only (*Loving v. Virginia* [1967] and *Zabolicki v. Redhail* [1978])

Right to live as a family (*Moore v. City of E. Cleveland* [1977])

Right to refuse medical attention (*Cruzan v. Director, Mo. Dept. of Health* [1990])

Strict Scrutiny and Rational Basis

The Supreme Court has developed tests to decide cases that involve a fundamental right. For fundamental rights, the Court uses the *strict scrutiny* test, and for all other cases, the Court uses the *rational basis* test. These are shorthand phrases that the Court developed to describe the type of test it will use when exercising judicial review.

Study Exhibit 6-3 to see which kinds of laws get special judicial scrutiny and which laws do not. If a law is a fundamental right, strict scrutiny will be used, and the law will likely be struck down as unconstitutional. The law at issue must be necessary to serve a compelling state interest and be the least restrictive way to achieve that interest. This is an extremely difficult test to pass, but when a fundamental right is involved, the Court will use its power of judicial review to nullify a law even though that law was passed by a majority vote in the state. In other words, a fundamental right can preempt a majority vote. For example, if a state agency issues a regulation that bans birth control devices, a court reviewing that rule would use the strict scrutiny test and strike the law down because the regulation violates the fundament right to use birth control as recognized by the Supreme Court.

On the other hand, if a regulation does not infringe on fundamental rights, the *rational basis* test is used, and the Court will not, as a general rule, exercise judicial review or overturn the law. To pass the rational basis test, the law or regulation only has to be rationally related to a legitimate state interest. For example, in *Johnson v. Phelan,* 69 F.3d 144 (7th Cir. 1995), a prisoner argued that he had a fundamental right, based on liberty of the Fourteenth Amendment, not to be monitored by female guards who could see him naked in the shower, cell, and toilet. The Court ruled that there is no such fundamental right; therefore, strict scrutiny would not be used. The prison regulation was related to further the legitimate interests of the prison system, which included making good use of the staff and reducing the potential conflict with antidiscrimination statutes.

These laws or regulations that do not touch on fundamental rights are only for the political process and not for the courts. The political process involves state legislatures passing laws under their police power. If the citizens of a state do not like the law, the citizens through elections have the authority to elect a new legislature to change the offensive law. As strong as majority rule is, there are certain areas so fundamental that the political process cannot be the final word. Judges can exercise their power of judicial review to protect fundamental rights and will uphold the law only if the state has a *compelling* justification for the

strict scrutiny

the test used to assess a law that implicates a fundamental right; the law must be necessary to further a compelling state interest.

rational basis

the test used to assess all laws that do not implicate a fundamental right; the law only needs to be rationally related to a legitimate state interest.

law. When deemed to be a fundamental right, an issue is essentially taken from the electoral process. This is precisely why Justice Harlan and others have stressed that this power should be used sparingly and that judges should be restrained while using reasoned judgment in utilizing substantive due process.

Sometimes the Supreme Court will apply the rational basis test and still strike down the law. For example, in *Lawrence v. Texas,* 539 U.S. 558 (2003), a sodomy statute that banned sodomy between consenting adults of the same sex, but not between consenting adults of different sexes, was not rationally related to a legitimate state interest. The Court in *Lawrence* emphasized the following:

> The present case does not involve minors. It does not involve persons who might be injured or coerced or who are situated in relationships where consent might not easily be refused. It does not involve public conduct or prostitution. It does not involve whether the government must give formal recognition to any relationship that homosexual persons seek to enter. The case does involve two adults who, with full and mutual consent from each other, engaged in sexual practices common to a homosexual lifestyle. The petitioners are entitled to respect for their private lives. The State cannot demean their existence or control their destiny by making their private sexual conduct a crime. Their right to liberty under the Due Process Clause gives them the full right to engage in their conduct without intervention of the government. It is a promise of the Constitution that there is a realm of personal liberty which the government may not enter. The Texas statute furthers no legitimate state interest which can justify its intrusion into the personal and private life of the individual. *Lawrence,* 539 U.S. at 578.

Note, however, that even in this ruling the Court did not elevate homosexual rights to fundamental status requiring strict scrutiny; the rational basis test was used. The Court simply stated without a lot of explanation that the Texas sodomy statute furthers no legitimate state interest which can justify its intrusion into the personal and private life of the individual. Although all administrative agencies must be aware of this decision when they attempt to regulate the private lives of individuals, it is unclear how the Supreme Court will apply this case to specific fact patterns.

Equal Protection

Along with the due process clause, the equal protection clause of the Fourteenth Amendment is a constitutional guarantee which is designed to protect the rights of people from governmental intrusion. The *equal protection clause* states that "no state shall deny to any person within its jurisdiction the equal protection of the laws." As with the due process clause of the Fourteenth Amendment, the equal protection clause restricts only the government, not private entities. The Supreme Court has ruled that administrative agencies must also adhere to the requirements of the equal protection clause. *New York City Transit Auth. v. Beazer,* 440 U.S. 568 (1979). Agencies at the federal, state, and local level must be mindful of the restrictions of the equal protection clause as they issue regulations and adjudications. Although the equal protection clause by its terms only restricts the states, the Supreme Court ruled in *Bolling v. Sharpe,* 347 U.S. 497 (1954), that the Fifth Amendment due process clause has an "equal protection" component that likewise restricts the federal government.

When will a court use due process as opposed to equal protection when analyzing an action of an administrative agency? Although these concepts can overlap, a good rule of thumb is as follows: If an agency action singles out and classifies groups of people for different treatment, equal protection is generally used. If the agency action applies across various group lines such as race or gender and deprives all of "liberty," then the due process clause is implicated. For example, a regulation that banned the use of contraceptives would violate the guarantee of liberty of the due process clause, but if the regulation only banned the sale of contraceptives to women and not to men, then equal protection would be violated. The word "equal" in equal protection does not mean equal treatment. A regulation that classifies people differently can treat groups "unequally" or dissimilarly as long as the law can be justified under one of the three constitutional "tests" that are analyzed in the following sections.

Classifications under Equal Protection

To decide if a given law or an agency action violates the equal protection clause of the Fourteenth Amendment, the Supreme Court has established three tests. The test used depends on the classification that the law creates. The three tests are:

1. Strict scrutiny for classifications which implicate fundamental rights or are based on race or national origin.
2. *Middle level scrutiny* for classifications based on gender and illegitimacy.
3. Rational basis test for all other classifications.

equal protection clause
the Fourteenth Amendment requirement that states not set up illegal categories to justify treating people unfairly

middle level scrutiny
the test used when a law classifies on the basis of gender or illegitimacy; the law must be substantially related to important governmental interests to be constitutional under the equal protection clause.

Equal Protection—Race, Strict Scrutiny

The central purpose of the equal protection clause is to prevent the states from discriminating between individuals on the basis of race. *Shaw v. Reno,* 509 U.S. 630 (1993). When laws classify people on the basis of race, the strict scrutiny test is used. Race is considered a *suspect class.* When laws classify using race, the Court is "suspicious" of the racial classification and will use the strict scrutiny test. This is the same test used when fundamental rights are infringed under "liberty" of due process. When strict scrutiny is invoked, the classification will be upheld only if it is *necessary* to promote a *compelling* governmental interest. The words *necessary* and *compelling* are used as shorthand terms to indicate that the Court is really scrutinizing the statute in question. The reason the Court began to give greater "scrutiny" of laws affecting racial and religious minorities is because of the prejudice these groups have endured. This prejudice over time has created a special condition, which does not allow for proper representation of people who are members of the suspect class in the normal political processes of voting and running for office. *United States v. Carolene Products,* 304 U.S. 144 (1938). A suspect class is one saddled with such disabilities, subjected to such a history of purposeful unequal treatment, or relegated to such a position of political powerlessness as to command extraordinary protection from the majoritarian political process. *San Antonio Independent School District v. Rodriguez,* 411 U.S. 1 (1973).

The purpose of strict scrutiny is to "smoke out" illegitimate uses of race by assuring that the legislative body is pursuing a goal important enough to warrant use of a highly suspect tool. The strict scrutiny test also ensures that the means chosen "fit" this compelling goal so closely that there is little or no possibility that the motive for the classification was illegitimate, racially prejudicial, or stereotype. *City of Richmond v. Croson,* 488 U.S. 469 (1989). If strict scrutiny is used, the Court will very likely strike down the law. In fact, *Korematsu v. United States,* 323 U.S. 214 (1944), involving imprisonment of Japanese Americans during World War II, was the rare case where strict scrutiny was used and the classification was upheld. After the bombing of Pearl Harbor on December 7, 1941 by Japan, the United States forced American citizens of Japanese decent into relocation camps. This was classification based on race, but it was upheld. The compelling governmental interest was national security. In a more recent case, the policy of the California Department of Corrections to racially segregate new or transferred inmates on a temporary basis was evaluated under strict scrutiny. *California v. Johnson,* 543 U.S. 499 (2005). The compelling governmental

suspect class

a group such as racial or ethnic minorities that has suffered historic, intentional discrimination and thus requires extraordinary protection by the courts interest to justify the racial classification was to prevent violence caused by racial and ethnic gangs. Justice Thomas commented on the ruling in *California v. Johnson* and stated that:

> Just last Term, this Court invalidated California's policy of racially segregating prisoners in its reception centers, notwithstanding that State's warning that its policy was necessary to prevent prison violence. California subsequently experienced several instances of severe race-based prison violence, including a riot that resulted in 2 fatalities and more than 100 injuries, and significant fighting along racial lines between newly arrived inmates, the very inmates that were subject to the policy invalidated by the Court in *Johnson. Beard v. Banks,* 126 S. Ct. 2572, 2582 (2006) (Thomas, J., concurring).

Although the use of racial classifications is subject to strict scrutiny, the classification can be justified by a compelling state interest. Preventing the loss of life and hundreds of injuries may be such a compelling interest.

As states have moved away from passing laws that intentionally discriminate, the focus under equal protection has shifted to the area of affirmative action, where race is used not to discriminate against racial minorities, but to remedy the effects of past discrimination. Affirmative action will be covered later in this chapter.

Equal Protection—Fundamental Rights, Strict Scrutiny

Just as fundamental rights are protected under the due process clause (see Exhibit 6-3), with the use of strict scrutiny, the courts will use the equal protection clause and strict scrutiny to judge classifications that interfere with a fundamental right. First Amendment rights, such as the right to procreate and the right to marry, can be protected by use of liberty of the Fourteenth Amendment or under equal protection. Sometimes the Court will use an equal protection analysis to decide a case, but the case will then stand for the legal principle that the right is a fundamental right and part of liberty. For example, the case of *Skinner v. Oklahoma,* 316 U.S. 535 (1942), stands for the principle that procreation is a fundamental liberty interest protected under due process. The Court actually decided the case on equal protection grounds. Similarly, in *Loving v. Virginia,* 388 U.S 1 (1967), and *Zablocki v. Redhail,* 434 U.S. 374 (1978), an equal protection analysis was used to find a fundamental right of marriage. In *Zablocki,* a state statute which required court approval for marriage for any parent who was subject to a child support obligation was ruled unconstitutional. In *Loving,* a state statute that banned interracial marriage was ruled unconstitutional under both due process and equal protection.

Another area where both due process and equal protection analysis is used is equal access to the courts. The cases have relied on both principles in holding that the Constitution does not require a state to grant an appeal but once granted an indigent defendant must be provided a free trial transcript, *Griffin v. Illinois,* 351 U.S. 12 (1956), and free attorney, *Douglas v. California,* 372 U.S. 353 (1963), for at least one appeal but not for a second appeal in the state court system nor to the United States Supreme Court, *Ross v. Moffitt,* 417 U.S. 600 (1974). The Court has also recognized that in civil cases, the state must provide access to the Courts. The Court has struck down laws on due process and equal protection grounds, laws that required a fee to obtain a divorce, *Boddie v. Connecticut,* 401 U.S. 371 (1971), and a law that required a fee before a mother could appeal from the termination of her parental rights, *M.L.B. v. S.L.J.,* 519 U.S. 102 (1996).

In *Shapiro v. Thompson,* 394 U.S. 618 (1969), the fundamental right to travel was established when the Court held that a one-year residency requirement for welfare assistance violated equal protection.

Equal Protection—Gender, Middle Level Scrutiny

The Supreme Court has recognized that the equal protection clause protects against discrimination in gender cases as well as race. When a law classifies on the basis of gender, the test used is called "middle level scrutiny," sometimes referred to as "intermediate scrutiny." Gender is not a suspect class, so *strict scrutiny is not* used. Under this less demanding test, the law must serve an *important* governmental interest, not a *compelling* interest. The means chosen must be *substantially* related to the objective of the statute. Under this test, sometimes the law is upheld, and sometimes it is struck down. For example, a law that excludes men from an all-women state-run nursing school violates equal protection. *Mississippi University for Women v. Hogan,* 458 U.S. 718 (1982). However, a law that requires *men* and not women to register for the draft does not. *Rostker v. Goldberg,* 453 U.S. 57 (1981). The objective of the draft law is to have a ready pool of potential combat soldiers. The Court held in *Rostker* that treating men different than women is *substantially* related to this *important* objective. A law that allowed *women* and not men to seek alimony violated equal protection. *Orr v. Orr,* 440 U.S. 268 (1979). The equal protection clause forbids intentional exclusion of women from juries because this kind of discrimination "serves to ratify and perpetuate invidious, archaic, and overbroad stereotypes about the relative abilities of men and women." *J.E.B. v. Alabama,* 511 U.S. 127, 131 (1994). A gender-based classification was at issue in *Michael M. v. Superior Court,* 450 U.S. 464 (1981), where the Court ruled that a statutory rape law did not violate the equal protection clause. The statute defined unlawful sexual intercourse as "an act of sexual intercourse accomplished with a female, not the wife of the perpetrator, where the female is under the age of 18 years." Thus males could be convicted under the statute but not females. The Court was satisfied that the justification for the statute (preventing illegitimate teenage pregnancies) justified the different treatment.

Equal Protection—Illegitimacy, Middle Level Scrutiny

Illegitimacy classifications that bar or restrict illegitimate children from collecting death benefits, recovering for the wrongful death of parents, and inheriting are judged under the middle level of review. For example, in *Trimble v. Gordon,* 430 U.S. 762 (1977), Illinois prohibited inheritance by nonmarital children from their fathers. Using the middle level of review the Court found that the interests of the state in protecting legitimate family relationships and preventing fraudulent claims were not substantially related to these interests because the law banned inheritance even when paternity was proven. In *Clark v. Jeter,* 486 U.S.456 (1988), the Court reviewed a Pennsylvania law that required an illegitimate child who was seeking child support from his or her father to file suit to establish paternity within six years of birth, while a legitimate child could seek support at any time. The six-year time limitation was not substantially related to the state's interest in avoiding fraudulent claims because Pennsylvania in a number of circumstances permitted paternity to be litigated more than six years after the child's birth. This cast doubt on this statute's purported interest in avoiding fraudulent claims.

Equal Protection—Economic and Social Classifications, Rational Basis

If a law does not classify on the basis of race, gender, alienage, or illegitimacy, the rational basis test is used. The vast majority of laws are in this category. These laws regulate business, taxes, inheritance, contracts, and real estate and are generally referred to as social-economic laws.

In the rational basis test, the Court looks to see if it is conceivable that the classification bears a rational relationship to the end that the government wants to achieve. The law is constitutional if there is a legitimate state interest and if the means rationally carry out that interest under *any* set of circumstances that the Court can envision. For example, a law that requires state police officers to retire at age 50 is constitutional under the rational basis test. This law classifies on the basis of age, so the rational basis test is used. The law *rationally* carries out the *legitimate* state interest of having an effective police force. It does not matter that many, if not most, of the officers are competent past the age of 50. It is rational to conclude that as age progresses performance will diminish. This is why most statutes are upheld. Age is not a "suspect" class. *Strict scrutiny is not used.* Age is not placed into the middle level either, so with the very minimum review by the Court, the law is upheld. *Massachusetts Board of Retirement v. Murgia,* 427 U.S. 307 (1976).

Under the rational basis test, the Court does not debate the wisdom of the statute. The statute in fact may be a failure in achieving its intended result. But whether the statute will achieve its goals is not the issue. The issue is if the state legislature *rationally could have believed that* the statute would achieve its goals. Is it rational that the legislature would conclude that a 50-year age requirement would improve the police force? If the answer is yes, then under the rational basis test, the statute is constitutional.

Equal Protection—Alienage, Strict Scrutiny and Rational Basis

The general rule is that laws that discriminate on the basis of alienage are adjudicated under strict scrutiny, since aliens are considered a suspect class. The Court has invalidated laws that denied aliens the right to pursue various occupations such as civil service jobs, *Sugarman v. Dougall,* 413 U.S. 634 (1973); engineering, *Examining Board v. Flores de Otero,* 426 U.S. 572 (1976); notary public, *Bernal v. Fainter,* 467 U.S. 216 (1983); and membership in state bar associations, *In re Griffiths,* 413 U.S. 717 (1973). The Court thereafter developed an exception to the rule that discrimination based on alienage triggers strict scrutiny. This exception is called the political function exception and applies to laws that exclude aliens from positions intimately related to the process of democratic self-government. Applying this exception, the Court ruled that aliens can be excluded from becoming police officers, *Foley v. Connelie,* 435 U.S. 291 (1978); teachers, *Ambach v. Norwick,* 441 U.S. 68 (1979); and probation officers, *Cabell v. Chavez-Salido,* 454 U.S. 432 (1982), because in these positions a person routinely exercises discretionary power, involving a basic governmental function that places them in a position of direct authority over other individuals. The rationale behind the political function exception is that a state may establish its own form of government and limit the right to govern to those who are full-fledged members of the political community.

Equal Protection—Other Classifications, Rational Basis

The following classifications are judged by the rational basis test:

Age—*Massachusetts Board of Retirement v. Murgia,* 427 U.S. 307 (1976)

Welfare assistance—*Dandridge v. Williams,* 397 U.S. 471 (1970)

Education—*San Antonio Independent School Dist. v. Rodriguez,* 411 U.S. 1 (1973); the Court left open the possibility that the Constitution might protect the right of education as a prerequisite to the right to speak or the right to vote.

Right to die: within the context of laws banning physician-assisted suicide—*Vacco v. Quill,* 521 U.S. 793 (1997)

Poverty and wealth classifications—*James v. Valtierra,* 402 U.S. 137 (1971)

Mental retardation—*City of Cleburne v. Cleburne Living Center,* 473 U.S. 432 (1985)

Sexual orientation—*Romer v. Evans,* 517 U.S. 620 (1996); a state constitutional amendment which prohibited all cities from enacting laws that prohibited discrimination of homosexuals, lesbians, or bisexuals was struck down as not rationally related to any legitimate state interest. The classification did not further a proper legislative end; instead it made homosexuals unequal to everyone else.

See Exhibit 6-4 for a breakdown of the classifications and the tests of equal protection.

EQUAL PROTECTION AND AFFIRMATIVE ACTION

Race has been used by government to classify individuals and then discriminate against these individuals. The classic case of race-based classification is *Plessy v. Ferguson,* 163 U.S. 537 (1896), where the Court ruled that a state law that imposed legal segregation in public transportation was legal if the accommodations were of equal quality. In *Brown v. Board of Education,* 347 U.S. 483 (1954), the Court ruled that state laws requiring children in public schools to be segregated by race violated the equal protection clause, and thus it overruled the separate

Exhibit 6-4

Equal Protection—Classifications and Tests

CLASSIFICATION	TEST	ANALYSIS
Race/ethnicity	Strict scrutiny	The law must be necessary to serve a compelling state interest and be narrowly tailored to achieve that interest.
Fundamental rights: Procreation, vote, access to courts, travel, marriage (heterosexual)	Strict scrutiny	The law must be necessary to serve a compelling state interest and be narrowly tailored to serve that interest.
Gender	Middle level	The law must be substantially related to serve an important state interest.
Illegitimacy	Middle level	The law must be substantially related to serve an important state interest.
Economic and social	Rational basis	The law must be rationally related to serve legitimate state interests.
Age		
Welfare assistance		
Right to die (assisted suicide laws)		
Poverty/wealth		
Mental retardation		
Sexual orientation		
Alienage	Strict scrutiny unless the law covers a political function; then rational basis	See preceding tests.

but equal doctrine of *Plessy*. This section will discuss the flip side of the issue: When can a federal, state, or local government and its agencies use race as a tool to remedy the effects of past discrimination?

The various programs designed to do this have been labeled *affirmative action*. These programs have different approaches and can be called set-asides, goals, or timetables. They attempt to include minorities in areas traditionally closed to them, such as higher education, certain professions and trades, labor unions, and others.

The constitutional problem with these programs involves the use of race by government to classify. When race is used, strict scrutiny is used even though the purpose of these laws is *not to discriminate,* but to *benefit*. When the city of Richmond passed an ordinance that required that 30 percent of the city's contracts must be awarded to minority contractors, the Court ruled that strict scrutiny must be used. *Croson v. City of Richmond*, 488 U.S. 469 (1989).

In *Adarand Constructors, Inc. v. Pena,* 515 U. S. 200 (1995), the federal government's affirmative action program was at issue. The affirmative action plan provided that 5 percent of certain federal contracts be awarded to Asian-Americans, Hispanics, African-Americans, and other minorities. The Supreme Court held that strict scrutiny must be used in evaluating the constitutionality of this federal affirmative action plan, just as *Croson* required strict scrutiny for state and local plans that use race. Because the use of race is immediately "suspect," this highest level of judicial scrutiny must be used. Past cases that used a lesser standard in evaluating race-based remedies were overruled. After *Adarand,* the federal government's race-based remedies are also subject to this highest level of scrutiny.

Does this mean that all affirmative action programs, federal and local, will be struck down? No. The Court stated in *Adarand* and other cases that some programs can withstand strict scrutiny. However, these programs must be *narrowly tailored* to further a *compelling interest*. Figuring out what kinds of affirmative action programs will pass the test of strict scrutiny was extremely difficult because the Court never fully explained what kinds of interests were compelling. In 1978, the Court issued an opinion in *Regents of the University v. Bakke*, 438 U.S. 265 (1978), and found a medical school's affirmative action plan which reserved 16 percent of the seats for members of certain minority groups to be an impermissible use of race. But *Bakke* did not produce a majority opinion and never settled on what interests are compelling interests that would satisfy strict scrutiny. In 2003, the Court issued two opinions *Gratz v. Bollinger,* 539 U.S. 244 (2003), and *Grutter v. Bollinger,* 539 U.S. 306 (2003), and finally explained which interests are compelling and which are not compelling.

affirmative action
programs designed to include disfavored minorities into areas where they have been excluded because of past discrimination

narrowly tailored
a requirement that is designed to ensure that the use of race furthers a compelling state interest

compelling interest
a strong enough reason for a state that justifies and makes constitutional the use of race

Not a Compelling Interest

Reducing the historic deficit of traditionally disfavored minorities in universities

Remedying societal discrimination

Increasing the number of professionals who will practice in communities that are underserved

Compelling Interests That Justify the Use of Racial Preferences

Remedying the effects of recent discrimination against disfavored minorities

Diversity

Whether diversity in college and law school education is a compelling state interest which can withstand strict scrutiny was the key question that went unanswered by the Court from 1978 until 2003. However, the use of race to achieve diversity must be narrowly tailored to achieve the goal of a diverse student body. Fortunately, in ruling in *Grutter* and *Gratz,* the Court spelled out what kinds of affirmative action plans are narrowly tailored and which are not.

In *Gratz,* the school selection committee assigned every underrepresented minority (e.g., African-Americans, Hispanics, Native Americans) an automatic 20-point bonus, one-fifth of the points needed, to guarantee admission to every single underrepresented minority applicant solely because of race, without consideration of the particular background, experience, or qualities of each individual applicant. In addition, this plan did not provide for any meaningful individualized review of the applicants and therefore was not narrowly tailored to achieve the interest in educational diversity.

On the other hand, in *Grutter,* the admissions process consisted of high school grades, scores on the Law School Admittance Test, and a number of variables such as personal recommendations, essays by the applicant, talents and experiences, quality of undergraduate institution, overcoming adversity, community service, and employment experiences. Race was one of several factors that was weighed in an individualized review of each applicant's application for admission. Race was used as a plus factor to achieve a critical mass of underrepresented minority students. A critical mass is not a fixed percentage but meaningful numbers that encourage underrepresented minorities to participate in the classroom and not feel isolated. The race of the applicant had to be considered to reach critical mass because underrepresented minority students could not be enrolled if admissions decisions were based solely on undergraduate grades and the Law School Admittance Test.

No fixed numbers of underrepresented minorities were set, and no one received an automatic bonus for race, as was the case in *Gratz.*

The narrow tailoring requirement is "to ensure that the means chosen fit the compelling goal so closely that there is little or no possibility that the motive for the classification was illegitimate racial prejudice or stereotype." To be narrowly tailored, a race-conscious admissions program cannot use a quota system nor place minority applicants on separate admissions tracks. "Quotas impose a fixed number or percentage which must be attained, or which cannot be exceeded." Race and ethnicity can be used as a plus factor more flexibly in the context of individualized consideration of each and every applicant and still be narrowly tailored. Narrow tailoring "requires that a race-conscious admissions program not unduly harm members of any racial group" including nonminorities. The plan in *Grutter* did not harm nonminority applicants because it considered all pertinent elements of diversity; it can and did "select nonminority applicants who have greater potential to enhance student body diversity over underrepresented minority applicants." *Grutter,* 539 U.S. at 333–341. All race-conscious admissions plans must have a termination point, and the Court set 25 years as a goal in which the use of racial preferences will no longer be required. As other affirmative action plans are challenged, it is likely that proponents of these plans will argue that their plan is just like *Grutter,* while the opponents will argue it is just like *Gratz.* Until the Supreme Court rules again, it will be up to the lower courts to decide. See Exhibit 6-5 for an outline of affirmative action and the use of race.

DELEGATED POWER AND JUDICIAL CONTROL

The previous sections described the constitutional issues that agencies face. Administrative agencies must respect procedural due process, substantive due process, and equal protection. Even where there is no constitutional interest at stake, the courts must also be sure that the agency has acted within the power that has been delegated to it by Congress, and in doing so, the court will look to the enabling act and to any subsequent statutes which may have transferred the power to the agency. For example, as noted in this chapter, the FDA acted outside its delegated power when it issued regulations concerning tobacco products because Congress never delegated the power to regulate tobacco to the FDA. *Brown and Williamson v. FDA,* 529 U.S. 120 (2000).

In what could be seen as the flip side of *Brown and Williamson,* the Environmental Protection Agency (EPA) asserted that Congress *did not* delegate power to the EPA to regulate carbon dioxide and other

---

Exhibit 6-5

Affirmative Action in Education

When race is used as a factor in the admissions process:

Strict scrutiny must be used because race is a suspect class under the equal protection clause.

The college must show a compelling interest to justify the use of race.

Compelling interests are:

Remedying the effects of recent discrimination against disfavored minorities

Diversity in the student body

The admissions plan then must be narrowly tailored to achieve the compelling interest.

Narrowly Tailored	Not Narrowly Tailored
A goal to produce a "critical mass" of underrepresented minorities.	Fixed quotas Separate admissions track for underrepresented minorities. Automatic 20-point bonus added to all underrepresented minorities.

---

greenhouse gases. In *Massachusetts v. EPA,* 127 S. Ct. 1438 (2007), the Supreme Court ruled that Congress, through the Clean Air Act (CAA), had delegated such powers to the EPA. (The case is found in Appendix D.) In reaching its conclusion, the Court looked at the relevant section of the CAA which states that:

> The [EPA] Administrator shall by regulation prescribe (and from time to time revise) in accordance with the provisions of this section, standards applicable to the emission of any air pollutant from any class or classes of new motor vehicles or new motor vehicle engines, which in his judgment cause, or contribute to, air pollution which may reasonably be anticipated to endanger public health or welfare. 42 U.S.C. § 7521(a)(1).

The EPA's position was that it had no authority to issue regulations because carbon dioxide is *not* an air pollutant under the CAA. The Court strongly disagreed with the EPA's assessment and held that because the CCA's expansive definition of air pollutant includes carbon dioxide, the EPA has the statutory authority to regulate the emissions of such gases from new motor vehicles.

The Court went on to say that it had little trouble in concluding that the CAA does include carbon dioxide and other greenhouse gases as air pollutants and stated that:

> In relevant part, § 202(a)(1) provides that EPA "shall by regulation prescribe...standards applicable to the emission of any air pollutant from any class or classes of new motor vehicles or new motor vehicle engines, which in [the Administrator's] judgment cause, or contribute to, air pollution which may reasonably be anticipated to endanger public health or welfare." Because EPA believes that Congress did not intend it to regulate substances that contribute to climate change, the agency maintains that carbon dioxide is not an "air pollutant" within the meaning of the provision. The statutory text forecloses EPA's reading. The Clean Air Act's sweeping definition of "air pollutant" includes "any air pollution agent or combination of such agents, including *any* physical, chemical . . . substance or matter which is emitted into or otherwise enters the ambient air . . . ." On its face, the definition embraces all airborne compounds of whatever stripe, and underscores that intent through the repeated use of the word "any." Carbon dioxide, methane, nitrous oxide, and hydrofluorocarbons are without a doubt "physical [and] chemical . . . substance[s] which [are] emitted into . . . the ambient air." The statute is unambiguous. *Massachusetts v. EPA,* 127 S. Ct. at 1460.

The EPA next argued that it could not regulate carbon dioxide emissions because doing so would require it to increase the vehicle fuel economy standards, which is a power Congress had delegated to the National Highway Traffic Safety Administration (NHTSA). The Court acknowledged that there may be overlap in the function of the agencies but saw no reason why both agencies could not administer their obligations and yet avoid inconsistency. The Court found the obligations of the EPA to be as follows:

> If EPA makes a finding of endangerment, the Clean Air Act requires the agency to regulate emissions of the deleterious pollutant from new motor vehicles. EPA no doubt has significant latitude as to the manner, timing, content, and coordination of its regulations with those of other agencies. [EPA's] reasons for action or inaction must conform to the authorizing statute. Under the clear terms of the Clean Air Act, EPA can avoid taking further action only if it determines that greenhouse gases do not contribute to climate change or if it provides some reasonable explanation as to why it cannot or will not exercise its discretion to determine whether they do. To the extent that this constrains

agency discretion to pursue other priorities of the Administrator or the President, this is the congressional design. *Massachusetts v. EPA,* 127 S. Ct. at 1462.

In sum, Congress had empowered the EPA to regulate carbon dioxide under the CAA, and therefore the EPA could not avoid its statutory obligations by refusing to do so.

JUDICIAL CONTROL AND AGENCY DISCRETION

Recall in Chapter 1 that discretion was defined as the ability of administrative agencies to make choices. Discretion is the power that agencies possess to act within the general guidelines set out by the legislature and includes the power and ability to make decisions on issues. When a legislature delegates rulemaking power (see Chapter 2), executive power (see Chapter 3), and judicial power (see Chapter 4) to an agency, it is granting much discretion to the agency so that the agency can perform its mandates as directed by the legislature. Statutes cannot provide what agencies can do in every instance. Agencies need flexibility to solve the problem at hand. Too much discretion leaves an agency with no guidelines to follow. Too little discretion ties the hands of the agency, and flexibility and efficiency are compromised. Let us look at three kinds of agency discretion. In each of these types of agency discretion, a court would be reluctant to change the decision of the agency.

- Policymaking discretion. Previous chapters contain numerous examples of policymaking discretion, such as the EPA banning lead in gasoline. Other examples of the use of policymaking discretion involve requiring hard toe shoes on construction sites, whether air bags should be required in vehicles, and how much testing should be done to protect against mad cow disease.

- Discretion to use rulemaking or adjudication to solve a problem. Review Exhibit 4-3, which compares rulemaking and adjudication. The decision by an agency to use rulemaking rather than adjudication is a form of discretion. For example, the Federal Trade Commission (FTC) is authorized by Congress to attack unfair trade practices by the use of administrative *adjudications* against individuals or businesses. The FTC is also authorized to issue *rules* against unfair trade practices. Generally, the courts will not interfere with the choice that the agencies make, especially when the agency supplies a clear reason why it is choosing adjudication over rulemaking, or vice versa.

- Prosecutorial discretion. Prosecutorial discretion involves the agency's decision to institute administrative proceedings. In criminal law, the decision by a district attorney to bring or not to bring criminal charges against someone who was involved in a fatal car accident is committed to the discretion of the district attorney. When a police officer decides to issue a warning and not give a ticket, the officer is exercising a form of prosecutorial discretion. When the Internal Revenue Service decides not to pursue criminal charges concerning an individual's tax return, that decision involves the agency's prosecutorial discretion. The decision by a local health board to issue a citation against a restaurant rather than close down the restaurant is another example of agency prosecutorial discretion. No agency has the resources to enforce every regulation and policy. The agency must make choices on whom to prosecute and what form the prosecution will take based on that agency's limited resources.

Agencies are called upon to find facts and then make conclusions of law based on those facts. For example, the EPA could find that a company violated a regulation by emitting too much lead into the air and thus impose a fine. As a general rule, the court is hesitant to use judicial review to overturn the agency's finding of fact. The court will defer to the decisions of the EPA in the previous example because the EPA has developed expertise in emission regulations which a court does not possess. When the court shows deference, it essentially respects the decisions of the agencies. Factual determinations will not be overturned lightly and are thus accorded deference. Because of the need of the agency to act flexibly and efficiently in implementing the law within the area of its jurisdiction and because of the expertise possessed by the agency and not the court, the courts will not easily overturn a ruling on a factual matter. This approach is consistent with the principle that a court will not interfere with the three kinds of discretion listed previously. Deference is also accorded to an agency because of the traditional role that the courts serve. Legislatures are the branch of government that is established to make policy choices. In turn, legislatures delegate much of this power to agencies to fill in gaps of statutes and make policy that is consistent with the intent of the legislature. On the other hand, the courts are not the policymakers but instead serve to interpret and act as a check and balance on the legislative and executive branches of government. Therefore, the court's role in judicial review of agency actions is limited. This limited role of the courts is manifest in our discussion of discretion and deference to an agency's actions.

Simply put, because the legislature has granted discretion to the agency, the court will exercise deference when reviewing the agency's use of that discretion.

However, when an agency decision calls for a legal interpretation of the Constitution or statutes, the court as a general rule will give less deference to the agency. This is so because the court is just as competent, if not more so, in reading the Constitution and statutes as is an agency. However, when an agency has made a legal interpretation of the statute under which it operates, the court will give what is referred to as *Chevron* deference, named after the case of *Chevron v. Natural Resources Defense Council,* 467 U.S. 837 (1984).

Chevron established a two-step test. First, the court must inquire if Congress has directly spoken to the precise question at issue. If so, that ends the inquiry, and the court must give effect to the unambiguous expressed intent of Congress. If the statute is silent or ambiguous, Congress has in effect left a gap in the statute for the agency to fill. If the agency in filling that gap has interpreted the statute in a reasonable manner, the court will give effect to that judgment, deferring to the agency, thus granting *Chevron* deference. Under *Chevron,* courts are to refrain from second-guessing agencies when they make policy decisions based on the statutes under which they operate.

The case of *FDA v. Brown and Williamson,* 529 U.S. 120 (2000), applied *Chevron* to the FDA's decision to regulate tobacco. The Court found that it was clearly not the intent of Congress to give such authority to the FDA, thus utilizing step one of *Chevron.* The Court ruled that Congress has clearly precluded the FDA from asserting jurisdiction over tobacco because such authority would be inconsistent with the intent expressed by Congress in the 1930 enactment of the Food, Drug and Cosmetic Act, the overall regulatory scheme, and Congress' intent in more recently enacted tobacco-specific legislation. In *Rust v. Sullivan,* 500 U.S. 173 (1991), the Supreme Court applied *Chevron* to uphold the validity of a regulation that banned medical personnel in federally funded family planning clinics from mentioning abortion as a medical option. For constitutional issues such as due process, the Court will not engage in *Chevron* deference but will base its decisions on its own independent review of the relevant constitutional provisions. (See previous discussion on constitutional issues in this chapter.)

How Much Judicial Review? Scope of Review

Society invests a lot of time, money, effort, and energy to set up the system of administrative law that we have been studying. We have noted that the legislature sets up the system of administrative law to more efficiently and effectively serve the public, especially in such highly technical areas as nuclear power and toxic emissions. It would be counterproductive to empower the agencies to do all this work and then have the court upset a decision of the agency by merely substituting its judgment for that of the agency. On the other hand, we need a check on the tremendous power possessed by agencies in modern society. One way that administrative law deals with this dilemma is by setting up a scope of judicial review for the courts to utilize that gives guidelines on how *closely* a court will scrutinize an agency action. See Exhibit 6-6, which is the Scope of Review section in the APA. The scope of review is designed not to assure a perfect decision, but only to set up minimum standards that seek to insure fairness in the administrative system.

Exhibit 6-6

§ 706 of APA, Scope of Review

To the extent necessary to decision and when presented, the reviewing court shall decide all relevant questions of law, interpret constitutional and statutory provisions, and determine the meaning or applicability of the terms of an agency action. The reviewing court shall —

· (1) compel agency action unlawfully withheld or unreasonably delayed; and

· (2) hold unlawful and set aside agency action, findings, and conclusions found to be —

  · (A) arbitrary, capricious, an abuse of discretion, or otherwise not in accordance with law;

  · (B) contrary to constitutional right, power, privilege, or immunity;

  · (C) in excess of statutory jurisdiction, authority, or limitations, or short of statutory right;

  · (D) without observance of procedure required by law;

  · (E) unsupported by substantial evidence in a case subject to sections 556 and 557 of this title or otherwise reviewed on the record of an agency hearing provided by statute; or

  · (F) unwarranted by the facts to the extent that the facts are subject to trial de novo by the reviewing court.

In making the foregoing determinations, the court shall review the whole record or those parts of it cited by a party, and due account shall be taken of the rule of prejudicial error.

de novo

trying a case as if no decision had been made

Before we discuss the terminology of the scope of review, please note that the terms cannot be defined with clarity and can more easily be described than defined. Courts often use overlapping definitions in attempting to deal with the scope of review, further adding to the confusion. With that in mind, think of the scope of review on a scale of 0 to 100. *De novo* review (see section 706(2)(F)) is complete, 100 percent review where the court *does* substitute its judgment for that of the agency. De novo is a complete review where the court rehears evidence and redecides the case. Consistent with the principles of judicial review and deference discussed previously, de novo review is very rare. A court's review of a Freedom of Information Request (FOIA) request is an example of de novo review. For FOIA requests, Congress wanted a court to do a complete review of the agency action to further the policy decision to keep agency documents open to the public. At the other end of the scale, 0 percent review is no review at all of agency action. This too is very rare. An example of no review at all is the decision of some state parole boards to deny a parole to an inmate. The inmate who is denied parole cannot appeal that decision to a court because the state legisla-

> The court to which the appeal goes is governed by statute. Sometimes the state or federal enabling act will specify the court. Jurisdictional statutes also designate where agency appeals are to be filed.

ture has mandated that the parole board, and not a court, shall have the final say on this issue. As another example, the decisions of a military base closure commission are not subject to judicial review. *Dalton v. Spector*, 511 U.S. 462 (1994).

Other categories within the scope of review such as arbitrary and capricious, abuse of discretion (706(2)(A)) and substantial evidence (706(2)(E)) fall somewhere between 0 percent and 100 percent. There are no fixed numbers that can be assigned. The substantial evidence standard is used in formal rulemaking and formal adjudications and is more demanding than the arbitrary and capricious standard which is used in informal proceedings.

The arbitrary and capricious standard has been defined as follows:

> Normally, an agency rule would be arbitrary and capricious if the agency has relied on factors which Congress has not intended it to consider, entirely failed to consider an important aspect of the

problem, offered an explanation for its decision that runs counter to the evidence before the agency, or is so implausible that it could not be ascribed to a difference in view or the product of agency expertise. *Motor Vehicle Mfrs. Ass'n v. State Farm,* 463 U.S. 29, 43 (1983).

thorough, probing, in-depth review . . . [the] inquiry into the facts is to be searching and careful, the ultimate standard of review is a narrow one. The court is not empowered to substitute its judgment for that of the agency. *Citizens to Preserve Overton Park, Inc. v. Volpe,* 401 U.S. 402, 415–416 (1971).

Substantial evidence can be described as follows:

It means such relevant evidence as a reasonable mind might accept as adequate to support a conclusion. *Universal Camera Corp. v. N.L.R.B.,* 340 U.S. 474, 477 (1951).

If you are still not clear after reading the preceding, do not be alarmed. The standards can overlap, are incapable of precision, and have therefore caused confusion, even with judges. In some state courts, the scope of review is based upon what is called a clearly erroneous standard. Under the clearly erroneous standard, the court can only reverse if it is firmly convinced that the agency's findings of fact were wrong or if the court is left with the firm and definite conviction that a mistake was made. For a student dealing with such terms as "arbitrary and capricious," "abuse of discretion," and "substantial evidence," it might be best to think of the court's review as follows: *If an agency's action in finding facts and reaching conclusions is reasonable, it will not be overturned.* The reasonableness standard keeps intact the mandates of judicial review, which are that courts are not to substitute their judgment for that of the agency but can reverse an agency in the interest of fairness if significant errors are made by the agency.

Note also that when reviewing the agency actions, the court is limited to reviewing the record that has been established at the agency. The record is all the evidence that the agency relied on to reach its decision. Even if a court uses judicial review to overturn a decision of the agency, the court in most instances will remand the case back to the agency so that the agency can reconsider its action and address the concerns of the court. On remand the agency might very well reach the same conclusion or might reach a different result, but either way the court has put the agency back on the proper path. That proper path involves making sure that the agency is furthering the intent of the legislative body that established the system of administrative law. See Exhibit 6-7, which illustrates the varying standards of judicial review.

Exhibit 6-7

Degree of Judicial Review/Review of Agency's Actions

	100% REVIEW	BETWEEN 100% AND 0% REVIEW, NO FIXED PERCENTAGE		0% REVIEW
Types of Review	De novo	Arbitrary and capricious or abuse of discretion	Substantial evidence	No review at all
Description	Complete review, essentially a retrial of the case. The court can substitute its judgment for that of the agency.	Agency must have articulated a rational connection between the facts found and the choice made. A rough, probing, in-depth review. The inquiry into the facts is to be searching and careful; the ultimate standard of review is a narrow one. The court is not empowered to substitute its judgment for that of the agency.	Evidence must be sufficient to support the conclusion of a reasonable person. Such relevant evidence as a reasonable mind might accept as adequate to support a conclusion.	There is no review. The agency decision stands.
Examples	FOIA requests	Informal rulemaking	Formal rulemaking	If the statute precludes

Exhibit 6-7 (Continued)

		Informal adjudication	Formal adjudication Rulemaking by the FTC and CPSC	review, if the action is committed to agency discretion, and there are no constitutional issues.
Frequency of Use	Rare	Most often used	Used sparingly	Rare

Questions of Law: High standard of review.
Whether the agency has violated the Constitution:

   a. Procedural due process

   b. Substantive due process

   c. Other constitutional issues

   Chevron deference—whether the agency has exceeded its power or misinterpreted the statute under which it operates

Judicial Review of Agency Inaction

A court gives much discretion to agency decisions *not* to act and is very reluctant to use judicial review in order to force an agency to act. A case that illustrates this point is *Heckler v. Chaney*, 470 U.S. 821 (1985). (See excerpt in Case Law at the end of the chapter.) In *Heckler*, the FDA refused to take any action against states that used drugs that had not been proven "safe and effective" for the purpose of carrying out the death penalty by lethal injection. The suit was filed by inmates who would be subjected to the lethal injection. The Court, in ruling on the FDA's decision not to act, stated that such agency decisions are presumed to be unreviewable. The Court recognized that the decision to take no action was a matter properly left to the discretion of agencies. A court should be reluctant to even hear a case that involves an agency decision not to act because the agencies must be free to balance a number of factors which are within the agency's expertise in the process of determining how to allocate their resources.

Barriers to Judicial Review

Statutes and various court-made doctrines place limits or barriers on the use of judicial review. These barriers will be discussed in the following sections.

- The statute precludes review
- The decision is committed to agency discretion
- Exhaustion of administrative remedies and ripeness
- Final agency action and deadlines to appeal
- Standing
- Primary jurisdiction

The Statute Precludes Review

Section 701(a)(1) of the Administrative Procedure Act states that there will be no judicial review if a statute so provides. If another statute such the enabling act expressly states "no judicial review," then this is controlling. However, even if a statute does not expressly preclude review, complete preclusion of judicial review is rare, and the Supreme Court has ruled that only if there is clear and convincing evidence should a court preclude judicial review. *Abbott Laboratories v. Gardner,* 387 U.S. 136 (1967). Where there is no express preclusion, the presumption of review is operative. Justice Souter's explanation of how Congress can preclude judicial review even without an express preclusion is very instructive:

> In sum, the text, structure, and purpose of the Act [Defense Base Closure and Realignment Act of 1990] clearly manifest congressional intent to confine the base-closing selection process within a narrow time frame before inevitable political opposition to an individual base closing could become overwhelming, to ensure that the decisions be implemented promptly, and to limit acceptance or rejection to a package of base closings as a whole, for the sake of political feasibility. While no one aspect of the Act, standing alone, would suffice to overcome the strong presumption in favor of judicial review, this structure (combined with the Act's provision for Executive and congressional review, . . .) can be understood no other way than as precluding judicial review of a base-closing decision under the scheme that Congress, out of its doleful experience, chose to enact. I conclude accordingly that the Act forecloses such judicial review. *Dalton v. Spector,* 511 U.S. 462, 483–484 (1994) (Souter, J., concurring).

Courts are more likely to agree that a statute precludes review in such areas as military affairs, foreign affairs, and national security matters. For example, in *Webster v. Doe*, 486 U.S. 592 (1988), the Supreme Court ruled that the decision of the Central Intelligence Agency (CIA) director to terminate an employee because of suspicion that he was a homosexual was precluded by statute and not subject to judicial review. The Court made similar rulings emphasizing national security concerns in *Snepp v. United States*, 444 U.S. 507 (1980) (concerning authorization of a book written by a former CIA employee), and in *Department of the Navy v. Egan*, 484 U.S. 518 (1988) (refusing to allow review of revocation of security clearance).

An example of a statute precluding judicial review at the state level can be found in Pennsylvania, where the decision of a parole board to deny parole is not subject to judicial review. *Barnhouse v. Pennsylvania Bd. of Probation and Parole*, 492 A.2d 1182 (1985).

Even if a statute precludes review, a court can still review issues of alleged constitutional violations which may include issues such as of freedom of speech and due process. In *Johnson v. Robison*, 415 U.S. 361 (1974), the Court ruled that a statute that barred judicial review of decisions of the Veterans Administration did not bar a review of the constitutional issues (freedom of religion) raised concerning a person's status as a conscientious objector.

The Decision Is Committed to Agency Discretion

Section 701(a)(2) of the Administrative Procedure Act and many provisions of state law limit judicial review by stating that judicial review is applicable except to the extent that statutes preclude judicial review or the agency action is committed to agency discretion. As noted in *Webster v. Doe* (the decision of the CIA director to terminate an employee not subject to judicial review), a statute can preclude judicial review. *Webster* also stands for the principle that if a decision of an agency is committed to agency discretion, that decision likewise is not subject to judicial review. *Heckler v. Chaney* (FDA decision not to take enforcement action against states that did not test drugs used in lethal injection not subject to judicial review) can likewise be viewed as a decision committed to the discretion of the agency. In *Barnhouse v. Pennsylvania Bd. of Probation and Parole*, a state legislature committed the decision to parole to agency discretion and thus precluded judicial review.

The Supreme Court in *Overton Park* and *State Farm* construed section 701(a)(1) in a way that still allows for judicial review even though the agency action was committed to agency discretion. In

Citizens to Preserve Overton Park, Inc. v. Volpe, 401 U.S. 402 (1971), the issue was the validity of the Secretary of Transportation's decision to fund a highway that went through a park. Although agreeing that such a decision was committed to the Secretary's discretion, the Court allowed review under the arbitrary and capricious standard of review to see if the decision was based on a consideration of relevant factors and whether there was a clear error of judgment. In *Motor Vehicle Mfrs. Ass'n v. State Farm,* 463 U.S. 29 (1983), the Court also allowed judicial review of the National Highway Transportation Safety Administration revocation of a rule that required new cars to have passive restraints (either automatic seat belts or air bags) by the year 1983, even though this decision was committed to agency discretion. Although committed to the agency's discretion, the Court ruled that NHTSA must *explain* how and why it used its discretion and explain why either air bags or automatic seat belts were no longer required. Although Section 701(a)(2) says there is no review of actions committed to agency discretion, under *Motor Vehicle* a court can still review the agency decision to make sure that there is a logical connection to the facts found and the choices made.

Exhaustion of Administrative Remedies and Ripeness

Before a court will even consider judicial review of an agency action, that action must be appealed all the way to the agency's highest decisionmaker. A person seeking to change a decision of an agency must *first* utilize the review procedures provided by the agency. If judicial review is sought while the agency action is still going on, the courts will dismiss for failure to exhaust administrative remedies. Review Exhibit 4-4 and note that if a claimant tried to take a Social Security claim into federal court before first going to the Appeals Council, the court would dismiss the case because of lack of ***exhaustion of administrative remedies***. Failure to exhaust the administrative remedies would make the case *not ripe* for a decision. Exhaustion of administrative remedies and ripeness can be seen as opposite sides of the same coin. One must exhaust administrative remedies for the case to be ripe to take to a court. If one has not exhausted the administrative remedies, the case is not ripe and cannot be reviewed in a court.

> The exhaustion requirement stresses both respect for agency prerogatives and principles of judicial economy by seeking to prevent premature interruption of the administrative process. The requirement prevents the frequent and deliberate flouting of administrative process [that] could weaken the effectiveness of an agency, and

exhaustion of administrative remedies
the principle that a court will not exercise judicial review before the review procedures inside the agency are completed

preserves agency autonomy by allowing it to exercise its discretion or apply its expertise. Requiring exhaustion also promotes judicial efficiency by avoiding needless repetition of administrative and judicial fact-finding, or by making possible a disposition by the agency that will obviate the need for judicial decision on this issue. *New York State Ophthalmological Soc. v. Bowen,* 854 F.2d 1379, 1387 (D.C. Cir. 1985).

Another kind of ***ripeness*** is illustrated in *Abbott Laboratories v. Gardner,* 387 U.S. 136 (1967), where a group of drug manufacturers sought review of a labeling regulation promulgated by the Commissioner of the FDA. However, the FDA had not yet instituted any enforcement action against the manufacturers. The manufacturers claimed that the FDA lacked statutory authority to impose the new labeling requirement; the FDA countered that the claim was not ripe for judicial review because there were no proceedings underway to enforce the regulation. The Court dealt with ripeness under a two-pronged test:

> Without undertaking to survey the intricacies of the ripeness doctrine it is fair to say that its basic rationale is to prevent the courts, through avoidance of premature adjudication, from entangling themselves in abstract disagreements over administrative policies, and also to protect the agencies from judicial interference until an administrative decision has been formalized and its effects felt in a concrete way by the challenging parties. The problem is best seen in a twofold aspect, requiring us to evaluate both the fitness of the issues for judicial decision and the hardship to the parties of withholding court consideration. *Abbot Laboratories,* 387 U.S. at 148–149.

In comparing exhaustion of administrative remedies and ripeness consider the following:

Exhaustion and ripeness advance substantially identical interests: (1) judicial economy (the proceedings before the agency may give the plaintiffs victory and thus moot the dispute); (2) agency autonomy (the agency's proceedings permit it to develop both a factual record and its own understanding and articulation of the issues); and (3) the proper functioning of the judiciary (judicial non-involvement until the conclusion of agency proceedings prevents the courts from becoming entangled in "abstract disagreements over administrative policies" unfit for judicial review). The clearest (and perhaps the only) difference between the doctrines is that exhaustion addresses the *plaintiff's* failure to employ available avenues of administrative relief, while ripeness addresses the status of *agency* activity, namely, the extent to which it has actually

ripeness

the doctrine whose basic rationale is to prevent the courts, through avoidance of premature adjudication, from entangling themselves in abstract disagreements over administrative policies and also to protect the agencies from judicial interference until an administrative decision has been formalized and its effects felt in a concrete way enforced its policies. *New York State Ophthalmological Soc. v. Bowen*, 854 F.2d 1379, 1392 (D.C. Cir.) (1988) (Williams, J., concurring in part and dissenting in part).

Final Agency Action and Deadlines to Appeal

Generally, only final actions can be appealed. Section 704 of the Administrative Procedure Act provides only final agency actions are subject to judicial review. This is true of most state statutes as well. An action is final when the decision-making process is completed so as to resolve the issue before the agency. For example, decisions by a military base closure commission were not reviewable by a court as a final decision. The commission had completed its work and had named the bases to be closed. However, because the ultimate decision on which bases to close rested with the president, there was no final agency action. *Dalton v. Specter*, 511 U.S. 462 (1994). In *FTC v. Standard Oil of California*, 449 U.S. 232 (1980), the FTC issued a complaint against major oil companies alleging that it had "reason to believe" that they were engaging in unfair methods of competition. When the issue was pending before an administrative law judge, the oil companies filed suit in federal court. The Court ruled that the FTC's issuance of the complaint was not:

> a definitive ruling or regulation. It had no legal force or practical effect upon [the oil companies'] daily business other than the dis-

Note that our discussion on exhaustion, ripeness, and finality is an overview of a very complex and interrelated series of issues. Our goal is to introduce you to the basic concepts. Courts themselves find it difficult to decide which doctrine to apply in a given case. For example, in the case of Ticor Title Insurance Co. v. FTC, 814 F.2d 731 (D.C. Cir. 1987), all three judges agreed that the court could not consider a decision of the FTC to initiate and prosecute complaints against various persons for engaging in unfair trade practices. However, one judge ruled that the reason was exhaustion of administrative remedies, one judged ruled that the reason was ripeness, and the third ruled that the reason was finality!

ruptions that accompany any major litigation. And immediate judicial review would serve neither efficiency nor enforcement of the Act. These pragmatic considerations counsel against the conclusion that the issuance of the complaint was final agency action. *FTC v. Standard Oil of California,* 449 U.S. at 243.

Once the agency's action becomes final, the appeal must be filed with the reviewing court within strict deadlines, which are usually 30 days. Failure to file on time is generally fatal to the appeal.

Standing

Standing focuses on whether the proper *person* is before the court. Parties must have a personal stake in the outcome of the case and a present or immediately threatened injury. That person must have a personal stake in the outcome of the case and an actual present or immediately threatened injury which would result from unlawful governmental conduct. In addition to suffering an injury-in-fact, the person before the court must be in the "zone of interest" sought to be protected by the statute under which the suit is brought. Compare this basic definition with the following cases.

Unions representing postal workers had no standing to challenge the Postal Service decision to allow private companies to deliver mail. The Court agreed that the unions may have suffered an injury-in-fact because the increased competition might cost jobs of postal workers. However, because the statute in question was passed to protect the interests of the public, the postal workers were not in the zone of interest and therefore had no standing to challenge the agency action. *Air Courier Conference of America v. American Postal Workers Union,* 498 U.S. 517 (1991).

A taxpayer who claimed that she was injured by the way the government taxes and spends will not have standing because this is a generalized grievance that is common to all taxpayers and better left for the electoral process. *Frothingham v. Mellon,* 262 U.S. 447 (1923).

The plaintiff could not challenge the CIA's refusal to publish its budget even though Article I, Sec. 9, cl.7 requires that "regular Statement and Account of the Receipts and Expenditures of all public Money shall be published from time to time." The plaintiff who claimed that the government acted in violation of this constitutional provision did not have standing because this was a generalized grievance about the conduct of government that all citizens possessed and was not personal to the plaintiff. *United States v. Richardson,* 418 U.S. 166 (1974).

standing
a person's right to bring a claim because he or she is directly affected by the issues raised

On the other hand, an esthetic interest can be the basis for standing. The interest to observe an animal species, *Japan Whaling Assn. v. American Cetacean Society,* 478 U.S. 221 (1986), and enjoy the beauty of a park or recreational area can be an injury-in-fact so as to justify standing, *Sierra Club v. Morton,* 405 U.S. 727 (1972). However, merely asserting "some day intentions without any descriptions of concrete plans, or indeed even any specifications of when the some day will be—do not support a finding of the actual or imminent injury" that the limitation of standing requires. *Lujan v. Defenders of Wildlife,* 504 U.S. 555, 564 (1992). The general rule is that a third party does not have standing to assert rights of persons not before the court; however, an association has standing to bring suit on behalf of its members if the members have standing in their own right and the members' participation is not required for the claim or relief requested. *Friends of the Earth v. Laidlaw,* 528 U.S. 167 (2000).

The Court discussed standing in the case of *Massachusetts v. EPA,* 127 S. Ct. 1438 (2007), the global warming case. In the case, various organizations and states sued to get the EPA to regulate greenhouse gases emitted from motor vehicles. The plaintiffs alleged that these emissions contribute to global warming. (The case is found in Appendix D.) The Court stated that there are three key elements of standing which were met in this case.

1. *Injury: A litigant must demonstrate that it has suffered a concrete and particularized injury that is either actual or imminent.* The Court found that a rise in sea levels associated with global warming has already harmed and will continue to harm Massachusetts.

2. *Causation: That the injury is fairly traceable to the defendant and that it is likely that a favorable decision will result.* The Court noted that the EPA did not dispute the existence of a causal connection between gas emissions and global warming. However, the EPA argued that there was no realistic possibility that the relief sought would mitigate global climate change because of predicted increases in greenhouse gas emissions from countries such as China and India. These increases would likely offset any marginal domestic decrease. The Court countered that the plaintiffs are not required to show that regulating gases would fix the entire problem but only show that this is a step in the right direction. Reducing U.S. emissions is such a step in light of the fact that the U.S. transportation sector emits an enormous quantity of greenhouse gases.

3. *Remedy/Redressibiliy: That a court has the ability to redress that injury; that is, to provide a remedy.* Even though regulating greenhouse gases will not by itself reverse global warming and even though China and India are increasing greenhouse emissions, a reduction in domestic emissions would slow the pace of global emissions. Therefore, redressibility was met because the risk of global warming would be reduced to some extent if the plaintiffs received the relief they seek.

Primary Jurisdiction

We have noted that a primary advantage of agencies is the level of technical expertise they develop which equips them to better solve society's problems. The doctrine of ***primary jurisdiction*** implements this agency advantage by allowing a court to decline to resolve an issue when that issue involves technical matters, such as chemical properties of particular products or the formulation of complex safety standards. Primary jurisdiction comes into play when *both* the court and the agency have jurisdiction to hear the case but the court defers to the agency to make the decision precisely because the agency's expertise will better settle the issue in dispute.

Other Methods of Judicial Control—Lawsuits

Persons who are harmed by agency decisions may be able to sue for money damages. With some exceptions, individuals can sue the federal government for the wrongful acts of its employees committed within the scope of their employment. Under the Federal Torts Claims Act (FTCA), the federal government would be liable in the same way that a private employer would be under the law of the state where the wrong occurred. For example, if an employee of a federal agency commits negligence that causes injury, the injured party could bring a suit against the federal government after first allowing the agency a chance to settle the matter. Generally, suits under the FTCA cannot be brought for such intentional acts as assault, battery, or false imprisonment unless these acts are done by a law enforcement or investigative officer. The FTCA also exempts the government from damages for any claim "based upon the exercise or performance or the failure to exercise or perform a discretionary function or duty on the part of a federal agency or an employee of the Government, whether or not the discretion involved be abused." A discretionary function would include high-level policy decisions concerning implementation of regulations. Many states have

primary jurisdiction
the principle that even if a court has the power to hear a case, if the case involves issues that are better decided by an administrative agency, the court will give the agency the first opportunity to resolve the issue

passed laws similar to the FTCA which regulate suits against state governments.

Under 42 U.S.C. Section 1983 of the federal statutes, state and local officials can be sued for violations of the federal Constitution. Section 1983 makes state or local government officials liable for actions that violate rights protected under the federal Constitution or federal statutes. For example, if prison officials put 20 prisoners into a cell designed for two people (cruel and unusual punishment under the Eight Amendment) or if a local police officer shot and killed an unarmed fleeing suspect (depriving a person of life under the Fourteenth Amendment), a suit under section 1983 could be filed.

Federal officials can also be sued for violation of the Constitution, *Bivens v. Six Unknown Named Agents of the Federal Bureau of Narcotics,* 403 U.S. 388 (1970). (See excerpt in Case Law at the end of the chapter.)

In *Bivens,* federal agents searched and arrested in their home members of an innocent family whom the federal agents believed to be drug dealers. The family could not sue under Section 1983 because that statute applies only to state and local officials. The family based its claim on the Fourth Amendment's prohibition against unreasonable search and seizures. The Court ruled that the cause of action could be based directly on the Fourth Amendment to the Constitution; a federal statute was not required for the courts to award money damages. The Supreme Court has been reluctant to extend the principles of *Bivens* to other settings. For example, in *Schweiker v. Chilichy,* 487 U.S. 412 (1988) (see excerpt in Case Law at the end of the chapter), plaintiffs were improperly denied Social Security disability benefits. Although the plaintiffs eventually were awarded the benefits retroactively, they sued claiming that their denials amounted to violations of due process. The Court framed the issue as follows:

> Whether a *Bivens* remedy should be implied for alleged due process violations in the denial of social security disability benefits.

The plaintiffs urged the Court, consistent with *Bivens,* to allow a cause of action for emotional distress. In rejecting the claim, the Court noted that the courts must be hesitant to create a new cause of action where Congress has created an administrative structure as detailed as the Social Security system and stated:

> When the design of a Government program suggests that Congress has provided what it considers adequate remedial mechanisms for constitutional violations that may occur in the course of its administration, we have not created additional *Bivens* remedies. *Schweiker v. Chilicky,* 487 U.S. at 424.

Congress and many state legislatures have enacted provisions in their statutes that authorize private individuals or groups to bring a lawsuit against an agency for enforcement of agency regulations. These citizen suits are common in environmental statutes. Examples of statutes that allow for such suits include the Clean Water Act, Clean Air Act, Safe Drinking Water Act, and Endangered Species Act. The citizen suit is intended to supplement the enforcement of statutes and can only be brought if federal or state authorities are not diligently prosecuting the action upon which the citizen suit is based.

CASE LAW

GOLDBERG v. KELLY
397 U.S. 254 (1970).

BRENNAN, J.:

The question for decision is whether a State that terminates public assistance payments to a particular recipient without affording him the opportunity for an evidentiary hearing prior to termination denies the recipient procedural due process in violation of the Due Process Clause of the Fourteenth Amendment.

[Recipients of the federally-assisted Aid to Families with Dependent Children (AFDC) or New York's general relief program sued in federal District Court. They alleged that New York state and city officials administering these programs terminated their aid without prior notice and hearing, thereby denying them due process of law.

The various plaintiffs complained that they had been dropped from the rolls for illegal or incorrect reasons. One plaintiff was terminated because she refused to cooperate with the city in suing her estranged husband; she contended that the cooperation requirement did not apply to her case. Another was dropped because he refused to accept counseling for drug addiction; he claimed he did not use drugs. A third was dropped for a factually erroneous reason; she fainted from lack of food while waiting at the welfare office to which her files had been transferred. Later she and her children were forced to go to the emergency room because of eating spoiled food donated by a neighbor. Her aid was reinstated after the suit was filed. Brief for Appellees, 83–84]

(*Continued*)

[Under recently adopted procedural rules] a caseworker who has doubts about the recipient's continued eligibility must first discuss them with the recipient. If the caseworker concludes that the recipient is no longer eligible, he recommends termination of aid to a unit supervisor. If the latter concurs, he sends the recipient a letter stating the reasons for proposing to terminate aid and notifying him that within seven days he may request that a higher official review the record, and may support the request with a written statement prepared personally or with the aid of an attorney or other person. If the reviewing official affirms the determination of ineligibility, aid is stopped immediately and the recipient is informed by letter of the reasons for the action. Appellees' challenge to this procedure emphasizes the absence of any provisions for the personal appearance of the recipient before the reviewing official, for oral presentation of evidence, and for confrontation and cross-examination of adverse witnesses. However, the letter does inform the recipient that he may request a post-termination "fair hearing." This is a proceeding before an independent state hearing officer at which the recipient may appear personally, offer oral evidence, confront and cross-examine the witnesses against him, and have a record made of the hearing. If the recipient prevails at the "fair hearing" he is paid all funds erroneously withheld. A recipient whose aid is not restored by a "fair hearing" decision may have judicial review. . . .

I

The constitutional issue to be decided, therefore, is the narrow one whether the Due Process Clause requires that the recipient be afforded an evidentiary hearing *before* the termination of benefits. The District Court held that only a pre-termination evidentiary hearing would satisfy the constitutional command, and rejected the argument of the state and city officials that the combination of the post-termination "fair hearing" with the informal pre-termination review disposed of all due process claims. The court said: "While post-termination review is relevant, there is one overpowering fact which controls here. By hypothesis, a welfare recipient is destitute, without funds or assets. . . . Suffice it to say that to cut off a welfare recipient in the face of . . . brutal need without a prior hearing of some sort is unconscionable, unless overwhelming considerations justify it." The court rejected the argument that the need to protect the public's tax revenues supplied the requisite "overwhelming consideration." "Against the justified desire to protect public funds must be weighed the individual's overpowering need in this unique situation not to be wrongfully deprived of assistance. . . . While the problem of additional expense must be kept in mind, it does not justify denying a hearing meeting the ordinary standards of due process. Under all the circumstances, we hold that due process requires an adequate hearing before termination of welfare benefits, and the fact that there is a later constitutionally fair proceeding does not alter the result." . . . .

Appellant does not contend that procedural due process is not applicable to the termination of welfare benefits. Such benefits are a matter of statutory entitlement for persons qualified to receive them.[1] Their termination involves state action that adjudicates important rights. The constitutional challenge cannot be answered by an argument that public assistance benefits are a "privilege" and not a "right." Relevant constitutional restraints apply as much to the withdrawal of public assistance benefits as to disqualification for unemployment compensation, . . . or to discharge from public employment. . . . The extent to which procedural due process must be afforded the recipient is influenced by the extent to which he may be "condemned to suffer grievous loss," *Joint Anti–Fascist Refugee Committee v. McGrath*, 341 U.S. 123 (1951) (Frankfurter, J., concurring), and depends upon whether the recipient's interest in avoiding that loss outweighs the governmental interest in summary adju-

---

[1] It may be realistic today to regard welfare entitlements as more like "property" than a "gratuity." Much of the existing wealth in this country takes the form of rights that do not fall within traditional common-law concepts of property. It has been aptly noted that "[s]ociety today is built around entitlement. The automobile dealer has his franchise, the doctor and lawyer their professional licenses, the worker his union membership, contract, and pension rights, the executive his contract and stock options; all are devices to aid security and independence. Many of the most important of these entitlements now flow from government: subsidies to farmers and businessmen, routes for airlines and channels for television stations; long term contracts for defense, space, and education; social security pensions for individuals. Such sources of security, whether private or public, are no longer regarded as luxuries or gratuities; to the recipients they are essentials, fully deserved, and in no sense a form of charity. It is only the poor whose entitlements, although recognized by public policy, have not been effectively enforced." Reich, Individual Rights and Social Welfare: The Emerging Legal Issues, 74 Yale L.J. 1245, 1255 (1965). See also Reich, The New Property, 73 Yale L.J. 733 (1964).

(*Continued*)

dication. Accordingly, as we said in *Cafeteria & Restaurant Workers Union v. McElroy*, 367 U.S. 886 (1961), "consideration of what procedures due process may require under any given set of circumstances must begin with a determination of the precise nature of the government function involved as well as of the private interest that has been affected by governmental action."

It is true, of course, that some governmental benefits may be administratively terminated without affording the recipient a pre-termination evidentiary hearing.[2] But we agree with the District Court that when welfare is discontinued, only a pre-termination evidentiary hearing provides the recipient with procedural due process.

For qualified recipients, welfare provides the means to obtain essential food, clothing, housing, and medical care. Thus the crucial factor in this context—a factor not present in the case of the black-listed government contractor, the discharged government employee, the taxpayer denied a tax exemption, or virtually anyone else whose governmental entitlements are ended—is that termination of aid pending resolution of a controversy over eligibility may deprive an *eligible* recipient of the very means by which to live while he waits. Since he lacks independent resources, his situation becomes immediately desperate. His need to concentrate upon finding the means for daily subsistence, in turn, adversely affects his ability to seek redress from the welfare bureaucracy.

Moreover, important governmental interests are promoted by affording recipients a pre-termination evidentiary hearing. From its founding the Nation's basic commitment has been to foster the dig-

---

[2]One Court of Appeals has stated: "In a wide variety of situations, it has long been recognized that where harm to the public is threatened, and the private interest infringed is reasonably deemed to be of less importance, an official body can take summary action pending a later hearing." *R.A. Holman & Co. v. SEC*, 299 F.2d 127 (1962) (suspension of exemption from stock registration requirement). See also, for example, *Ewing v. Mytinger & Casselberry, Inc.*, 339 U.S. 594 (1950) (seizure of mislabeled vitamin product); *North American Cold Storage Co. v. Chicago*, 211 U.S. 306 (1908) (seizure of food not fit for human use); . . . In *Cafeteria & Restaurant Workers Union v. McElroy*, supra, summary dismissal of a public employee was upheld because "[i]n [its] proprietary military capacity, the Federal Government . . . has traditionally exercised unfettered control," and because the case involved the Government's "dispatch of its own internal affairs."

nity and well-being of all persons within its borders. . . . Welfare, by meeting the basic demands of subsistence, can help bring within the reach of the poor the same opportunities that are available to others to participate meaningfully in the life of the community. At the same time, welfare guards against the societal malaise that may flow from a widespread sense of unjustified frustration and insecurity. Public assistance, then, is not mere charity, but a means to "promote the general Welfare, and secure the Blessings of Liberty to ourselves and our Posterity." The same governmental interests that counsel the provision of welfare, counsel as well its uninterrupted provision to those eligible to receive it; pre-termination evidentiary hearings are indispensable to that end.

Appellant does not challenge the force of these considerations but argues that they are outweighed by countervailing governmental interests in conserving fiscal and administrative resources. These interests, the argument goes, justify the delay of any evidentiary hearing until after discontinuance of the grants. Summary adjudication protects the public fisc by stopping payments promptly upon discovery of reason to believe that a recipient is no longer eligible. Since most terminations are accepted without challenge, summary adjudication also conserves both the fisc and administrative time and energy by reducing the number of evidentiary hearings actually held.

We agree with the District Court, however, that these governmental interests are not overriding in the welfare context. The requirement of a prior hearing doubtless involves some greater expense, and the benefits paid to ineligible recipients pending decision at the hearing probably cannot be recouped, since these recipients are likely to be judgment-proof. But the State is not without weapons to minimize these increased costs. Much of the drain on fiscal and administrative resources can be reduced by developing procedures for prompt pre-termination hearings and by skillful use of personnel and facilities. Indeed, the very provision for a post-termination evidentiary hearing in New York's Home Relief program is itself cogent evidence that the State recognizes the primacy of the public interest in correct eligibility determinations and therefore in the provision of procedural safeguards. Thus, the interest of the eligible recipient in uninterrupted receipt of public assistance, coupled with the State's interest that his payments not be erroneously terminated, clearly outweighs the State's competing concern to prevent any increase in its fiscal and administrative burdens. . . .

(Continued)

II

We also agree with the District Court, however, that the pre-termination hearing need not take the form of a judicial or quasi-judicial trial. We bear in mind that the statutory "fair hearing" will provide the recipient with a full administrative review.[3] Accordingly, the pre-termination hearing has one function only: to produce an initial determination of the validity of the welfare department's grounds for discontinuance of payments in order to protect a recipient against an erroneous termination of his benefits. Thus, a complete record and a comprehensive opinion, which would serve primarily to facilitate judicial review and to guide future decisions, need not be provided at the pre-termination stage. We recognize, too, that both welfare authorities and recipients have an interest in relatively speedy resolution of questions of eligibility, that they are used to dealing with one another informally, and that some welfare departments have very burdensome caseloads. These considerations justify the limitation of the pre-termination hearing to minimum procedural safeguards, adapted to the particular characteristics of welfare recipients, and to the limited nature of the controversies to be resolved. We wish to add that we, no less than the dissenters, recognize the importance of not imposing upon the States or the Federal Government in this developing field of law any procedural requirements beyond those demanded by rudimentary due process. . . .

The hearing must be "at a meaningful time and in a meaningful manner." In the present context these principles require that a recipient have timely and adequate notice detailing the reasons for a proposed termination, and an effective opportunity to defend by confronting any adverse witnesses and by presenting his own arguments and evidence orally. These rights are important in cases such as those before us, where recipients have challenged proposed terminations as resting on incorrect or misleading factual premises or on misapplication of rules or policies to the facts of particular cases.[4]

---

[3] Due process does not, of course, require two hearings. If, for example, a State simply wishes to continue benefits until after a "fair" hearing there will be no need for a preliminary hearing.

[4] This case presents no question requiring our determination whether due process requires only an opportunity for written submission, or an opportunity both for written submission and oral argument, where there are no factual issues in dispute or where the application of the rule of law is not interwined with factual issues.

We are not prepared to say that the seven-day notice currently provided by New York City is constitutionally insufficient per se, although there may be cases where fairness would require that a longer time be given. Nor do we see any constitutional deficiency in the content or form of the notice. New York employs both a letter and a personal conference with a caseworker to inform a recipient of the precise questions raised about his continued eligibility. Evidently the recipient is told the legal and factual bases for the Department's doubts. This combination is probably the most effective method of communicating with recipients.

The city's procedures presently do not permit recipients to appear personally with or without counsel before the official who finally determines continued eligibility. Thus a recipient is not permitted to present evidence to that official orally, or to confront or cross-examine adverse witnesses. These omissions are fatal to the constitutional adequacy of the procedures.

The opportunity to be heard must be tailored to the capacities and circumstances of those who are to be heard. It is not enough that a welfare recipient may present his position to the decisionmaker in writing or secondhand through his caseworker. Written submissions are an unrealistic option for most recipients, who lack the educational attainment necessary to write effectively and who cannot obtain professional assistance. Moreover, written submissions do not afford the flexibility of oral presentations; they do not permit the recipient to mold his argument to the issues the decisionmaker appears to regard as important. Particularly where credibility and veracity are at issue, as they must be in many termination proceedings, written submissions are a wholly unsatisfactory basis for decision. The secondhand presentation to the decisionmaker by the caseworker has its own deficiencies; since the caseworker usually gathers the facts upon which the charge of ineligibility rests, the presentation of the recipient's side of the controversy cannot safely be left to him. Therefore a recipient must be allowed to state his position orally. Informal procedures will suffice; in this context due process does not require a particular order of proof or mode of offering evidence.

In almost every setting where important decisions turn on questions of fact, due process requires an opportunity to confront and cross-examine adverse witnesses. . . . Welfare recipients must therefore be given an opportunity to confront and cross-examine the witnesses relied on by the department.

(Continued)

"The right to be heard would be, in many cases, of little avail if it did not comprehend the right to be heard by counsel." We do not say that counsel must be provided at the pre-termination hearing, but only that the recipient must be allowed to retain an attorney if he so desires. Counsel can help delineate the issues, present the factual contentions in an orderly manner, conduct cross-examination, and generally safeguard the interests of the recipient. We do not anticipate that this assistance will unduly prolong or otherwise encumber the hearing. . . . Finally, the decisionmaker's conclusion as to a recipient's eligibility must rest solely on the legal rules and evidence adduced at the hearing. To demonstrate compliance with this elementary requirement, the decisionmaker should state the reasons for his determination and indicate the evidence he relied on, though his statement need not amount to a full opinion or even formal findings of fact and conclusions of law. And, of course, an impartial decisionmaker is essential. We agree with the District Court that prior involvement in some aspects of a case will not necessarily bar a welfare official from acting as a decisionmaker. He should not, however, have participated in making the determination under review.

Affirmed.

MR. JUSTICE BLACK, dissenting. . . .

The Court [today] relies upon the Fourteenth Amendment and in effect says that failure of the government to pay a promised charitable instalment to an individual deprives that individual of *his own property*, in violation of the Due Process Clause of the Fourteenth Amendment. It somewhat strains credulity to say that the government's promise of charity to an individual is property belonging to that individual when the government denies that the individual is honestly entitled to receive such a payment.

I would have little, if any, objection to the majority's decision in this case if it were written as the report of the House Committee on Education and Labor, but as an opinion ostensibly resting on the language of the Constitution I find it woefully deficient. Once the verbiage is pared away it is obvious that this Court today adopts the views of the District Court "that to cut off a welfare recipient in the face of . . . 'brutal need' without a prior hearing of some sort is unconscionable," and therefore, says the Court, unconstitutional. The majority reaches this result by a process of weighing "the recipient's interest in avoiding" the termination of welfare benefits against "the governmental interest in summary adjudication." Today's balancing act requires a "pre-termination evidentiary hearing," yet there is nothing that indicates what tomorrow's balance will be. Although the majority attempts to bolster its decision with limited quotations from prior cases, it is obvious that today's result does not depend on the language of the Constitution itself or the principles of other decisions, but solely on the collective judgment of the majority as to what would be a fair and humane procedure in this case. . . .

The Court apparently feels that this decision will benefit the poor and needy. In my judgment the eventual result will be just the opposite. While today's decision requires only an administrative, evidentiary hearing, the inevitable logic of the approach taken will lead to constitutionally imposed, time-consuming delays of a full adversary process of administrative and judicial review. In the next case the welfare recipients are bound to argue that cutting off benefits before judicial review of the agency's decision is also a denial of due process. Since, by hypothesis, termination of aid at that point may still "deprive an *eligible* recipient of the very means by which to live while he waits," I would be surprised if the weighing process did not compel the conclusion that termination without full judicial review would be unconscionable. After all, at each step, as the majority seems to feel, the issue is only one of weighing the government's pocketbook against the actual survival of the recipient, and surely that balance must always tip in favor of the individual. Similarly today's decision requires only the opportunity to have the benefit of counsel at the administrative hearing, but it is difficult to believe that the same reasoning process would not require the appointment of counsel, for otherwise the right to counsel is a meaningless one since these people are too poor to hire their own advocates. Thus the end result of today's decision may well be that the government, once it decides to give welfare benefits, cannot reverse that decision until the recipient has had the benefits of full administrative and judicial review, including, of course, the opportunity to present his case to this Court. Since this process will usually entail a delay of several years, the inevitable result of such a constitutionally imposed burden will be that the government will not put a claimant on the rolls initially until it has made an exhaustive investigation to determine his eligibility. While this Court will perhaps have insured that no needy person will be taken off the rolls without a full "due process" proceeding, it will also have insured that many will never get on the rolls, or at least that they will remain destitute during the lengthy proceedings followed to determine initial eligibility.

(*Continued*)

For the foregoing reasons I dissent from the Court's holding. The operation of a welfare state is a new experiment for our Nation. For this reason, among others, I feel that new experiments in carrying out a welfare program should not be frozen into our constitutional structure. They should be left, as are other legislative determinations, to the Congress and the legislatures that the people elect to make our laws.

MR. CHIEF JUSTICE BURGER, with whom MR. JUSTICE BLACK joins, dissenting. . . .

The Court's action today seems another manifestation of the now familiar constitutionalizing syndrome: once some presumed flaw is observed, the Court then eagerly accepts the invitation to find a constitutionally "rooted" remedy. If no provision is explicit on the point, it is then seen as "implicit" or commanded by the vague and nebulous concept of "fairness." . . . .

I would wait until more is known about the problems before fashioning solutions in the rigidity of a constitutional holding.

By allowing the administrators to deal with these problems we leave room for adjustments if, for example, it is found that a particular hearing process is too costly. The history of the complexity of the administrative process followed by judicial review as we have seen it for the past 30 years should suggest the possibility that new layers of procedural protection may become an intolerable drain on the very funds earmarked for food, clothing, and other living essentials.[5]

Aside from the administrative morass that today's decision could well create, the Court should also be cognizant of the legal precedent it may be setting. The majority holding raises intriguing possibilities concerning the right to a hearing at other stages in the welfare process which affect the total sum of assistance, even though the action taken might fall short of complete termination. For example, does the Court's holding embrace welfare reductions or denial of increases as opposed to terminations, or decisions concerning initial applications or requests for special assistance? The Court supplies no distinguishable considerations and leaves these crucial questions unanswered.

---

[5]We are told, for example, that Los Angeles County alone employs 12,500 welfare workers to process grants to 500,000 people under various welfare programs. The record does not reveal how many more employees will be required to give this newly discovered "due process" to every welfare recipient whose payments are terminated for fraud or other factors of ineligibility or those whose initial applications are denied.

Reprinted from Asimow, M.; Bonfield, A.; and Levin, R. State and Federal Administrative Law, 2nd ed. ©1998, with permission of Thomson West.

CASE LAW

MATHEWS v. ELDRIDGE
424 U.S. 319 (1976).

POWELL, J.:

The issue in this case is whether the Due Process Clause of the Fifth Amendment requires that prior to the termination of Social Security disability benefit payments the recipient be afforded an opportunity for an evidentiary hearing.... Respondent Eldridge was first awarded benefits in June 1968. In March 1972, he received a questionnaire from the state agency charged with monitoring his medical condition. Eldridge completed the questionnaire, indicating that his condition had not improved and identifying the medical sources, including physicians, from whom he had received treatment recently. The state agency then obtained reports from his physician and a psychiatric consultant. After considering these reports and other information in his file the agency informed Eldridge by letter that it had made a tentative determination that his disability had ceased in May 1972. The letter included a statement of reasons for the proposed termination of benefits, and advised Eldridge that he might request reasonable time in which to obtain and submit additional information pertaining to his condition.

In his written response, Eldridge disputed one characterization of his medical condition and indicated that the agency already had enough evidence to establish his disability. The state agency then made its final determination that he had ceased to be disabled in May 1972. This determination was accepted by the Social Security Administration (SSA), which notified Eldridge in July that his benefits would terminate after that month. The notification also advised him of his right to seek reconsideration by the state agency of this initial determination within six months.

Instead of requesting reconsideration Eldridge commenced this action challenging the constitutional validity of the administrative procedures established by the Secretary of Health, Education, and Welfare for assessing whether there exists a continuing disability. He sought an immediate reinstatement of benefits pending a hearing on the issue of his disability.... In support of his contention that due process requires a pre-termination hearing, Eldridge relied exclusively upon this Court's decision in *Goldberg v. Kelly*....

(Continued)

A

Procedural due process imposes constraints on governmental decisions which deprive individuals of "liberty" or "property" interests within the meaning of the Due Process Clause of the Fifth or Fourteenth Amendment. The Secretary does not contend that procedural due process is in applicable to terminations of Social Security disability benefits. He recognizes . . . that the interest of an individual in continued receipt of these benefits is a statutorily created "property" interest protected by the Fifth Amendment. Rather, the Secretary contends that the existing administrative procedures, detailed below, provide all the process that is constitutionally due before a recipient can be deprived of that interest.

This Court consistently has held that some form of hearing is required before an individual is finally deprived of a property interest. The "right to be heard before being condemned to suffer grievous loss of any kind, even though it may not involve the stigma and hardships of a criminal conviction, is a principle basic to our society." The fundamental requirement of due process is the opportunity to be heard "at a meaningful time and in a meaningful manner."

In recent years this Court increasingly has had occasion to consider the extent to which due process requires an evidentiary hearing prior to the deprivation of some type of property interest even if such a hearing is provided thereafter. In only one case, *Goldberg v. Kelly*, has the Court held that a hearing closely approximating a judicial trial is necessary. In other cases requiring some type of pretermination hearing as a matter of constitutional right the Court has spoken sparingly about the requisite procedures. . . .

These decisions underscore the truism that "[d]ue process, unlike some legal rules, is not a technical conception with a fixed content unrelated to time, place and circumstances." "[D]ue process is flexible and calls for such procedural protections as the particular situation demands."

Accordingly, resolution of the issue whether the administrative procedures provided here are constitutionally sufficient requires analysis of the governmental and private interests that are affected. More precisely, our prior decisions indicate that identification of the specific dictates of due process generally requires consideration of three distinct factors: First, the private interest that will be affected by the official action; second, the risk *of an erroneous deprivation of such interest through the procedures used, and the probable value, if any, of additional or substitute procedural safeguards;* and finally, the Government's interest, including the function involved and the fiscal and administrative burdens that the additional or substitute procedural requirement would entail.

We turn first to a description of the procedures for the termination of Social Security disability benefits and thereafter consider the factors bearing upon the constitutional adequacy of these procedures.

B

The disability insurance program is administered jointly by state and federal agencies. State agencies make the initial determination whether a disability exists, when it began, and when it ceased.... In order to establish initial and continued entitlement to disability benefits a worker must demonstrate that he is unable

> to engage in any substantial gainful activity by reason of any medically determinable physical or mental impairment which can be expected to result in death or which has lasted or can be expected to last for a continuous period of not less than 12 months....

To satisfy this test the worker bears a continuing burden of showing, by means of "medically acceptable clinical and laboratory diagnostic techniques," that he has a physical or mental impairment of such severity that

> "he is not only unable to do his previous work but cannot, considering his age, education, and work experience, engage in any other kind of substantial gainful work which exists in the national economy, regardless of whether such work exists in the immediate area in which he lives, or whether a specific job vacancy exists for him, or whether he would be hired if he applied for work."

.... The continuing-eligibility investigation is made by a state agency acting through a "team" consisting of a physician and a non-medical person trained in disability evaluation. The agency periodically communicates with the disabled worker, usually by mail—in which case he is sent a detailed questionnaire—or by telephone, and requests information concerning his present condition, including current medical restrictions and sources of treatment, and any additional information that he considers relevant to his continued entitlement to benefits. Information regarding the recipient's current condition is also obtained from his sources of medical treatment.

(Continued)

If there is a conflict between the information provided by the beneficiary and that obtained from medical sources such as his physician, or between two sources of treatment, the agency may arrange for an examination by an independent consulting physician. Whenever the agency's tentative assessment of the beneficiary's condition differs from his own assessment, the beneficiary is informed that benefits may be terminated, provided a summary of the evidence upon which the proposed determination to terminate is based, and afforded an opportunity to review the medical reports and other evidence in his case file. He also may respond in writing and submit additional evidence. The state agency then makes its final determination, which is reviewed by an examiner in the SSA Bureau of Disability Insurance. If, as is usually the case, the SSA accepts the agency determination it notifies the recipient in writing, informing him of the reasons for the decision, and of his right to seek *de novo* reconsideration by the state agency. Upon acceptance by the SSA, benefits are terminated effective two months after the month in which medical recovery is found to have occurred.

If the recipient seeks reconsideration by the state agency and the determination is adverse, the SSA reviews the reconsideration determination and notifies the recipient of the decision. He then has a right to an evidentiary hearing before an SSA administrative law judge.

The hearing is nonadversary, and the SSA is not represented by counsel. As at all prior and subsequent stages of the administrative process, however, the claimant may be represented by counsel or other spokesmen. If this hearing results in an adverse decision, the claimant is entitled to request discretionary review by the SSA Appeals Council, and finally may obtain judicial review.[1]

Should it be determined at any point after termination of benefits, that the claimant's disability extended beyond the date of cessation initially established, the worker is entitled to retroactive payments. . . . If, on the other hand, a beneficiary receives any payments to which he is later determined not to be entitled, the statute authorizes the Secretary to attempt to recoup these funds in specified circumstances.

C

Despite the elaborate character of the administrative procedures provided by the Secretary, the courts below held them to be constitu-

---

[1] Unlike all prior levels of review, which are *de novo*, the district court is required to treat findings of fact as conclusive if supported by substantial evidence.

tionally inadequate, concluding that due process requires an evidentiary hearing prior to termination. In light of the private and governmental interests at stake here and the nature of the existing procedures, we think this was error.

Since a recipient whose benefits are terminated is awarded full retroactive relief if he ultimately prevails, his sole interest is in the uninterrupted receipt of this source of income pending final administrative decision on his claim. His potential injury is thus similar in nature to that of the welfare recipient in *Goldberg*. . . .

Only in *Goldberg* has the Court held that due process requires an evidentiary hearing prior to a temporary deprivation. It was emphasized there that welfare assistance is given to persons on the very margin of subsistence:

> "The crucial factor in this context—a factor not present in the case of . . . virtually anyone else whose governmental entitlements are ended—is that termination of aid pending resolution of a controversy over eligibility may deprive an *eligible* recipient of the very means by which to live while he waits."

Eligibility for disability benefits, in contrast, is not based upon financial need. Indeed, it is wholly unrelated to the worker's income or support from many other sources, such as earnings of other family members, workmen's compensation awards, tort claims awards, savings, private insurance, public or private pensions, veterans' benefits, food stamps, public assistance, or the "many other important programs, both public and private, which contain provisions for disability payments affecting a substantial portion of the work force. . . ."

As *Goldberg* illustrates, the degree of potential deprivation that may be created by a particular decision is a factor to be considered in assessing the validity of any administrative decisionmaking process. The potential deprivation here is generally likely to be less than in *Goldberg*, although the degree of difference can be overstated. As the District Court emphasized, to remain eligible for benefits a recipient must be "unable to engage in substantial gainful activity." Thus, in contrast to the discharged federal employee in *Arnett,* there is little possibility that the terminated recipient will be able to find even temporary employment to ameliorate the interim loss.

. . . [T]he possible length of wrongful deprivation of . . . benefits [also] is an important factor in assessing the impact of official action on the private interests. The Secretary concedes that the delay between a request for a hearing before an administrative law judge

(Continued)

and a decision on the claim is currently between 10 and 11 months. Since a terminated recipient must first obtain a reconsideration decision as a prerequisite to invoking his right to an evidentiary hearing, the delay between the actual cutoff of benefits and final decision after a hearing exceeds one year.

In view of the torpidity of this administrative review process and the typically modest resources of the family unit of the physically disabled worker,[2] the hardship imposed upon the erroneously terminated disability recipient may be significant. Still, the disabled worker's need is likely to be less than that of a welfare recipient. In addition to the possibility of access to private resources, other forms of government assistance will become available where the termination of disability benefits places a worker or his family below the subsistence level.[3]

In view of these potential sources of temporary income, there is less reason here than in *Goldberg* to depart from the ordinary principle, established by our decisions, that something less than an evidentiary hearing is sufficient prior to adverse administrative action.

D

An additional factor to be considered here is the fairness and reliability of the existing pretermination procedures, and the probable

---

[2] *Amici* cite statistics compiled by the Secretary which indicate that in 1965 the mean income of the family unit of a disabled worker was $3,803, while the median income for the unit was $2,836. The mean liquid assets—*i.e.*, cash, stocks, bonds—of these family units was $4,862; the median was $940. These statistics do not take into account the family unit's nonliquid assets—*i.e.*, automobile, real estate, and the like.

[3] *Amici* emphasize that because an identical definition of disability is employed in both the Title II Social Security Program and in the companion welfare system for the disabled, Supplemental Security Income (SSI), the terminated disability-benefits recipient will be ineligible for the SSI Program. There exist, however, state and local welfare programs which may supplement the worker's income. In addition, the worker's household unit can qualify for food stamps if it meets the financial need requirements. Finally, in 1974, 480,000 of the approximately 2,000,000 disabled workers receiving Social Security benefits also received SSI benefits. Since financial need is a criterion for eligibility under the SSI program, those disabled workers who are most in need will in the majority of cases be receiving SSI benefits when disability insurance aid is terminated. And, under the SSI program, a pretermination evidentiary hearing is provided, if requested.

value, if any, of additional procedural safeguards. Central to the evaluation of any administrative process is the nature of the relevant inquiry. In order to remain eligible for benefits the disabled worker must demonstrate by means of "medically acceptable clinical and laboratory diagnostic techniques" that he is unable "to engage in any substantial gainful activity by reason of any *medically determinable* physical or mental impairment . . ." In short, a medical assessment of the worker's physical or mental condition is required. This is a more sharply focused and easily documented decision than the typical determination of welfare entitlement. In the latter case, a wide variety of information may be deemed relevant, and issues of witness credibility and veracity often are critical to the decisionmaking process. *Goldberg* noted that in such circumstances "written submissions are a wholly unsatisfactory basis for decision."

By contrast, the decision whether to discontinue disability benefits will turn, in most cases, upon "routine, standard, and unbiased medical reports by physician specialists" concerning a subject whom they have personally examined.[4] In *Richardson v. Perales*, 402 U.S. 389, 404 (1971), the Court recognized the "reliability and probative worth of written medical reports," emphasizing that while there may be "professional disagreement with the medical conclusions" the "specter of questionable credibility and veracity is not present." To be sure, credibility and veracity may be a factor in the ultimate disability assessment in some cases. But procedural due process rules are shaped by the risk of error inherent in the truthfinding process as applied to the generality of cases, not the rare exceptions. The poten-

---

[4]The decision is not purely a question of the accuracy of a medical diagnosis since the ultimate issue which the state agency must resolve is whether in light of the particular worker's "age, education, and work experience" he cannot "engage in any . . . substantial gainful work which exists in the national economy". . . . Yet information concerning each of these worker characteristics is amenable to effective written presentation. The value of an evidentiary hearing, or even a limited oral presentation, to an accurate presentation of those factors to the decisionmaker does not appear substantial. Similarly, resolution of the inquiry as to the types of employment opportunities that exist in the national economy for a physically impaired worker with a particular set of skills would not necessarily be advanced by an evidentiary hearing. The statistical information relevant to this judgment is more amenable to written than to oral presentation.

(*Continued*)

tial value of an evidentiary hearing, or even oral presentation to the decisionmaker, is substantially less in this context than in *Goldberg*.

The decision in *Goldberg* also was based on the Court's conclusion that written submissions were an inadequate substitute for oral presentation because they did not provide an effective means for the recipient to communicate his case to the decisionmaker. Written submissions were viewed as an unrealistic option, for most recipients lacked the "educational attainment necessary to write effectively" and could not afford professional assistance. In addition, such submissions would not provide the "flexibility of oral presentations" or "permit the recipient to mold his argument to the issues the decision maker appears to regard as important." In the context of the disability-benefits-entitlement assessment the administrative procedures under review here fully answer these objections.

The detailed questionnaire which the state agency periodically sends the recipient identifies with particularity the information relevant to the entitlement decision, and the recipient is invited to obtain assistance from the local SSA office in completing the questionnaire. More important, the information critical to the entitlement decision usually is derived from medical sources, such as the treating physician. Such sources are likely to be able to communicate more effectively through written documents than are welfare recipients or the lay witnesses supporting their cause. The conclusions of physicians often are supported by X-rays and the results of clinical or laboratory tests, information typically more amenable to written than to oral presentation.

A further safeguard against mistake is the policy of allowing the disability recipient's representative full access to all information relied upon by the state agency. In addition, prior to the cutoff of benefits the agency informs the recipient of its tentative assessment, the reasons therefor, and provides a summary of the evidence that it considers most relevant. Opportunity is then afforded the recipient to submit additional evidence or arguments, enabling him to challenge directly the accuracy of information in his file as well as the correctness of the agency's tentative conclusions. These procedures, again as contrasted with those before the Court in *Goldberg*, enable the recipient to "mold" his argument to respond to the precise issues which the decisionmaker regards as crucial.

Despite these carefully structured procedures, *amici* point to the significant reversal rate for appealed cases as clear evidence that the current process is inadequate. Depending upon the base selected and the line of analysis followed, the relevant reversal rates urged by the contending parties vary from a high of 58.6% for appealed reconsideration decisions to an overall reversal rate of only 3.3%. Bare statistics rarely provide a satisfactory measure of the fairness of a decision-making process. Their adequacy is especially suspect here since the administrative review system is operated on an open-file basis. A recipient may always submit new evidence, and such submissions may result in additional medical examinations. Such fresh examinations were held in approximately 30% to 40% of the appealed cases, in fiscal 1973, either at the reconsideration or evidentiary hearing stage of the administrative process. In this context, the value of reversal rate statistics as one means of evaluating the adequacy of the pretermination process is diminished. Thus, although we view such information as relevant, it is certainly not controlling in this case.

E

In striking the appropriate due process balance the final factor to be assessed is the public interest. This includes the administrative burden and other societal costs that would be associated with requiring, as a matter of constitutional right, an evidentiary hearing upon demand in all cases prior to the termination of disability benefits. The most visible burden would be the incremental cost resulting from the increased number of hearings and the expense of providing benefits to ineligible recipients pending decision. No one can predict the extent of the increase, but the fact that full benefits would continue until after such hearings would assure the exhaustion in most cases of this attractive option. Nor would the theoretical right of the Secretary to recover undeserved benefits result, as a practical matter, in any substantial offset to the added outlay of public funds. The parties submit widely varying estimates of the probable additional financial cost. We only need say that experience with the constitutionalizing of government procedures suggests that the ultimate additional cost in terms of money and administrative burden would not be insubstantial.

Financial cost alone is not a controlling weight in determining whether due process requires a particular procedural safeguard prior to some administrative decision. But the Government's interest, and hence that of the public, in conserving scarce fiscal and administrative resources is a factor that must be weighed. At some point the benefit of an additional safeguard to the individual affected by the administrative action and to society in terms of increased assurance that the action is just, may be outweighed by

(*Continued*)

the cost. Significantly, the cost of protecting those whom the preliminary administrative process has identified as likely to be found undeserving may in the end come out of the pockets of the deserving since resources available for any particular program of social welfare are not unlimited.

But more is implicated in cases of this type than ad hoc weighing of fiscal and administrative burdens against the interests of a particular category of claimants. The ultimate balance involves a determination as to when, under our constitutional system, judicial-type procedures must be imposed upon administrative action to assure fairness. We reiterate the wise admonishment of Mr. Justice Frankfurter that differences in the origin and function of administrative agencies "preclude wholesale transplantation of the rules of procedure, trial and review which have evolved from the history and experience of courts." The judicial model of an evidentiary hearing is neither a required, nor even the most effective, method of decisionmaking in all circumstances. The essence of due process is the requirement that "a person in jeopardy of serious loss [be given] notice of the case against him and opportunity to meet it." All that is necessary is that the procedures be tailored, in light of the decision to be made, to "the capacities and circumstances of those who are to be heard," *Goldberg v. Kelly*, to insure that they are given a meaningful opportunity to present their case. In assessing what process is due in this case, substantial weight must be given to the good-faith judgments of the individuals charged by Congress with the administration of social welfare programs that the procedures they have provided assure fair consideration of the entitlement claims of individuals. This is especially so where, as here, the prescribed procedures not only provide the claimant with an effective process for asserting his claim prior to any administrative action, but also assure a right to an evidentiary hearing, as well as to subsequent judicial review, before the denial of his claim becomes final.

We conclude that an evidentiary hearing is not required prior to the termination of disability benefits and that the present administrative procedures fully comport with due process.

The judgment of the Court of Appeals is *Reversed.*

[BRENNAN and MARSHALL, JJ. dissented. They observed:]. . . .
The Court's consideration that a discontinuance of disability benefits may cause the recipient to suffer only a limited deprivation is no argu-

ment. It is speculative. . . . Indeed in the present case, it is indicated that because disability benefits were terminated, there was a foreclosure on the Eldridge home and the family's furniture was repossessed, forcing Eldridge, his wife and children to sleep in one bed. . . .

Reprinted from Asimow, M.; Bonfield, A.; and Levin, R. State and Federal Administrative Law, 2nd ed. ©1998, with permission of Thomson West.

CASE LAW

HECKLER v. CHANEY
470 U.S. 821, 105 S.Ct. 1649, 84 L.Ed.2d 714 (1985).

JUSTICE REHNQUIST delivered the opinion of the Court.

I

Respondents have been sentenced to death by lethal injection of drugs under the laws of the States of Oklahoma and Texas. . . . Respondents first petitioned the Food and Drug Administration (FDA), claiming that the drugs used by the States for this purpose, although approved by the FDA for the medical purposes stated on their labels, were not approved for use in human executions. They alleged that the drugs had not been tested for the purpose for which they were to be used, and that, given that the drugs would likely be administered by untrained personnel, it was also likely that the drugs would not induce the quick and painless death intended. They urged that use of these drugs for human execution was the "unapproved use of an approved drug" and constituted a violation of the Act's prohibitions against "misbranding." They also suggested that the Federal Food, Drug, and Cosmetics Act's (FDCA) requirements for approval of "new drugs" applied, since these drugs were now being used for a new purpose. Accordingly, respondents claimed that the FDA was required to approve the drugs as "safe and effective" for human execution before they could be distributed in interstate commerce. They therefore requested the FDA to take various investigatory and enforcement actions to prevent these perceived violations. . . .

The FDA Commissioner responded, refusing to take the requested actions. The Commissioner first detailed his disagreement with respondents' understanding of the scope of FDA jurisdiction over the unapproved use of approved drugs for human execution, concluding that FDA jurisdiction in the area was generally unclear

(Continued)

but in any event should not be exercised to interfere with this particular aspect of state criminal justice systems. He went on to state:

> "Were FDA clearly to have jurisdiction in the area, moreover, we believe we would be authorized to decline to exercise it under our inherent discretion to decline to pursue certain enforcement matters. The unapproved use of approved drugs is an area in which the case law is far from uniform. Generally, enforcement proceedings in this area are initiated only when there is a serious danger to the public health or a blatant scheme to defraud. We cannot conclude that those dangers are present under State lethal injection laws, which are duly authorized statutory enactments in furtherance of proper State functions. . . ." . . .

II

. . . Petitioner urges that the decision of the FDA to refuse enforcement is an action "committed to agency discretion by law" under § 701(a)(2).

This Court has not had occasion to interpret this second exception in § 701(a) in any great detail. On its face, the section does not obviously lend itself to any particular construction; indeed, one might wonder what difference exists between § (a)(1) and § (a)(2). The former section seems easy in application; it requires construction of the substantive statute involved to determine whether Congress intended to preclude judicial review of certain decisions. . . . But one could read the language "committed to agency discretion by law" in § (a)(2) to require a similar inquiry. In addition, commentators have pointed out that construction of § (a)(2) is further complicated by the tension between a literal reading of § (a)(2), which exempts from judicial review those decisions committed to agency "discretion," and the primary scope of review prescribed by § 706(2)(A)—whether the agency's action was "arbitrary, capricious, or an abuse of discretion." . . .

This Court first discussed § (a)(2) in *Citizens to Preserve Overton Park v. Volpe*. That case dealt with the Secretary of Transportation's approval of the building of an interstate highway through a park in Memphis, Tennessee. . . . Interested citizens challenged the Secretary's approval under the APA, arguing that he had not satisfied the substantive statute's requirements. This Court first addressed the "threshold question" of whether the agency's action was at all reviewable. After setting out the language of § 701(a), the Court stated:

"In this case, there is no indication that Congress sought to prohibit judicial review and there is most certainly no 'showing of "clear and convincing evidence" of a . . . legislative intent' to restrict access to judicial review. *Abbott Laboratories v. Gardner.*

"Similarly, the Secretary's decision here does not fall within the exception for action 'committed to agency discretion.' This is a very narrow exception. . . . The legislative history of the Administrative Procedure Act indicates that it is applicable in those rare instances where 'statutes are drawn in such broad terms that in a given case there is no law to apply.'"

The above quote answers several of the questions raised by the language of § 701(a), although it raises others. First, it clearly separates the exception provided by § (a)(1) from the § (a)(2) exception. The former applies when Congress has expressed an intent to preclude judicial review. The latter applies in different circumstances; even where Congress has not affirmatively precluded review, review is not to be had if the statute is drawn so that a court would have no meaningful standard against which to judge the agency's exercise of discretion. In such a case, the statute ("law") can be taken to have "committed" the decisionmaking to the agency's judgment absolutely. This construction avoids conflict with the "abuse of discretion" standard of review in § 706—if no judicially manageable standards are available for judging how and when an agency should exercise its discretion, then it is impossible to evaluate agency action for "abuse of discretion." . . .

To this point our analysis does not differ significantly from that of the Court of Appeals. That court purported to apply the "no law to apply" standard of *Overton Park*. We disagree, however, with that court's insistence that the "narrow construction" of § (a)(2) required application of a presumption of reviewability even to an agency's decision not to undertake certain enforcement actions. Here we think the Court of Appeals broke with tradition, case law, and sound reasoning.

Overton Park did not involve an agency's refusal to take requested enforcement action. It involved an affirmative act of approval under a statute that set clear guidelines for determining when such approval should be given. Refusals to take enforcement steps generally involve precisely the opposite situation, and in that situation we think the presumption is that judicial review is not available. This Court has recognized on several occasions over

(Continued)

many years that an agency's decision not to prosecute or enforce, whether through civil or criminal process, is a decision generally committed to an agency's absolute discretion. This recognition of the existence of discretion is attributable in no small part to the general unsuitability for judicial review of agency decisions to refuse enforcement.

The reasons for this general unsuitability are many. First, an agency decision not to enforce often involves a complicated balancing of a number of factors which are peculiarly within its expertise. Thus, the agency must not only assess whether a violation has occurred, but whether agency resources are best spent on this violation or another, whether the agency is likely to succeed if it acts, whether the particular enforcement action requested best fits the agency's overall policies, and, indeed, whether the agency has enough resources to undertake the action at all. An agency generally cannot act against each technical violation of the statute it is charged with enforcing. The agency is far better equipped than the courts to deal with the many variables involved in the proper ordering of its priorities. . . .

In addition to these administrative concerns, we note that when an agency refuses to act it generally does not exercise its coercive power over an individual's liberty or property rights, and thus does not infringe upon areas that courts often are called upon to protect. Similarly, when an agency does act to enforce, that action itself provides a focus for judicial review, inasmuch as the agency must have exercised its power in some manner. . . . Finally, we recognize that an agency's refusal to institute proceedings shares to some extent the characteristics of the decision of a prosecutor in the Executive Branch not to indict—a decision which has long been regarded as the special province of the Executive Branch, inasmuch as it is the Executive who is charged by the Constitution to "take Care that the Laws be faithfully executed." U.S. Const., Art. II, § 3.

We of course only list the above concerns to facilitate understanding of our conclusion that an agency's decision not to take enforcement action should be presumed immune from judicial review under § 701(a)(2). For good reasons, such a decision has traditionally been "committed to agency discretion," and we believe that the Congress enacting the APA did not intend to alter that tradition. In so stating, we emphasize that the decision is only presumptively unreviewable; the presumption may be rebutted where the substantive statute has provided guidelines for the agency to follow in exercising its enforcement powers.[1] Thus, in establishing this presumption in the APA, Congress did not set agencies free to disregard legislative direction in the statutory scheme that the agency administers. Congress may limit an agency's exercise of enforcement power if it wishes, either by setting substantive priorities, or by otherwise circumscribing an agency's power to discriminate among issues or cases it will pursue. How to determine when Congress has done so is the question left open by *Overton Park.*

Dunlop v. Bachowski, 421 U.S. 560 (1975), relied upon heavily by respondents and the majority in the Court of Appeals, presents an example of statutory language which supplied sufficient standards to rebut the presumption of unreviewability. [The law there] provided that, upon filing of a complaint by a union member, "[t]he Secretary shall investigate such complaint and, if he finds probable cause to believe that a violation . . . has occurred . . . he shall . . . bring a civil action. . . ." . . . This Court held that review was available. It rejected the Secretary's argument that the statute precluded judicial review, and in a footnote it stated its agreement with the conclusion of the Court of Appeals that the decision was not "an unreviewable exercise of prosecutorial discretion." . . . The Court of Appeals, in turn, had found the "principle of absolute prosecutorial discretion" inapplicable, because the language of the [Act] indicated that the Secretary was required to file suit if certain "clearly defined" factors were present. The decision therefore was not "'beyond the judicial capacity to supervise.'"

Dunlop is thus consistent with a general presumption of unreviewability of decisions not to enforce. The statute being administered quite clearly withdrew discretion from the agency and provided guidelines for exercise of its enforcement power. . . . The danger that agencies may not carry out their delegated powers with sufficient

---

[1]We do not have in this case a refusal by the agency to institute proceedings based solely on the belief that it lacks jurisdiction. Nor do we have a situation where it could justifiably be found that the agency has "consciously and expressly adopted a general policy" that is so extreme as to amount to an abdication of its statutory responsibilities. Although we express no opinion on whether such decisions would be unreviewable under § 701(a)(2), we note that in those situations the statute conferring authority on the agency might indicate that such decisions were not "committed to agency discretion."

(Continued)

vigor does not necessarily lead to the conclusion that courts are the most appropriate body to police this aspect of their performance. That decision is in the first instance for Congress, and we therefore turn to the FDCA to determine whether in this case Congress has provided us with "law to apply." If it has indicated an intent to circumscribe agency enforcement discretion, and has provided meaningful standards for defining the limits of that discretion, there is "law to apply" under § 701 (a)(2), and courts may require that the agency follow that law; if it has not, then an agency refusal to institute proceedings is a decision "committed to agency discretion by law" within the meaning of that section.

III

. . . The Act's general provision for enforcement provides only that "[t]he Secretary is authorized to conduct examinations and investigations. . . ." Unlike the statute at issue in *Dunlop*, [the FDCA] gives no indication of when an injunction should be sought, and [the section] providing for seizures, is framed in the permissive—the offending food, drug, or cosmetic "shall be liable to be proceeded against." The section on criminal sanctions states baldly that any person who violates the Act's substantive prohibitions "shall be imprisoned . . . or fined." Respondents argue that this statement mandates criminal prosecution of every violator of the Act but they adduce no indication in case law or legislative history that such was Congress' intention in using this language, which is commonly found in the criminal provisions of Title 18 of the United States Code. We are unwilling to attribute such a sweeping meaning to this language, particularly since the Act charges the Secretary only with recommending prosecution; any criminal prosecutions must be instituted by the Attorney General. The Act's enforcement provisions thus commit complete discretion to the Secretary to decide how and when they should be exercised. . . .

IV

We therefore conclude that the presumption that agency decisions not to institute proceedings are unreviewable under 5 U.S.C. § 701(a)(2) is not overcome by the enforcement provisions of the FDCA. The FDA's decision not to take the enforcement actions requested by respondents is therefore not subject to judicial review under the APA. The general exception to reviewability provided by § 701(a)(2) for action "committed to agency discretion" remains a narrow one, but within that exception are included agency refusals to institute investigative or enforcement proceedings, unless Congress has indicated otherwise. In so holding, we essentially leave to Congress, and not to the courts, the decision as to whether an agency's refusal to institute proceedings should be judicially reviewable. No colorable claim is made in this case that the agency's refusal to institute proceedings violated any constitutional rights of respondents, and we do not address the issue that would be raised in such a case.

JUSTICE BRENNAN, concurring.

Today the Court holds that individual decisions of the Food and Drug Administration not to take enforcement action in response to citizen requests are presumptively not reviewable under the Administrative Procedure Act. I concur in this decision. This general presumption is based on the view that, in the normal course of events, Congress intends to allow broad discretion for its administrative agencies to make particular enforcement decisions, and there often may not exist readily discernible "law to apply" for courts to conduct judicial review of nonenforcement decisions.

I also agree that, despite this general presumption, "Congress did not set agencies free to disregard legislative direction in the statutory scheme that the agency administers." Thus the Court properly does not decide today that nonenforcement decisions are unreviewable in cases where (1) an agency flatly claims that it has no statutory jurisdiction to reach certain conduct; (2) an agency engages in a pattern of nonenforcement of clear statutory language, as in *Adams v. Richardson*, 480 F.2d 1159 (1973)(en banc); (3) an agency has refused to enforce a regulation lawfully promulgated and still in effect; or (4) a nonenforcement decision violates constitutional rights. It is possible to imagine other nonenforcement decisions made for entirely illegitimate reasons, for example, nonenforcement in return for a bribe, judicial review of which would not be foreclosed by the nonreviewability presumption. It may be presumed that Congress does not intend administrative agencies, agents of Congress' own creation, to ignore clear jurisdictional, regulatory, statutory, or constitutional commands, and in some circumstances including those listed above the statutes or regulations at issue may well provide "law to apply" under 5 U.S.C. § 701(a)(2). Individual, isolated nonenforcement decisions, however, must be made by hundreds of agencies each day. It is entirely permissible to presume that Congress has not intended courts to review such mundane matters,

(Continued)

absent either some indication of congressional intent to the contrary or proof of circumstances such as those set out above.

JUSTICE MARSHALL, concurring in the judgment.

Easy cases at times produce bad law, for in the rush to reach a clearly ordained result, courts may offer up principles, doctrines, and statements that calmer reflection, and a fuller understanding of their implications in concrete settings, would eschew. In my view, the "presumption of unreviewability" announced today is a product of that lack of discipline that easy cases make all too easy. . . .

I write separately to argue for a different basis of decision: that refusals to enforce, like other agency actions, are reviewable in the absence of a "clear and convincing" congressional intent to the contrary, but that such refusals warrant deference when, as in this case, there is nothing to suggest that an agency with enforcement discretion has abused that discretion. . . .

When a statute does not mandate full enforcement, I agree with the Court that an agency is generally "far better equipped than the courts to deal with the many variables involved in the proper ordering of its priorities." As long as the agency is choosing how to allocate finite enforcement resources, the agency's choice will be entitled to substantial deference, for the choice among valid alternative enforcement policies is precisely the sort of choice over which agencies generally have been left substantial discretion by their enabling statutes. On the merits, then, a decision not to enforce that is based on valid resource-allocation decisions will generally not be "arbitrary, capricious, an abuse of discretion, or otherwise not in accordance with law." The decision in this case is no exception to this principle.

The Court, however, is not content to rest on this ground. Instead, the Court transforms the arguments for deferential review on the merits into the wholly different notion that "enforcement" decisions are presumptively unreviewable altogether—unreviewable whether the resource-allocation rationale is a sham, unreviewable whether enforcement is declined out of vindictive or personal motives, and unreviewable whether the agency has simply ignored the request for enforcement. . . .

Moreover, for at least two reasons it is inappropriate to rely on notions of prosecutorial discretion to hold agency inaction unreviewable. First, . . . even in the area of criminal prosecutions, prosecutorial discretion is not subject to a "presumption of unreviewability." If a plaintiff makes a sufficient threshold showing that a prosecutor's discretion has been exercised for impermissible reasons, judicial review is available.

Second, arguments about prosecutorial discretion do not necessarily translate into the context of agency refusals to act. . . . Criminal prosecutorial decisions vindicate only intangible interests, common to society as a whole, in the enforcement of the criminal law. The conduct at issue has already occurred; all that remains is society's general interest in assuring that the guilty are punished. . . . In contrast, requests for administrative enforcement typically seek to prevent concrete and future injuries that Congress has made cognizable—injuries that result, for example, from misbranded drugs, such as alleged in this case, or unsafe nuclear power plants—or to obtain palpable benefits that Congress has intended to bestow—such as labor union elections free of corruption. Entitlements to receive these benefits or to be free of these injuries often run to specific classes of individuals whom Congress has singled out as statutory beneficiaries. The interests at stake in review of administrative enforcement decisions are thus more focused and in many circumstances more pressing than those at stake in criminal prosecutorial decisions. A request that a nuclear plant be operated safely or that protection be provided against unsafe drugs is quite different from a request that an individual be put in jail or his property confiscated as punishment for past violations of the criminal law.

Perhaps most important, the *sine qua non* of the APA was to alter inherited judicial reluctance to constrain the exercise of discretionary administrative power—to rationalize and make fairer the exercise of such discretion. Since passage of the APA, the sustained effort of administrative law has been to "continuously narro[w] the category of actions considered to be so discretionary as to be exempted from review." . . . Judicial review is available under the APA in the absence of a clear and convincing demonstration that Congress intended to preclude it precisely so that agencies, whether in rulemaking, adjudicating, acting or failing to act, do not become stagnant backwaters of caprice and lawlessness. . . .

Reprinted from Funk, W.; Shapiro, S.; and Weaver, R. Administrative Procedure and Practice: Problems and Cases. © 2006, with permission of Thomson West.

CASE LAW

BIVENS v. SIX UNKNOWN NAMED AGENTS OF FEDERAL BUREAU OF NARCOTICS
Supreme Court of the United States, 1971.
403 U.S. 388, 91 S.Ct. 1999, 29 L.Ed.2d 619.

MR. JUSTICE BRENNAN delivered the opinion of the Court. The Fourth Amendment provides that:

> "The right of the people to be secure in their persons, houses, papers, and effects, against unreasonable searches and seizures, shall not be violated. . . ."

In *Bell v. Hood*, 327 U.S. 678, 66 S.Ct. 773, 90 L.Ed. 939 (1946), we reserved the question whether violation of that command by a federal agent acting under color of his authority gives rise to a cause of action for damages consequent upon his unconstitutional conduct. Today we hold that it does.

This case has its origin in an arrest and search carried out on the morning of November 26, 1965. Petitioner's complaint alleged that on that day respondents, agents of the Federal Bureau of Narcotics acting under claim of federal authority, entered his apartment and arrested him for alleged narcotics violations. The agents manacled petitioner in front of his wife and children, and threatened to arrest the entire family. They searched the apartment from stem to stern. Thereafter, petitioner was taken to the federal courthouse in Brooklyn, where he was interrogated, booked, and subjected to a visual strip search.

On July 7, 1967, petitioner brought suit in Federal District Court. In addition to the allegations above, his complaint asserted that the arrest and search were effected without a warrant, and that unreasonable force was employed in making the arrest; fairly read, it alleges as well that the arrest was made without probable cause. Petitioner claimed to have suffered great humiliation, embarrassment, and mental suffering as a result of the agents' unlawful conduct, and sought $15,000 damages from each of them. The District Court, on respondents' motion, dismissed the complaint on the ground, *inter alia*, that it failed to state a cause of action [, and the Court of Appeals affirmed]. We reverse.

I

Respondents do not argue that petitioner should be entirely without remedy for an unconstitutional invasion of his rights by federal agents. In respondents' view, however, the rights that petitioner asserts—primarily rights of privacy—are creations of state and not of federal law. Accordingly, they argue, petitioner may obtain money damages to redress invasion of these rights only by an action in tort, under state law, in the state courts. In this scheme the Fourth Amendment would serve merely to limit the extent to which the agents could defend the state law tort suit by asserting that their actions were a valid exercise of federal power: if the agents were shown to have violated the Fourth Amendment, such a defense would be lost to them and they would stand before the state law merely as private individuals. Candidly admitting that it is the policy of the Department of Justice to remove all such suits from the state to the federal courts for decision, respondents nevertheless urge that we uphold dismissal of petitioner's complaint in federal court, and remit him to filing an action in the state courts in order that the case may properly be removed to the federal court for decision on the basis of state law.

We think that respondents' thesis rests upon an unduly restrictive view of the Fourth Amendment's protection against unreasonable searches and seizures by federal agents, a view that has consistently been rejected by this Court. Respondents seek to treat the relationship between a citizen and a federal agent unconstitutionally exercising his authority as no different from the relationship between two private citizens. In so doing, they ignore the fact that power, once granted, does not disappear like a magic gift when it is wrongfully used. An agent acting—albeit unconstitutionally—in the name of the United States possesses a far greater capacity for harm than an individual trespasser exercising no authority other than his own. Cf. *Amos v. United States*, 255 U.S. 313, 317, 41 S.Ct. 266, 267–268, 65 L.Ed. 654 (1921); *United States v. Classic*, 313 U.S. 299, 326, 61 S.Ct. 1031, 1043, 85 L.Ed. 1368 (1941). Accordingly, as our cases make clear, the Fourth Amendment operates as a limitation upon the exercise of federal power regardless of whether the State in whose jurisdiction that power is exercised would prohibit or penalize the identical act if engaged in by a private citizen. . . .

First. Our cases have long since rejected the notion that the Fourth Amendment proscribes only such conduct as would, if engaged in by private persons, be condemned by state law. . . . *Gambino v. United States*, 275 U.S. 310, 48 S.Ct. 137, 72 L.Ed. 293 (1927). . . .

(*Continued*)

Second. The interests protected by state laws regulating trespass and the invasion of privacy, and those protected by the Fourth Amendment's guarantee against unreasonable searches and seizures, may be inconsistent or even hostile. Thus, we may bar the door against an unwelcome private intruder, or call the police if he persists in seeking entrance. The availability of such alternative means for the protection of privacy may lead the State to restrict imposition of liability for any consequent trespass. A private citizen, asserting no authority other than his own, will not normally be liable in trespass if he demands, and is granted, admission to another's house. See W. Prosser, The Law of Torts § 18, pp. 109–110 (3d ed., 1964); 1 F. Harper & F. James, The law of Torts § 1.11 (1956). But one who demands admission under a claim of federal authority stands in a far different position. Cf. *Amos v. United States,* 255 U.S. 313, 317, 41 S.Ct. 266, 267–268, 65 L.Ed. 654 (1921). The mere invocation of federal power by a federal law enforcement official will normally render futile any attempt to resist an unlawful entry or arrest by resort to the local police; and a claim of authority to enter is likely to unlock the door as well. See *Weeks v. United States,* 232 U.S. 383, 386, 34 S.Ct. 341, 342, 58 L.Ed. 652 (1914); *Amos v. United States, supra.* "In such cases there is no safety for the citizen except in the protection of the judicial tribunals, for rights which have been invaded by the officers of the government, professing to act in its name. There remains to him but the alternative of resistance, which may amount to crime." *United States v. Lee,* 106 U.S. 196, 219, 1 S.Ct. 240, 259, 27 L.Ed. 171 (1882). Nor is it adequate to answer that state law may take into account the different status of one clothed with the authority of the Federal Government. For just as state law may not authorize federal agents to violate the Fourth Amendment, *Weeks v. United States,* supra; *In re Ayers,* 123 U.S. 443, 507, 8 S.Ct. 164, 183–184, 31 L.Ed. 216 (1887), neither may state law undertake to limit the extent to which federal authority can be exercised. *In re Neagle,* 135 U.S. 1, 10 S.Ct. 658, 34 L.Ed. 55 (1890). . . .

Third. That damages may be obtained for injuries consequent upon a violation of the Fourth Amendment by federal officials should hardly seem a surprising proposition. Historically, damages have been regarded as the ordinary remedy for an invasion of personal interests in liberty. See *Nixon v. Condon,* 286 U.S. 73, 52 S.Ct. 484, 76 L.Ed. 984 (1932); Katz, The Jurisprudence of Remedies: Constitutional Legality and the Law of Torts in *Bell v. Hood,*

117 U.Pa.L.Rev. 1, 8–33 (1968). Of course, the Fourth Amendment does not in so many words provide for its enforcement by an award of money damages for the consequences of its violation. But "it is . . . well settled that where legal rights have been invaded, and a federal statute provides for a general right to sue for such invasion, federal courts may use any available remedy to make good the wrong done." *Bell v. Hood,* 327 U.S. at 684, 66 S.Ct., at 777 (footnote omitted). The present case involves no special factors counseling hesitation in the absence of affirmative action by Congress. We are not dealing with a question of "federal fiscal policy," as in *United States v. Standard Oil Co.,* 332 U.S. 301, 311; 67 S.Ct. 1604, 1609–1610, 91 L.Ed. 2067 (1947). In that case we refused to infer from the Government-soldier relationship that the United States could recover damages from one who negligently injured a soldier and thereby caused the Government to pay his medical expenses and lose his services during the course of his hospitalization. Nothing that Congress was normally quite solicitous where the federal purse was involved, we pointed out that "the United States [was] the party plaintiff to the suit. And the United States has power at any time to create the liability." Id. at 316, 67 S.Ct., at 1612; see *United States v. Gilman,* 347 U.S. 507, 74 S.Ct. 695, 98 L.Ed. 898 (1954). Nor are we asked in this case to impose liability upon a congressional employee for actions contrary to no constitutional prohibition, but merely said to be in excess of the authority delegated to him by the Congress. *Wheeldin v. Wheeler,* 373 U.S. 647, 83 S.Ct. 1441, 10 L.Ed.2d 605 (1963). Finally, we cannot accept respondents' formulation of the question as whether the availability of money damages is necessary to enforce the Fourth Amendment. For we have here no explicit congressional declaration that persons injured by a federal officer's violation of the Fourth Amendment may not recover money damages from the agents, but must instead be remitted to another remedy, equally effective in the view of Congress. The question is merely whether petitioner, if he can demonstrate an injury consequent upon the violation by federal agents of his Fourth Amendment rights, is entitled to redress his injury through a particular remedial mechanism normally available in the federal courts. . . . "The very essence of civil liberty certainly consists in the right of every individual to claim the protection of the laws, whenever he receives an injury." *Marbury v. Madison,* 1 Cranch 137, 163, 2 L.Ed. 60 (1803). Having concluded that petitioner's complaint states a cause of action

(Continued)

under the Fourth Amendment, . . . we hold that petitioner is entitled to recover money damages for any injuries he has suffered as a result of the agents' violation of the Amendment. . . .

Judgment reversed and case remanded.

MR. JUSTICE HARLAN, concurring in the judgment. . . .

[T]he interest which Bivens claims—to be free from official conduct in contravention of the Fourth Amendment—is a federally protected interest. Therefore, the question of judicial *power* to grant Bivens damages is not a problem of the "source" of the "right"; instead, the question is whether the power to authorize damages as a judicial remedy for the vindication of a federal constitutional right is placed by the Constitution itself exclusively in Congress' hands.

The contention that the federal courts are powerless to accord a litigant damages for a claimed invasion of his federal constitutional rights until Congress explicitly authorizes the remedy cannot rest on the notion that the decision to grant compensatory relief involves a resolution of policy considerations not susceptible of judicial discernment. [We have, for example, implied damages remedies under federal statutes which lack an express provision for a cause of action. We have similarly implied injunctive remedies for constitutional violations, so there is nothing unique in the status of constitutional provisions that makes them inappropriate for implication of remedies.] . . .

[The government's] arguments for a more stringent test to govern the grant of damages in constitutional cases seem to be adequately answered by the point that the judiciary has a particular responsibility to assure the vindication of constitutional interests such as those embraced by the Fourth Amendment. To be sure, "it must be remembered that legislatures are ultimate guardians of the liberties and welfare of the people in quite as great a degree as the courts." *Missouri, Kansas & Texas R. Co. of Texas v. May,* 194 U.S. 267, 270, 24 S.Ct. 638, 639, 48 L.Ed. 971 (1904). But it must also be recognized that the Bill of Rights is particularly intended to vindicate the interests of the individual in the face of the popular will as expressed in legislative majorities; at the very least, it strikes me as no more appropriate to await express congressional authorization of traditional judicial relief with regard to these legal interests than with respect to interests protected by federal statutes.

The question then, is, as I see it, whether compensatory relief is "necessary" or "appropriate" to the vindication of the interest asserted. In resolving that question, it seems to me that the range of policy considerations we may take into account is at least as broad as the range a legislature would consider with respect to an express statutory authorization of a traditional remedy. In this regard I agree with the Court that the appropriateness of according Bivens compensatory relief does not turn simply on the deterrent effect liability will have on federal official conduct. Damages as a traditional form of compensation for invasion of a legally protected interest may be entirely appropriate even if no substantial deterrent effects on future official lawlessness might be thought to result. Bivens, after all, has invoked judicial processes claiming entitlement to compensation for injuries resulting from allegedly lawless official behavior, if those injuries are properly compensable in money damages. I do not think a court of law—vested with the power to accord a remedy—should deny him his relief simply because he cannot show that future lawless conduct will thereby be deterred.

And I think it is clear that Bivens advances a claim of the sort that, if proved, would be properly compensable in damages. The personal interests protected by the Fourth Amendment are those we attempt to capture by the notion of "privacy"; while the Court today properly points out that the type of harm which officials can inflict when they invade protected zones of an individual's life are different from the types of harm private citizens inflict on one another, the experience of judges in dealing with private trespass and false imprisonment claims supports the conclusion that courts of law are capable of making the types of judgment concerning causation and magnitude of injury necessary to accord meaningful compensation for invasion of Fourth Amendment rights. . . .

MR. CHIEF JUSTICE BURGER, dissenting.

I dissent from today's holding which judicially creates a damage remedy not provided for by the Constitution and not enacted by Congress. We would more surely preserve the important values of the doctrine of separation of powers—and perhaps get a better result—by recommending a solution to the Congress as the branch of government in which the Constitution has vested the legislative power. Legislation is the business of the Congress, and it has the facilities, and competence for that task—as we do not. . . .

. . .

MR. JUSTICE BLACK, dissenting.

In my opinion for the Court in *Bell v. Hood*, we did as the Court states, reserve the question whether an unreasonable search

(Continued)

made by a federal officer in violation of the Fourth Amendment gives the subject of the search a federal cause of action for damages against the officers making the search. There can be no doubt that Congress could create a federal cause of action for damages for an unreasonable search in violation of the Fourth Amendment. Although Congress has created such a federal cause of action against *state* officials acting under color of state law, it has never created such a cause of action against federal officials. If it wanted to do so, Congress could, of course, create a remedy against federal officials who violate the Fourth Amendment in the performance of their duties. But the point of this case and the fatal weakness in the Court's judgment is that neither Congress nor the State of New York has enacted legislation creating such a right of action. For us to do so is, in my judgment, an exercise of power that the Constitution does not give us.

Even if we had the legislative power to create a remedy, there are many reasons why we should decline to create a cause of action where none has existed since the formation of our Government. The courts of the United States as well as those of the States are choked with lawsuits. The number of cases on the docket of this Court have reached an unprecedented volume in recent years. . . . Unfortunately, there have also been a growing number of frivolous lawsuits, particularly actions for damages against law enforcement officers whose conduct has been judicially sanctioned by state trial and appellate courts and in many instances even by this Court. . . . Of course, there are instances of legitimate grievances, but legislators might well desire to devote judicial resources to other problems of a more serious nature.

. . .

Reprinted from Abernathy, C. Civil Rights and Constitutional Litigation, 3rd ed. © 2000, with permission of Thomson West.

CASE LAW

SCHWEIKER v. CHILICKY

Supreme Court of the United States, 1988.
487 U.S. 412, 108 S.Ct. 2460, 101 L.Ed.2d 370.

JUSTICE O'CONNOR delivered the opinion of the Court.

This case requires us to decide whether the improper denial of Social Security disability benefits, allegedly resulting from violations of due process by government officials who administered the Federal Social Security program, may give rise to a cause of action for money damages against those officials. We conclude that such a remedy, not having been included in the elaborate remedial scheme devised by Congress, is unavailable.

[Plaintiffs had lost disability benefits due them under the federal Social Security Act, allegedly because of procedural due process violation in the termination of their previously awarded benefits. Federal officials had allegedly encouraged the denial of benefits through its "continuing disability review" (CDR) process, a complicated system of forcing beneficiaries to establish their eligibility repeatedly. Each plaintiff had actually sought and recovered a retroactive award of benefits under procedures made available by the Social Security Act itself, but the Act provided no damages for the emotional distress that the plaintiffs had suffered during their periods of lost benefits. The Court gave a very sympathetic description of the widespread economic and social distress that resulted from the defendants' alleged wrongdoing.]

Our more recent decisions have responded cautiously to suggestions that *Bivens* remedies be extended into new contexts. The absence of statutory relief for a constitutional violation, for example, does not by any means necessarily imply that courts should award money damages against the officers responsible for the violation. Thus, in *Chappell v. Wallace*, 462 U.S. 296, 103 S.Ct. 2362, 76 L.Ed.2d 586 (1983), we refused—unanimously—to create a *Bivens* action for enlisted military personnel who alleged that they had been injured by the unconstitutional actions of their superior officers and who had no remedy against the Government itself:

> "The special nature of military life—the need for unhesitating and decisive action by military officers and equally disciplined responses by enlisted personnel—would be undermined by a judicially created remedy exposing officers to personal liability at the hands of those they are charged to command . . . ."

(Continued)

. . .

Similarly, we refused—again unanimously—to create a *Bivens* remedy for a First Amendment violation "aris[ing] out of an employment relationship that is governed by comprehensive procedural and substantive provisions giving meaningful remedies against the United States." *Bush v. Lucas*, 462 U.S. 367, 368, 103 S.Ct. 2404, 2406, 76 L.Ed.2d 648 (1983). . . . The Court stressed that the case involved policy questions in an area that had received careful attention from Congress. Noting that the Legislature is far more competent than the Judiciary to carry out the necessary "balancing [of] governmental efficiency and the rights of employees," we refused to "decide whether or not it would be good policy to permit a federal employee to recover damages from a supervisor who has improperly disciplined him for exercising his First Amendment rights."

In sum, the concept of "special factors counselling hesitation in the absence of affirmative action by Congress" has proved to include an appropriate judicial deference to indications that congressional inaction has not been inadvertent. When the design of a government program suggests that Congress has provided what it considers adequate remedial mechanisms for constitutional violations that may occur in the course of its administration, we have not created additional *Bivens* remedies.

B

The administrative structure and procedures of the Social Security system, which affects virtually every American, "are of a size and extent difficult to comprehend." *Richardson v. Perales*, 402 U.S. 389, 399, 91 S.Ct. 1420, 1426, 28 L.Ed.2d 842 (1971). Millions of claims are filed every year under the Act's disability benefits programs alone, and these claims are handled under "an unusually protective [multi]-step process for the review and adjudication of disputed claims." *Heckler v. Day*, 467 U.S. 104, 106, 104 S.Ct. 2249, 2251, 81 L.Ed.2d 88 (1984).

[The Court described the various steps of administrative review available under the Social Security Act. These are supplemented by a right to judicial review in the federal district court. The Act specifically includes a right to assert constitutional complaints. Nevertheless, the Act provides only for retroactive benefits awards, not damages for any violations of statutory or constitutional rights.]

The case before us cannot reasonably be distinguished from *Bush v. Lucas*. Here, exactly as in *Bush*, Congress has failed to provide for "complete relief": respondents have not been given a remedy in damages for emotional distress or for other hardships suffered because of delays in their receipt of Social Security benefits. The creation of a *Bivens* remedy would obviously offer the prospect of relief for injuries that must now go unredressed. Congress, however, has not failed to provide meaningful safeguards or remedies for the rights of persons situated as respondents were. Indeed, the system for protecting their rights is, if anything, considerably more elaborate than the civil service system considered in *Bush*. The prospect of personal liability for official acts, moreover, would undoubtedly lead to new difficulties and expense in recruiting administrators for the programs Congress has established. Congressional competence at "balancing governmental efficiency and the rights of [individuals]," *Bush*, is no more questionable in the social welfare context than it is in the civil service context.

Congressional attention to problems that have arisen in the administration of CDR (including the very problems that gave rise to this case) has, moreover, been frequent and intense. See, *e.g.*, H.R.Rep. No. 98–618, pp. 2, 4 (1984); S.Rep. No. 98–466, pp. 10, 17–18 (1984), U.S. Code Cong. & Admin. News 1984, p. 3038. Congress itself required that the CDR program be instituted. Within two years after the program began, Congress enacted emergency legislation providing for the continuation of benefits even after a finding of ineligibility by a state agency. Less than two years after passing that law, and fully aware of the results of extensive investigations of the practices that led to respondents' injuries, Congress again enacted legislation aimed at reforming the administration of CDR; that legislation again specifically addressed the problem that had provoked the earlier emergency legislation. At each step, Congress chose specific forms and levels of protection for the rights of persons affected by incorrect eligibility determinations under CDR. At no point did Congress choose to extend to any person the kind of remedies that respondents seek in this lawsuit. Cf. 130 Cong.Rec. H1960–1961 (Mar. 27, 1984) (Rep. Perkins) (expressing regret that the bill eventually enacted as the 1984 Reform Act did not provide additional relief for persons improperly terminated during the early years of CDR). Thus, congressional unwillingness to provide consequential damages for unconstitutional deprivations of a statutory right is at least as clear in the context of this case as it was in *Bush*.

· · ·

[W]e, declined in *Bush* "'to create a new substantive legal liability . . .' because we are convinced that Congress is in a better position

(Continued)

to decide whether or not the public interest would be served by creating it." 462 U.S., at 390, 103 S.Ct., at 2417 (citation omitted). That reasoning applies as much, or more, in this case as it did in *Bush* itself.

. . .

In the end, respondents' various arguments are rooted in their insistent and vigorous contention that they simply have not been adequately recompensed for their injuries. They say, for example:

> "Respondents are disabled workers who were dependent upon their Social Security benefits when petitioners unconstitutionally terminated them. Respondents needed those benefits, at the time they were wrongfully withheld, to purchase food, shelter, medicine, and life's other necessities. The harm they suffered as a result bears no relation to the dollar amount of the benefits unjustly withheld from them. For the Government to offer belated restoration of back benefits in a lump sum and attempt to call it quits, after respondents have suffered deprivation for months on end, is not only to display gross insensitivity to the damage done to respondents' lives, but to trivialize the seriousness of petitioners' offense." Brief for Respondents 11.

We agree that suffering months of delay in receiving the income on which one has depended for the very necessities of life cannot be fully remedied by the "belated restoration of back benefits." The trauma to respondents, and thousands of others like them, must surely have gone beyond what anyone of normal sensibilities would wish to see imposed on innocent disabled citizens. Nor would we care to "trivialize" the nature of the wrongs alleged in this case. Congress, however, has addressed the problems created by state agencies' wrongful termination of disability benefits. Whether or not we believe that its response was the best response, Congress is the body charged with making the inevitable compromises required in the design of a massive and complex welfare benefits program. Cf. *Dandridge v. Williams*, 397 U.S. 471, 487, 90 S.Ct. 1153, 1162, 25 L.Ed.2d 491 (1970). Congress has discharged that responsibility to the extent that it affects the case before us, and we see no legal basis that would allow us to revise its decision.[1]

---

[1]The Solicitor General contends that Congress has explicitly precluded the creation of a *Bivens* remedy for respondents' claims. Cf. *Bivens*. His argument rests on 42 U.S.C. § 405(h) (1982 ed. Supp. III), which provides:

Because the relief sought by respondents is unavailable as a matter of law, the case must be dismissed. The judgment of the Court of Appeals to the contrary is therefore

Reversed.

JUSTICE STEVENS, concurring in part and concurring in the judgment. [Omitted]

JUSTICE BRENNAN, with whom JUSTICE MARSHALL and JUSTICE BLACKMUN join, dissenting.

. . .

I agree that in appropriate circumstances we should defer to a congressional decision to substitute alternative relief for a judicially created remedy. Neither the design of Title II's administrative review process, however, nor the debate surrounding its reform contain any suggestion that Congress meant to preclude recognition of a *Bivens* action for persons whose constitutional rights are violated by those charged with administering the program, or that Congress viewed this process as an adequate substitute remedy for such violations. Indeed, Congress never mentioned, let alone debated, the desirability of providing a statutory remedy for such constitutional wrongs. Because I believe legislators of "normal sensibilities" would not wish to leave such traumatic injuries unrecompensed, I find it inconceivable that Congress meant by mere silence to bar all redress for such injuries.

. . .

Here, as the legislative history of the 1984 Reform Act makes abundantly clear, Congress did not attempt to achieve a delicate balance between the constitutional rights of Title II beneficiaries on the one hand, and administrative concerns on the other. Rather than fine-tuning "an elaborate remedial scheme that ha[d] been constructed step by step" over the better part of a century, Congress confronted a paralyzing breakdown in a vital social program, which it sought to rescue from near-total anarchy. . . .

. . .

At no point during the lengthy legislative debate, however, did any Member of Congress so much as hint that the substantive eligibility criteria, notice requirements, and interim payment provisions that would govern *future* disability reviews adequately redressed the harms that beneficiaries may have suffered as a result of the unconstitutional actions of individual state and federal officials in *past* proceedings, or that the constitutional rights of those unjustly deprived

(Continued)

of benefits in the past had to be sacrificed in the name of administrative efficiency or any other governmental interest. The Court today identifies no legislative compromise, "inevitable" or otherwise, in which lawmakers expressly declined to afford a remedy for such past wrongs. Nor can the Court point to any legislator who suggested that state and federal officials should be shielded from liability for any unconstitutional acts taken in the course of administering the review program, or that exposure to liability for such acts would be inconsistent with Congress' comprehensive and carefully crafted remedial scheme.

Although the Court intimates that Congress consciously chose not to afford any remedies beyond the prospective protections set out in the 1984 Reform Act itself, the one legislator the Court identifies as bemoaning the Act's inadequate response to past wrongs argued only that the legislation should have permitted all recipients, including those whose benefits were terminated before December 31, 1984, to seek a redetermination of their eligibility under the new review standards. See 130 Cong.Rec. H1961 (Mar. 27, 1984) (remarks of Rep. Perkins). Neither this legislator nor any other, however, discussed the possibility or desirability of redressing injuries flowing from the temporary loss of benefits in those cases where the benefits were ultimately restored on administrative appeal. The possibility that courts might act in the absence of congressional measures was never even discussed, let alone factored into Congress' response to the emergency it faced.

> "The findings and decision of the Secretary after a hearing shall be binding upon all individuals who were parties to such hearing. No findings of fact or decision of the Secretary shall be reviewed by any person, tribunal, or governmental agency except as herein provided. No action against the United States, the Secretary, or any officer or employee thereof shall be brought under section 1331 or 1346 of title 28 to recover on any claim arising under [Title II]." Relying on *Heckler v. Ringer*, 466 U.S. 602, 614–616, 620–626, 104 S.Ct. 2013, 2021–2022, 2024–2028, 80 L.Ed.2d 622 (1984), and *Weinberger v. Salfi*, 422 U.S. 749, 756–762, 95 S.Ct. 2457, 2462–2465, 45 L.Ed.2d 522 (1975), the Solicitor General has previously argued that the third sentence of this provision prevents any exercise of general federal-question jurisdiction under § 1331. See *Bowen v. Michigan Academy of Family Physicians*, 476 U.S.

667, 679, 106 S.Ct. 2133, 2140, 90 L.Ed.2d 623 (1986). Without deciding the question, we noted that arguments could be made for and against the Solicitor General's position. We continue to believe that the exact scope of the third sentence's restriction on federal-question jurisdiction is not free from doubt; because we hold on other grounds that a *Bivens* remedy is precluded in this case, we need not decide whether § 405(h) would have the same effect.

Reprinted from Abernathy, C. Civil Rights and Constitutional Litigation, 3rd ed. © 2000, with permission of Thomson West.

CHAPTER SUMMARY

Once an agency has reached a final decision on a matter before it, that decision can be taken into a court of law and reviewed. The decision can be a denial of benefits or a ruling that an individual or business has violated a regulation. When a court examines a decision of an agency, the court is engaging in judicial review. While engaging in judicial review, the court looks to see if the agency has violated constitutional rights in the form of procedural due process, substantive due process, and equal protection. The court will also look to see if the agency has gone beyond its delegated powers. Courts defer to agency actions when the agency has exercised its discretion. Examples of agency discretion are policy-making discretion, discretion to choose rulemaking or adjudication, and prosecutorial discretion. Courts give less deference to agency interpretations of the Constitution and statutes. The scope of review examines how closely a court will scrutinize an agency action. At one end of the spectrum, de novo review is a complete review; at the other end is no review at all. In between are the standards of substantial evidence, arbitrary and capricious, and abuse of discretion. In general, a court, when engaging in judicial review, will look to see if the agency acted reasonably. If the agency acted reasonably and gave a reasoned decision, the court will not change the agency action. Various barriers to judicial review must be overcome to get the agency decision into a court for review. These barriers include exhaustion of administrative remedies, ripeness, standing, and primary jurisdiction. In addition, the appeal to the court must be filed within specified deadlines. Lawsuits can also be filed. Citizen suits, generally in environmental law, can be filed to compel agencies to enforce statutes and regulations.

KEY TERMS

affirmative action

compelling interest

de novo

due process clause of the Fifth Amendment

due process clause of the Fourteenth Amendment

entitlements

equal protection clause

exhaustion of administrative remedies

fundamental rights

judicial review

liberty

middle level scrutiny

narrowly tailored

primary jurisdiction

procedural due process

rational basis

ripeness

standing

state action

strict scrutiny

substantive due process

suspect class

REVIEW QUESTIONS

1. Explain two reasons for judicial review.
2. Explain how the term judicial review is used generally and in administrative law.
3. Distinguish procedural and substantive due process.
4. Are agencies bound to follow the Constitution? Explain.
5. State three interests that are protected by the Constitution under substantive due process and explain how these interests are established.
6. State the three main elements of procedural due process.
   a. What are the three levels of scrutiny used for the equal protection analysis?
   b. Match the three levels of equal protection scrutiny with the type of classification.
   c. What role does discretion play in judicial review of agency action?
   d. Discuss the scope of review and review of agency action.
   e. List and explain three barriers to judicial review.

MORE INFORMATION

1. To access the Attorney General's Report on the APA, go to http://www.oalj.dol.gov and click on APA/ALJs.
2. To learn about state court systems throughout the country, go to http://www.ncsonline.org/index.html.

PRACTICAL APPLICATIONS

1. A city housing authority operates city-owned rental property. The Housing Authority issued the following regulation:

"'Family' means a number of individuals related to the nominal head of the household or to the spouse of the nominal head of the household living as a single housekeeping unit in a single dwelling unit, but limited to the following:

   (a) Husband or wife of the nominal head of the household.

   (b) Unmarried children of the nominal head of the household or of the spouse of the nominal head of the household, provided, however, that such unmarried children have no children residing with them.

   (c) Father or mother of the nominal head of the household or of the spouse of the nominal head of the household.

   (d) Notwithstanding the provisions of subsection (b) hereof, a family may include not more than one dependent married or unmarried child of the nominal head of the household or of the spouse of the nominal head of the household and the spouse and dependent children of such dependent child. For the purpose of this subsection, a dependent person is one who has more than fifty percent of his total support furnished for him by the nominal head of the household and the spouse of the nominal head of the household.

   (e) A family may consist of one individual."

Mary Jones lives in the city together with her son, Dale Jones Sr., and her two grandsons, Dale Jr. and John Jones Jr. The two boys are first cousins rather than brothers. Mary Jones received a notice of violation from the Housing Authority, stating that John was an "illegal occupant" and directing her to comply with the ordinance. When she failed to remove him from her home, the city filed a criminal charge. What defense can Mrs. Jones raise to the charge?

2. Using the three tests of equal protection analysis, read the following actions of an administrative agency and state the constitutional test that a court would use to analyze the agency action.

   A. A state liquor control agency regulation allows men to apply for a state liquor license at age 25 but women can apply at age 21.

   B. A city housing authority institutes an affirmative action plan that requires that 30 percent of all contracts must be awarded to minority groups.

   C. A state prison system segregates newly arrived prisoners by race and ethnicity.

3. Read the following actions of an administrative agency and state the constitutional test under the due process clause that a court would use to analyze the agency action.

   A. Following the state's statute, the Marriage License Bureau refuses to issue a license to a same-sex couple.

B. A state health board issues a regulation that bans all forms of contraception.

4. For each of the following examples, state the standard of review that a court most likely would apply to a decision of an administrative agency:
   A. Informal adjudication
   B. Informal rulemaking
   C. Formal adjudication
   D. Formal rulemaking
   E. A request under the Freedom of Information Act (FOIA).

5. Go to the Web site of your state's court system and do the following:
   A. Diagram your state's court system from the trial court to the highest court in your state.
   B. Does your state have a court that deals primarily with appeals from state agencies? If so, state the name of the court.

@ LEARN ABOUT THE AGENCIES

Go to the Web sites of the following agencies and state their function.

1. FWS—Fish and Wildlife Service—http://www.fws.gov
2. BIA—Bureau of Indian Affairs—http://www.doi.gov/bureau-indian-affairs.html
3. OSM—Office of Surface Mining—http://www.osmre.gov
4. BLS—Bureau of Labor Statistics—http://www.stats.bls.gov
5. CFTC—Commodity Futures Trading Commission—http://www.cftc.gov

CHAPTER 7

Legislative Control of Administrative Agencies

CHAPTER OBJECTIVES

After reading this chapter, you should be able to:

- Assess the various methods of legislative control of administrative agencies.

- Evaluate how a legislature calibrates the power that it delegates to administrative agencies.

- Assess the role of the enabling act and new legislation as a control over an agency.

- Identify statutes that are designed to control the actions of administrative agencies.

CHAPTER OUTLINE

INTRODUCTION TO LEGISLATIVE CONTROL

Chapter 6 covered judicial control of administrative agencies and judicial review of administrative decisions. Recall the vital but limited nature of judicial review. In exercising judicial review, the courts are not to substitute their judgment for that of the agency but instead act as a key check on agency power to ensure fairness in the system of administrative law. For a legislature, the control is virtually total. This is so because agencies are creatures of the legislative branch, created to carry out the intent of the legislature. Just as the legislature can create an agency, it can likewise abolish it. Furthermore, once a regulation is enacted by an agency, Congress or a state legislature can simply erase it by passing a law. For example, if the Food and Drug Administration (FDA) issues a rule that no vending machines may be stocked with cigarettes, Congress can pass a law that negates that regulation. Other methods of legislative control, such as funding the agency, approving the agency officials, and political controls, will be covered in this chapter.

Control by the Enabling Act

The initial control is the enabling act which creates the agency. Recall from Chapter 1 how the enabling act delegates the power to the agency and tells the agency what it can and cannot do. Recall further the concept of discretion. Discretion is the ability to make choices. If the legislature gives a broad mandate to the agency, much discretion is delegated, but if specific guidance and restrictions are set out in the statute, the agency gets less discretion to act. By calibrating the power and discretion given to the agency, the legislature can control the agency. For example, Congress might limit discretion by setting out specific statutory provisions to the FDA on how certain drugs may be licensed. On the other hand, the delegation to the Federal Communications Commission (FCC) is to regulate the public airwaves "in the public interest," a broad delegation of power with much discretion.

See how Congress created the Department of Labor.

> There shall be an executive department in the Government to be called the Department of Labor, with a Secretary of Labor, who shall be the head thereof, to be appointed by the President, by and with the advice and consent of the Senate, and whose tenure of office shall be like that of the heads of the other executive departments. . . . The purpose of the Department of Labor shall be to foster, promote, and develop the welfare of the wage earners of the United States, to improve their working conditions, and to

advance their opportunities for profitable employment. 29 U.S.C. § 551.

Now note how Congress delegated power to the Secretary of Labor and the other cabinet departments.

> The head of an Executive department or military department may prescribe regulations for the government of his department, the conduct of its employees, the distribution and performance of its business, and the custody, use, and preservation of its records, papers, and property. This section does not authorize withholding information from the public or limiting the availability of records to the public. 5 U.S.C. § 301.

The entire list of Executive Departments is as follows:

The Department of State

The Department of the Treasury

The Department of Defense

The Department of Justice

The Department of the Interior

The Department of Agriculture

The Department of Commerce

The Department of Labor

The Department of Health and Human Services

The Department of Housing and Urban Development

The Department of Transportation

The Department of Energy

The Department of Education

The Department of Veterans Affairs

The Department of Homeland Security

5 U.S.C. § 101.

Refer to Exhibit 1-12, which lists not only the Executive Department (also known as the president's cabinet), but also many of the subcabinet agencies.

Another way that a legislature controls the agency through the enabling act is through the delegation of the traditional power wielded by the agency. Recall that many agencies possess three powers: legislative power in the form of rulemaking (see Chapter 2), executive power to enforce its regulations (see Chapter 3), and judicial power to adjudicate disputes (see Chapter 4). The enabling act can delegate all three powers or withhold certain of these powers. For example, the Federal

Trade Commission (FTC) and the FDA have all three powers, while the U.S. Commission on Civil Rights has no power to issue regulations, enforce regulations, or adjudicate disputes but is confined to investigating and fact gathering. The Equal Employment Opportunity Commission (EEOC) can adjudicate disputes with respect to sexual harassment but only has the power to issue "guidelines" and not binding regulations in this area. State legislatures pass enabling acts to control their state agencies in a similar fashion.

Control by Abolition and Sunset

What the legislature can create it can also abolish. See Exhibit 7-1, which is an excerpt of a bill that abolished the Interstate Commerce Commission.

The life of an agency can be regulated by a provision in the enabling act which terminates the agency at a certain time unless renewed by a new statute. This is called a *sunset provision*. Examples of agencies that have been sunseted include:

sunset provision
a provision of an enabling act that calls for the termination of an agency after a fixed time period

- War Claims Commission—created to adjudicate claims for victims who suffered personal injury or property damage at the hands of the enemy in World War II
- J.F.K. Assassination Review Board—created to obtain all documents related to the Kennedy assassination
- 9-11 Compensation Fund—created to compensate victims of the 9-11 attacks
- Office of Independent Counsel—created to investigate and prosecute high officials of the federal government

Exhibit 7-1
Congress Abolishes the Interstate Commerce Commission
H.R.2539
ICC Termination Act of 1995 (Enrolled as Agreed to or Passed by Both House and Senate)
TITLE I–ABOLITION OF INTERSTATE COMMERCE COMMISSION **SEC. 101. ABOLITION.**
The Interstate Commerce Commission is abolished.

Source: http://thomas.loc.gov

Statutes can also have sunset provisions that terminate specified sections of an act unless reenacted. Tax provisions and specified sections of the Patriot Act are examples of statutes which include sunset provisions.

Control by New Legislation

There are times when Congress or state legislatures want to change the scope and power of an agency after it is created. The change can enhance or decrease the power and discretion of an agency and can add or withdraw certain responsibilities. A legislature can even pass legislation that negates a regulation issued by an agency.

Control by new Congressional enactment is illustrated by the case of *Public Citizen v. Dept. of Health and Human Services*, 831 F.2d 1108 (D.C. Cir. 1987). The case involved the FDA listing as safe certain food color additives which studies revealed caused cancer in laboratory test animals. The actual risk to humans was extremely small to the point of being trivial. For example, one additive was calculated to have one in a 19 billion lifetime cancer risk. Nevertheless, the court reversed the FDA ruling that the additives were safe because Congress stated in what was known as the Delaney Clause of the Color Additive Amendments that a color additive shall be deemed unsafe, if tests revealed that the additives were found to "to induce cancer in man or animal . . ." It was undisputed that the additives caused cancer in animals. The FDA did not have the power to declare the additives safe because Congress delegated no discretion to the FDA on this issue.

A major annoyance to millions of Americans is the inevitable telephone call (many times during the dinner hour) by telemarketers, intent on exposing the virtues of their products. As a result of such intrusions, the FTC and the FCC began to implement rules to protect the public. See the following comments in Exhibit 7-2 received by the FTC on the issue of telemarketers.

Congress responded in 2003 to make it clear that the FTC had the power to establish a do-not-call registry by specifically delegating that power to the FTC. See Exhibit 7-3.

Some other examples of Congress exerting control over agencies by passing new legislation include:

- Congress prohibited the Consumer Product Safety Commission from regulating firearms. Pub.L. 94-284, § 3(e).
- Congress started in the 1970s to require agencies to consider the environmental impact of their policies and regulations. 42 U.S.C. 4332(1)(c).

Exhibit 7-2

Comments from the Public on Telemarketers

— Telemarketers should be prohibited from blocking telephone caller ID systems' access to the telemarketer's company name and telephone number. It is totally unfair that the consumer should be left totally helpless in the face of an intruder who knows where the consumer lives and the telephone number at which he/she can be reached, yet the consumer is denied the means to identify who and where the intruder is, for what company the intruder works and with whom the consumer can file a complaint for abuse, disrespect, intrusion, etc.

— I am fed up with telemarketers. We receive an average of three calls per night and even on Sunday afternoons. I used to be courteous and tell them I wouldn't be interested. I have found they either continue with their sales pitch or hang up on me. I have not found any who don't get very rude once they find out they will not make a sale. I have tried telling them to remove me from their calling list and it seems they are being taught to hang up before you can verify they are removing your name. When they call back, they say they have no record of you asking to be removed.

— We're still receiving too many calls. Last week, for example, someone called at 10:00 in the evening and others would not take no for an answer and kept phoning at other inappropriate times even when asked to remove our name and number off the list.

— We greatly appreciate the help by the Federal Trade Commission to put a stop to abusive and deceptive practices by telemarketers. We would like to see (and hear) the total termination of them all!

http://www.ftc.gov/bcp/rulemaking/tsr/comments/index.html

Exhibit 7-3

Authorization from Congress

(a) Authority.–The Federal Trade Commission is authorized under section 3(a)(3)(A) of the Telemarketing and Consumer Fraud and Abuse Prevention Act (15 U.S.C. 6102(a)(3)(A)) to implement and enforce a national do-not-call registry.

(b) Ratification.–The do-not-call registry provision of the Telemarketing Sales Rule (16 C.F.R. 310.4(b)(1)(iii)), which was promulgated by the Federal Trade Commission, effective March 31, 2003, is ratified.

Source: P.L. 108-82

- Congress stopped the FDA from banning the food sweetener saccharin. P.L. 95-203.

- Congress prevented the National Highway & Transportation Safety Administration (NHTSA) from requiring seat belt systems which prevented the car from starting or sounding a continuous buzzer when the belt was not fastened. 15 U.S.C. § 1410b.

- Congress was considering raising the maximum fines that the FCC can impose to $500,000 after the Janet Jackson "exposure" incident at the halftime show of the Super Bowl.

That Congress can act and change a policy of an agency when faced with public pressure is evidenced in the case of the food additive saccharin. In March of 1977 the Food and Drug Administration (FDA) proposed a ban on the use of saccharin which was at that time the only artificial non-nutritive sweetener available in the country for use in foods and beverages. The FDA stated that it was acting on scientific reports that showed that saccharin, when fed in high doses to rats, caused cancer. The proposed ban caused a public uproar which prompted Congress to act to save saccharin for Americans. Source: S. Rep. 95-353 (1977)

Control by Funding

Under Article I of the Constitution, Congress controls the spending of all federal dollars and can therefore control an agency by increasing or decreasing the annual budgets of the agencies. Although the president plays a key role in the budgetary process and there is much give and take in the political arena on how the money gets spent, it is up to Congress to allocate spending.

Many factors go into how agencies are funded. Agency budgets reflect national and state priorities. With the collapse of the Soviet Union and the end of the Cold War in the late 1980s, defense spending decreased. After the events of 9/11, funding was substantially increased, not only for defense, but also for the nation's intelligence agencies. The budget for the National Aeronautics and Space Administration (NASA) rose dramatically when exploration of space and getting a man on the moon was a priority in the 1960s. Preparation for an anticipated bird flu outbreak will swell the budgets of the health and science agencies, while a case of mad cow disease will do the same for agencies charged with safeguarding the nation's food supply. Each year the governors and the state legislatures go through a similar process in the state capitals.

> To see the budget of the United States and the agencies, go to the Congressional Budget Office (CBO) at http://www.cbo.gov, which prepares the budget for Congress.
> The Office of Management and Budget (OMB), at http://www.whitehouse.gov/omb, prepares the budget for the president.

A method of specific control used by Congress over the funding of an agency is through the use of appropriations riders. Appropriations riders are passed as part of larger spending bills and put strict and specific limits on how agencies can spend their funds. For example, in 1994, Congress passed an appropriations rider which stated:

(1) $1,500,000 are rescinded from the amounts available for making determinations whether a species is a threatened or endangered species and whether habitat is critical habitat under the Endangered Species Act of 1973 . . . and

(2) none of the remaining funds appropriated under that heading may be made available for making a final determination that a species is threatened or endangered or that habitat constitutes critical habitat (except a final determination that a species previously determined to be endangered is no longer endangered but continues to be threatened). P.L. 104-06.

Because of this rider and its restrictions on the expenditure of funds, the Secretary of the Interior was unable to place the California red-legged frog on the Endangered Species list. This use of the appropriations rider was approved, *Environmental Defense Center v. Babbitt,* 73 F.3d 867 (9th Cir. 1995).

Another example is the appropriations rider which prevented the Occupational Safety and Health Administration (OSHA) from issuing regulations on ergonomics. Ergonomics is the study of requirements of work in relation to the physical and psychological capabilities and limitations of people and focuses on harm caused to the body from long-term repetitive motions rather than acute trauma. See the following and also see the discussion of ergonomics later in the chapter under Control by the Congressional Review Act.

> None of the funds made available in this Act may be used by the Occupational Safety and Health Administration to promulgate or issue any proposed or final standard regarding ergonomic protection before September 30, 1998: Provided, That nothing in this section shall be construed to limit the Occupational Safety and Health Administration from issuing voluntary guidelines on ergonomic protection or from developing a proposed standard regarding ergonomic protection: Provided further, That no funds made available in this Act may be used by the Occupational Safety and Health Administration to enforce voluntary ergonomics guidelines . . . P.L. 105-78, § 104.

Control by Approval of Agency Officials

The president and governors appoint the heads of the agencies. For many appointments, the Senate of the U.S. Congress or the senates in the state legislature must approve the nominations. For example, as noted in Chapter 1, the president nominates the Secretaries of State and Defense and the Attorney General of the United States, but the Senate must approve these nominations. For the most part, the Senate confirms the president's choice. There are rare instances when the Senate rejects a presidential appointment, such as the case in 1989, when the Senate rejected the nomination of John Tower as Secretary of Defense because, in part, of allegations of an alcohol problem. Once in office, however, Congress cannot remove a cabinet officer except by impeachment. It is also fair to say that most governors get their cabinet appointments approved unless an extraordinarily controversial person is selected.

Control by Oversight

Congress and state legislatures form committees that have jurisdiction over the various agencies. The committees oversee the work of the agencies in a variety of ways. First, the Senate committees hold hearings on the nominations of the heads of agencies. The committee will vote on whether to approve the president's nomination. For example, the Senate Judiciary Committee holds hearings on the president's nomination for Attorney General. The Senate Armed Services Committee does the same for the Secretary of Defense. The Foreign Relations Committee approves the president's nomination for Secretary of State. The full Senate must then vote on the nomination. During the hearings, senators question the nominee about his or her qualifications and policy issues before casting their votes.

> To read a transcript of the testimony of Donald Rumsfeld when he appeared before the Senate Armed Services Committee in connection with his nomination as Secretary of Defense, go to: http://armed-services.senate.gov/hearings.

The House of Representatives is not tasked under the Constitution with approving nominations of agency officials, but like the Senate, the House does conduct other kinds of hearings.

Both houses of Congress and state legislatures through their committees and subcommittees exert oversight of the agencies over which they have jurisdiction. For example, the House and Senate have Intelligence Committees that oversee the intelligence agencies, including the Central Intelligence Agency (CIA) and military intelligence agencies such as the National Security Agency (NSA) and the Defense Intelligence Agency (DIA). Both the House and Senate have Homeland Security Committees that oversee the Department of Homeland Security.

On the House side, the Committee on Transportation and Infrastructure has several committees that specialize in oversight of various agencies. For example, the Subcommittee on Aviation has jurisdiction over most aspects of the Federal Aviation Administration (FAA), the Transportation Security Administration (TSA), and the National Transportation Safety Board (NTSB). On the Senate side, the U.S. Senate Committee on Commerce, Science, and Transportation handles issues that include communications, highways, aviation, rail, shipping, transportation security, merchant marine, the Coast Guard, oceans, fisheries, climate change, disasters, science, space, interstate commerce, tourism, consumer issues, economic development, technology, competitiveness, product safety, and insurance. Some of the subcommittees include Aviation, Space and Science, Fisheries and Coast Guard, and Trade, Tourism, and Economic Development.

The committees and subcommittees can call the heads of the agency to testify about the workings of the agency and policy matters confronting the agency. Sometimes there is an event or disaster that will trigger an oversight hearing. For example, if there is a train wreck or a plane crash, a committee of Congress will call the Secretary of Transportation or the head of the NTSB to testify. If there is a threat of an infectious disease such as SARS or bird flu, the head of the Centers for Disease Control (CDC) or the Secretary of Health and Human Services will be called.

The head of the Mine Safety and Health Administration will likely be called to testify if miners are trapped in an underground mine. See Exhibit 7-4, which is an excerpt of a hearing conducted by the Senate after fourteen miners were trapped in the Sago Mine in West Virginia in January 2006. Note that the senators will give an opening statement followed by statements by the witnesses. The senators will then ask questions of the witnesses.

Also testifying at this hearing were representatives of the Sago Mine and union officials. Within two months of this hearing, Senators Spector and Byrd introduced the Mine Safety and Health Act of 2006. Key provisions of the Act would require an operator of a mine to make available to each miner a wireless emergency tracking device and a wireless text messaging device. The operator of the mine would also have to establish oxygen stations with not less than a four-day supply of oxygen. Penalties for violation of mine safety would be substantially increased. Ultimately, the Mine Improvement and New Emergency Response Act of 2006 (P.L. 109-236) passed Congress and was signed into law by the president. The specific improvements listed here were not included. Included in the law, however, was the requirement that mine operators are required to submit a plan of mine safety improvement to the Secretary of Labor that meets specified safety requirements. Note how Congress responded to this disaster. Congress felt compelled to respond directly and not through the Mine Safety and Health Administration (MSHA), the federal regulatory agency. Congress adopted legislation that directly addressed mine safety rather than merely passing a law that would require the agency to issue new safety regulations. No doubt this was so because of the high publicity level of the case and the high loss of life.

The committees and subcommittees at times conduct hearings to investigate scandals. Some examples include Watergate, Iran Contra, and the corporate scandals such as WorldCom, Enron, and the savings and loan scandals of the 1980s and 1990s.

During all hearings witness are called to testify. The witnesses include not only the heads of the agency, but also agency staff, experts, local, federal and state politicians, and members of the general public.

Exhibit 7-4

Excerpt of Senate Hearing

SAGO MINE DISASTER AND AN OVERVIEW OF MINE SAFETY

HEARING before a Subcommittee of the Committee on Appropriations

SPECIAL HEARING

JANUARY 23, 2006–WASHINGTON, DC

Subcommittee on Departments of Labor, Health and Human Services, and Education, and Related Agencies

ARLEN SPECTER, Pennsylvania, Chairman

SAGO MINE DISASTER AND AN OVERVIEW OF MINE SAFETY

U.S. Senate,

Subcommittee on Labor, Health and Human

Services, Education, and Related Agencies,

Committee on Appropriations,

Washington, DC.

The subcommittee met at 11 a.m., in room SH-216, Hart

Senate Office Building, Senator Arlen Specter (chairman) presiding.

Present: Senators Specter, DeWine, Harkin, and Byrd.

OPENING STATEMENT OF SENATOR ARLEN SPECTER

Senator Specter. Good morning, ladies and gentlemen. The Appropriations Subcommittee on Labor, Health and Human Services and Education will now proceed with this hearing, which will inquire into mine safety on coal mines.

This hearing is prompted by the disaster at the Sago Mine on January 2. There have since been two more fatal accidents in West Virginia. I thank the distinguished ranking member of the full committee former president pro tempore Senator Byrd for his requesting the hearing. This subcommittee has been active on the investigation of mine disasters in the past, notably the Quecreek, which occurred in Pennsylvania in the year 2002, and there are very, very important questions on the issue on what has happened at these mine incidents, focusing on Sago. . . .

STATEMENT OF HON. DAVID G. DYE, ACTING ASSISTANT

SECRETARY, MINE SAFETY AND HEALTH

ADMINISTRATION, DEPARTMENT OF LABOR

ACCOMPANIED BY:

Exhibit 7-4 (Continued)

RAY McKINNEY, ADMINISTRATOR FOR COAL MINE SAFETY AND HEALTH, MINE SAFETY AND HEALTH ADMINISTRATION, DEPARTMENT OF LABOR

ROBERT M. FRIEND, ADMINISTRATOR FOR METAL AND NONMETAL MINE SAFETY AND HEALTH, MINE SAFETY AND HEALTH ADMINISTRATION, DEPARTMENT OF LABOR

ED CLAIR, ASSOCIATE SOLICITOR, DEPARTMENT OF LABOR

Mr. Dye. Thank you, Mr. Chairman, Senator Byrd, members of the committee. Thank you for this opportunity to appear before you to discuss the work of the Mine Safety and Health Administration and its performance related to the January 2 Sago Mine Explosion in Tallmansville, West Virginia.

My heart is especially heavy today as I appear before you just days after the Aracoma Mine accident in Melville, West Virginia, that claimed two lives. I would like to commend the 21 rescue teams involved in the Aracoma Mine rescue efforts this weekend and the 13 mine rescue teams involved at Sago Mine who put their own lives on the line in the quest to save their fellow miners. Most of these brave rescuers are volunteers. All of them willingly face danger and give generously of their time and in constant training. We cannot thank them enough for their help and their sacrifice; they are the embodiment of American spirit, selflessness and courage.

. . .

Senator Specter. Thank you, Mr. McKinney. We'll now start 5-minute rounds for each of the senators on the panel, and I would like everybody to stay within the time limits. We can go to a second round if necessary, and I will stay within the limit myself.

Mr. McKinney starting with you, there was a report that 11 of the miners had been reported alive, 12 miners reported alive, and it was especially cruel and to then find out that it was wrong, that they had died. Was there any way that report, false report, could have been avoided to save so much pain and suffering?

Mr. McKinney. I think it is sad, and I think it saddened all of us. There was a lot of people who felt very good for a short period of time and then were deeply saddened by that loss.

Senator Specter. Could it have been prevented?

Mr. McKinney. As I said earlier, those communications were coming from the underground. They were relayed several times before they reached the surface. We always ask repeat that, and you get a

(Continued)

Exhibit 7-4 (Continued)

response back what you have, but by the time it reaches the surface, you have to go back through six people again, and I think that's exactly what happened.

Senator Specter. Let me move on to another question because of limited time. The Sago Mine had 208 citations in the year 2005. Was any of those citations a causative factor in this disaster? Any of the facts uncovered in the citations a causative factor for this disaster?

Mr. McKinney. I think we're still investigating the disaster itself, and that will be determined by the investigation team if there's anything there we saw through the course of those inspections.

Senator Specter. Is it a possibility that one or more of these violations might have been the cause of the disaster?

Mr. McKinney. All of those 208 violations had been abated and corrected. The only outstanding violations that we had, had to do with roof conditions and tunnel liners being cushioned, and things of that nature. The other conditions had been corrected.

Senator Specter. I noted that these 208 citations resulted in fines of slightly in excess of $27,000. Was that sufficiently tough punishment for so many citations, Mr. Dye?

Mr. Dye. Nine of the most serious violations have been appealed. Those that haven't been assessed yet could double or triple the amount already assessed.

Senator Specter. Was the $27,000 in fines sufficient for those which hadn't been subject to appeal?

Mr. Dye. Those assessments are determined through a formula under our guidelines.

Senator Specter. We're going to take a close look at that, and I would like to have your one-by-one itemization of all of these violations specifying exactly what was involved and what penalty was imposed so this subcommittee can make an evaluation.

Mr. Dye. We will supply that for the record.

[Furnished as questions for the record.]

Senator Specter. Pardon me for moving on, but there's very little time, and we want to pinpoint the questions and the answers. Your unit had its funding reduced by $2,800,000 by virtue of a 1 percent across-the-board cut. Had the allocation remained without the 1 percent cut that this subcommittee had put into effect, we would have met the budget request for the administration. But with the 1 percent cut,

---

Exhibit 7-4 (Continued)

there was that reduction of $2,800,000, and I note that you've lost 183 positions as a result of budget insufficiency. Was that cut causative of the reductions in personnel, and were the reductions in personnel a causative factor in the Sago Mine tragedy?

Mr. Dye. Please allow me to answer the last question first. No, I don't think so. We have dealt with rescissions for several years in a row. Our strategy has been, where we have had to reduce personnel, to try to reduce them in administrative and support positions, to try to reorganize in a way that maximizes our ability to keep our enforcement personnel out there. In fact, the Congress directed us to do that, and we have tried to manage them that way.

Senator Specter. We would like a specification of what you would have done with the additional $2,800,000 had you been allocated that, and we would also like a written followup as to what were these 183 positions which you had to cut and what the impact has been on those cuts in terms of what your ability is to improvise mine safety. . .

Senator Specter. Senator Byrd. . .

---

http://www.gpoaccess.gov/congress

To access the United States House of Representatives Committees and Subcommittees, go to: http://www.house.gov. To access the United States Senate Committees and Subcommittees, go to: http://www.senate.gov.

In addition to holding hearings, Congress requires the agencies to submit written reports, generally on an annual basis.

Control by Direct Contact

Direct contact involves a member of the legislature or staff contacting a member of the public. Direct contact can happen when a constituent asks a legislator for help with finding a lost Social Security check or a veteran's benefit. Generally, direct contact is a legitimate and uncontroversial way for a legislator to help the public in its dealings with administrative agencies. However, if a legislator crosses the line and pressures an administrator into doing a "favor" for a constituent or a campaign contributor, serious ethical issues can arise. For example, the Senate Ethics Committee investigated five senators (the Keating 5) with respect to their meetings with the head of the Federal Home Loan Bank Board (FHLBB). The senators were having direct contact with this agency (which regulates savings and loans) on behalf of the president of Lincoln Savings and Loan Association (Lincoln), Charles Keating, who had arranged for thousands of dollars to be contributed to the campaigns of the senators. The senators were interested in an ongoing investigation of Lincoln and whether the FHLBB should make changes in rules that were favorable to Lincoln. Lincoln eventually collapsed, and many people lost their life savings. Keating was ordered to pay back over $36,000,000 and served time in prison on federal and state fraud charges. Although the Senate Ethics Committee did not say that the senators violated any criminal laws, the investigation found various ethical breaches for imposing undue pressure on the FHLBB. See *Keating v. OTS,* 45 F.3d 322 (9th Cir. 1994) and S. Rep No.102-223 (1991).

Control by Sunshine Provisions

sunshine laws

a law requiring open meetings of government agencies

State and federal laws require that government agencies conduct their business in full view of the public. These laws are called *sunshine laws.* The federal Sunshine Act, 5 U.S.C. § 552b, requires that meetings of an agency be open to the public so that the public may have the chance to examine the workings of agencies. Most meetings of agencies of multimember agencies such as the FCC are covered. Meetings must generally be publicly announced at least one week before they are held. Meetings are covered under the Sunshine Act when the agency members take action on behalf of the agency and where deliberations of the agency dispose of official business. The exceptions to the Sunshine Act are similar to the Freedom of Information Act (FOIA) exemptions. See Chapter 5 for a list of FOIA exemptions.

Control by Legislative Veto

legislative veto

the power of the legislative branch to cancel or veto a decision of an agency

The term *legislative veto* seems out of place since it is the president and most governors that have the veto power. However, in hundreds of laws, Congress has reserved to itself the power to cancel or "veto" a decision of an agency. The Supreme Court ruled that the legislative veto was unconstitutional in *INS v. Chadha*, 462 U.S. 919 (1983). (See excerpt in Case Law later in the chapter.) In *Chadha*, the Immigration and Naturalization Service (INS) issued an order that Chadha, an alien, could remain in the United States. The House of Representatives, acting without the Senate or president voted to cancel or veto the order of the INS. The court ruled that the legislative veto was unconstitutional for two reasons. First, the legislative veto violated the Presentment Clause, Article I, Section 7, Clause 2, because the issue was never presented to the president for his signature. Second, Article I, Sections 1 and 7, require that no law can take effect unless *both* the House and the Senate concur. Here, only the House acted; therefore *bicameralism* was violated.

Control by the Congressional Review Act

One response to the Supreme Court's ruling declaring the legislative veto unconstitutional was the enactment of the Congressional Review Act (CRA). The Act attempts to regain a bit of lost control after the legislative veto was declared to be unconstitutional by forcing agencies to submit any major rule (one with an annual impact of $100 million or more) to Congress before it can be a final, binding regulation. The rule cannot take effect until 60 days after it is submitted to Congress or after it is published in the *Federal Register*, whichever is later. If both houses of Congress thereafter pass a resolution of disapproval which is then signed by the president, the regulation is killed. The agency is forbidden to issue another rule that is similar to the disapproved rule. Because both houses act and because the resolution of disapproval is presented to the president, the CRA avoids both unconstitutional aspects of the legislative veto as found in *Chadha*.

Congress has not chosen to use the CRA very often but did so in 2001 for the ergonomics rule. 57 Fed. Reg. 34192-01. Recall that ergonomics is the study of requirements of work in relation to the physical and psychological capabilities and limitations of people and focuses on harm caused to the body from long-term repetitive motions rather than acute trauma. The rule required businesses to address ergonomics hazards. Using the CRA, both houses of Congress voted to disapprove the rule, President Bush agreed, and the ergonomics rule was stopped. See Exhibit 7-5.

bicameralism

the principle that requires both house of Congress to pass a bill before the bill can be presented to the president

> **Exhibit 7-5**
>
> ## Congress Rejects Ergonomics Rule
>
> **One Hundred Seventh Congress**
> **of the**
> **United States of America**
>
> **AT THE FIRST SESSION**
>
> Begun and held at the City of Washington on Wednesday, the third day of January, two thousand and one.
>
> Joint Resolution
>
> Providing for congressional disapproval of the rule submitted by the Department of Labor under chapter 8 of title 5, United States Code, relating to ergonomics.
>
> *Resolved by the Senate and House of Representatives of the United States of America in Congress assembled,* That Congress disapproves the rule submitted by the Department of Labor relating to ergonomics (published at 65 Fed. Reg. 68261 [2000]), and such rule shall have no force or effect.

Source: P.L. 107-5

Paperwork Reduction Act

The Paperwork Reduction Act (44 U.S.C. §§ 3501–3520) was passed to try to limit the government's ability to require records and to lessen the cost to the government of collecting and maintaining the information. The Act applies when an agency of the federal government attempts to require reporting or recordkeeping that applies to ten or more people. The main purposes of the Act are to:

> minimize the paperwork burden for individuals, small businesses, educational and nonprofit institutions, Federal contractors, State, local and tribal governments, and other persons resulting from the collection of information by or for the Federal Government; and ensure the greatest possible public benefit from and maximize the utility of information created, collected, maintained, used, shared and disseminated by or for the Federal Government.

The main purposes of the Act are achieved by forcing agencies to justify their recordkeeping rules and to get approval from the Office of Information and Regulatory Affairs (OIRA) before the rules are operative. OIRA is an agency within the Office of Management and Budget (OMB). OMB assists the president in overseeing the preparation of the federal budget.

Regulatory Flexibility Act and Unfunded Mandates Act

Agency regulations in many instances impose additional costs on the public and businesses. The Regulatory Flexibility Act (5 U.S.C. §§ 601–612) requires agencies to study the economic effects of their regulations on small businesses. The Act also requires the agency to minimize the economic effect on businesses and to consider alternatives where possible.

The Unfunded Mandates Act (2 U.S.C.A. § 1532) addresses the cost of regulations on state and local governments, or the private sector, and requires preparation of a written cost-benefit analysis and selection of the least costly, most cost-effective, or least burdensome alternative that achieves the objectives of the rule. The Act applies to any proposed rule that adds $100 million per year in costs on state and local governments or private businesses.

Agencies to Oversee Other Agencies

Congress created the Congressional Research Service (CRS) and the Office of Technology Assessment (OTA) to conduct studies of agency activities. The CRS and OTA work exclusively for members of Congress to analyze issues to produce reports on issues, legislation, and activities of agencies. The General Accountability Office (GAO) is the most powerful congressional agency that conducts investigations and issues reports on the work of agencies. Many times reports from these agencies will trigger oversight hearings.

> To see reports generated by the CRS, OTA (no longer in operation), and GAO, go to:
> CRS: http://fas.org/man/crs
> OTS: http://www.wws.princeton.edu/ota/ns20/pubs_f.html
> GAO: http://www.gao.gov

Advisory Committees

Many agencies have advisory committees to assist them in their work. The advisory committees consist of experts in the field for which the agency is responsible. For example, the FDA is an agency that uses many advisory committees. See the following advisory committees for medical devices and radiation-emitting products.

Committee
Anesthesiology and Respiratory Therapy Devices Panel
Circulatory System Devices Panel
Clinical Chemistry and Clinical Toxicology Devices Panel
Dental Products Panel
Device Good Manufacturing Practice Advisory Committee
Ear, Nose, and Throat Devices Panel
Gastroenterology and Urology Devices Panel
General and Plastic Surgery Devices Panel
General Hospital and Personal Use Devices Panel
Hematology and Pathology Devices Panel
Immunology Devices Panel
Medical Devices Dispute Resolution Panel
Microbiology Devices Panel
Molecular and Clinical Genetics Panel
National Mammography Quality Assurance Advisory Committee
Neurological Devices Panel
Obstetrics and Gynecology Devices Panel
Ophthalmic Devices Panel
Orthopaedic and Rehabilitation Devices Panel
Radiological Devices Panel
Technical Electronic Product Radiation Safety Standards Committee

The many other advisory committees of the FDA, lists of members, and transcripts of the meetings are available. (See: http://www.fda.gov/oc/advisory/default.htm.) Congress passed the Federal Advisory Committees Act, Appendix 2 to title 5 of the United States Code, in an effort to keep the workings of the advisory committees in the open and subject to public scrutiny. The Act, in general, requires that meetings be open to the public and allows the public a chance to attend and participate and to have access to the records of the advisory committees.

CASE LAW

IMMIGRATION AND NATURALIZATION SERVICE [INS]
v. CHADHA
462 U.S. 919 (1983).

[Section 244(a)(1) of the Immigration and Nationality Act provides that the Attorney General shall have discretion to "suspend" the deportation of an otherwise deportable alien who meets certain statutory standards, one of which is that deportation would cause "extreme hardship." The Attorney General delegated this power to the INS.

Chadha was an East Indian who had been born in Kenya and held a British passport; he had been admitted on a student visa but had overstayed the expiration date. Following an on-the-record hearing, an immigration judge held that Chadha was deportable but ordered that deportation be suspended because Chadha met the "extreme hardship" requirements of the statute.

Section 244(c)(1) provides that the Attorney General must report all suspensions of deportation to Congress; and § 244(c)(2) provides that if, during the legislative session in which the suspension is reported or the next session, either the House or the Senate passes a resolution "stating in substance that it does not favor the suspension of such deportation," the effect will be to "veto" the suspension.

> "Every Order, Resolution, or Vote to which the Concurrence of the Senate and House of Representatives may be necessary (except on a question of Adjournment) *shall be* presented to the President of the United States; and before the Same shall take Effect, *shall be* approved by him, or being disapproved by him, shall be repassed by two thirds of the Senate and House of Representatives, according to the Rules and Limitations prescribed in the Case of a Bill." Art. I, § 7, cl. 3.

These provisions of Art. I are integral parts of the constitutional design for the separation of powers. . . . [T]he purposes underlying the Presentment Clauses, Art. I, § 7, cls. 2, 3, and the bicameral requirement of Art. I, § 1 and § 7, cl. 2, guide our resolution of the important question presented in this case. . . .

The records of the Constitutional Convention reveal that the requirement that all legislation be presented to the President before becoming law was uniformly accepted by the Framers. Presentment to

(Continued)

the President and the Presidential veto were considered so imperative that the draftsmen took special pains to assure that these requirements could not be circumvented. During the final debate on Art. I, § 7, cl. 2, James Madison expressed concern that it might easily be evaded by the simple expedient of calling a proposed law a "resolution" or "vote" rather than a "bill." As a consequence, Art. I, § 7, cl. 3, was added.

The decision to provide the President with a limited and qualified power to nullify proposed legislation by veto was based on the profound conviction of the Framers that the powers conferred on Congress were the powers to be most carefully circumscribed. It is beyond doubt that lawmaking was a power to be shared by both Houses and the President. In The Federalist No. 73 (H. Lodge ed. 1888), Hamilton focused on the President's role in making laws:

> "If even no propensity had ever discovered itself in the legislative body to invade the rights of the Executive, the rules of just reasoning and theoretic propriety would of themselves teach us that the one ought not to be left to the mercy of the other, but ought to possess a constitutional and effectual power of self-defense." *Id.*, at 457–458. . . .

The President's role in the lawmaking process also reflects the Framers' careful efforts to check whatever propensity a particular Congress might have to enact oppressive, improvident, or ill-considered measures. . . .

The bicameral requirement of Art. I, §§ 1, 7 was of scarcely less concern to the Framers than was the Presidential veto and indeed the two concepts are interdependent. By providing that no law could take effect without the concurrence of the prescribed majority of the Members of both Houses, the Framers reemphasized their belief, already remarked upon in connection with the Presentment Clauses, that legislation should not be enacted unless it has been carefully and fully considered by the Nation's elected officials. . . .

We see therefore that the Framers were acutely conscious that the bicameral requirement and the Presentment Clauses would serve essential constitutional functions. The President's participation in the legislative process was to protect the Executive Branch from Congress and to protect the whole people from improvident laws. The division of the Congress into two distinctive bodies assures that the legislative power would be exercised only after opportunity for full study and debate in separate settings. The President's unilateral veto power, in turn, was limited by the power of two thirds of both Houses of Congress to overrule a veto thereby precluding final arbitrary action of one person. It emerges clearly that the prescription for legislative action in Art. I, §§ 1, 7 represents the Framers' decision that the legislative power of the Federal government be exercised in accord with a single, finely wrought and exhaustively considered, procedure. . . .

When any Branch acts, it is presumptively exercising the power the Constitution has delegated to it. See *J W Hampton Jr. & Co. v. United States*, 276 U.S. 394, 406 (1928). When the Executive acts, it presumptively acts in an executive or administrative capacity as defined in Art. II. And when, as here, one House of Congress purports to act, it is presumptively acting within its assigned sphere.

Beginning with this presumption, we must nevertheless establish that the challenged action under § 244(c)(2) is of the kind to which the procedural requirements of Art. I, § 7 apply. Not every action taken by either House is subject to the bicameralism and presentment requirements of Art. I. Whether actions taken by either House are, in law and fact, an exercise of legislative power depends not on their form but upon "whether they contain matter which is properly to be regarded as legislative in its character and effect."

Examination of the action taken here by one House pursuant to § 244(c)(2) reveals that it was essentially legislative in purpose and effect. In purporting to exercise power defined in Art. I, § 8, cl. 4 to "establish an uniform Rule of Naturalization," the House took action that had the purpose and effect of altering the legal rights, duties and relations of persons, including the Attorney General, Executive Branch officials and Chadha, all outside the legislative branch. . . .

The legislative character of the one-House veto in this case is confirmed by the character of the Congressional action it supplants. Neither the House of Representatives nor the Senate contends that, absent the veto provision in § 244(c)(2), either of them, or both of them acting together, could effectively require the Attorney General to deport an alien once the Attorney General, in the exercise of legislatively delegated authority,[1] had determined the alien should remain in the United States. Without the challenged provision in §

---

[1]Congress protests that affirming the Court of Appeals in these cases will sanction "lawmaking by the Attorney General. . . . Why is the Attorney General exempt from submitting his proposed changes in the law to the full bicameral process?" To be sure, some administrative agency action—rulemaking, for

(Continued)

244(c)(2), this could have been achieved, if at all, only by legislation requiring deportation. . . .

The nature of the decision implemented by the one-House veto in this case further manifests its legislative character. After long experience with the clumsy, time consuming private bill procedure, Congress made a deliberate choice to delegate to the Executive Branch, and specifically to the Attorney General, the authority to allow deportable aliens to remain in this country in certain specified circumstances. It is not disputed that this choice to delegate authority is precisely the kind of decision that can be implemented only in accordance with the procedures set out in Art. I. Disagreement with the Attorney General's decision on Chadha's deportation—that is, Congress' decision to deport Chadha—no less than Congress' origi-

example—may resemble "lawmaking." See 5 U.S.C. § 551(4), which defines an agency's "rule" as "the whole or part of an agency statement of general or particular applicability and future effect designed to implement, interpret, or prescribe *law* or policy. . . ." This Court has referred to agency activity as being "quasi-legislative" in character. Clearly, however, "[i]n the framework of our Constitution, the President's power to see that the laws are faithfully executed refutes the idea that he is to be a lawmaker."

When the Attorney General performs his duties pursuant to § 244, he does not exercise "legislative" power. The bicameral process is not necessary as a check on the Executive's administration of the laws because his administrative activity cannot reach beyond the limits of the statute that created it—a statute duly enacted pursuant to Art. I, §§ 1, 7. The constitutionality of the Attorney General's execution of the authority delegated to him by § 244 involves only a question of delegation doctrine. The courts, when a case or controversy arises, can always "ascertain whether the will of Congress has been obeyed," and can enforce adherence to statutory standards.

It is clear, therefore, that the Attorney General acts in his presumptively Art. II capacity when he administers the Immigration and Nationality Act. Executive action under legislatively delegated authority that might resemble "legislative" action in some respects is not subject to the approval of both Houses of Congress and the President for the reason that the Constitution does not so require. That kind of Executive action is always subject to check by the terms of the legislation that authorized it; and if that authority is exceeded it is open to judicial review as well as the power of Congress to modify or revoke the authority entirely. A one-House veto is clearly legislative in both character and effect and is not so checked; the need for the check provided by Art. I, §§ 1, 7, is therefore clear. Congress' authority to delegate portions of its power to administrative agencies provides no support for the argument that Congress can constitutionally control administration of the laws by way of a congressional veto.

nal choice to delegate to the Attorney General the authority to make that decision, involves determinations of policy that Congress can implement in only one way; bicameral passage followed by presentment to the President. Congress must abide by its delegation of authority until that delegation is legislatively altered or revoked. . . .

. . . There are but four provisions in the Constitution, explicit and unambiguous, by which one House may act alone with the unreviewable force of law, not subject to the President's veto: [initiation of impeachments by the House; and impeachment trials, approval of presidential appointments, and ratification of treaties by the Senate]. These carefully defined exceptions from presentment and bicameralism underscore the difference between the legislative functions of Congress and other unilateral but important and binding one-House acts provided for in the Constitution. . . .

Since it is clear that the action by the House under § 244(c)(2) was not within any of the express constitutional exceptions authorizing one House to act alone, and equally clear that it was an exercise of legislative power, that action was subject to the standards prescribed in Article I. . . .

The veto authorized by § 244(c)(2) doubtless has been in many respects a convenient shortcut; the "sharing" with the Executive by Congress of its authority over aliens in this manner is, on its face, an appealing compromise. In purely practical terms, it is obviously easier for action to be taken by one House without submission to the President; but it is crystal clear from the records of the Convention, contemporaneous writings and debates, that the Framers ranked other values higher than efficiency. The records of the Convention and debates in the States preceding ratification underscore the common desire to define and limit the exercise of the newly created federal powers affecting the states and the people. There is unmistakable expression of a determination that legislation by the national Congress be a step-by-step, deliberate and deliberative process.

The choices we discern as having been made in the Constitutional Convention impose burdens on governmental processes that often seem clumsy, inefficient, even unworkable, but those hard choices were consciously made by men who had lived under a form of government that permitted arbitrary governmental acts to go unchecked. There is no support in the Constitution or decisions of this Court for the proposition that the cumbersomeness and delays often encountered in complying with explicit Constitutional standards may be avoided, either by the Congress or by the President. . . .

(Continued)

We hold that the Congressional veto provision in § 244(c)(2) is severable from the Act and that it is unconstitutional.

POWELL, J., concurring in the judgment.

The Court's decision, based on the Presentment Clauses, Art. I, § 7, cls. 2 and 3, apparently will invalidate every use of the legislative veto. The breadth of this holding gives one pause. Congress has included the veto in literally hundreds of statutes, dating back to the 1930s. Congress clearly views this procedure as essential to controlling the delegation of power to administrative agencies. One reasonably may disagree with Congress' assessment of the veto's utility, but the respect due its judgment as a coordinate branch of Government cautions that our holding should be no more extensive than necessary to decide this case. In my view, the case may be decided on a narrower ground. When Congress finds that a particular person does not satisfy the statutory criteria for permanent residence in this country it has assumed a judicial function in violation of the principle of separation of powers. Accordingly, I concur only in the judgment. . . .

Functionally, the [separation of powers] doctrine may be violated in two ways. One branch may interfere impermissibly with the other's performance of its constitutionally assigned function. Alternatively, the doctrine may be violated when one branch assumes a function that more properly is entrusted to another. This case presents the latter situation. . . .

On its face, the House's action appears clearly adjudicatory. The House did not enact a general rule; rather it made its own determination that six specific persons did not comply with certain statutory criteria. It thus undertook the type of decision that traditionally has been left to other branches. Even if the House did not make a *de novo* determination, but simply reviewed the Immigration and Naturalization Service's findings, it still assumed a function ordinarily entrusted to the federal courts. See 5 U.S.C. § 704 (providing generally for judicial review of final agency action). Where, as here, Congress has exercised a power "that cannot possibly be regarded as merely in aid of the legislative function of Congress," the decisions of this Court have held that Congress impermissibly assumed a function that the Constitution entrusted to another branch.

The impropriety of the House's assumption of this function is confirmed by the fact that its action raises the very danger the Framers sought to avoid—the exercise of unchecked power. In deciding whether Chadha deserves to be deported, Congress is not subject to any internal constraints that prevent it from arbitrarily depriving him of the right to remain in this country. Unlike the judiciary or an administrative agency, Congress is not bound by established substantive rules. Nor is it subject to the procedural safeguards, such as the right to counsel and a hearing before an impartial tribunal, that are present when a court or an agency adjudicates individual rights. The only effective constraint on Congress' power is political, but Congress is most accountable politically when it prescribes rules of general applicability. When it decides rights of specific persons, those rights are subject to "the tyranny of a shifting majority."

. . . In my view, when Congress undertook to apply its rules to Chadha, it exceeded the scope of its constitutionally prescribed authority. I would not reach the broader question whether legislative vetoes are invalid under the Presentment Clauses.

WHITE, J., dissenting.

Today the Court not only invalidates § 244(c)(2) of the Immigration and Nationality Act, but also sounds the death knell for nearly 200 other statutory provisions in which Congress has reserved a "legislative veto." For this reason, the Court's decision is of surpassing importance. And it is for this reason that the Court would have been well-advised to decide the case, if possible, on the narrower grounds of separation of powers, leaving for full consideration the constitutionality of other congressional review statutes operating on such varied matters as war powers and agency rulemaking, some of which concern the independent regulatory agencies.

The prominence of the legislative veto mechanism in our contemporary political system and its importance to Congress can hardly be overstated. It has become a central means by which Congress secures the accountability of executive and independent agencies. Without the legislative veto, Congress is faced with a Hobson's choice: either to refrain from delegating the necessary authority, leaving itself with a hopeless task of writing laws with the requisite specificity to cover endless special circumstances across the entire policy landscape, or in the alternative, to abdicate its lawmaking function to the executive branch and independent agencies. To choose the former leaves major national problems unresolved; to opt for the latter risks unaccountable policymaking by those not elected to fill that role. Accordingly, over the past five decades, the legislative veto has been placed in nearly 200 statutes. The device is known in every field of governmental concern:

(Continued)

reorganization, budgets, foreign affairs, war powers, and regulation of trade, safety, energy, the environment and the economy. . . .

Even this brief review suffices to demonstrate that the legislative veto is more than "efficient, convenient, and useful." It is an important if not indispensable political invention that allows the President and Congress to resolve major constitutional and policy differences, assures the accountability of independent regulatory agencies, and preserves Congress' control over lawmaking. Perhaps there are other means of accommodation and accountability, but the increasing reliance of Congress upon the legislative veto suggests that the alternatives to which Congress must now turn are not entirely satisfactory.

The history of the legislative veto also makes clear that it has not been a sword with which Congress has struck out to aggrandize itself at the expense of the other branches—the concerns of Madison and Hamilton. Rather, the veto has been a means of defense, a reservation of ultimate authority necessary if Congress is to fulfill its designated role under Article I as the nation's lawmaker. While the President has often objected to particular legislative vetoes, generally those left in the hands of congressional committees, the Executive has more often agreed to legislative review as the price for a broad delegation of authority. To be sure, the President may have preferred unrestricted power, but that could be precisely why Congress thought it essential to retain a check on the exercise of delegated authority. . . .

The Court holds that the disapproval of a suspension of deportation by the resolution of one House of Congress is an exercise of legislative power without compliance with the prerequisites for lawmaking set forth in Art. I of the Constitution. Specifically, the Court maintains that the provisions of § 244(c)(2) are inconsistent with the requirement of bicameral approval, implicit in Art. I, § 1, and the requirement that all bills and resolutions that require the concurrence of both Houses be presented to the President, Art. I, § 7, cl. 2 and 3.

I do not dispute the Court's truismatic exposition of these clauses. There is no question that a bill does not become a law until it is approved by both the House and the Senate, and presented to the President. Similarly, I would not hesitate to strike an action of Congress in the form of a concurrent resolution which constituted an exercise of original lawmaking authority. I agree with the Court that the President's qualified veto power is a critical element in the distribution of powers under the Constitution, widely endorsed among the Framers, and intended to serve the President as a defense against legislative encroachment and to check the "passing of bad laws through haste, inadvertence, or design." The Federalist No. 73, at 458 (A. Hamilton). The records of the Convention reveal that it is the first purpose which figured most prominently but I acknowledge the vitality of the second. *Id.*, at 443. I also agree that the bicameral approval required by Art. I, §§ 1, 7 "was of scarcely less concern to the Framers than was the Presidential veto," and that the need to divide and disperse legislative power figures significantly in our scheme of Government. All of this . . . is entirely unexceptionable.

It does not, however, answer the constitutional question before us. The power to exercise a legislative veto is not the power to write new law without bicameral approval or presidential consideration. The veto must be authorized by statute and may only negative what an Executive department or independent agency has proposed. On its face, the legislative veto no more allows one House of Congress to make law than does the presidential veto confer such power upon the President. Accordingly, the Court properly recognizes that it "must establish that the challenged action under § 244(c)(2) is of the kind to which the procedural requirements of Art. I, § 7 apply" and admits that "not every action taken by either House is subject to the bicameralism and presentation requirements of Art. I." . . .

It is long-settled that Congress may "exercise its best judgment in the selection of measures, to carry into execution the constitutional powers of the government," and "avail itself of experience, to exercise its reason, and to accommodate its legislation to circumstances." *McCulloch v. Maryland,* 4 Wheat. 316, 415–416, 420 (1819).

The Court heeded this counsel in approving the modern administrative state. The Court's holding today that all legislative-type action must be enacted through the lawmaking process ignores that legislative authority is routinely delegated to the Executive branch, to the independent regulatory agencies, and to private individuals and groups. . . .

This Court's decisions sanctioning such delegations make clear that Article I does not require all action with the effect of legislation to be passed as a law. . . .

If Congress may delegate lawmaking power to independent and executive agencies, it is most difficult to understand Article I as forbidding Congress from also reserving a check on legislative power for itself. Absent the veto, the agencies receiving delegations of legislative or quasi-legislative power may issue regulations having the

(Continued)

force of law without bicameral approval and without the President's signature. It is thus not apparent why the reservation of a veto over the exercise of that legislative power must be subject to a more exacting test. In both cases, it is enough that the initial statutory authorizations comply with the Article I requirements.

Nor are there strict limits on the agents that may receive such delegations of legislative authority so that it might be said that the legislature can delegate authority to others but not to itself. While most authority to issue rules and regulations is given to the executive branch and the independent regulatory agencies, statutory delegations to private persons have also passed this Court's scrutiny. . . . [T]he Court's decision today suggests that Congress may place a "veto" power over suspensions of deportation in private hands or in the hands of an independent agency, but is forbidden from reserving such authority for itself. Perhaps this odd result could be justified on other constitutional grounds, such as the separation of powers, but certainly it cannot be defended as consistent with the Court's view of the Article I presentment and bicameralism commands. . . .

The Court also takes no account of perhaps the most relevant consideration: However resolutions of disapproval under § 244(c)(2) are formally characterized, in reality, a departure from the status quo occurs only upon the concurrence of opinion among the House, Senate, and President. Reservations of legislative authority to be exercised by Congress should be upheld if the exercise of such reserved authority is consistent with the distribution of and limits upon legislative power that Article I provides. . . .

The central concern of the presentation and bicameralism requirements of Article I is that when a departure from the legal status quo is undertaken, it is done with the approval of the President and both Houses of Congress—or, in the event of a presidential veto, a two-thirds majority in both Houses. This interest is fully satisfied by the operation of § 244(c)(2). The President's approval is found in the Attorney General's action in recommending to Congress that the deportation order for a given alien be suspended. The House and the Senate indicate their approval of the Executive's action by not passing a resolution of disapproval within the statutory period. Thus, a change in the legal status quo—the deportability of the alien—is consummated only with the approval of each of the three relevant actors. The disagreement of any one of the three maintains the alien's pre-existing status. . . .

It is true that the purpose of separating the authority of government is to prevent unnecessary and dangerous concentration of power in one branch. For that reason, the Framers saw fit to divide and balance the powers of government so that each branch would be checked by the others. Virtually every part of our constitutional system bears the mark of this judgment.

But the history of the separation of powers doctrine is also a history of accommodation and practicality. . . . This is the teaching of *Nixon v. Administrator of General Services,* 433 U.S. 425 (1977), which, in rejecting a separation of powers objection to a law requiring that the Administrator take custody of certain presidential papers, set forth a framework for evaluating such claims:

> [I]n determining whether the Act disrupts the proper balance between the coordinate branches, the proper inquiry focuses on the extent to which it prevents the Executive Branch from accomplishing its constitutionally assigned functions. Only where the potential for disruption is present must we then determine whether that impact is justified by an overriding need to promote objectives within the constitutional authority of Congress.

Section 244(c)(2) survives this test. The legislative veto provision does not "prevent the Executive Branch from accomplishing its constitutionally assigned functions." . . .

A legislative check on an inherently executive function, for example that of initiating prosecutions, poses an entirely different question. But the legislative veto device here—and in many other settings—is far from an instance of legislative tyranny over the Executive. It is a necessary check on the unavoidably expanding power of the agencies, both executive and independent, as they engage in exercising authority delegated by Congress.

I regret that I am in disagreement with my colleagues on the fundamental questions that this case presents. But even more I regret the destructive scope of the Court's holding. It reflects a profoundly different conception of the Constitution than that held by the Courts which sanctioned the modern administrative state. Today's decision strikes down in one fell swoop provisions in more laws enacted by Congress than the Court has cumulatively invalidated in

(Continued)

> its history. I fear it will now be more difficult "to insure that the fundamental policy decisions in our society will be made not by an appointed official but by the body immediately responsible to the people."
>
> [Justice Rehnquist dissented, arguing that the suspension and veto provisions were not severable. Justice White agreed.]

Reprinted from Asimow, M.; Bonfield, A.; and Levin, R. State and Federal Administrative Law, 2nd Ed. © 1998, with permission of Thomson West.

CHAPTER SUMMARY

Agencies are created by the legislative branch and are therefore ultimately controlled by Congress and state legislatures. The initial control is the enabling act which creates the agency and delegates power to the agency. A legislature can abolish any agency and can pass statutes that countermand regulations and/or change agency jurisdiction. A sunset provision calls for the abolition of the agency after a set period of time. Sunshine laws require agencies to do their business in open view of the public. Other controls include setting the levels of funding for the agencies, approval of agency officials, and legislative oversight. Control by direct contact or casework, where members of the legislature deal directly with agency officials, is a legitimate source of control as long as the legislators do not improperly influence agency officials to do special favors for constituents or campaign contributors. The legislative veto, where one house of Congress or both could nullify an agency action without presidential approval, was declared unconstitutional by the Supreme Court. This limitation on legislative power was addressed by the Congressional Review Act which gives Congress control over major agency regulations.

KEY TERMS

bicameralism
legislative veto

sunset provision
sunshine law

REVIEW QUESTIONS

1. List and describe three legislative controls of administrative agencies.
2. Explain how Congress uses the enabling act and new legislation to control the powers of administrative agencies.
3. Discuss the role of committee hearings with respect to legislative oversight of administrative agencies.
4. Why was the legislative veto ruled unconstitutional?
5. List some other statutes that seek to control administrative agencies.

MORE INFORMATION

1. Go to the Web site of the United States Commission on Civil Rights to see what power has been delegated to this agency. Click on "mission and powers." http://www.usccr.gov
2. Go to http://www.senate.gov and click on "committees" to see a list of Senate committees and the areas over which the committees have jurisdiction.
3. Go to http://www.house.gov/house and click on "committees" to see a list of House committees and the areas over which the committees have jurisdiction.
4. Go to http://www.nrc.gov to see how the Nuclear Regulatory Commission was established and to see which laws govern its operations.

PRACTICAL APPLICATIONS

1. Go to http://www.gao.gov, the Web site for the Government Accountability Office (GAO).
   A. What is the function of the GAO?
   B. What was the prior name of this agency?
   C. Is the GAO subject to FOIA?
   D. What is the name and title of the person who heads the GAO?
   E. What is the term of office for the head of the GAO?
2. Go to the Web site of the Government Printing Office at http://www.gpoaccess.gov/chearings/index.html and answer the following questions.

Search the 109th Congress for the House and put in the search "boxing." Click on the fourth hit.

   A. What is the name of the subcommittee that conducted the hearing?
   B. Who is the chairman of the subcommittee?

C. What is the date that the hearing was held?

3. Answer the following questions after reviewing Exhibit 7-4.

A. What committee of Congress conducted the hearing?

B. Over which agencies does this committee have oversight responsibilities?

C. What was the date of the hearing?

D. What was the subject matter of the hearing?

E. What senators were present?

F. Identify Mr. McKinney and Mr. Dye and the agency they represented.

4. In the aftermath of the Sago Mine tragedy, Congress introduced corrective legislation. Find the bill and answer the following questions.

Go to thomasloc.gov.

Select the 109 Congress.

Select Search Bill Text.

Put in as your search "S 2308" or "Mine Safety and Health Act of 2006."

A. To what committee was the bill referred?

B. What existing statute does this bill amend?

C. Under Section 2 of the bill, state three requirements that improve mine safety.

D. Under Section 5 of the bill, what is the time period within which an operator must inform the Secretary of Labor of a disaster, and what is the penalty for failing to do so?

L E A R N   A B O U T   T H E   A G E N C I E S

Go to the Web sites of the following agencies and state their function.

1. OSHA—Occupational Safety and Health Administration—http://www.osha.gov

2. NSA—National Security Agency—http://www.nsa.gov

3. DHS—Department of Homeland Security— http://www.dhs.gov/dhspublic/index.jsp

4. CDC—Centers for Disease Control—http://www.cdc.gov

5. FCC—Federal Communications Communication—http://www.fcc.gov

CHAPTER 8

Executive Control of Administrative Agencies

CHAPTER OBJECTIVES

After reading this chapter, you should be able to:

- List and describe the various methods of executive control of administrative agencies.

- Analyze the legal sources of executive power over administrative agencies.

- Assess the role of the principle of separation of powers with respect to presidential power over administrative agencies.

CHAPTER OUTLINE

INTRODUCTION TO EXECUTIVE CONTROL

The president and the governors of the states have an array of powers that exert control over administrative agencies. Although the specific nature of the power of governors differs from the president's and varies from state to state, some common examples of the powers of the president and governors of the states are:

- power to appoint the heads of agencies
- power over the budget
- power to issue executive orders
- power to set policy
- power to veto legislative bills
- power to direct litigation
- power of reorganization
- power to pardon

Some states allow the governor to approve regulations and to rescind regulations that have been enacted. However, the president cannot exert such direct control over agency regulations.

With respect to the president, there is no specific provision of the Constitution that can be cited for executive authority over administrative agencies. Over the years, presidents have cited the following provisions of Article II as their constitutional authority.

- Article II, Section 1, invests the president with executive power.
- Article II, Section 2, provides that the president is the commander-in-chief of the armed forces.
- Article II Section 2, gives the president the appointment power.
- Article II, Section 3, obligates the president to take care that the laws be faithfully executed.
- Article II, Section 2, authorizes the president to require the opinions in writing of the heads of the executive departments.

The following sections will discuss aspects of executive control over administrative agencies.

APPOINTMENT/REMOVAL POWER AND SEPARATION OF POWERS

appointments clause
a provision in the Constitution, Article II, Section 2, that vests power in the president to appoint officials to the federal government

The president is given the power in Article II, Section 2, in what is known as the *appointments clause*, to appoint people to the federal government. The appointments clause states that the president shall "nominate and by and with the Advice and Consent of the Senate, shall appoint Ambassadors . . . Judges of the supreme Court, and all other Officers of the United States." Further, Congress "may by Law vest Appointment of such inferiors Officers, as they may think proper, in the President alone, in thc Courts of Law, or in the Heads of Departments." This section establishes two classes of appointees—principal officers and inferior officers. The principal officers are the high-level officers of government that serve directly under the president. For example, members of the president's cabinet, such as the Secretary of State or Secretary of Defense are principal officers who are appointed by the president and must be approved by the Senate. The Secretary of Defense is said to serve at the pleasure of the president and can be removed by the president at any time. Congress cannot restrict the president's power to remove the Secretary of Defense.

The second class of appointees is inferior officers. Congress can vest the appointment of these inferior officers in the president alone, the courts, or in the Cabinet officers. The president's power to remove the inferior officers can be restricted by Congress if Congress places fixed terms for the inferior officer to serve or provides that the officer cannot be *removed except for cause.* Congress can neither appoint nor remove principal or inferior officers except by the process of impeachment. For example, Congress can remove a federal judge or cabinet officer only by impeachment. Congress places these restrictions most often in the enabling act when it creates administrative agencies. The purpose of these restrictions is to give the agency a degree of independence from the president to better serve the public interest. See Chapter 1 for a discussion of the different kinds of administrative agencies.

The cases of *Buckley v. Valeo,* 424 U.S. 1 (1976), *Morrison v. Olson,* 487 U.S. 654 (1988), and *Bowsher v. Synar,* 478 U.S. 714 (1986), illustrate the basic principles of appointment and removal and the interrelated constitutional principle of separation of powers. In *Buckley,* Congress established an agency called the Federal Election Commission (FEC). The FEC was given powers to issue and enforce regulations concerning federal elections. Some of the commissioners were appointed by members of Congress. Since these commissioners were inferior officers with executive power, Congress had no right to appoint them; therefore separation of powers was violated.

At issue in *Morrison* was the constitutionality of a law that authorized the creation of an "independent counsel" to investigate and prosecute certain high-ranking government officials. The independent counsel was appointed by a special federal court, not the president. The

removal for cause

the principle that an official does not serve at the pleasure of the president and can be removed only for misconduct or incapacity president through the Attorney General could only remove the independent counsel for cause. The Court ruled that the independent counsel was an inferior officer who performed executive functions. Although the president's power of removal was restricted by the removal for cause requirement, the law did not interfere with the president's constitutional duty to take care that the laws be faithfully executed, and thus neither separation of powers nor the appointments clause were violated.

At issue in *Bowsher* was a deficit control statute known as the Gramm-Rudman-Hollings Act which set a maximum deficit amount for federal spending toward a goal of a zero budget deficit. If Congress did not meet the goals, the Act required the Comptroller General to make across-the-board cuts in most government programs. The Comptroller General is a legislative officer removable by Congress. The Court found that in making the automatic cuts that the statute required, the Comptroller General was performing an executive function. The statute violated the doctrine of separation of powers because it gave executive power to an officer in the legislative branch.

As these cases illustrate, the Constitution set up a structure of separation of powers between the president and Congress with respect to the appointment and removal process of government officials, including the heads of the administrative agencies. The Supreme Court as the coequal third branch must decide if an agency structure of appointment and removal of the officials is constitutional. Justice Jackson captured the principle of separation of powers when he stated:

> While the Constitution diffuses power the better to secure liberty, it also contemplates that practice will integrate the dispersed powers into a workable government. It enjoins upon its branches separateness but interdependence, autonomy but reciprocity. *Youngstown Sheet & Tube Co. v. Sawyer*, 343 U.S. 579, 635 (1952) (Jackson, J., concurring).

POWER OVER THE BUDGET

Although under Article I of the Constitution Congress has the power to spend, the president plays an important role in formulating the budgets of the agencies. The president, through the Office of Management and Budget (OMB), submits an annual budget to Congress. The OMB is an agency inside the Executive Office of the President. Most agencies must submit their budgets to the OMB for clearance before the overall budget is submitted to Congress. Budget requests will reflect the policy choices of the president and governors. Domestic concerns and even international issues can cause a president to ask for more money for an agency. For example, in 2005, President Bush announced a budget plan that would increase funding for health agencies to fight the possibility of a bird flu pandemic. Governors throughout the country are taking similar measures.

One tool that is available to many governors, but not to the president, is the *line-item veto*. The line-item veto allows the president or governor to "line out" or cancel individual spending items, while allowing the rest of the spending in the bill to become law. The Supreme Court ruled in *Clinton v. New York*, 524 U.S. 417 (1998), that the line-item veto is unconstitutional because Article I, Section 7, Clause 2 of the Constitution requires the president to either veto or approve the *entire* bill. *Clinton v. New York* applies only to the federal government. Governors in many states have the line-item veto because the constitutions of those states make it legal.

line-item veto
a law that gives authority to the president or a governor to cancel individual items of spending

EXECUTIVE ORDERS

An *executive order* is a directive issued by the president or a governor that implements a policy but need not be passed by a legislature. Presidents and governors use executive orders to gain influence over agencies and to assure that most agencies of the government are in compliance with administrative policy. Presidents issue hundreds of executive orders during the course of their administration. Many executive orders have significant effects on a broad range of policies affecting how agencies operate. For example, President Johnson issued an executive order prohibiting discrimination in public employment. President Ford also issued an executive order prohibiting assassination of foreign leaders by any agencies of the United States. Executive orders are issued by number and are published in the *Federal Register*.

executive order
a directive issued by the president or governors to agencies or officials

Executive orders are a powerful tool of the president because they do not have to be approved by Congress. However, to be a valid exercise of power, the executive order must be based on the president's constitutional powers stemming from Article II (see preceding listing of presidential powers) *or* be based on power delegated to the president by Congress. If a president were to issue an executive order without such authority, the president would be encroaching on the powers of Congress and violating principles of separation of powers because Article I of the Constitution vests legislative power only in Congress. One of the key Supreme Court cases which set the parameters of presidential powers involved the legality of an executive order issued by President

This executive order made many federal employees very happy.

Executive Order 13,281 of December 19, 2002

Half-Day Closing of Executive Departments and Agencies of the Federal Government on Tuesday, December 24, 2002

By the authority vested in me as President by the Constitution and the laws of the United States of America, it is hereby ordered as follows:

Section 1. All executive branch departments and agencies of the Federal Government shall be closed and their employees excused from duty for the last half of the scheduled workday on Tuesday, December 24, 2002, the day before Christmas Day, except as provided in section 2 below.

Sec. 2. The heads of executive branch departments and agencies may determine that certain offices and installations of their organizations, or parts thereof, must remain open and that certain employees must report for duty for the full scheduled workday on December 24, 2002, for reasons of national security or defense or other public reasons.

Sec. 3. Tuesday, December 24, 2002, shall be considered as falling within the scope of Executive Order 11,582 of February 11, 1971, and of 5 U.S.C. 5546 and 6103(b) and other similar statutes insofar as they relate to the pay and leave of employees of the United States.

George W. Bush

THE WHITE HOUSE,
December 19, 2002.

Truman during the Korean War. *Youngstown Sheet & Tube Co. v. Sawyer,* 343 U.S. 579 (1952). (See excerpt in Case Law at the end of the chapter.) Known as the Steel Seizure case, the President Truman issued an executive order to the Secretary of Commerce to take control of steel mills and keep them running because of a pending nationwide strike. The Supreme Court first looked to see if Congress had delegated power to the President authorizing the executive order. No such statute existed, so if President Truman had the authority to issue the order, that authority had to be found in the Constitution. The Court could find no such authority in the president's Article II powers. The Court stated:

The President's power, if any, to issue the order must stem either from an act of Congress or from the Constitution itself. There is no statute that expressly authorizes the President to take possession of property as he did here. Nor is there any act of Congress to which our attention has been directed from which such a power can fairly be implied. Indeed, we do not understand the Government to rely on statutory authorization for this seizure. There are two statutes which do authorize the President to take both personal and real property under certain conditions. However, the Government admits that these conditions were not met and that the President's order was not rooted in either of the statutes.

It is clear that if the President had authority to issue the order he did, it must be found in some provisions of the Constitution. And it is not claimed that express constitutional language grants this power to the President. The contention is that presidential power should be implied from the aggregate of his powers under the Constitution. Particular reliance is placed on provisions in Article II which say that 'the executive Power shall be vested in a President' . . . that 'he shall take Care that the Laws be faithfully executed'; and that he 'shall be Commander in Chief of the Army and Navy of the United States.'

The order cannot properly be sustained as an exercise of the President's military power as Commander in Chief of the Armed Forces. *Youngstown Sheet & Tube Co. v. Sawyer,* 343 U.S. 585–587.

The president's order could not stand as he attempted to take private property when such an action is a legislative function reserved for Congress under Article I. Therefore, the president violated the separation of powers by performing a legislative function in encroaching on the powers reserved to Congress. Justice Jackson's concurring opinion has been a model on how courts should examine all presidential actions including executive orders. The Steel Seizure case is also important because of the concurring opinion of Justice Jackson, which provides a three-category framework to review the validity of presidential actions.

1. When the President acts pursuant to an express or implied authorization from Congress, his authority is at its maximum, for it includes all that he possesses in his own right, plus all that Congress can delegate. . . . 2. When the President acts in the absence of either a congressional grant or denial of authority, he can only rely upon his own independent powers, but there is a zone of twilight in which he and Congress may have concurrent authority, or in which its distribution is uncertain. . . . 3. When the President takes measures incompatible with the express or implied will of Congress, his power is at its lowest ebb, for then he can only rely upon

his own constitutional powers minus any constitutional powers of Congress over the matter. *Youngstown Sheet & Tube Co. v. Sawyer,* 343 U.S. 579, 635–637 (1952) (Jackson, J., concurring).

For Justice Jackson, the president acted contrary to the will of Congress and thus placed the Steel Seizure case into the third category, portraying the president at his lowest ebb and finding that the president had exceeded his Article II powers.

See Exhibit 8-1, which is Executive Order 13,295. This executive order revised the list of quarantinable communicable diseases to add the disease SARS to the list. Note that the executive order first states under what authority the president is acting. For this executive order, the president is relying on the presidential powers vested in him by Article II of the Constitution. (See the Article II powers listed in the Introduction to Executive Control section of this chapter.) In addition to such constitutional powers, the order also states that the president is relying on powers delegated to him under the Public Health Service Act. Also note that Section 5 revokes a previous executive order. Presidents can unilaterally revoke executive orders that they have issued or orders that their predecessors have issued.

An executive order may be invalid because it conflicts with a statute. In 1995, the president issued an executive order barring the federal government from contracting with employers who hire permanent replacements during a lawful strike. The order was held to be invalid because it conflicted with the National Labor Relations Act. *Chamber of Commerce v. Reich,* 74 F.3d 1322 (D.C. Cir. 1996).

All officials of the government, including the president, must deal with the costs of any program and must balance the time, personnel, and dollars expended against the benefits to be gained by the policy. Agencies struggle with these issues each time a regulation is issued. For example, what is the cost versus the benefit to the public when the food industry is required to provide detailed labeling of ingredients on food packages? What is the cost of environmental regulations on businesses?

In order to gain more control over the cost of regulations to the public and industry, presidents have issued executive orders to force agencies to use cost benefit analyses when formulating regulations. For example, Executive Order 12,866 issued by President Clinton requires agencies to submit major rules (those rules that have a $100 million effect on the economy) to the Office of Information and Regulatory Affairs (OIRA), which is a branch of the Office of Management and Budget. The agencies must demonstrate that the benefits of the regulation outweigh the cost before implementing the regulation. See Appendix C for the text of Executive Order 12,866.

Exhibit 8-1

Executive Order Quarantinable Communicable Diseases

Federal Register/Vol. 68, No. 68 /Wednesday, April 9, 2003/Presidential Documents 17255

Executive Order 13,295 of April 4, 2003

Revised List of Quarantinable Communicable Diseases

By the authority vested in me as President by the Constitution and the laws of the United States of America, including section 361(b) of the Public Health Service Act (42 U.S.C. 264(b)), it is hereby ordered as follows:

Section 1. Based upon the recommendation of the Secretary of Health and Human Services (the "Secretary"), in consultation with the Surgeon General, and for the purpose of specifying certain communicable diseases for regulations providing for the apprehension, detention, or conditional release of individuals to prevent the introduction, transmission, or spread of suspected communicable diseases, the following communicable diseases are hereby specified pursuant to section 361(b) of the Public Health Service Act:

(a) Cholera; Diphtheria; infectious Tuberculosis; Plague; Smallpox; Yellow Fever; and Viral Hemorrhagic Fevers (Lassa, Marburg, Ebola, Crimean-Congo, South American, and others not yet isolated or named).

(b) Severe Acute Respiratory Syndrome (SARS), which is a disease associated with fever and signs and symptoms of pneumonia or other respiratory illness, is transmitted from person to person predominantly by the aerosolized or droplet route, and, if spread in the population, would have severe public health consequences.

Sec. 2. The Secretary, in the Secretary's discretion, shall determine whether a particular condition constitutes a communicable disease of the type specified in section 1 of this order.

Sec. 3. The functions of the President under sections 362 and 364(a) of the Public Health Service Act (42 U.S.C. 265 and 267(a)) are assigned to the Secretary.

Sec. 4. This order is not intended to, and does not, create any right or benefit enforceable at law or equity by any party against the United States, its departments, agencies, entities, officers, employees or agents, or any other person.

Sec. 5. Executive Order 12,452 of December 22, 1983, is hereby revoked.

THE WHITE HOUSE,

April 4, 2003.

GEORGE W. BUSH

List of Executive Orders
Presidents and the number of times they used executive orders. The list is the total number of executive orders including executive orders affecting administrative agencies.

Franklin Roosevelt—3,728
Harry Truman—896
Dwight Eisenhower—486
John Kennedy—214
Lyndon Johnson—324
Richard Nixon—346
Gerald Ford—169
Jimmy Carter—320
Ronald Reagan—381
George Bush—166
Bill Clinton—346
George W. Bush—197

Source: http://www.archives.gov

Executive orders are also intended to assure that the agencies are pursuing policies that are consistent with the policies of the president. By requiring submission of any proposed regulation, the president can ensure compliance with many of his polices.

CONTROL BY POLICY SETTING

Every president comes into office with an agenda, priorities, and a set of policy goals and objectives. The policies are reflected to a great degree in the campaign promises articulated in the presidential campaign and are generally consistent with the platform of the political party of which he is a member. The programs and policies cover the whole range of government activities including international affairs, domestic policy, and the direction of the agencies. As we have seen, presidents can establish policies by the appointments they make, the budgets they recommend, and the executive orders they issue. Presidents also set administrative policy through the issuance of directives to various agencies of the government. For example, soon after President Clinton took office in 1993, he issued a series of directives that reversed the policies of the previous administrations. One such directive ordered the Secretary of

Health and Human Services to rescind a ban that had been placed on RU-486, commonly know as the "abortion pill." See Exhibit 8-2. Another directive to the Secretary of Health and Human Services directed the secretary to lift a moratorium on federal funding of fetal tissue research. See Exhibit 8-3.

Exhibit 8-2

Memorandum to the Secretary of Health and Human Services

Memorandum

Weekly Compilation of Presidential Documents

http://www.gpoaccess.gov/

Monday, January 25, 1993

Volume 29–Number 3

Pages 57-91

Administration of William J. Clinton

Memorandum on Importation of **RU-486**

January 22, 1993

Memorandum for the Secretary of Health and Human Services

Subject: Importation of **RU-486**

In Import Alert 66-47, the Food and Drug Administration ("FDA") excluded the drug Mifepristine–commonly known as **RU-486**–from the list of drugs that individuals can import into the United States for their "personal use," although the drugs have not yet been approved for distribution by the FDA. (See FDA Regulatory Procedures Manual, Chapter 9-71.) Import Alert 66-47 effectively bans the importation into this Nation of a drug that is used in other nations as a nonsurgical means of abortion.

I am informed that in excluding **RU-486** from the personal use importation exemption, the FDA appears to have based its decision on factors other than an assessment of the possible health and safety risks of the drug. Accordingly, I hereby direct that you promptly instruct the FDA to determine whether there is sufficient evidence to warrant exclusion of **RU-486** from the list of drugs that qualify for the personal use importation exemption. Furthermore, if the FDA concludes that **RU-486** meets the criteria for the personal use importation exemption, I direct that you immediately take steps to rescind Import Alert 66-47.

(Continued)

Exhibit 8-2 (Continued)

In addition, I direct that you promptly assess initiatives by which the Department of Health and Human Services can promote the testing, licensing, and manufacturing in the United States of **RU-486** or other antiprogestins.

You are hereby authorized and directed to publish this memorandum in the Federal Register.

William J. Clinton

Exhibit 8-3

Memorandum to the Secretary of Health and Human Services

Weekly Compilation of Presidential Documents

http://www.gpoaccess.gov/

Monday, January 25, 1993

Volume 29–Number 3

Pages 57-91

Administration of William J. Clinton

Memorandum on Fetal Tissue Transplantation Research

January 22, 1993

Memorandum for the Secretary of Health and Human Services

Subject: Federal Funding of Fetal Tissue Transplantation Research

On March 22, 1988, the Assistant Secretary for Health of Health and Human Services ("HHS") imposed a temporary moratorium on Federal funding of research involving transplantation of fetal tissue from induced abortions. Contrary to the recommendations of a National Institutes of Health advisory panel, on November 2, 1989, the Secretary of Health and Human Services extended the moratorium indefinitely. This moratorium has significantly hampered the development of possible treatments for individuals afflicted with serious diseases and disorders, such as Parkinson's disease, Alzheimer's disease, diabetes, and leukemia. Accordingly, I hereby direct that you immediately lift the moratorium.

You are hereby authorized and directed to publish this memorandum in the Federal Register.

William J. Clinton

A third memorandum to the Secretary of Health and Human Services lifted the regulations know as the "Gag Rule" issued in February 1988, which prohibited health professionals at federally funded health clinics from providing their patients with information, counseling, or referrals concerning abortion. Previously, the Supreme Court had upheld the "Gag Rule" in the case of *Rust v. Sullivan,* 500 U.S. 173 (1991). (See excerpt in Case Law at the end of the chapter.) See Exhibit 8-4.

Exhibit 8-4

Memorandum to the Secretary of Health and Human Services

[Weekly Compilation of Presidential Documents]

http://www.gpoaccess.gov/

[Page 87-88]

Monday, January 25, 1993

Volume 29–Number 3

Pages 57-91

Administration of William J. Clinton

Memorandum on the Title X "Gag Rule"

January 22, 1993

Memorandum for the Secretary of Health and Human Services

Subject: The Title X "Gag Rule"

Title X of the Public Health Services Act provides Federal funding for family planning clinics to provide services for low-income patients.

The Act specifies that Title X funds may not be used for the performance of abortions, but places no restrictions on the ability of clinics that receive Title X funds to provide abortion counseling and referrals or to perform abortions using non-Title X funds. During the first 18 years of the program, medical professionals at Title X clinics provided complete, uncensored information, including nondirective abortion counseling. In February 1988, the Department of Health and Human Services adopted regulations, which have become known as the "Gag Rule," prohibiting Title X recipients from providing their patients with information, counseling, or referrals concerning abortion. Subsequent attempts by the Bush Administration to modify the Gag Rule and ensuing litigation have created confusion and uncertainty about the current legal status of the regulations.

(Continued)

> ### Exhibit 8-4 (Continued)
>
> The Gag Rule endangers women's lives and health by preventing them from receiving complete and accurate medical information and interferes with the doctor-patient relationship by prohibiting information that medical professionals are otherwise ethically and legally required to provide to their patients. Furthermore, the Gag Rule contravenes the clear intent of a majority of the members of both the United States Senate and House of Representatives, which twice passed legislation to block the Gag Rule's enforcement but failed to override Presidential vetoes.
>
> For these reasons, you have informed me that you will suspend the Gag Rule pending the promulgation of new regulations in accordance with the "notice and comment" procedures of the Administrative Procedure Act. I hereby direct you to take that action as soon as possible. I further direct that, within 30 days, you publish in the Federal Register new proposed regulations for public comment.
>
> You are hereby authorized and directed to publish this memorandum in the Federal Register.
>
> William J. Clinton

Exhibit 8-5 is a memorandum to the Secretary of Defense directing the secretary to lift a ban and permit abortion services to be provided at U.S. military facilities if paid entirely by private funds.

These four directives changed policies of previous administrations and are illustrative of how a president can inject his policy preferences into agency policy.

POWER TO VETO

The president and most governors have the power to veto bills passed by the legislature. If the president does not like a bill that creates an agency or one that modifies the powers of an agency, the president can stop it with a veto. If Congress passes a law that rescinds a regulation of an agency, the president can stop this law by the veto. However, Congress can override the veto with a two-thirds (2/3) vote of both Houses, but this is extremely difficult to do.

POWER OVER LITIGATION

The Department of Justice is headed by the Attorney General of the United States, who is appointed by the president with the approval

---

Exhibit 8-5

Memorandum to the Secretary of Defense

[Weekly Compilation of Presidential Documents]

http://www.gpoaccess.gov/

[Page 88]

Monday, January 25, 1993

Volume 29–Number 3

Pages 57-91

Administration of William J. Clinton

Memorandum on Abortions in Military Hospitals

January 22, 1993

Memorandum for the Secretary of Defense

Subject: Privately Funded Abortions at Military Hospitals

Section 1093 of title 10 of the United States Code prohibits the use of Department of Defense ("DOD") funds to perform abortions except where the life of a woman would be endangered if the fetus were carried to term. By memoranda of December 21, 1987, and June 21, 1988, DOD has gone beyond what I am informed are the requirements of the statute and has banned all abortions at U.S. military facilities, even where the procedure is privately funded. This ban is unwarranted. Accordingly, I hereby direct that you reverse the ban immediately and permit abortion services to be provided, if paid for entirely with non-DOD funds and in accordance with other relevant DOD policies and procedures.

You are hereby authorized and directed to publish this memorandum in the Federal Register.

William J. Clinton

---

of the Senate. The Attorney General is charged with enforcing federal law. Recall from Chapter 6 that a person or business can challenge the legality of a regulation in a court. Most agencies rely on the Department of Justice to represent them if the legality of a regulation is litigated. A presidential administration can exert influence over administrative agencies in the selection of the regulations it chooses to defend and the enthusiasm with which it defends them. In *FDA v. Brown and Williamson*, 529 U.S. 120 (2000), the Clinton administration defended regulations issued by the FDA that regulated tobacco. Because of the policy differences between presidential administrations, it is highly unlikely that the Reagan administration or either Bush administrations would have defended the tobacco regulations.

REORGANIZATION

In an attempt to make the numerous and varied agencies of the government more efficient and to promote better management of the agencies, Congress has from time to time delegated to the president the power to reorganize the agencies of the executive branch. A good example of presidential reorganization was the creation of the Environmental Protection Agency by President Nixon. Under the terms of Reorganization Plan No.3 of 1970, the following functions moved to the new Environmental Protection Agency:

- The functions carried out by the Federal Water Quality Administration (from the Department of the Interior).
- Functions with respect to pesticides studies now vested in the Department of the Interior.
- The functions carried out by the National Air Pollution Control Administration (from the Department of Health, Education, and Welfare).
- The functions carried out by the Bureau of Solid Waste Management and the Bureau of Water Hygiene, and portions of the functions carried out by the Bureau of Radiological Health of the Environmental Control Administration (from the Department of Health, Education, and Welfare).
- Certain functions with respect to pesticides carried out by the Food and Drug Administration (from the Department of Health, Education, and Welfare).
- Authority to perform studies relating to ecological systems now vested in the Council on Environmental Quality.
- Certain functions respecting radiation criteria and standards now vested in the Atomic Energy Commission and the Federal Radiation Council.
- Functions respecting pesticides registration and related activities now carried out by the Agricultural Research Service (from the Department of Agriculture).

POWER TO PARDON

The president, under Article II, Section 2 of the Constitution, can pardon people who have or may have committed federal crimes. The governor can pardon persons convicted of state crimes. One of the most famous pardons in history was the pardon by President Ford of ex–President Nixon in 1974, in the aftermath of the Watergate scandal. In 1992, President Bush pardoned officials involved in the Iran-Contra scandal, including ex-Secretary of Defense Casper Weinberger. See Exhibit 8-6. The pardon is the last word because a pardon is not reviewable by a court. See Exhibit 8-7, which is the pardon granted by President Carter to those who evaded the draft during the Vietnam War.

Exhibit 8-6
Presidential Pardon
57 FR 62145, Pres. Proc. No. 6518
Proclamation 6518
Grant of Executive Clemency
December 24, 1992
By the President of the United States of America
A Proclamation
Today I am exercising my power under the Constitution to pardon former Secretary of Defense Caspar Weinberger and others for their conduct related to the Iran-Contra affair. For more than 6 years now, the American people have invested enormous resources into what has become the most thoroughly investigated matter of its kind in our history. During that time, the last American hostage has come home to freedom, worldwide terrorism has declined, the people of Nicaragua have elected a democratic government, and the Cold War has ended in victory for the American people and the cause of freedom we championed. . . .
I have also decided to pardon five other individuals for their conduct related to the Iran-Contra affair: Elliott Abrams, Duane Clarridge, Alan Fiers, Clair George, and Robert McFarlane. First, the common denominator of their motivation—whether their actions were right or wrong—was patriotism. Second, they did not profit or seek to profit from their conduct. Third, each has a record of long and distinguished service to this country. And finally, all five have already paid a price—in depleted savings, lost careers, anguished families—grossly disproportionate to any misdeeds or errors of judgment they may have committed . . .

(Continued)

Exhibit 8-6 (Continued)

*62147 For more than 30 years in public service, I have tried to follow three precepts: honor, decency, and fairness. I know, from all those years of service, that the American people believe in fairness and fair play. In granting these pardons today, I am doing what I believe honor, decency, and fairness require.

NOW, THEREFORE, I, GEORGE BUSH, President of the United States of America, pursuant to my powers under Article II, Section 2, of the Constitution, do hereby grant a full, complete, and unconditional pardon to Elliott Abrams, Duane R. Clarridge, Alan Fiers, Clair George, Robert C. McFarlane, and Caspar W. Weinberger for all offenses charged or prosecuted by Independent Counsel Lawrence E. Walsh or other member of his office, or committed by these individuals and within the jurisdiction of that office.

IN WITNESS WHEREOF, I have hereunto set my hand this twenty-fourth day of December, in the year of our Lord nineteen hundred and ninety-two, and of the Independence of the United States of America the two hundred and seventeenth.

GEORGE BUSH

Exhibit 8-7

Presidential Pardon

Proclamation 4483–Granting pardon for violations of the Selective Service Act, August 4, 1964, to March 28, 1973

Source: The provisions of Proclamation 4483 of Jan. 21, 1977, appear at 42 FR 4391, 3 CFR, 1977

Acting pursuant to the grant of authority in Article II, Section 2, of the Constitution of the United States, I, Jimmy Carter, President of the United States, do hereby grant a full, complete and unconditional pardon to: (1) all persons who may have committed any offense between August 4, 1964 and March 28, 1973 in violation of the Military Selective Service Act or any rule or regulation promulgated thereunder; and (2) all persons heretofore convicted, irrespective of the date of conviction, of any offense committed between August 4, 1964 and March 28, 1973 in violation of the Military Selective Service Act, or any rule or regulation promulgated thereunder, restoring to them full political, civil and other rights.

This pardon does not apply to the following who are specifically excluded therefrom:

Exhibit 8-7 (Continued)

(1) All persons convicted of or who may have committed any offense in violation of the Military Selective Service Act, or any rule or regulation promulgated thereunder, involving force or violence; and

(2) All persons convicted of or who may have committed any offense in violation of the Military Selective Service Act, or any rule or regulation promulgated thereunder, in connection with duties or responsibilities arising out of employment as agents, officers or employees of the Military Selective Service system.

IN WITNESS WHEREOF, I have hereunto set my hand this 21st day of January, in the year of our Lord nineteen hundred and seventy-seven, and of the Independence of the United States of America the two hundred and first.

Jimmy Carter

CASE LAW

SECTION 1. PRESIDENTIAL ACTION AFFECTING "CONGRESSIONAL" POWERS
YOUNGSTOWN SHEET & TUBE CO. v. SAWYER
[THE STEEL SEIZURE CASE]
343 U.S. 579, 72 S.Ct. 863, 96 L.Ed. 1153 (1952).

JUSTICE BLACK delivered the opinion of the Court. . . .
We are asked to decide whether [President Truman] was acting within his constitutional power when he issued an order directing the Secretary of Commerce [Sawyer] to take possession of and operate most of the Nation's steel mills. The mill owners argue that the President's order amounts to lawmaking, a legislative function which the Constitution has expressly confided to the Congress and not to the President. The Government's position is that the order was made on findings of the President and that his action was necessary to avert a national catastrophe which would inevitably result from a stoppage of steel production [during the Korean War].

[When efforts to settle a labor dispute—including reference to the Federal Wage Stabilization Board—failed, the union called a nationwide strike to begin April 9, 1952. Finding that such a strike

(Continued)

would jeopardize national defense, a few hours before the strike deadline the President issued Executive Order 10340, directing the Secretary of Commerce to take possession of most of the country's steel mills and keep them operating. The President sent a message to Congress reporting his actions on the next day. On May 3, the Court granted certiorari for direct review of a U.S. District Court order that had enjoined the Secretary's continued possession of the steel mills, and set argument for May 12. On June 2, the Court upheld the injunction, ruling the seizure unconstitutional.]

The President's power, if any, to issue the order must stem either from an act of Congress or from the Constitution itself.

[T]he use of the seizure techniques [to] prevent work stoppage was not only unauthorized by any congressional enactment; prior to this controversy, Congress had refused to adopt that method of settling labor disputes. When the Taft–Hartley Act [Labor Management Relations Act of 1947] was under [consideration], Congress rejected an amendment which would have authorized such governmental seizures in cases of emergency. [Instead], the plan sought to bring about settlements by use of the customary devices of mediation, conciliation, investigation by boards of inquiry, and public reports. In some instances temporary injunctions were authorized to provide cooling-off periods. All this failing, unions were left free to strike after a secret vote by employees. . . .[a]

It is clear that if the President had authority to issue the order he did, it must be found in some provision of the Constitution. [The] contention is that presidential power should be implied from the aggregate of his powers under the Constitution. Particular reliance is placed on provisions in Article II which say that "The executive Power shall be vested in a President"; that "he shall take Care that the Laws be faithfully executed"; and that he "shall be Commander in Chief of the Army and Navy of the United States."

---

[a]Sections 206–210 of the Act provided that "[w]henever in the opinion of the President [a] threatened or actual strike [will], if permitted to occur or to continue, imperil the national health or safety," on the President's initiative, the strike could be enjoined while a board of inquiry studied the dispute, but that the strike could continue after 80 days if the employees reject the employer's last offer of settlement. The President was then obligated under the Act to report on the emergency to Congress.

. . . We cannot with faithfulness to our constitutional system hold that the Commander in Chief of the Armed Forces has the ultimate power as such to take possession of private property in order to keep labor disputes from stopping production. This is a job for the Nation's lawmakers, not for its military authorities.

Nor can the seizure order be sustained because of the several constitutional provisions that grant executive power to the President. In the framework of our Constitution, the President's power to see that the laws are faithfully executed refutes the idea that he is to be a lawmaker. The Constitution limits his functions in the lawmaking process to the recommending of laws he thinks wise and the vetoing of laws he thinks bad. And the Constitution is neither silent nor equivocal about who shall make laws which the President is to execute. The first section of the first article says that "All legislative Powers herein granted shall be vested in a Congress of the United States." . . .

The President's order does not direct that a congressional policy be executed in a manner prescribed by Congress—it directs that a presidential policy be executed in a manner prescribed by the President. The preamble of the order itself, like that of many statutes, sets out reasons why the President believes certain policies should be adopted, proclaims these policies as rules of conduct to be followed, and again, like a statute, authorizes a government official to promulgate additional rules and regulations consistent with the policy proclaimed and needed to carry that policy into execution. The power of Congress to adopt such public policies as those proclaimed by the order is beyond question. It can authorize the taking of private property for public use. It can make laws regulating the relationships between employers and employees, prescribing rules designed to settle labor disputes, and fixing wages and working conditions in certain fields of our economy. The Constitution did not subject this lawmaking power of Congress to presidential or military supervision or control.

It is said that other Presidents without congressional authority have taken possession of private business enterprises in order to settle labor disputes. But even if this be true, Congress has not thereby lost its exclusive constitutional authority to make laws necessary and proper to carry out the powers vested by the Constitution "in the Government of the United States."

Affirmed.

JUSTICE FRANKFURTER, concurring in the judgment and opinion of the Court.

(*Continued*)

Although the considerations relevant to the legal enforcement of the principle of separation of powers seem to me more complicated and flexible than may appear from what Mr. Justice Black has written, I join his opinion because I thoroughly agree with the application of the principle to this case. . . .

[We] must [put] to one side consideration of what powers the President would have had if there had been no legislation whatever bearing on the authority asserted by the seizure, or if the seizure had been only for a short, explicitly temporary period, to be terminated automatically unless Congressional approval were given. These and other questions, like or unlike, are not now here. . . .

[It] cannot be contended that the President would have had power to issue this order had Congress explicitly negated such authority in formal legislation. [And Congress's decision reflected in the Labor Management Relations Act of 1947 should be given the same effect, since] Congress has expressed its will to withhold this power from the President as though it had said so in so many words. [It has] said to the President, "You may not seize. Please report to us and ask for seizure power if you think it is needed in a specific [situation]."

[The] content of the three authorities of government is not to be derived from an abstract analysis. The areas are partly interacting, not wholly disjointed. The Constitution is a framework for government. Therefore the way the framework has consistently operated fairly establishes that it has operated according to its true nature. Deeply embedded traditional ways of conducting government cannot supplant the Constitution or legislation, but they give meaning to the words of a text. [But the] list of executive assertions of the power of seizure in circumstances comparable to the present reduces to three in the six-month period from June to December of 1941. [T]hese three isolated instances do not add up [to] the kind of executive construction of the Constitution [necessary to justify the action here]. Nor do they come to us sanctioned by the long-continued acquiescence of Congress. . . .

JUSTICE DOUGLAS, concurring in the judgment and opinion of the Court.

[The] President might seize and the Congress by subsequent action might ratify the seizure. But until and unless Congress acted, no condemnation would be lawful. The branch of government that has the power to pay compensation for a seizure is the only one able to authorize a seizure or make lawful one that the President has effected. That seems to me to be the necessary result of the condemnation provision in the Fifth Amendment.

JUSTICE JACKSON, concurring in the judgment and opinion of the Court.

The actual art of governing under our Constitution does not and cannot conform to judicial definitions of the power of any of its branches based on isolated clauses or even single Articles torn from context. While the Constitution diffuses power the better to secure liberty, it also contemplates that practice will integrate the dispersed powers into a workable government. It enjoins upon its branches separateness but interdependence, autonomy but reciprocity. Presidential powers are not fixed but fluctuate, depending upon their disjunction or conjunction with those of Congress. We may well begin by a somewhat over-simplified grouping of practical situations in which a President may doubt, or others may challenge, his powers, and by distinguishing roughly the legal consequences of this factor of relativity.

1. When the President acts pursuant to an express or implied authorization of Congress, his authority is at its maximum, for it includes all that he possesses in his own right plus all that Congress can delegate. . . .

2. When the President acts in absence of either a congressional grant or denial or authority, he can only rely upon his own independent powers, but there is a zone of twilight in which he and Congress may have concurrent authority, or in which its distribution is uncertain. Therefore, congressional inertia, indifference or quiescence may sometimes, at least as a practical matter, enable, if not invite, measures on independent presidential responsibility. In this area, any actual test of power is likely to depend on the imperatives of events and contemporary imponderables rather than on abstract theories of law.

3. When the President takes measures incompatible with the expressed or implied will of Congress, his power is at its lowest ebb, for then he can rely only upon his own constitutional powers minus any constitutional powers of Congress over the matter. Courts can sustain exclusive Presidential control in such a case only by disabling the Congress from acting upon the subject. Presidential claim to a power at once so conclusive and preclusive must be scrutinized with caution, for what is at stake is the equilibrium established by our constitutional system.

Into which of these classifications does this executive seizure of the steel industry fit? It is eliminated from the first by admission, for

(Continued)

it is conceded that no congressional authorization exists for this seizure. . . .

[It] seems clearly eliminated from [the "second category"] because Congress has not left seizure of private property an open field but has covered it by three statutory policies inconsistent with this seizure [none of which] were invoked. In choosing a different and inconsistent way of his own, the President cannot claim that it is necessitated or invited by failure of Congress to legislate upon the occasions, grounds and methods for seizure of industrial properties.

This leaves the current seizure to be justified only by the severe tests under the third grouping, [where] we can sustain the President only by holding that seizure of such strike-bound industries is within his domain and beyond control by Congress. . . .

[I] cannot accept the view that [Art. II, § 1. cl. 1, vesting "the executive power" in the President] is a grant in bulk of all conceivable executive power but regard it as an allocation to the presidential office of the generic powers thereafter stated.

The [Commander in Chief] appellation is sometimes advanced as support for any presidential action, internal or external, involving use of force, the idea being that it vests power to do anything, anywhere, that can be done with an army or navy. [However, the] Constitution expressly places in Congress power "to raise and *support* Armies" and "to *provide* and *maintain* a Navy." (Emphasis supplied.) This certainly lays upon Congress primary responsibility for supplying the armed forces. Congress alone controls the raising of revenues and their appropriation and may determine in what manner and by what means they shall be spent for military and naval procurement. I suppose no one would doubt that Congress can take over war supply as a Government enterprise. . . .

The third clause in which the Solicitor General finds seizure powers is that "he shall take Care that the Laws be faithfully executed." That authority must be matched against [the due process clause of the fifth amendment]. One [clause] gives a governmental authority that reaches so far as there is law, the other gives a private right that authority shall go no farther. . . .

The Solicitor General lastly grounds support of the seizure upon nebulous, inherent powers never expressly granted but said to have accrued to the office from the customs and claims of preceding administrations. The plea is for a resulting power to deal with a crisis or an emergency according to the necessities of the case, the unarticulated assumption being that necessity knows no law. Loose and irresponsible use of adjectives colors all non-legal and much legal discussion of presidential powers. "Inherent" powers, "implied" powers, "incidental" powers, "plenary" powers, "war" powers and "emergency" powers are used, often interchangeably and without fixed or ascertainable meanings. . . .

In view of the ease, expedition and safety with which Congress can grant and has granted large emergency powers, certainly ample to embrace this crisis, I am quite unimpressed with the argument that we should affirm possession of them without statute. Such power either has no beginning or it has no end. If it exists, it need submit to no legal restraint. I am not alarmed that it would plunge us straightway into dictatorship, but it is at least a step in that wrong direction.

[The]Executive, except for recommendation and veto, has no legislative power. The executive action we have here originates in the individual will of the President and represents an exercise of authority without law. [With] all its defects, delays, and inconveniences, men have discovered no technique for long preserving free government except that the Executive be under the law, and that the law be made by parliamentary deliberations.[b]

CHIEF JUSTICE VINSON, with whom JUSTICE REED and JUSTICE MINTON join, dissenting.

[The dissent emphasized the country's international commitments for economic and military aid to preserve the free world and the congressional action directing the President to strengthen the armed forces. It called attention to the legislation directly related to supporting the Korean War. It quoted affidavits showing the enormous demand for steel in vital defense programs and attesting that a work stoppage would imperil the national defense.]

Accordingly, if the President has any power under the Constitution to meet a critical situation in the absence of express statutory authorization, there is no basis whatever for criticizing the exercise of such power in this case.

---

[b]Burton, J., also concurred in Black, J.'s opinion but also wrote a separate concurrence, similar in thrust to those of Frankfurter and Jackson, JJ., stressing that "the President's [order] invaded the jurisdiction of Congress," which "reserved to itself" the remedy of seizure. Clark, J., concurred in the judgment because "Congress had prescribed methods to be followed by the President in meeting the emergency at hand, [but] in the absence of such action by Congress, the President's independent power to act depends upon the gravity of the situation confronting the nation."

(Continued)

[Our] Presidents have on many occasions exhibited the leadership contemplated by the Framers when they made the President Commander in Chief, and imposed upon him the trust to "take Care that the Laws be faithfully executed." With or without explicit statutory authorization, Presidents have [dealt] with national emergencies by acting promptly [to] enforce legislative programs, at least to save those programs until Congress could act. Congress and the courts have responded to such executive initiative with consistent approval. [Historic episodes from George Washington to Franklin D. Roosevelt were summarized in 17 pages. A brief excerpt follows:]

Some six months before Pearl Harbor, a dispute at a single aviation [plant] interrupted a segment of the production of military aircraft. [President] Roosevelt ordered the seizure of the plant "pursuant to the powers vested in [him] by the Constitution and laws of the United States, as President of the United States of America and Commander in Chief of the Army and Navy of the United States." The Attorney General (Jackson) vigorously proclaimed that the President had the moral duty to keep this Nation's defense effort a "going concern." [A]lso prior to Pearl Harbor, the President ordered the seizure of a ship-building company and an aircraft parts plant. Following the declaration of war, [five] additional industrial concerns were seized to avert interruption of needed production. During the same period, the President directed seizure of the Nation's coal mines to remove an obstruction to the effective prosecution of the war.

[This] is but a cursory summary of executive leadership. But it amply demonstrates that Presidents have taken prompt action to enforce the laws and protect the country whether or not Congress happened to provide in advance for the particular method of execution. [T]he fact that Congress and the courts have consistently recognized and given their support to such executive action indicates that such a power of seizure has been accepted throughout our history.

Flexibility as to mode of execution [of the laws] to meet critical situations is a matter of practical necessity. [The] broad executive power granted by Article II [cannot], it is said, be invoked to avert disaster. Instead, the President must confine himself to sending a message to Congress recommending action. Under this messenger-boy concept of the Office, the President cannot even act to preserve legislative programs from destruction so that Congress will have something left to act upon.

[T]here [is no] question of unlimited executive power in this case. The President himself closed the door to any such claim when he sent his Message to Congress stating his purpose to abide by any action of Congress, whether approving or disapproving his seizure action. [There] is no question that the possession was other than temporary in character and subject to congressional direction— either approving, disapproving or regulating the manner in which the mills were to be administered and returned to the owners. [Judicial], legislative and executive precedents throughout our history demonstrate that in this case the President acted in full conformity with his duties under the Constitution.

Reprinted from Choper, J.; Kasmir, Y.; Shiffrin, S.; and Fallon, R. The American Constitution, 9th ed. © 2001, with permission of Thomson West.

CASE LAW

RUST v. SULLIVAN
Supreme Court of the United States, 1991.
500 U.S. 173, 111 S.Ct. 1759, 114 L.Ed.2d 233.

CHIEF JUSTICE REHNQUIST delivered the opinion of the Court. These cases concern a facial challenge to Department of Health and Human Services (HHS) regulations which limit the ability of Title X fund recipients to engage in abortion-related activities. The United States Court of Appeals for the Second Circuit upheld the regulations, finding them to be a permissible construction of the statute as well as consistent with the First and Fifth Amendments of the Constitution. We granted certiorari to resolve a split among the Courts of Appeals. We affirm.

[The Public Health Service Act of 1970 authorized the federal government to give grants for the creation of family planning centers, provided that the money not be used for abortions. The Secretary of Health in the Reagan Administration construed the Act to prohibit the expenditure of federal funds to counsel women or refer them elsewhere for an abortion. Recipients are also forbidden, as a condition of federal funding, to use their own funds for such counseling or to provide abortions through a parallel facility. (In effect, the regulations were designed to ensure that grant recipients did not use other funds available to them to promote abortions.) Health care

(Continued)

providers challenged the regulations on several grounds, including the claim that they violated their Due Process and First Amendment rights. The lower courts rejected the claims.]

There is no question but that the statutory prohibition contained in § 1008 is constitutional. In *Maher v. Roe*, 432 U.S. 464, 97 S.Ct. 2376, 53 L.Ed.2d 484 (1977), we upheld a state welfare regulation under which Medicaid recipients received payments for services related to childbirth, but not for nontherapeutic abortions. The Court rejected the claim that this unequal subsidization worked a violation of the Constitution. . . .

The Government can, without violating the Constitution, selectively fund a program to encourage certain activities it believes to be in the public interest, without at the same time funding an alternate program which seeks to deal with the problem in another way. In so doing, the Government has not discriminated on the basis of viewpoint; it has merely chosen to fund one activity to the exclusion of the other. . . . [The First Amendment is not violated.]

To hold that the Government unconstitutionally discriminates on the basis of viewpoint when it chooses to fund a program dedicated to advance certain permissible goals, because the program in advancing those goals necessarily discourages alternate goals, would render numerous government programs constitutionally suspect. When Congress established a National Endowment for Democracy to encourage other countries to adopt democratic principles, 22 U.S.C. § 4411(b), it was not constitutionally required to fund a program to encourage competing lines of political philosophy such as Communism and Fascism. Petitioners' assertions ultimately boil down to the position that if the government chooses to subsidize one protected right, it must subsidize analogous counterpart rights. But the Court has soundly rejected that proposition. Within far broader limits than petitioners are willing to concede, when the government appropriates public funds to establish a program it is entitled to define the limits of that program.

. . .

Petitioners also contend that the restrictions on the subsidization of abortion-related speech contained in the regulations are impermissible because they condition the receipt of a benefit, in this case Title X funding, on the relinquishment of a constitutional right, the right to engage in abortion advocacy and counseling. Relying on *Perry v. Sindermann*, 408 U.S. 593, 597 (1972), and *FCC v. League of Women Voters of Cal.*, 468 U.S. 364 (1984), petitioners argue that "even though the government may deny [a] . . . benefit for any number of reasons, there are some reasons upon which the government may not rely. It may not deny a benefit to a person on a basis that infringes his constitutionally protected interests—especially, his interest in freedom of speech."

Petitioners' reliance on these cases is unavailing, however, because here the government is not denying a benefit to anyone, but is instead simply insisting that public funds be spent for the purposes for which they were authorized. The Secretary's regulations do not force the Title X grantee to give up abortion-related speech; they merely require that the grantee keep such activities separate and distinct from Title X activities. Title X expressly distinguishes between a Title X *grantee* and a Title X *project*. . . . The regulations govern the scope of the Title X *project's* activities, and leave the grantee unfettered in its other activities. The Title X *grantee* can continue to perform abortions, provide abortion-related services, and engage in abortion advocacy; it simply is required to conduct those activities through programs that are separate and independent from the project that receives Title X funds. 42 CFR 59.9 (1989).

. . .

Petitioners contend, [finally], that most Title X clients are effectively precluded by indigency and poverty from seeing a health care provider who will provide abortion-related services. But once again, even these Title X clients are in no worse position than if Congress had never enacted Title X. "The financial constraints that restrict an indigent woman's ability to enjoy the full range of constitutionally protected freedom of choice are the product not of governmental restrictions on access to abortion, but rather of her indigency." [*Harris v. McRae*, 448 U.S. 297, 316, 100 S.Ct. 2671, 2687, 65 L.Ed.2d 784 (1980).]

The Secretary's regulations are a permissible construction of Title X and do not violate either the First or Fifth Amendments to the Constitution. Accordingly, the judgment of the Court of Appeals is

Affirmed.

JUSTICE BLACKMUN, with whom JUSTICE MARSHALL joins, with whom JUSTICE STEVENS joins as to Parts II and III, and with whom JUSTICE O'CONNOR joins as to Part I, dissenting.

[Part I held that the regulations were void because they were inconsistent with the 1970 Act.]

[II]

Until today, the Court never has upheld viewpoint-based suppression of speech simply because that suppression was a condition

(Continued)

upon the acceptance of public funds. Whatever may be the Government's power to condition the receipt of its largess upon the relinquishment of constitutional rights, it surely does not extend to a condition that suppresses the recipient's cherished freedom of speech based solely upon the content or viewpoint of that speech. *Speiser v. Randall*, 357 U.S. 513, 518–519 (1958) ("To deny an exemption to claimants who engage in certain forms of speech is in effect to penalize them for such speech. . . . The denial is 'frankly aimed at the suppression of dangerous ideas'"). . . .

. . .

Remarkably, the majority concludes that "the Government has not discriminated on the basis of viewpoint; it has merely chosen to fund one activity to the exclusion of another." But the majority's claim that the Regulations merely limit a Title X project's speech to preventive or preconceptional services rings hollow in light of the broad range of non-preventive services that the Regulations authorize Title X projects to provide. By refusing to fund those family-planning projects that advocate abortion *because* they advocate abortion, the Government plainly has targeted a particular viewpoint. Cf. *Ward v. Rock Against Racism*, 491 U.S. 781 (1989). The majority's reliance on the fact that the Regulations pertain solely to funding decisions simply begs the question. Clearly, there are some bases upon which government may not rest its decision to fund or not to fund. For example, the Members of the majority surely would agree that government may not base its decision to support an activity upon considerations of race. See, e.g., *Yick Wo v. Hopkins*, 118 U.S. 356 (1886). As demonstrated above, our cases make clear that ideological viewpoint is a similarly repugnant ground upon which to base funding decisions.

Reprinted from Abernathy, C. Civil Rights and Constitutional Litigation, 3rd ed. © 2000, with permission of Thomson West.

CHAPTER SUMMARY

Presidents and governors exert control over administrative agencies through the power of appointment and removal, influence over the budget, issuance of executive orders, power to set policy, power to veto, power to control litigation, power of reorganization, and power to pardon. Presidents have issued executive orders to force agencies to do cost/benefit analyses among other activities. Presidents and governors use a variety of these powers to shape the policies of the agencies to conform to administrative policy.

KEY TERMS

appointments clause

executive order

line-item veto

removal for cause

REVIEW QUESTIONS

1. List and describe the various methods used by presidents and governors to control agencies.
2. What provisions of the Constitution give the president the power over agencies?
3. State two powers over agency regulations possessed by some governors but not by the president.
4. Why was the line-item veto declared unconstitutional by the Supreme Court?
5. What are executive orders, and why are they important to the president's power over administrative agencies?

MORE INFORMATION

1. To access presidential executive orders, go to http://www.archives.gov.
2. To obtain information about the Watergate scandal and the presidential pardon of President Nixon by President Ford, go to http://www.google.com. Search the term "Watergate."
3. To read a transcript of a congressional hearing concerning the use of executive orders, go to Hearing of the Subcommittee on Legislative and Budget Process, The Impact of Executive Orders on the Legislative Process: Executive Lawmaking? at http://www.rules.house.gov/archives/rules_cox08.htm.

PRACTICAL APPLICATIONS

1. Go to http://thomas.loc.gov.
   Scroll down to Presidential Nominations.
   Go to the 101st Congress.
   Search John Tower.
   A. What happened to the nomination?
      Stay in the 101st Congress. Search Richard B. Chaney and add Wyoming as the state of the nominee.
   B. What happened to the nomination?

2. Go to http://www.firstgov.gov. List the agencies that are included in the Executive Office of the President.

3. Sometimes presidents direct the Secretary of Treasury through an executive order to freeze the assets of heads of countries who have been deposed and who have assets in the United States.
   Go to http://www.archives.gov/federal-register.
   State the head and name of the country affected by:
   A. Executive Order 12,274
   B. Executive Order 12,588

4. Find the Executive Order that stated the following:
   (g) Prohibition of Assassination. No employee of the United States Government shall engage in, or conspire to engage in, political assassination.

5. Justice Jackson in the Steel Seizure case provided the framework to analyze exertions of presidential power. Refer to the discussion of this case in the text and then place the following presidential actions into one of the three categories:
   A. The president authorizes the Secretary of Defense to deliver fighter jets to the government of Brazil to suppress a revolution. Congress had passed a statute that reads in part "the United States shall not directly or indirectly give military aid to the government of Brazil."
   B. Congress passes a statute that authorizes the president to sell out-of-date aircraft carriers to Switzerland. The president then directs the Secretary of the Treasury to make the necessary arrangements.
   C. The president orders the Secretary of Defense to send two U.S. aircraft carriers to the coast of Australia.

LEARN ABOUT THE AGENCIES

Go to the Web sites of the following agencies and state their function.

1. DOL—Department of Labor—http://www.dol.gov
2. DOD—Department of Defense—http://www.defenselink.mil
3. NSA—National Security Agency—http://www.nsa.gov
4. USDA—United States Department of Agriculture—http://www.usda.gov
5. ATF—Bureau of Alcohol, Tobacco, and Firearms—http://www.atf.treas.gov

THE CONSTITUTION OF THE
UNITED STATES: HTTP://WWW.ARCHIVES.GOV

Note: *The following text is a transcription of the Constitution in its* ***original*** *form.*

Items that are underlined have since been amended or superseded.

We the People of the United States, in Order to form a more perfect Union, establish Justice, insure domestic Tranquility, provide for the common defence, promote the general Welfare, and secure the Blessings of Liberty to ourselves and our Posterity, do ordain and establish this Constitution for the United States of America.

Article. I.

Section. 1.
All legislative Powers herein granted shall be vested in a Congress of the United States, which shall consist of a Senate and House of Representatives.

Section. 2.
The House of Representatives shall be composed of Members chosen every second Year by the People of the several States, and the Electors in each State shall have the Qualifications requisite for Electors of the most numerous Branch of the State Legislature.

No Person shall be a Representative who shall not have attained to the Age of twenty five Years, and been seven Years a Citizen of the United States, and who shall not, when elected, be an Inhabitant of that State in which he shall be chosen.

<u>Representatives and direct Taxes shall be apportioned among the several States which may be included within this Union, according to their respective Numbers, which shall be determined by adding to the whole Number of free Persons, including those bound to Service for a Term of Years, and excluding Indians not taxed, three fifths of all other Persons.</u> The actual Enumeration shall be made within three Years after the first Meeting of the Congress of the United States, and within every subsequent Term of ten Years, in such Manner as they shall by Law direct. The Number of Representatives shall not exceed one for every thirty Thousand, but each State shall have at Least one Representative; and until such enumeration shall be made, the State of New Hampshire shall be entitled to chuse three, Massachusetts eight, Rhode-Island and Providence Plantations one, Connecticut five, New-York six, New Jersey four, Pennsylvania eight, Delaware one, Maryland six, Virginia ten, North Carolina five, South Carolina five, and Georgia three.

When vacancies happen in the Representation from any State, the Executive Authority thereof shall issue Writs of Election to fill such Vacancies.

The House of Representatives shall chuse their Speaker and other Officers; and shall have the sole Power of Impeachment.

Section. 3.

The Senate of the United States shall be composed of two Senators from each State, <u>chosen by the Legislature</u> thereof for six Years; and each Senator shall have one Vote.

Immediately after they shall be assembled in Consequence of the first Election, they shall be divided as equally as may be into three Classes. The Seats of the Senators of the first Class shall be vacated at the Expiration of the second Year, of the second Class at the Expiration of the fourth Year, and of the third Class at the Expiration of the sixth Year, so that one third may be chosen every second Year; <u>and if Vacancies happen by Resignation, or otherwise, during the Recess of the Legislature of any State, the Executive thereof may make temporary Appointments until the next Meeting of the Legislature, which shall then fill such Vacancies.</u>

No Person shall be a Senator who shall not have attained to the Age of thirty Years, and been nine Years a Citizen of the United States, and who shall not, when elected, be an Inhabitant of that State for which he shall be chosen.

The Vice President of the United States shall be President of the Senate, but shall have no Vote, unless they be equally divided.

The Senate shall chuse their other Officers, and also a President pro tempore, in the Absence of the Vice President, or when he shall exercise the Office of President of the United States.

The Senate shall have the sole Power to try all Impeachments. When sitting for that Purpose, they shall be on Oath or Affirmation. When the President of the United States is tried, the Chief Justice shall preside: And no Person shall be convicted without the Concurrence of two thirds of the Members present.

Judgment in Cases of Impeachment shall not extend further than to removal from Office, and disqualification to hold and enjoy any Office of honor, Trust or Profit under the United States: but the Party convicted shall nevertheless be liable and subject to Indictment, Trial, Judgment and Punishment, according to Law.

Section. 4.

The Times, Places and Manner of holding Elections for Senators and Representatives, shall be prescribed in each State by the Legislature thereof; but the Congress may at any time by Law make or alter such Regulations, except as to the Places of chusing Senators.

The Congress shall assemble at least once in every Year, and such Meeting shall <u>be on the first Monday in December,</u> unless they shall by Law appoint a different Day.

Section. 5.

Each House shall be the Judge of the Elections, Returns and Qualifications of its own Members, and a Majority of each shall constitute a Quorum to do Business; but a smaller Number may adjourn from day to day, and may be authorized to compel the Attendance of absent Members, in such Manner, and under such Penalties as each House may provide.

Each House may determine the Rules of its Proceedings, punish its Members for disorderly Behaviour, and, with the Concurrence of two thirds, expel a Member.

Each House shall keep a Journal of its Proceedings, and from time to time publish the same, excepting such Parts as may in their Judgment require Secrecy; and the Yeas and Nays of the Members of either House on any question shall, at the Desire of one fifth of those Present, be entered on the Journal.

Neither House, during the Session of Congress, shall, without the Consent of the other, adjourn for more than three days, nor to any other Place than that in which the two Houses shall be sitting.

Section. 6.

The Senators and Representatives shall receive a Compensation for their Services, to be ascertained by Law, and paid out of the Treasury of the United States. They shall in all Cases, except Treason, Felony and Breach of the Peace, be privileged from Arrest during their

Attendance at the Session of their respective Houses, and in going to and returning from the same; and for any Speech or Debate in either House, they shall not be questioned in any other Place.

No Senator or Representative shall, during the Time for which he was elected, be appointed to any civil Office under the Authority of the United States, which shall have been created, or the Emoluments whereof shall have been encreased during such time; and no Person holding any Office under the United States, shall be a Member of either House during his Continuance in Office.

Section. 7.

All Bills for raising Revenue shall originate in the House of Representatives; but the Senate may propose or concur with Amendments as on other Bills.

Every Bill which shall have passed the House of Representatives and the Senate, shall, before it become a Law, be presented to the President of the United States: If he approve he shall sign it, but if not he shall return it, with his Objections to that House in which it shall have originated, who shall enter the Objections at large on their Journal, and proceed to reconsider it. If after such Reconsideration two thirds of that House shall agree to pass the Bill, it shall be sent, together with the Objections, to the other House, by which it shall likewise be reconsidered, and if approved by two thirds of that House, it shall become a Law. But in all such Cases the Votes of both Houses shall be determined by yeas and Nays, and the Names of the Persons voting for and against the Bill shall be entered on the Journal of each House respectively. If any Bill shall not be returned by the President within ten Days (Sundays excepted) after it shall have been presented to him, the Same shall be a Law, in like Manner as if he had signed it, unless the Congress by their Adjournment prevent its Return, in which Case it shall not be a Law.

Every Order, Resolution, or Vote to which the Concurrence of the Senate and House of Representatives may be necessary (except on a question of Adjournment) shall be presented to the President of the United States; and before the Same shall take Effect, shall be approved by him, or being disapproved by him, shall be repassed by two thirds of the Senate and House of Representatives, according to the Rules and Limitations prescribed in the Case of a Bill.

Section. 8.

The Congress shall have Power to lay and collect Taxes, Duties, Imposts and Excises, to pay the Debts and provide for the common Defence and general Welfare of the United States; but all Duties, Imposts and Excises shall be uniform throughout the United States;

To borrow Money on the credit of the United States;

To regulate Commerce with foreign Nations, and among the several States, and with the Indian Tribes;

To establish an uniform Rule of Naturalization, and uniform Laws on the subject of Bankruptcies throughout the United States;

To coin Money, regulate the Value thereof, and of foreign Coin, and fix the Standard of Weights and Measures;

To provide for the Punishment of counterfeiting the Securities and current Coin of the United States;

To establish Post Offices and post Roads;

To promote the Progress of Science and useful Arts, by securing for limited Times to Authors and Inventors the exclusive Right to their respective Writings and Discoveries;

To constitute Tribunals inferior to the supreme Court;

To define and punish Piracies and Felonies committed on the high Seas, and Offences against the Law of Nations;

To declare War, grant Letters of Marque and Reprisal, and make Rules concerning Captures on Land and Water;

To raise and support Armies, but no Appropriation of Money to that Use shall be for a longer Term than two Years;

To provide and maintain a Navy;

To make Rules for the Government and Regulation of the land and naval Forces;

To provide for calling forth the Militia to execute the Laws of the Union, suppress Insurrections and repel Invasions;

To provide for organizing, arming, and disciplining, the Militia, and for governing such Part of them as may be employed in the Service of the United States, reserving to the States respectively, the Appointment of the Officers, and the Authority of training the Militia according to the discipline prescribed by Congress;

To exercise exclusive Legislation in all Cases whatsoever, over such District (not exceeding ten Miles square) as may, by Cession of particular States, and the Acceptance of Congress, become the Seat of the Government of the United States, and to exercise like Authority over all Places purchased by the Consent of the Legislature of the State in which the Same shall be, for the Erection of Forts, Magazines, Arsenals, dock-Yards, and other needful Buildings;–And

To make all Laws which shall be necessary and proper for carrying into Execution the foregoing Powers, and all other Powers vested by this Constitution in the Government of the United States, or in any Department or Officer thereof.

Section. 9.

The Migration or Importation of such Persons as any of the States now existing shall think proper to admit, shall not be prohibited by the Congress prior to the Year one thousand eight hundred and eight, but a Tax or duty may be imposed on such Importation, not exceeding ten dollars for each Person.

The Privilege of the Writ of Habeas Corpus shall not be suspended, unless when in Cases of Rebellion or Invasion the public Safety may require it.

No Bill of Attainder or ex post facto Law shall be passed.

No Capitation, or other direct, Tax shall be laid, <u>unless in Proportion to the Census or enumeration herein before directed to be taken.</u>

No Tax or Duty shall be laid on Articles exported from any State.

No Preference shall be given by any Regulation of Commerce or Revenue to the Ports of one State over those of another; nor shall Vessels bound to, or from, one State, be obliged to enter, clear, or pay Duties in another.

No Money shall be drawn from the Treasury, but in Consequence of Appropriations made by Law; and a regular Statement and Account of the Receipts and Expenditures of all public Money shall be published from time to time.

No Title of Nobility shall be granted by the United States: And no Person holding any Office of Profit or Trust under them, shall, without the Consent of the Congress, accept of any present, Emolument, Office, or Title, of any kind whatever, from any King, Prince, or foreign State.

Section. 10.

No State shall enter into any Treaty, Alliance, or Confederation; grant Letters of Marque and Reprisal; coin Money; emit Bills of Credit; make any Thing but gold and silver Coin a Tender in Payment of Debts; pass any Bill of Attainder, ex post facto Law, or Law impairing the Obligation of Contracts, or grant any Title of Nobility.

No State shall, without the Consent of the Congress, lay any Imposts or Duties on Imports or Exports, except what may be absolutely necessary for executing it's inspection Laws: and the net Produce of all Duties and Imposts, laid by any State on Imports or Exports, shall be for the Use of the Treasury of the United States; and all such Laws shall be subject to the Revision and Controul of the Congress.

No State shall, without the Consent of Congress, lay any Duty of Tonnage, keep Troops, or Ships of War in time of Peace, enter into any Agreement or Compact with another State, or with a foreign Power, or engage in War, unless actually invaded, or in such imminent Danger as will not admit of delay.

Article. II.

Section. 1.

The executive Power shall be vested in a President of the United States of America. He shall hold his Office during the Term of four Years, and, together with the Vice President, chosen for the same Term, be elected, as follows:

Each State shall appoint, in such Manner as the Legislature thereof may direct, a Number of Electors, equal to the whole Number of Senators and Representatives to which the State may be entitled in the Congress: but no Senator or Representative, or Person holding an Office of Trust or Profit under the United States, shall be appointed an Elector.

The Electors shall meet in their respective States, and vote by Ballot for two Persons, of whom one at least shall not be an Inhabitant of the same State with themselves. And they shall make a List of all the Persons voted for, and of the Number of Votes for each; which List they shall sign and certify, and transmit sealed to the Seat of the Government of the United States, directed to the President of the Senate. The President of the Senate shall, in the Presence of the Senate and House of Representatives, open all the Certificates, and the Votes shall then be counted. The Person having the greatest Number of Votes shall be the President, if such Number be a Majority of the whole Number of Electors appointed; and if there be more than one who have such Majority, and have an equal Number of Votes, then the House of Representatives shall immediately chuse by Ballot one of them for President; and if no Person have a Majority, then from the five highest on the List the said House shall in like Manner chuse the President. But in chusing the President, the Votes shall be taken by States, the Representation from each State having one Vote; A quorum for this purpose shall consist of a Member or Members from two thirds of the States, and a Majority of all the States shall be necessary to a Choice. In every Case, after the Choice of the President, the Person having the greatest Number of Votes of the Electors shall be the Vice President. But if there should remain two or more who have equal Votes, the Senate shall chuse from them by Ballot the Vice President.

The Congress may determine the Time of chusing the Electors, and the Day on which they shall give their Votes; which Day shall be the same throughout the United States.

No Person except a natural born Citizen, or a Citizen of the United States, at the time of the Adoption of this Constitution, shall be eligible to the Office of President; neither shall any Person be eligible to that Office who shall not have attained to the Age of thirty five Years, and been fourteen Years a Resident within the United States.

In Case of the Removal of the President from Office, or of his Death, Resignation, or Inability to discharge the Powers and Duties of the said Office, the Same shall devolve on the Vice President, and the Congress may by Law provide for the Case of Removal, Death, Resignation or Inability, both of the President and Vice President, declaring what Officer shall then act as President, and such Officer shall act accordingly, until the Disability be removed, or a President shall be elected.

The President shall, at stated Times, receive for his Services, a Compensation, which shall neither be increased nor diminished during the Period for which he shall have been elected, and he shall not receive within that Period any other Emolument from the United States, or any of them.

Before he enter on the Execution of his Office, he shall take the following Oath or Affirmation:–"I do solemnly swear (or affirm) that I will faithfully execute the Office of President of the United States, and will to the best of my Ability, preserve, protect and defend the Constitution of the United States."

Section. 2.

The President shall be Commander in Chief of the Army and Navy of the United States, and of the Militia of the several States, when called into the actual Service of the United States; he may require the Opinion, in writing, of the principal Officer in each of the executive Departments, upon any Subject relating to the Duties of their respective Offices, and he shall have Power to grant Reprieves and Pardons for Offences against the United States, except in Cases of Impeachment.

He shall have Power, by and with the Advice and Consent of the Senate, to make Treaties, provided two thirds of the Senators present concur; and he shall nominate, and by and with the Advice and Consent of the Senate, shall appoint Ambassadors, other public Ministers and Consuls, Judges of the supreme Court, and all other Officers of the United States, whose Appointments are not herein otherwise provided for, and which shall be established by Law: but the Congress may by Law vest the Appointment of such inferior Officers, as they think proper, in the President alone, in the Courts of Law, or in the Heads of Departments.

The President shall have Power to fill up all Vacancies that may happen during the Recess of the Senate, by granting Commissions which shall expire at the End of their next Session.

Section. 3.

He shall from time to time give to the Congress Information of the State of the Union, and recommend to their Consideration such

Measures as he shall judge necessary and expedient; he may, on extraordinary Occasions, convene both Houses, or either of them, and in Case of Disagreement between them, with Respect to the Time of Adjournment, he may adjourn them to such Time as he shall think proper; he shall receive Ambassadors and other public Ministers; he shall take Care that the Laws be faithfully executed, and shall Commission all the Officers of the United States.

Section. 4.

The President, Vice President and all civil Officers of the United States, shall be removed from Office on Impeachment for, and Conviction of, Treason, Bribery, or other high Crimes and Misdemeanors.

Article III.

Section. 1.

The judicial Power of the United States shall be vested in one supreme Court, and in such inferior Courts as the Congress may from time to time ordain and establish. The Judges, both of the supreme and inferior Courts, shall hold their Offices during good Behaviour, and shall, at stated Times, receive for their Services a Compensation, which shall not be diminished during their Continuance in Office.

Section. 2.

The judicial Power shall extend to all Cases, in Law and Equity, arising under this Constitution, the Laws of the United States, and Treaties made, or which shall be made, under their Authority;–to all Cases affecting Ambassadors, other public Ministers and Consuls;–to all Cases of admiralty and maritime Jurisdiction;–to Controversies to which the United States shall be a Party;–to Controversies between two or more States;– between a State and Citizens of another State;–between Citizens of different States;–between Citizens of the same State claiming Lands under Grants of different States, and between a State, or the Citizens thereof, and foreign States, Citizens or Subjects.

In all Cases affecting Ambassadors, other public Ministers and Consuls, and those in which a State shall be Party, the supreme Court shall have original Jurisdiction. In all the other Cases before mentioned, the supreme Court shall have appellate Jurisdiction, both as to Law and Fact, with such Exceptions, and under such Regulations as the Congress shall make.

The Trial of all Crimes, except in Cases of Impeachment, shall be by Jury; and such Trial shall be held in the State where the said Crimes shall have been committed; but when not committed within any State, the Trial shall be at such Place or Places as the Congress may by Law have directed.

Section. 3.

Treason against the United States, shall consist only in levying War against them, or in adhering to their Enemies, giving them Aid and Comfort. No Person shall be convicted of Treason unless on the Testimony of two Witnesses to the same overt Act, or on Confession in open Court.

The Congress shall have Power to declare the Punishment of Treason, but no Attainder of Treason shall work Corruption of Blood, or Forfeiture except during the Life of the Person attainted.

Article. IV.

Section. 1.

Full Faith and Credit shall be given in each State to the public Acts, Records, and judicial Proceedings of every other State. And the Congress may by general Laws prescribe the Manner in which such Acts, Records and Proceedings shall be proved, and the Effect thereof.

Section. 2.

The Citizens of each State shall be entitled to all Privileges and Immunities of Citizens in the several States.

A Person charged in any State with Treason, Felony, or other Crime, who shall flee from Justice, and be found in another State, shall on Demand of the executive Authority of the State from which he fled, be delivered up, to be removed to the State having Jurisdiction of the Crime.

No Person held to Service or Labour in one State, under the Laws thereof, escaping into another, shall, in Consequence of any Law or Regulation therein, be discharged from such Service or Labour, but shall be delivered up on Claim of the Party to whom such Service or Labour may be due.

Section. 3.

New States may be admitted by the Congress into this Union; but no new State shall be formed or erected within the Jurisdiction of any other State; nor any State be formed by the Junction of two or more States, or Parts of States, without the Consent of the Legislatures of the States concerned as well as of the Congress.

The Congress shall have Power to dispose of and make all needful Rules and Regulations respecting the Territory or other Property belonging to the United States; and nothing in this Constitution shall be so construed as to Prejudice any Claims of the United States, or of any particular State.

Section. 4.

The United States shall guarantee to every State in this Union a Republican Form of Government, and shall protect each of them against Invasion; and on Application of the Legislature, or of the Executive (when the Legislature cannot be convened), against domestic Violence.

Article. V.

The Congress, whenever two thirds of both Houses shall deem it necessary, shall propose Amendments to this Constitution, or, on the Application of the Legislatures of two thirds of the several States, shall call a Convention for proposing Amendments, which, in either Case, shall be valid to all Intents and Purposes, as Part of this Constitution, when ratified by the Legislatures of three fourths of the several States, or by Conventions in three fourths thereof, as the one or the other Mode of Ratification may be proposed by the Congress; Provided that no Amendment which may be made prior to the Year One thousand eight hundred and eight shall in any Manner affect the first and fourth Clauses in the Ninth Section of the first Article; and that no State, without its Consent, shall be deprived of its equal Suffrage in the Senate.

Article. VI.

All Debts contracted and Engagements entered into, before the Adoption of this Constitution, shall be as valid against the United States under this Constitution, as under the Confederation.

This Constitution, and the Laws of the United States which shall be made in Pursuance thereof; and all Treaties made, or which shall be made, under the Authority of the United States, shall be the supreme Law of the Land; and the Judges in every State shall be bound thereby, any Thing in the Constitution or Laws of any State to the Contrary notwithstanding.

The Senators and Representatives before mentioned, and the Members of the several State Legislatures, and all executive and judicial Officers, both of the United States and of the several States, shall be bound by Oath or Affirmation, to support this Constitution; but no religious Test shall ever be required as a Qualification to any Office or public Trust under the United States.

Article. VII.

The Ratification of the Conventions of nine States, shall be sufficient for the Establishment of this Constitution between the States so ratifying the Same.

The Word, "the," being interlined between the seventh and eighth Lines of the first Page, the Word "Thirty" being partly written on an Erazure in the fifteenth Line of the first Page, The Words "is tried" being interlined between the thirty second and thirty third Lines of the first Page and the Word "the" being interlined between the forty third and forty fourth Lines of the second Page.

Attest William Jackson Secretary

Done in Convention by the Unanimous Consent of the States present the Seventeenth Day of September in the Year of our Lord one thousand seven hundred and Eighty seven and of the Independence of the United States of America the Twelfth In witness whereof We have hereunto subscribed our Names,

G°. Washington
Presidt and deputy from Virginia

Delaware
Geo: Read
Gunning Bedford jun
John Dickinson
Richard Bassett
Jaco: Broom

Maryland
James McHenry
Dan of St Thos. Jenifer
Danl. Carroll

Virginia
John Blair
James Madison Jr.

North Carolina
Wm. Blount
Richd. Dobbs Spaight
Hu Williamson

South Carolina
J. Rutledge
Charles Cotesworth Pinckney
Charles Pinckney
Pierce Butler

Georgia
William Few
Abr Baldwin

New Hampshire
John Langdon
Nicholas Gilman

Massachusetts
Nathaniel Gorham
Rufus King

Connecticut
Wm. Saml. Johnson
Roger Sherman

New York
Alexander Hamilton

New Jersey
Wil: Livingston
David Brearley
Wm. Paterson
Jona: Dayton

Pennsylvania
B Franklin
Thomas Mifflin
Robt. Morris
Geo. Clymer
Thos. FitzSimons
Jared Ingersoll
James Wilson
Gouv Morris

Amendment I

Congress shall make no law respecting an establishment of religion, or prohibiting the free exercise thereof; or abridging the freedom of speech, or of the press; or the right of the people peaceably to assemble, and to petition the Government for a redress of grievances.

Amendment II

A well regulated Militia, being necessary to the security of a free State, the right of the people to keep and bear Arms, shall not be infringed.

Amendment III

No Soldier shall, in time of peace be quartered in any house, without the consent of the Owner, nor in time of war, but in a manner to be prescribed by law.

Amendment IV

The right of the people to be secure in their persons, houses, papers, and effects, against unreasonable searches and seizures, shall not be violated, and no Warrants shall issue, but upon probable cause, supported by Oath or affirmation, and particularly describing the place to be searched, and the persons or things to be seized.

Amendment V

No person shall be held to answer for a capital, or otherwise infamous crime, unless on a presentment or indictment of a Grand Jury, except in cases arising in the land or naval forces, or in the Militia, when in actual service in time of War or public danger; nor shall any person be subject for the same offence to be twice put in jeopardy of life or limb; nor shall be compelled in any criminal case to be a witness against himself, nor be deprived of life, liberty, or property, without due process of law; nor shall private property be taken for public use, without just compensation.

Amendment VI

In all criminal prosecutions, the accused shall enjoy the right to a speedy and public trial, by an impartial jury of the State and district wherein the crime shall have been committed, which district shall have been previously ascertained by law, and to be informed of the nature and cause of the accusation; to be confronted with the witnesses against him; to have compulsory process for obtaining witnesses in his favor, and to have the Assistance of Counsel for his defence.

Amendment VII

In Suits at common law, where the value in controversy shall exceed twenty dollars, the right of trial by jury shall be preserved, and no fact tried by a jury, shall be otherwise re-examined in any Court of the United States, than according to the rules of the common law.

Amendment VIII

Excessive bail shall not be required, nor excessive fines imposed, nor cruel and unusual punishments inflicted.

Amendment IX

The enumeration in the Constitution, of certain rights, shall not be construed to deny or disparage others retained by the people.

Amendment X

The powers not delegated to the United States by the Constitution, nor prohibited by it to the States, are reserved to the States respectively, or to the people.

AMENDMENT XI

Passed by Congress March 4, 1794. Ratified February 7, 1795.

Note: Article III, section 2, of the Constitution was modified by amendment 11.
The Judicial power of the United States shall not be construed to extend to any suit in law or equity, commenced or prosecuted against one of the United States by Citizens of another State, or by Citizens or Subjects of any Foreign State.

AMENDMENT XII

Passed by Congress December 9, 1803. Ratified June 15, 1804.

Note: A portion of Article II, section 1, of the Constitution was superseded by the 12th amendment.

The Electors shall meet in their respective states and vote by ballot for President and Vice-President, one of whom, at least, shall not be an inhabitant of the same state with themselves; they shall name in their ballots the person voted for as President, and in distinct ballots the person voted for as Vice-President, and they shall make distinct lists of all persons voted for as President, and of all persons voted for as Vice-President, and of the number of votes for each, which lists they shall sign and certify, and transmit sealed to the seat of the government of the United States, directed to the President of the Senate; – the President of the Senate shall, in the presence of the Senate and House of Representatives, open all the certificates and the votes shall then be counted; – The person having the greatest number of votes for President, shall be the President, if such number be a majority of the whole number of Electors appointed; and if no person have such majority, then from the persons having the highest numbers not exceeding three on the list of those voted for as President, the House of Representatives shall choose immediately, by ballot, the President. But in choosing the President, the votes shall be taken by states, the representation from each state having one vote; a quorum for this purpose shall consist of a member or members from two-thirds of the states, and a majority of all the states shall be necessary to a choice. [And if the House of Representatives shall not choose a President whenever the right of choice shall devolve upon them, before the fourth day of March next following, then the Vice-President shall act as President, as in case of the death or other constitutional disability of the President. –]* The person having the greatest number of votes as Vice-President, shall be the Vice-President, if such number be a majority of the whole number of Electors appointed, and if no person have a majority, then from the two highest numbers on the list, the Senate shall choose the Vice-President; a quorum for the purpose shall consist of two-thirds of the whole number of Senators, and a majority of the whole number shall be necessary to a choice. But no person constitutionally ineligible to the office of President shall be eligible to that of Vice-President of the United States.

Superseded by section 3 of the 20th amendment.

AMENDMENT XIII
Passed by Congress January 31, 1865. Ratified December 6, 1865.

Note: A portion of Article IV, section 2, of the Constitution was superseded by the 13th amendment.

Section 1.
Neither slavery nor involuntary servitude, except as a punishment for crime whereof the party shall have been duly convicted, shall

exist within the United States, or any place subject to their jurisdiction.

Section 2.

Congress shall have power to enforce this article by appropriate legislation.

AMENDMENT XIV

Passed by Congress June 13, 1866. Ratified July 9, 1868.

Note: Article I, section 2, of the Constitution was modified by section 2 of the 14th amendment.

Section 1.

All persons born or naturalized in the United States, and subject to the jurisdiction thereof, are citizens of the United States and of the State wherein they reside. No State shall make or enforce any law which shall abridge the privileges or immunities of citizens of the United States; nor shall any State deprive any person of life, liberty, or property, without due process of law; nor deny to any person within its jurisdiction the equal protection of the laws.

Section 2.

Representatives shall be apportioned among the several States according to their respective numbers, counting the whole number of persons in each State, excluding Indians not taxed. But when the right to vote at any election for the choice of electors for President and Vice-President of the United States, Representatives in Congress, the Executive and Judicial officers of a State, or the members of the Legislature thereof, is denied to any of the male inhabitants of such State, being twenty-one years of age,* and citizens of the United States, or in any way abridged, except for participation in rebellion, or other crime, the basis of representation therein shall be reduced in the proportion which the number of such male citizens shall bear to the whole number of male citizens twenty-one years of age in such State.

Changed by section 1 of the 26th amendment.

Section 3.

No person shall be a Senator or Representative in Congress, or elector of President and Vice-President, or hold any office, civil or military, under the United States, or under any State, who, having previously taken an oath, as a member of Congress, or as an officer of the United States, or as a member of any State legislature, or as an executive or judicial officer of any State, to support the Constitution of the United States, shall have engaged in insurrection or rebellion against the same, or given aid or comfort to the enemies thereof. But Congress may by a vote of two-thirds of each House, remove such disability.

Section 4.

The validity of the public debt of the United States, authorized by law, including debts incurred for payment of pensions and bounties for services in suppressing insurrection or rebellion, shall not be questioned. But neither the United States nor any State shall assume or pay any debt or obligation incurred in aid of insurrection or rebellion against the United States, or any claim for the loss or emancipation of any slave; but all such debts, obligations and claims shall be held illegal and void.

Section 5.

The Congress shall have the power to enforce, by appropriate legislation, the provisions of this article.

AMENDMENT XV

Passed by Congress February 26, 1869. Ratified February 3, 1870.

Section 1.

The right of citizens of the United States to vote shall not be denied or abridged by the United States or by any State on account of race, color, or previous condition of servitude.

Section 2.

The Congress shall have the power to enforce this article by appropriate legislation.

AMENDMENT XVI

Passed by Congress July 2, 1909. Ratified February 3, 1913.

Note: Article I, section 9, of the Constitution was modified by amendment 16.

The Congress shall have power to lay and collect taxes on incomes, from whatever source derived, without apportionment among the several States, and without regard to any census or enumeration.

AMENDMENT XVII

Passed by Congress May 13, 1912. Ratified April 8, 1913.

Note: Article I, section 3, of the Constitution was modified by the 17th amendment.

The Senate of the United States shall be composed of two Senators from each State, elected by the people thereof, for six years; and each Senator shall have one vote. The electors in each State shall have the qualifications requisite for electors of the most numerous branch of the State legislatures.

When vacancies happen in the representation of any State in the Senate, the executive authority of such State shall issue writs of election to fill such vacancies: *Provided,* That the legislature of any State may empower the executive thereof to make temporary appointments until the people fill the vacancies by election as the legislature may direct.

This amendment shall not be so construed as to affect the election or term of any Senator chosen before it becomes valid as part of the Constitution.

AMENDMENT XVIII

Passed by Congress December 18, 1917. Ratified January 16, 1919. Repealed by amendment 21.

Section 1.

After one year from the ratification of this article the manufacture, sale, or transportation of intoxicating liquors within, the importation thereof into, or the exportation thereof from the United States and all territory subject to the jurisdiction thereof for beverage purposes is hereby prohibited.

Section 2.

The Congress and the several States shall have concurrent power to enforce this article by appropriate legislation.

Section 3.

This article shall be inoperative unless it shall have been ratified as an amendment to the Constitution by the legislatures of the several States, as provided in the Constitution, within seven years from the date of the submission hereof to the States by the Congress.

AMENDMENT XIX

Passed by Congress June 4, 1919. Ratified August 18, 1920.

The right of citizens of the United States to vote shall not be denied or abridged by the United States or by any State on account of sex.

Congress shall have power to enforce this article by appropriate legislation.

AMENDMENT XX

Passed by Congress March 2, 1932. Ratified January 23, 1933.

Note: Article I, section 4, of the Constitution was modified by section 2 of this amendment. In addition, a portion of the 12th amendment was superseded by section 3.

Section 1.

The terms of the President and the Vice President shall end at noon on the 20th day of January, and the terms of Senators and Representatives at noon on the 3d day of January, of the years in which such terms would have ended if this article had not been ratified; and the terms of their successors shall then begin.

Section 2.

The Congress shall assemble at least once in every year, and such meeting shall begin at noon on the 3d day of January, unless they shall by law appoint a different day.

Section 3.

If, at the time fixed for the beginning of the term of the President, the President elect shall have died, the Vice President elect shall become President. If a President shall not have been chosen before the time fixed for the beginning of his term, or if the President elect shall have failed to qualify, then the Vice President elect shall act as President until a President shall have qualified; and the Congress may by law provide for the case wherein neither a President elect nor a Vice President shall have qualified, declaring who shall then act as President, or the manner in which one who is to act shall be selected, and such person shall act accordingly until a President or Vice President shall have qualified.

Section 4.

The Congress may by law provide for the case of the death of any of the persons from whom the House of Representatives may choose a President whenever the right of choice shall have devolved upon them, and for the case of the death of any of the persons from whom the Senate may choose a Vice President whenever the right of choice shall have devolved upon them.

Section 5.

Sections 1 and 2 shall take effect on the 15th day of October following the ratification of this article.

Section 6.

This article shall be inoperative unless it shall have been ratified as an amendment to the Constitution by the legislatures of three-fourths of the several States within seven years from the date of its submission.

AMENDMENT XXI

Passed by Congress February 20, 1933. Ratified December 5, 1933.

Section 1.

The eighteenth article of amendment to the Constitution of the United States is hereby repealed.

Section 2.

The transportation or importation into any State, Territory, or Possession of the United States for delivery or use therein of intoxicating liquors, in violation of the laws thereof, is hereby prohibited.

Section 3.

This article shall be inoperative unless it shall have been ratified as an amendment to the Constitution by conventions in the several States, as provided in the Constitution, within seven years from the date of the submission hereof to the States by the Congress.

AMENDMENT XXII
Passed by Congress March 21, 1947. Ratified February 27, 1951.

Section 1.

No person shall be elected to the office of the President more than twice, and no person who has held the office of President, or acted as President, for more than two years of a term to which some other person was elected President shall be elected to the office of President more than once. But this Article shall not apply to any person holding the office of President when this Article was proposed by Congress, and shall not prevent any person who may be holding the office of President, or acting as President, during the term within which this Article becomes operative from holding the office of President or acting as President during the remainder of such term.

Section 2.

This article shall be inoperative unless it shall have been ratified as an amendment to the Constitution by the legislatures of three-fourths of the several States within seven years from the date of its submission to the States by the Congress.

AMENDMENT XXIII
Passed by Congress June 16, 1960. Ratified March 29, 1961.

Section 1.

The District constituting the seat of Government of the United States shall appoint in such manner as Congress may direct:

A number of electors of President and Vice President equal to the whole number of Senators and Representatives in Congress to which the District would be entitled if it were a State, but in no event more than the least populous State; they shall be in addition to those appointed by the States, but they shall be considered, for the purposes of the election of President and Vice President, to be electors appointed by a State; and they shall meet in the District and perform such duties as provided by the twelfth article of amendment.

Section 2.

The Congress shall have power to enforce this article by appropriate legislation.

AMENDMENT XXIV
Passed by Congress August 27, 1962. Ratified January 23, 1964.

Section 1.
The right of citizens of the United States to vote in any primary or other election for President or Vice President, for electors for President or Vice President, or for Senator or Representative in Congress, shall not be denied or abridged by the United States or any State by reason of failure to pay poll tax or other tax.

Section 2.
The Congress shall have power to enforce this article by appropriate legislation.

AMENDMENT XXV
Passed by Congress July 6, 1965. Ratified February 10, 1967.

Note: Article II, section 1, of the Constitution was affected by the 25th amendment.

Section 1.
In case of the removal of the President from office or of his death or resignation, the Vice President shall become President.

Section 2.
Whenever there is a vacancy in the office of the Vice President, the President shall nominate a Vice President who shall take office upon confirmation by a majority vote of both Houses of Congress.

Section 3.
Whenever the President transmits to the President pro tempore of the Senate and the Speaker of the House of Representatives his written declaration that he is unable to discharge the powers and duties of his office, and until he transmits to them a written declaration to the contrary, such powers and duties shall be discharged by the Vice President as Acting President.

Section 4.
Whenever the Vice President and a majority of either the principal officers of the executive departments or of such other body as Congress may by law provide, transmit to the President pro tempore of the Senate and the Speaker of the House of Representatives their written declaration that the President is unable to discharge the powers and duties of his office, the Vice President shall immediately assume the powers and duties of the office as Acting President.

Thereafter, when the President transmits to the President pro tempore of the Senate and the Speaker of the House of Representatives his written declaration that no inability exists, he shall resume the powers and duties of his office unless the Vice

President and a majority of either the principal officers of the executive department or of such other body as Congress may by law provide, transmit within four days to the President pro tempore of the Senate and the Speaker of the House of Representatives their written declaration that the President is unable to discharge the powers and duties of his office. Thereupon Congress shall decide the issue, assembling within forty-eight hours for that purpose if not in session. If the Congress, within twenty-one days after receipt of the latter written declaration, or, if Congress is not in session, within twenty-one days after Congress is required to assemble, determines by two-thirds vote of both Houses that the President is unable to discharge the powers and duties of his office, the Vice President shall continue to discharge the same as Acting President; otherwise, the President shall resume the powers and duties of his office.

AMENDMENT XXVI
Passed by Congress March 23, 1971. Ratified July 1, 1971.

Note: Amendment 14, section 2, of the Constitution was modified by section 1 of the 26th amendment.

Section 1.
The right of citizens of the United States, who are eighteen years of age or older, to vote shall not be denied or abridged by the United States or by any State on account of age.

Section 2.
The Congress shall have power to enforce this article by appropriate legislation.

AMENDMENT XXVII
Originally proposed Sept. 25, 1789. Ratified May 7, 1992.

No law, varying the compensation for the services of the Senators and Representatives, shall take effect, until an election of representatives shall have intervened.

A P P E N D I X B

SELECTED SECTIONS OF THE
ADMINISTRATIVE PROCEDURE ACT TITLE 5, U.S. CODE

§ 551. **Definitions**

For the purpose of this subchapter–

(1) "agency" means each authority of the Government of the United States, whether or not it is within or subject to review by another agency, but does not include–

   (A) the Congress;

   (B) the courts of the United States;

   (C) the governments of the territories or possessions of the United States;

   (D) the government of the District of Columbia; or except as to the requirements of section 552 of this title–

   (E) agencies composed of representatives of the parties or of representatives of organizations of the parties to the disputes determined by them;

   (F) courts martial and military commissions;

   (G) military authority exercised in the field in time of war or in occupied territory; or

   (H) functions conferred by sections 1738, 1739, 1743, and 1744 of title 12; chapter 2 of title 41; subchapter II of chapter 471 of title 49; or sections 1884, 1891-1902, and former section 1641(b)(2), of title 50, appendix;

(2) "person" includes an individual, partnership, corporation, association, or public or private organization other than an agency;

(3) "party" includes a person or agency named or admitted as a party, or properly seeking and entitled as of right to be admitted as a party, in an agency proceeding, and a person or agency admitted by an agency as a party for limited purposes;

(4) "rule" means the whole or a part of an agency statement of general or particular applicability and future effect designed to implement, interpret, or prescribe law or policy or describing the organization, procedure, or practice requirements of an agency and includes the approval or prescription for the future of rates, wages, corporate or financial structures or reorganizations thereof, prices, facilities, appliances, services or allowances therefor or of valuations, costs, or accounting, or practices bearing on any of the foregoing;

(5) "rule making" means agency process for formulating, amending, or repealing a rule;

(6) "order" means the whole or a part of a final disposition, whether affirmative, negative, injunctive, or declaratory in form, of an agency in a matter other than rule making but including licensing;

(7) "adjudication" means agency process for the formulation of an order;

(8) "license" includes the whole or a part of an agency permit, certificate, approval, registration, charter, membership, statutory exemption or other form of permission;

(9) "licensing" includes agency process respecting the grant, renewal, denial, revocation, suspension, annulment, withdrawal, limitation, amendment, modification, or conditioning of a license;

(10) "sanction" includes the whole or a part of an agency—

    (A) prohibition, requirement, limitation, or other condition affecting the freedom of a person;

    (B) withholding of relief;

    (C) imposition of penalty or fine;

    (D) destruction, taking, seizure, or withholding of property;

    (E) assessment of damages, reimbursement, restitution, compensation, costs, charges, or fees;

    (F) requirement, revocation, or suspension of a license; or

    (G) taking other compulsory or restrictive action;

(11) "relief" includes the whole or a part of an agency—

    (A) grant of money, assistance, license, authority, exemption, exception, privilege, or remedy;

    (B) recognition of a claim, right, immunity, privilege, exemption, or exception; or

    (C) taking of other action on the application or petition of, and beneficial to, a person;

(12) "agency proceeding" means an agency process as defined by paragraphs (5), (7), and (9) of this section;

(13) "agency action" includes the whole or a part of an agency rule, order, license, sanction, relief, or the equivalent or denial thereof, or failure to act; and

(14) "ex parte communication" means an oral or written communication not on the public record with respect to which reasonable prior notice to all parties is not given, but it shall not include requests for status reports on any matter or proceeding covered by this subchapter.

§ 552.   Public information; agency rules, opinions, orders, records, and proceedings

(a) Each agency shall make available to the public information as follows:

(1) Each agency shall separately state and currently publish in the Federal Register for the guidance of the public–

(A) descriptions of its central and field organization and the established places at which, the employees (and in the case of a uniformed service, the members) from whom, and the methods whereby, the public may obtain information, make submittals or requests, or obtain decisions;

(B) statements of the general course and method by which its functions are channeled and determined, including the nature and requirements of all formal and informal procedures available;

(C) rules of procedure, descriptions of forms available or the places at which forms may be obtained, and instructions as to the scope and contents of all papers, reports, or examinations;

(D) substantive rules of general applicability adopted as authorized by law, and statements of general policy or interpretations of general applicability formulated and adopted by the agency; and

(E) each amendment, revision, or repeal of the foregoing.

Except to the extent that a person has actual and timely notice of the terms thereof, a person may not in any manner be required to resort to, or be adversely affected by, a matter required to be published in the Federal Register and not so published. For the purpose of this paragraph, matter reasonably available to the class of persons affected thereby is deemed published in the Federal Register when incorporated by reference therein with the approval of the Director of the Federal Register.

(2) Each agency, in accordance with published rules, shall make available for public inspection and copying–

(A) final opinions, including concurring and dissenting opinions, as well as orders, made in the adjudication of cases;

(B) those statements of policy and interpretations which have been adopted by the agency and are not published in the Federal Register;

(C) administrative staff manuals and instructions to staff that affect a member of the public;

(D) copies of all records, regardless of form or format, which have been released to any person under paragraph (3) and which, because of the nature of their subject matter, the agency determines have become or are likely to become the subject of subsequent requests for substantially the same records; and

(E) a general index of the records referred to under subparagraph (D);

unless the materials are promptly published and copies offered for sale. For records created on or after November 1, 1996, within one year after such date, each agency shall make such records available, including by computer telecommunications or, if computer telecommunications means have not been established by the agency, by other electronic means. To the extent required to prevent a clearly unwarranted invasion of personal privacy, an agency may delete identifying details when it makes available or publishes an opinion, statement of policy, interpretation, staff manual, instruction, or copies of records referred to in subparagraph (D). However, in each case the justification for the deletion shall be explained fully in writing, and the extent of such deletion shall be indicated on the portion of the record which is made available or published, unless including that indication would harm an interest protected by the exemption in subsection (b) under which the deletion is made. If technically feasible, the extent of the deletion shall be indicated at the place in the record where the deletion was made. Each agency shall also maintain and make available for public inspection and copying current indexes providing identifying information for the public as to any matter issued, adopted, or promulgated after July 4, 1967, and required by this paragraph to be made available or published. Each agency shall promptly publish, quarterly or more frequently, and distribute (by sale or otherwise) copies of each index or supplements thereto unless it determines by order published in the Federal Register that the publication would be unnecessary and impracticable, in which case the agency shall nonetheless provide copies of such index on request at a cost not to exceed the direct cost of duplication. Each agency shall make the index referred to in subparagraph (E) available by computer telecommunications by December 31, 1999. A final order, opinion, statement of policy, interpretation, or staff manual or instruction that affects a member of the public may be relied on, used, or cited as precedent by an agency against a party other than an agency only if–

(i)   it has been indexed and either made available or published as provided by this paragraph; or

(ii) the party has actual and timely notice of the terms thereof.

(3) (A) Except with respect to the records made available under paragraphs (1) and (2) of this subsection, and except as provided in subparagraph (E), each agency, upon any request for records which (i) reasonably describes such records and (ii) is made in accordance with published rules stating the time, place, fees (if any), and procedures to be followed, shall make the records promptly available to any person.

(B) In making any record available to a person under this paragraph, an agency shall provide the record in any form or format requested by the person if the record is readily reproducible by the agency in that form or format. Each agency shall make reasonable efforts to maintain its records in forms or formats that are reproducible for purposes of this section.

(C) In responding under this paragraph to a request for records, an agency shall make reasonable efforts to search for the records in electronic form or format, except when such efforts would significantly interfere with the operation of the agency's automated information system.

(D) For purposes of this paragraph, the term "search" means to review, manually or by automated means, agency records for the purpose of locating those records which are responsive to a request.

(E) An agency, or part of an agency, that is an element of the intelligence community (as that term is defined in section 3(4) of the National Security Act of 1947 (50 U.S.C. 401a(4))) shall not make any record available under this paragraph to–

(i)   any government entity, other than a State, territory, commonwealth, or district of the United States, or any subdivision thereof; or

(ii) a representative of a government entity described in clause (i).

(4)(A)(i) In order to carry out the provisions of this section, each agency shall promulgate regulations, pursuant to notice and receipt of public comment, specifying the schedule of fees applicable to the processing of requests under this section and establishing procedures and guidelines for determining when such fees should be waived or reduced. Such schedule shall conform to the guidelines which shall be promulgated, pursuant to notice and receipt of public comment, by the Director of the Office of Management and Budget and which shall provide for a uniform schedule of fees for all agencies.

(ii) Such agency regulations shall provide that–

(I) fees shall be limited to reasonable standard charges for document search, duplication, and review, when records are requested for commercial use;

(II) fees shall be limited to reasonable standard charges for document duplication when records are not sought for commercial use and the request is made by an educational or noncommercial scientific institution, whose purpose is scholarly or scientific research; or a representative of the news media; and

(III) for any request not described in (I) or (II), fees shall be limited to reasonable standard charges for document search and duplication.

(iii) Documents shall be furnished without any charge or at a charge reduced below the fees established under clause (ii) if disclosure of the information is in the public interest because it is likely to contribute significantly to public understanding of the operations or activities of the government and is not primarily in the commercial interest of the requester.

(iv) Fee schedules shall provide for the recovery of only the direct costs of search, duplication, or review. Review costs shall include only the direct costs incurred during the initial examination of a document for the purposes of determining whether the documents must be disclosed under this section and for the purposes of withholding any portions exempt from disclosure under this section. Review costs may not include any costs incurred in resolving issues of law or policy that may be raised in the course of processing a request under this section. No fee may be charged by any agency under this section–

(I) if the costs of routine collection and processing of the fee are likely to equal or exceed the amount of the fee; or

(II) for any request described in clause (ii)(II) or (III) of this subparagraph for the first two hours of search time or for the first one hundred pages of duplication.

(v) No agency may require advance payment of any fee unless the requester has previously failed to pay fees in a timely fashion, or the agency has determined that the fee will exceed $250.

(vi) Nothing in this subparagraph shall supersede fees chargeable under a statute specifically providing for setting the level of fees for particular types of records.

(vii) In any action by a requester regarding the waiver of fees under this section, the court shall determine the matter de novo: *Provided,* That the court's review of the matter shall be limited to the record before the agency.

(B) On complaint, the district court of the United States in the district in which the complainant resides, or has his principal place of business, or in which the agency records are situated, or in the District of Columbia, has jurisdiction to enjoin the agency from withholding agency records and to order the production of any agency records improperly withheld from the complainant. In such a case the court shall determine the matter de novo, and may examine the contents of such agency records in camera to determine whether such records or any part thereof shall be withheld under any of the exemptions set forth in subsection (b) of this section, and the burden is on the agency to sustain its action. In addition to any other matters to which a court accords substantial weight, a court shall accord substantial weight to an affidavit of an agency concerning the agency's determination as to technical feasibility under paragraph (2)(C) and subsection (b) and reproducibility under paragraph (3)(B).

(C) Notwithstanding any other provision of law, the defendant shall serve an answer or otherwise plead to any complaint made under this subsection within thirty days after service upon the defendant of the pleading in which such complaint is made, unless the court otherwise directs for good cause shown.

(D) Repealed. Pub. L. 98-620, Title IV, § 402(2), Nov. 8, 1984, 98 Stat. 3357

(E) The court may assess against the United States reasonable attorney fees and other litigation costs reasonably incurred in any case under this section in which the complainant has substantially prevailed.

(F) Whenever the court orders the production of any agency records improperly withheld from the complainant and assesses against the United States reasonable attorney fees and other litigation costs, and the court additionally issues a written finding that the circumstances surrounding the withholding raise questions whether agency personnel acted arbitrarily or capriciously with respect to the withholding, the Special Counsel shall promptly initiate a proceeding to determine whether disciplinary action is warranted against the officer or employee who was primarily responsible for the withholding. The Special Counsel, after investigation and consideration of the evidence submitted, shall submit his findings and recommendations to the administrative authority of the agency concerned and shall send copies of the findings and recommendations to the officer or employee or his representative. The administrative authority shall take the corrective action that the Special Counsel recommends.

(G) In the event of noncompliance with the order of the court, the district court may punish for contempt the responsible employee, and in the case of a uniformed service, the responsible member.

(5) Each agency having more than one member shall maintain and make available for public inspection a record of the final votes of each member in every agency proceeding.

(6)(A) Each agency, upon any request for records made under paragraph (1), (2), or (3) of this subsection, shall–

(i) determine within 20 days (excepting Saturdays, Sundays, and legal public holidays) after the receipt of any such request whether to comply with such request and shall immediately notify the person making such request of such determination and the reasons therefor, and of the right of such person to appeal to the head of the agency any adverse determination; and

(ii) make a determination with respect to any appeal within twenty days (excepting Saturdays, Sundays, and legal public holidays) after the receipt of such appeal. If on appeal the denial of the request for records is in whole or in part upheld, the agency shall notify the person making such request of the provisions for judicial review of that determination under paragraph (4) of this subsection.

(B) (i) In unusual circumstances as specified in this subparagraph, the time limits prescribed in either clause (i) or clause (ii) of subparagraph (A) may be extended by written notice to the person making such request setting forth the unusual circumstances for such extension and the date on which a determination is expected to be dispatched. No such notice shall specify a date that would result in an extension for more than ten working days, except as provided in clause (ii) of this subparagraph.

(ii) With respect to a request for which a written notice under clause (i) extends the time limits prescribed under clause (i) of subparagraph (A), the agency shall notify the person making the request if the request cannot be processed within the time limit specified in that clause and shall provide the person an opportunity to limit the scope of the request so that it may be processed within that time limit or an opportunity to arrange with the agency an alternative time frame for processing the request or a modified request. Refusal by the person to reasonably modify the request or arrange such an alternative time frame shall be considered as a factor in determining whether exceptional circumstances exist for purposes of subparagraph (C).

(iii) As used in this subparagraph, "unusual circumstances" means, but only to the extent reasonably necessary to the proper processing of the particular requests—

(I) the need to search for and collect the requested records from field facilities or other establishments that are separate from the office processing the request;

(II) the need to search for, collect, and appropriately examine a voluminous amount of separate and distinct records which are demanded in a single request; or

(III) the need for consultation, which shall be conducted with all practicable speed, with another agency having a substantial interest in the determination of the request or among two or more components of the agency having substantial subject-matter interest therein.

(iv) Each agency may promulgate regulations, pursuant to notice and receipt of public comment, providing for the aggregation of certain requests by the same requestor, or by a group of requestors acting in concert, if the agency reasonably believes that such requests actually constitute a single request, which would otherwise satisfy the unusual circumstances specified in this subparagraph, and the requests involve clearly related matters. Multiple requests involving unrelated matters shall not be aggregated.

(C) (i) Any person making a request to any agency for records under paragraph (1), (2), or (3) of this subsection shall be deemed to have exhausted his administrative remedies with respect to such request if the agency fails to comply with the applicable time limit provisions of this paragraph. If the Government can show exceptional circumstances exist and that the agency is exercising due diligence in responding to the request, the court may retain jurisdiction and allow the agency additional time to complete its review of the records. Upon any determination by an agency to comply with a request for records, the records shall be made promptly available to such person making such request. Any notification of denial of any request for records under this subsection shall set forth the names and titles or positions of each person responsible for the denial of such request.

(ii) For purposes of this subparagraph, the term "exceptional circumstances" does not include a delay that results from a predictable agency workload of requests under this section, unless the agency demonstrates reasonable progress in reducing its backlog of pending requests.

(iii) Refusal by a person to reasonably modify the scope of a request or arrange an alternative time frame for processing a request (or a modified request) under clause (ii) after being given an opportunity to do so by the agency to whom the person made the request shall be considered as a factor in determining whether exceptional circumstances exist for purposes of this subparagraph.

(D) (i) Each agency may promulgate regulations, pursuant to notice and receipt of public comment, providing for multitrack processing of requests for records based on the amount of work or time (or both) involved in processing requests.

(ii) Regulations under this subparagraph may provide a person making a request that does not qualify for the fastest multitrack processing an opportunity to limit the scope of the request in order to qualify for faster processing.

(iii) This subparagraph shall not be considered to affect the requirement under subparagraph (C) to exercise due diligence.

(E) (i) Each agency shall promulgate regulations, pursuant to notice and receipt of public comment, providing for expedited processing of requests for records–

(I) in cases in which the person requesting the records demonstrates a compelling need; and

(II) in other cases determined by the agency.

(ii) Notwithstanding clause (i), regulations under this subparagraph must ensure–

(I)   that a determination of whether to provide expedited processing shall be made, and notice of the determination shall be provided to the person making the request, within 10 days after the date of the request; and

(II) expeditious consideration of administrative appeals of such determinations of whether to provide expedited processing.

(iii) An agency shall process as soon as practicable any request for records to which the agency has granted expedited processing under this subparagraph. Agency action to deny or affirm denial of a request for expedited processing pursuant to this subparagraph, and failure by an agency to respond in a timely manner to such a request shall be subject to judicial review under paragraph (4), except that the judicial review shall be based on the record before the agency at the time of the determination.

(iv) A district court of the United States shall not have jurisdiction to review an agency denial of expedited processing of a request for records after the agency has provided a complete response to the request.

(v) For purposes of this subparagraph, the term "compelling need" means–

(I)   that a failure to obtain requested records on an expedited basis under this paragraph could reasonably be expected to pose an imminent threat to the life or physical safety of an individual; or

(II) with respect to a request made by a person primarily engaged in disseminating information, urgency to inform the public concerning actual or alleged Federal Government activity.

(vi) A demonstration of a compelling need by a person making a request for expedited processing shall be made by a statement certified by such person to be true and correct to the best of such person's knowledge and belief.

(F) In denying a request for records, in whole or in part, an agency shall make a reasonable effort to estimate the volume of any requested matter the provision of which is denied, and shall provide any such estimate to the person making the request, unless providing such estimate would harm an interest protected by the exemption in subsection (b) pursuant to which the denial is made.

(b)   This section does not apply to matters that are–

(1)(A) specifically authorized under criteria established by an Executive order to be kept secret in the interest of national defense or foreign policy and (B) are in fact properly classified pursuant to such Executive order;

(2)   related solely to the internal personnel rules and practices of an agency;

(3)   specifically exempted from disclosure by statute (other than section 552b of this title), provided that such statute (A) requires that the matters be withheld from the public in such a manner as to leave no discretion on the issue, or (B) establishes particular criteria for withholding or refers to particular types of matters to be withheld;

(4)   trade secrets and commercial or financial information obtained from a person and privileged or confidential;

(5)   inter-agency or intra-agency memorandums or letters which would not be available by law to a party other than an agency in litigation with the agency;

(6)   personnel and medical files and similar files the disclosure of which would constitute a clearly unwarranted invasion of personal privacy;

(7)   records or information compiled for law enforcement purposes, but only to the extent that the production of such law enforcement records or information (A) could reasonably be expected to interfere with enforcement proceedings, (B) would deprive a person of a right to a fair trial or an impartial adjudication, (C) could reasonably be expected to constitute an unwarranted invasion of personal privacy, (D) could reasonably be expected to disclose the identity of a confidential source, including a State, local, or foreign agency or authority or any private institution which furnished information on a confidential basis, and, in the case of a record or information compiled by criminal law enforcement authority in the course of a criminal investigation or by an agency conducting a lawful national security intelligence investigation, information furnished by a confidential source, (E) would disclose techniques and procedures for law enforcement investigations or prosecutions, or would disclose guidelines for law enforcement investigations or prosecutions if such disclosure could reasonably be expected to risk circumvention of the law, or (F) could reasonably be expected to endanger the life or physical safety of any individual;

(8)   contained in or related to examination, operating, or condition reports prepared by, on behalf of, or for the use of an agency responsible for the regulation or supervision of financial institutions; or

(9)   geological and geophysical information and data, including maps, concerning wells.

Any reasonably segregable portion of a record shall be provided to any person requesting such record after deletion of the portions which are exempt under this subsection. The amount of information deleted shall be indicated on the released portion of the record, unless including that indication would harm an interest protected by the exemption in this subsection under which the deletion is made. If technically feasible, the amount of the information deleted shall be indicated at the place in the record where such deletion is made.

(c)(1) Whenever a request is made which involves access to records described in subsection (b)(7)(A) and–

    (A) the investigation or proceeding involves a possible violation of criminal law; and

    (B) there is reason to believe that (i) the subject of the investigation or proceeding is not aware of its pendency, and (ii) disclosure of the existence of the records could reasonably be expected to interfere with enforcement proceedings, the agency may, during only such time as that circumstance continues, treat the records as not subject to the requirements of this section.

  (2) Whenever informant records maintained by a criminal law enforcement agency under an informant's name or personal identifier are requested by a third party according to the informant's name or personal identifier, the agency may treat the records as not subject to the requirements of this section unless the informant's status as an informant has been officially confirmed.

  (3) Whenever a request is made which involves access to records maintained by the Federal Bureau of Investigation pertaining to foreign intelligence or counterintelligence, or international terrorism, and the existence of the records is classified information as provided in subsection (b)(1), the Bureau may, as long as the existence of the records remains classified information, treat the records as not subject to the requirements of this section.

  (d) This section does not authorize withholding of information or limit the availability of records to the public, except as specifically stated in this section. This section is not authority to withhold information from Congress.

(e)(1) On or before February 1 of each year, each agency shall submit to the Attorney General of the United States a report which shall cover the preceding fiscal year and which shall include–

    (A) the number of determinations made by the agency not to comply with requests for records made to such agency under subsection (a) and the reasons for each such determination;

(B) (i) the number of appeals made by persons under subsection (a)(6), the result of such appeals, and the reason for the action upon each appeal that results in a denial of information; and

(ii) a complete list of all statutes that the agency relies upon to authorize the agency to withhold information under subsection (b)(3), a description of whether a court has upheld the decision of the agency to withhold information under each such statute, and a concise description of the scope of any information withheld;

(C) the number of requests for records pending before the agency as of September 30 of the preceding year, and the median number of days that such requests had been pending before the agency as of that date;

(D) the number of requests for records received by the agency and the number of requests which the agency processed;

(E) the median number of days taken by the agency to process different types of requests;

(F) the total amount of fees collected by the agency for processing requests; and

(G) the number of full-time staff of the agency devoted to processing requests for records under this section, and the total amount expended by the agency for processing such requests.

(2) Each agency shall make each such report available to the public including by computer telecommunications, or if computer telecommunications means have not been established by the agency, by other electronic means.

(3) The Attorney General of the United States shall make each report which has been made available by electronic means available at a single electronic access point. The Attorney General of the United States shall notify the Chairman and ranking minority member of the Committee on Government Reform and Oversight of the House of Representatives and the Chairman and ranking minority member of the Committees on Governmental Affairs and the Judiciary of the Senate, no later than April 1 of the year in which each such report is issued, that such reports are available by electronic means.

(4) The Attorney General of the United States, in consultation with the Director of the Office of Management and Budget, shall develop reporting and performance guidelines in connection with reports required by this subsection by October 1, 1997, and may establish additional requirements

for such reports as the Attorney General determines may be useful.

(5) The Attorney General of the United States shall submit an annual report on or before April 1 of each calendar year which shall include for the prior calendar year a listing of the number of cases arising under this section, the exemption involved in each case, the disposition of such case, and the cost, fees, and penalties assessed under subparagraphs (E), (F), and (G) of subsection (a)(4). Such report shall also include a description of the efforts undertaken by the Department of Justice to encourage agency compliance with this section.

(f)   For purposes of this section, the term–

(1) "agency" as defined in section 551(1) of this title includes any executive department, military department, Government corporation, Government controlled corporation, or other establishment in the executive branch of the Government (including the Executive Office of the President), or any independent regulatory agency; and

(2) "record" and any other term used in this section in reference to information includes any information that would be an agency record subject to the requirements of this section when maintained by an agency in any format, including an electronic format.

(g)   The head of each agency shall prepare and make publicly available upon request, reference material or a guide for requesting records or information from the agency, subject to the exemptions in subsection (b), including–

(1) an index of all major information systems of the agency;

(2) a description of major information and record locator systems maintained by the agency; and

(3) a handbook for obtaining various types and categories of public information from the agency pursuant to chapter 35 of title 44, and under this section.

§ 552a.   Records maintained on individuals

(a)   Definitions.–For purposes of this section–

(1) the term "agency" means agency as defined in section 552(e) of this title;

(2) the term "individual" means a citizen of the United States or an alien lawfully admitted for permanent residence;

(3) the term "maintain" includes maintain, collect, use, or disseminate;

(4) the term "record" means any item, collection, or grouping of information about an individual that is maintained by an agency, including, but not limited to, his education, financial

transactions, medical history, and criminal or employment history and that contains his name, or the identifying number, symbol, or other identifying particular assigned to the individual, such as a finger or voice print or a photograph;

(5) the term "system of records" means a group of any records under the control of any agency from which information is retrieved by the name of the individual or by some identifying number, symbol, or other identifying particular assigned to the individual;

(6) the term "statistical record" means a record in a system of records maintained for statistical research or reporting purposes only and not used in whole or in part in making any determination about an identifiable individual, except as provided by section 8 of title 13;

(7) the term "routine use" means, with respect to the disclosure of a record, the use of such record for a purpose which is compatible with the purpose for which it was collected;

(8) the term "matching program"–

(A) means any computerized comparison of–

(i) two or more automated systems of records or a system of records with non-Federal records for the purpose of–

(I) establishing or verifying the eligibility of, or continuing compliance with statutory and regulatory requirements by, applicants for, recipients or beneficiaries of, participants in, or providers of services with respect to, cash or in-kind assistance or payments under Federal benefit programs, or

(II) recouping payments or delinquent debts under such Federal benefit programs, or

(ii) two or more automated Federal personnel or payroll systems of records or a system of Federal personnel or payroll records with non-Federal records,

(B) but does not include–

(i) matches performed to produce aggregate statistical data without any personal identifiers;

(ii) matches performed to support any research or statistical project, the specific data of which may not be used to make decisions concerning the rights, benefits, or privileges of specific individuals;

(iii) matches performed, by an agency (or component thereof) which performs as its principal function any activity pertaining to the enforcement of criminal laws, subsequent to the initiation of a specific criminal or civil law enforcement investigation of a named person or persons for the purpose of gathering evidence against such person or persons;

   (iv) matches of tax information (I) pursuant to section 6103(d) of the Internal Revenue Code of 1986, (II) for purposes of tax administration as defined in section 6103(b)(4) of such Code, (III) for the purpose of intercepting a tax refund due an individual under authority granted by section 404(e), 464, or 1137 of the Social Security Act; or (IV) for the purpose of intercepting a tax refund due an individual under any other tax refund intercept program authorized by statute which has been determined by the Director of the Office of Management and Budget to contain verification, notice, and hearing requirements that are substantially similar to the procedures in section 1137 of the Social Security Act;

   (v) matches–

   (I) using records predominantly relating to Federal personnel, that are performed for routine administrative purposes (subject to guidance provided by the Director of the Office of Management and Budget pursuant to subsection (v)); or

   (II) conducted by an agency using only records from systems of records maintained by that agency;

if the purpose of the match is not to take any adverse financial, personnel, disciplinary, or other adverse action against Federal personnel [FN1]

   (vi) matches performed for foreign counterintelligence purposes or to produce background checks for security clearances of Federal personnel or Federal contractor personnel;

   (vii) matches performed incident to a levy described in section 6103(k)(8) of the Internal Revenue Code of 1986; or

   (viii) matches performed pursuant to section 202(x)(3) or 1611(e)(1) of the Social Security Act (42 U.S.C. 402(x)(3), 1382(e)(1));

  (9) the term "recipient agency" means any agency, or contractor thereof, receiving records contained in a system of records from a source agency for use in a matching program;

  (10) the term "non-Federal agency" means any State or local government, or agency thereof, which receives records contained in a system of records from a source agency for use in a matching program;

  (11) the term "source agency" means any agency which discloses records contained in a system of records to be used in a

matching program, or any State or local government, or agency thereof, which discloses records to be used in a matching program;

(12) the term "Federal benefit program" means any program administered or funded by the Federal Government, or by any agent or State on behalf of the Federal Government, providing cash or in-kind assistance in the form of payments, grants, loans, or loan guarantees to individuals; and

(13) the term "Federal personnel" means officers and employees of the Government of the United States, members of the uniformed services (including members of the Reserve Components), individuals [FN2] entitled to receive immediate or deferred retirement benefits under any retirement program of the Government of the United States (including survivor benefits).

(b) Conditions of disclosure.–No agency shall disclose any record which is contained in a system of records by any means of communication to any person, or to another agency, except pursuant to a written request by, or with the prior written consent of, the individual to whom the record pertains, unless disclosure of the record would be–

(1) to those officers and employees of the agency which maintains the record who have a need for the record in the performance of their duties;

(2) required under section 552 of this title;

(3) for a routine use as defined in subsection (a)(7) of this section and described under subsection (e)(4)(D) of this section;

(4) to the Bureau of the Census for purposes of planning or carrying out a census or survey or related activity pursuant to the provisions of title 13;

(5) to a recipient who has provided the agency with advance adequate written assurance that the record will be used solely as a statistical research or reporting record, and the record is to be transferred in a form that is not individually identifiable;

(6) to the National Archives and Records Administration as a record which has sufficient historical or other value to warrant its continued preservation by the United States Government, or for evaluation by the Archivist of the United States or the designee of the Archivist to determine whether the record has such value;

(7) to another agency or to an instrumentality of any governmental jurisdiction within or under the control of the United States for a civil or criminal law enforcement activity if the activity is authorized by law, and if the head of the agency or instrumentality has made a written request to the agency which maintains the record specifying the particular

portion desired and the law enforcement activity for which the record is sought;

(8) to a person pursuant to a showing of compelling circumstances affecting the health or safety of an individual if upon such disclosure notification is transmitted to the last known address of such individual;

(9) to either House of Congress, or, to the extent of matter within its jurisdiction, any committee or subcommittee thereof, any joint committee of Congress or subcommittee of any such joint committee;

(10) to the Comptroller General, or any of his authorized representatives, in the course of the performance of the duties of the Government Accountability Office;

(11) pursuant to the order of a court of competent jurisdiction; or

(12) to a consumer reporting agency in accordance with section 3711(e) of title 31.

(c) **Accounting of certain disclosures.**–Each agency, with respect to each system of records under its control, shall–

(1) except for disclosures made under subsections (b)(1) or (b)(2) of this section, keep an accurate accounting of–

(A) the date, nature, and purpose of each disclosure of a record to any person or to another agency made under subsection (b) of this section; and

(B) the name and address of the person or agency to whom the disclosure is made;

(2) retain the accounting made under paragraph (1) of this subsection for at least five years or the life of the record, whichever is longer, after the disclosure for which the accounting is made;

(3) except for disclosures made under subsection (b)(7) of this section, make the accounting made under paragraph (1) of this subsection available to the individual named in the record at his request; and

(4) inform any person or other agency about any correction or notation of dispute made by the agency in accordance with subsection (d) of this section of any record that has been disclosed to the person or agency if an accounting of the disclosure was made.

(d) **Access to records.**–Each agency that maintains a system of records shall–

(1) upon request by any individual to gain access to his record or to any information pertaining to him which is contained in the system, permit him and upon his request, a person of his own choosing to accompany him, to review the record and have a copy made of all or any portion thereof in a form comprehensible to him, except that the agency may require

the individual to furnish a written statement authorizing discussion of that individual's record in the accompanying person's presence;

(2) permit the individual to request amendment of a record pertaining to him and–

   (A) not later than 10 days (excluding Saturdays, Sundays, and legal public holidays) after the date of receipt of such request, acknowledge in writing such receipt; and

   (B) promptly, either–

   (i) make any correction of any portion thereof which the individual believes is not accurate, relevant, timely, or complete; or

   (ii) inform the individual of its refusal to amend the record in accordance with his request, the reason for the refusal, the procedures established by the agency for the individual to request a review of that refusal by the head of the agency or an officer designated by the head of the agency, and the name and business address of that official;

(3) permit the individual who disagrees with the refusal of the agency to amend his record to request a review of such refusal, and not later than 30 days (excluding Saturdays, Sundays, and legal public holidays) from the date on which the individual requests such review, complete such review and make a final determination unless, for good cause shown, the head of the agency extends such 30-day period; and if, after his review, the reviewing official also refuses to amend the record in accordance with the request, permit the individual to file with the agency a concise statement setting forth the reasons for his disagreement with the refusal of the agency, and notify the individual of the provisions for judicial review of the reviewing official's determination under subsection (g)(1)(A) of this section;

(4) in any disclosure, containing information about which the individual has filed a statement of disagreement, occurring after the filing of the statement under paragraph (3) of this subsection, clearly note any portion of the record which is disputed and provide copies of the statement and, if the agency deems it appropriate, copies of a concise statement of the reasons of the agency for not making the amendments requested, to persons or other agencies to whom the disputed record has been disclosed; and

(5) nothing in this section shall allow an individual access to any information compiled in reasonable anticipation of a civil action or proceeding.

(e) **Agency requirements.**–Each agency that maintains a system of records shall–

(1) maintain in its records only such information about an individual as is relevant and necessary to accomplish a purpose of the agency required to be accomplished by statute or by executive order of the President;

(2) collect information to the greatest extent practicable directly from the subject individual when the information may result in adverse determinations about an individual's rights, benefits, and privileges under Federal programs;

(3) inform each individual whom it asks to supply information, on the form which it uses to collect the information or on a separate form that can be retained by the individual–

(A) the authority (whether granted by statute, or by executive order of the President) which authorizes the solicitation of the information and whether disclosure of such information is mandatory or voluntary;

(B) the principal purpose or purposes for which the information is intended to be used;

(C) the routine uses which may be made of the information, as published pursuant to paragraph (4)(D) of this subsection; and

(D) the effects on him, if any, of not providing all or any part of the requested information;

(4) subject to the provisions of paragraph (11) of this subsection, publish in the Federal Register upon establishment or revision a notice of the existence and character of the system of records, which notice shall include–

(A) the name and location of the system;

(B) the categories of individuals on whom records are maintained in the system;

(C) the categories of records maintained in the system;

(D) each routine use of the records contained in the system, including the categories of users and the purpose of such use;

(E) the policies and practices of the agency regarding storage, retrievability, access controls, retention, and disposal of the records;

(F) the title and business address of the agency official who is responsible for the system of records;

(G) the agency procedures whereby an individual can be notified at his request if the system of records contains a record pertaining to him;

(H) the agency procedures whereby an individual can be notified at his request how he can gain access to any record pertaining to him contained in the system of records, and how he can contest its content; and

(I)   the categories of sources of records in the system;

(5)   maintain all records which are used by the agency in making any determination about any individual with such accuracy, relevance, timeliness, and completeness as is reasonably necessary to assure fairness to the individual in the determination;

(6)   prior to disseminating any record about an individual to any person other than an agency, unless the dissemination is made pursuant to subsection (b)(2) of this section, make reasonable efforts to assure that such records are accurate, complete, timely, and relevant for agency purposes;

(7)   maintain no record describing how any individual exercises rights guaranteed by the First Amendment unless expressly authorized by statute or by the individual about whom the record is maintained or unless pertinent to and within the scope of an authorized law enforcement activity;

(8)   make reasonable efforts to serve notice on an individual when any record on such individual is made available to any person under compulsory legal process when such process becomes a matter of public record;

(9)   establish rules of conduct for persons involved in the design, development, operation, or maintenance of any system of records, or in maintaining any record, and instruct each such person with respect to such rules and the requirements of this section, including any other rules and procedures adopted pursuant to this section and the penalties for noncompliance;

(10)   establish appropriate administrative, technical, and physical safeguards to insure the security and confidentiality of records and to protect against any anticipated threats or hazards to their security or integrity which could result in substantial harm, embarrassment, inconvenience, or unfairness to any individual on whom information is maintained;

(11)   at least 30 days prior to publication of information under paragraph (4)(D) of this subsection, publish in the Federal Register notice of any new use or intended use of the information in the system, and provide an opportunity for interested persons to submit written data, views, or arguments to the agency; and

(12)   if such agency is a recipient agency or a source agency in a matching program with a non-Federal agency, with respect to any establishment or revision of a matching program, at least 30 days prior to conducting such program, publish in the Federal Register notice of such establishment or revision.

    (f) Agency rules.–In order to carry out the provisions of this section, each agency that maintains a system of records shall promulgate rules, in accordance with the requirements (including general notice) of section 553 of this title, which shall–

(1) establish procedures whereby an individual can be notified in response to his request if any system of records named by the individual contains a record pertaining to him;

(2) define reasonable times, places, and requirements for identifying an individual who requests his record or information pertaining to him before the agency shall make the record or information available to the individual;

(3) establish procedures for the disclosure to an individual upon his request of his record or information pertaining to him, including special procedure, if deemed necessary, for the disclosure to an individual of medical records, including psychological records, pertaining to him;

(4) establish procedures for reviewing a request from an individual concerning the amendment of any record or information pertaining to the individual, for making a determination on the request, for an appeal within the agency of an initial adverse agency determination, and for whatever additional means may be necessary for each individual to be able to exercise fully his rights under this section; and

(5) establish fees to be charged, if any, to any individual for making copies of his record, excluding the cost of any search for and review of the record.

The Office of the Federal Register shall biennially compile and publish the rules promulgated under this subsection and agency notices published under subsection (e)(4) of this section in a form available to the public at low cost.

(g)(1) **Civil remedies.**–Whenever any agency

    (A) makes a determination under subsection (d)(3) of this section not to amend an individual's record in accordance with his request, or fails to make such review in conformity with that subsection;

    (B) refuses to comply with an individual request under subsection (d)(1) of this section;

    (C) fails to maintain any record concerning any individual with such accuracy, relevance, timeliness, and completeness as is necessary to assure fairness in any determination relating to the qualifications, character, rights, or opportunities of, or benefits to the individual that may be made on the basis of such record, and consequently a determination is made which is adverse to the individual; or

(D) fails to comply with any other provision of this section, or any rule promulgated thereunder, in such a way as to have an adverse effect on an individual, the individual may bring a civil action against the agency, and the district courts of the United States shall have jurisdiction in the matters under the provisions of this subsection.

(2) (A) In any suit brought under the provisions of subsection (g)(1)(A) of this section, the court may order the agency to amend the individual's record in accordance with his request or in such other way as the court may direct. In such a case the court shall determine the matter de novo.

(B) The court may assess against the United States reasonable attorney fees and other litigation costs reasonably incurred in any case under this paragraph in which the complainant has substantially prevailed.

(3) (A) In any suit brought under the provisions of subsection (g)(1)(B) of this section, the court may enjoin the agency from withholding the records and order the production to the complainant of any agency records improperly withheld from him. In such a case the court shall determine the matter de novo, and may examine the contents of any agency records in camera to determine whether the records or any portion thereof may be withheld under any of the exemptions set forth in subsection (k) of this section, and the burden is on the agency to sustain its action.

(B) The court may assess against the United States reasonable attorney fees and other litigation costs reasonably incurred in any case under this paragraph in which the complainant has substantially prevailed.

(4) In any suit brought under the provisions of subsection (g)(1)(C) or (D) of this section in which the court determines that the agency acted in a manner which was intentional or willful, the United States shall be liable to the individual in an amount equal to the sum of–

(A) actual damages sustained by the individual as a result of the refusal or failure, but in no case shall a person entitled to recovery receive less than the sum of $1,000; and

(B) the costs of the action together with reasonable attorney fees as determined by the court.

(5) An action to enforce any liability created under this section may be brought in the district court of the United States in

the district in which the complainant resides, or has his principal place of business, or in which the agency records are situated, or in the District of Columbia, without regard to the amount in controversy, within two years from the date on which the cause of action arises, except that where an agency has materially and willfully misrepresented any information required under this section to be disclosed to an individual and the information so misrepresented is material to establishment of the liability of the agency to the individual under this section, the action may be brought at any time within two years after discovery by the individual of the misrepresentation. Nothing in this section shall be construed to authorize any civil action by reason of any injury sustained as the result of a disclosure of a record prior to September 27, 1975.

   (h) **Rights of legal guardians.**–For the purposes of this section, the parent of any minor, or the legal guardian of any individual who has been declared to be incompetent due to physical or mental incapacity or age by a court of competent jurisdiction, may act on behalf of the individual.

(i)(1) **Criminal penalties.**–Any officer or employee of an agency, who by virtue of his employment or official position, has possession of, or access to, agency records which contain individually identifiable information the disclosure of which is prohibited by this section or by rules or regulations established thereunder, and who knowing that disclosure of the specific material is so prohibited, willfully discloses the material in any manner to any person or agency not entitled to receive it, shall be guilty of a misdemeanor and fined not more than $5,000.

  (2) Any officer or employee of any agency who willfully maintains a system of records without meeting the notice requirements of subsection (e)(4) of this section shall be guilty of a misdemeanor and fined not more than $5,000.

  (3) Any person who knowingly and willfully requests or obtains any record concerning an individual from an agency under false pretenses shall be guilty of a misdemeanor and fined not more than $5,000.

   (j) **General exemptions.**–The head of any agency may promulgate rules, in accordance with the requirements (including general notice) of sections 553(b)(1), (2), and (3), (c), and (e) of this title, to exempt any system of records within the agency from any part of this section except subsections (b), (c)(1) and (2), (e)(4)(A) through (F), (e)(6), (7), (9), (10), and (11), and (i) if the system of records is–

(1) maintained by the Central Intelligence Agency; or

(2) maintained by an agency or component thereof which performs as its principal function any activity pertaining to the enforcement of criminal laws, including police efforts to prevent, control, or reduce crime or to apprehend criminals, and the activities of prosecutors, courts, correctional, probation, pardon, or parole authorities, and which consists of (A) information compiled for the purpose of identifying individual criminal offenders and alleged offenders and consisting only of identifying data and notations of arrests, the nature and disposition of criminal charges, sentencing, confinement, release, and parole and probation status; (B) information compiled for the purpose of a criminal investigation, including reports of informants and investigators, and associated with an identifiable individual; or (C) reports identifiable to an individual compiled at any stage of the process of enforcement of the criminal laws from arrest or indictment through release from supervision.

At the time rules are adopted under this subsection, the agency shall include in the statement required under section 553(c) of this title, the reasons why the system of records is to be exempted from a provision of this section.

(k) **Specific exemptions.**–The head of any agency may promulgate rules, in accordance with the requirements (including general notice) of sections 553(b)(1), (2), and (3), (c), and (e) of this title, to exempt any system of records within the agency from subsections (c)(3), (d), (e)(1), (e)(4)(G), (H), and (I) and (f) of this section if the system of records is–

(1) subject to the provisions of section 552(b)(1) of this title;

(2) investigatory material compiled for law enforcement purposes, other than material within the scope of subsection (j)(2) of this section: *Provided, however,* That if any individual is denied any right, privilege, or benefit that he would otherwise be entitled by Federal law, or for which he would otherwise be eligible, as a result of the maintenance of such material, such material shall be provided to such individual, except to the extent that the disclosure of such material would reveal the identity of a source who furnished information to the Government under an express promise that the identity of the source would be held in confidence, or, prior to the effective date of this section, under an implied promise that the identity of the source would be held in confidence;

(3) maintained in connection with providing protective services to the President of the United States or other individuals pursuant to section 3056 of title 18;

(4) required by statute to be maintained and used solely as statistical records;

(5) investigatory material compiled solely for the purpose of determining suitability, eligibility, or qualifications for Federal civilian employment, military service, Federal contracts, or access to classified information, but only to the extent that the disclosure of such material would reveal the identity of a source who furnished information to the Government under an express promise that the identity of the source would be held in confidence, or, prior to the effective date of this section, under an implied promise that the identity of the source would be held in confidence;

(6) testing or examination material used solely to determine individual qualifications for appointment or promotion in the Federal service the disclosure of which would compromise the objectivity or fairness of the testing or examination process; or

(7) evaluation material used to determine potential for promotion in the armed services, but only to the extent that the disclosure of such material would reveal the identity of a source who furnished information to the Government under an express promise that the identity of the source would be held in confidence, or, prior to the effective date of this section, under an implied promise that the identity of the source would be held in confidence.

At the time rules are adopted under this subsection, the agency shall include in the statement required under section 553(c) of this title, the reasons why the system of records is to be exempted from a provision of this section.

(*l*)(1) **Archival records.**–Each agency record which is accepted by the Archivist of the United States for storage, processing, and servicing in accordance with section 3103 of title 44 shall, for the purposes of this section, be considered to be maintained by the agency which deposited the record and shall be subject to the provisions of this section. The Archivist of the United States shall not disclose the record except to the agency which maintains the record, or under rules established by that agency which are not inconsistent with the provisions of this section.

(2) Each agency record pertaining to an identifiable individual which was transferred to the National Archives of the United States as a record which has sufficient historical or other

value to warrant its continued preservation by the United States Government, prior to the effective date of this section, shall, for the purposes of this section, be considered to be maintained by the National Archives and shall not be subject to the provisions of this section, except that a statement generally describing such records (modeled after the requirements relating to records subject to subsections (e)(4)(A) through (G) of this section) shall be published in the Federal Register.

(3) Each agency record pertaining to an identifiable individual which is transferred to the National Archives of the United States as a record which has sufficient historical or other value to warrant its continued preservation by the United States Government, on or after the effective date of this section, shall, for the purposes of this section, be considered to be maintained by the National Archives and shall be exempt from the requirements of this section except subsections (e)(4)(A) through (G) and (e)(9) of this section.

(m) (1) **Government contractors.**–When an agency provides by a contract for the operation by or on behalf of the agency of a system of records to accomplish an agency function, the agency shall, consistent with its authority, cause the requirements of this section to be applied to such system. For purposes of subsection (i) of this section any such contractor and any employee of such contractor, if such contract is agreed to on or after the effective date of this section, shall be considered to be an employee of an agency.

(2) A consumer reporting agency to which a record is disclosed under section 3711(e) of title 31 shall not be considered a contractor for the purposes of this section.

(n) **Mailing lists.**–An individual's name and address may not be sold or rented by an agency unless such action is specifically authorized by law. This provision shall not be construed to require the withholding of names and addresses otherwise permitted to be made public.

(o) **Matching agreements.**–(1) No record which is contained in a system of records may be disclosed to a recipient agency or non-Federal agency for use in a computer matching program except pursuant to a written agreement between the source agency and the recipient agency or non-Federal agency specifying–

(A) the purpose and legal authority for conducting the program;

(B) the justification for the program and the anticipated results, including a specific estimate of any savings;

(C) a description of the records that will be matched, including each data element that will be used, the approximate number of records that will be matched, and the projected starting and completion dates of the matching program;

(D) procedures for providing individualized notice at the time of application, and notice periodically thereafter as directed by the Data Integrity Board of such agency (subject to guidance provided by the Director of the Office of Management and Budget pursuant to subsection (v)), to–

(i) applicants for and recipients of financial assistance or payments under Federal benefit programs, and

(ii) applicants for and holders of positions as Federal personnel, that any information provided by such applicants, recipients, holders, and individuals may be subject to verification through matching programs;

(E) procedures for verifying information produced in such matching program as required by subsection (p);

(F) procedures for the retention and timely destruction of identifiable records created by a recipient agency or non-Federal agency in such matching program;

(G) procedures for ensuring the administrative, technical, and physical security of the records matched and the results of such programs;

(H) prohibitions on duplication and redisclosure of records provided by the source agency within or outside the recipient agency or the non-Federal agency, except where required by law or essential to the conduct of the matching program;

(I) procedures governing the use by a recipient agency or non-Federal agency of records provided in a matching program by a source agency, including procedures governing return of the records to the source agency or destruction of records used in such program;

(J) information on assessments that have been made on the accuracy of the records that will be used in such matching program; and

(K) that the Comptroller General may have access to all records of a recipient agency or a non-Federal agency that the Comptroller General deems necessary in order to monitor or verify compliance with the agreement.

(2) (A) A copy of each agreement entered into pursuant to paragraph (1) shall–

(i) be transmitted to the Committee on Governmental Affairs of the Senate and the Committee on Government Operations of the House of Representatives; and

(ii) be available upon request to the public.

(B) No such agreement shall be effective until 30 days after the date on which such a copy is transmitted pursuant to subparagraph (A)(i).

(C) Such an agreement shall remain in effect only for such period, not to exceed 18 months, as the Data Integrity Board of the agency determines is appropriate in light of the purposes, and length of time necessary for the conduct, of the matching program.

(D) Within 3 months prior to the expiration of such an agreement pursuant to subparagraph (C), the Data Integrity Board of the agency may, without additional review, renew the matching agreement for a current, ongoing matching program for not more than one additional year if–

(i) such program will be conducted without any change; and

(ii) each party to the agreement certifies to the Board in writing that the program has been conducted in compliance with the agreement.

(p) **Verification and opportunity to contest findings.**–(1) In order to protect any individual whose records are used in a matching program, no recipient agency, non-Federal agency, or source agency may suspend, terminate, reduce, or make a final denial of any financial assistance or payment under a Federal benefit program to such individual, or take other adverse action against such individual, as a result of information produced by such matching program, until–

(A) (i) the agency has independently verified the information; or

(ii) the Data Integrity Board of the agency, or in the case of a non-Federal agency the Data Integrity Board of the source agency, determines in accordance with guidance issued by the Director of the Office of Management and Budget that–

(I) the information is limited to identification and amount of benefits paid by the source agency under a Federal benefit program; and

(II) there is a high degree of confidence that the information provided to the recipient agency is accurate;

(B)   the individual receives a notice from the agency containing a statement of its findings and informing the individual of the opportunity to contest such findings; and

(C)   (i)   the expiration of any time period established for the program by statute or regulation for the individual to respond to that notice; or

   (ii)   in the case of a program for which no such period is established, the end of the 30-day period beginning on the date on which notice under subparagraph (B) is mailed or otherwise provided to the individual.

(2)   Independent verification referred to in paragraph (1) requires investigation and confirmation of specific information relating to an individual that is used as a basis for an adverse action against the individual, including where applicable investigation and confirmation of–

(A)   the amount of any asset or income involved;

(B)   whether such individual actually has or had access to such asset or income for such individual's own use; and

(C)   the period or periods when the individual actually had such asset or income.

(3)   Notwithstanding paragraph (1), an agency may take any appropriate action otherwise prohibited by such paragraph if the agency determines that the public health or public safety may be adversely affected or significantly threatened during any notice period required by such paragraph.

(q)   **Sanctions.**–(1) Notwithstanding any other provision of law, no source agency may disclose any record which is contained in a system of records to a recipient agency or non-Federal agency for a matching program if such source agency has reason to believe that the requirements of subsection (p), or any matching agreement entered into pursuant to subsection (o), or both, are not being met by such recipient agency.

(2)   No source agency may renew a matching agreement unless–

(A)   the recipient agency or non-Federal agency has certified that it has complied with the provisions of that agreement; and

(B)   the source agency has no reason to believe that the certification is inaccurate.

(r)   **Report on new systems and matching programs.**–Each agency that proposes to establish or make a significant change in a system of records or a matching program shall provide adequate advance notice of any such proposal (in duplicate) to the

Committee on Government Operations of the House of Representatives, the Committee on Governmental Affairs of the Senate, and the Office of Management and Budget in order to permit an evaluation of the probable or potential effect of such proposal on the privacy or other rights of individuals.

(s) Biennial report.–The President shall biennially submit to the Speaker of the House of Representatives and the President pro tempore of the Senate a report–

(1) describing the actions of the Director of the Office of Management and Budget pursuant to section 6 of the Privacy Act of 1974 during the preceding 2 years;

(2) describing the exercise of individual rights of access and amendment under this section during such years;

(3) identifying changes in or additions to systems of records;

(4) containing such other information concerning administration of this section as may be necessary or useful to the Congress in reviewing the effectiveness of this section in carrying out the purposes of the Privacy Act of 1974.

(t)(1) Effect of other laws.–No agency shall rely on any exemption contained in section 552 of this title to withhold from an individual any record which is otherwise accessible to such individual under the provisions of this section.

(2) No agency shall rely on any exemption in this section to withhold from an individual any record which is otherwise accessible to such individual under the provisions of section 552 of this title.

(u) **Data Integrity Boards.**–(1) Every agency conducting or participating in a matching program shall establish a Data Integrity Board to oversee and coordinate among the various components of such agency the agency's implementation of this section.

(2) Each Data Integrity Board shall consist of senior officials designated by the head of the agency, and shall include any senior official designated by the head of the agency as responsible for implementation of this section, and the inspector general of the agency, if any. The inspector general shall not serve as chairman of the Data Integrity Board.

(3) Each Data Integrity Board–

(A) shall review, approve, and maintain all written agreements for receipt or disclosure of agency records for matching programs to ensure compliance with subsection (o), and all relevant statutes, regulations, and guidelines;

(B) shall review all matching programs in which the agency has participated during the year, either as a source agency or recipient agency, determine compliance with applicable laws, regulations, guidelines, and agency agreements, and assess the costs and benefits of such programs;

(C) shall review all recurring matching programs in which the agency has participated during the year, either as a source agency or recipient agency, for continued justification for such disclosures;

(D) shall compile an annual report, which shall be submitted to the head of the agency and the Office of Management and Budget and made available to the public on request, describing the matching activities of the agency, including–

(i) matching programs in which the agency has participated as a source agency or recipient agency;

(ii) matching agreements proposed under subsection (o) that were disapproved by the Board;

(iii) any changes in membership or structure of the Board in the preceding year;

(iv) the reasons for any waiver of the requirement in paragraph (4) of this section for completion and submission of a cost-benefit analysis prior to the approval of a matching program;

(v) any violations of matching agreements that have been alleged or identified and any corrective action taken; and

(vi) any other information required by the Director of the Office of Management and Budget to be included in such report;

(E) shall serve as a clearinghouse for receiving and providing information on the accuracy, completeness, and reliability of records used in matching programs;

(F) shall provide interpretation and guidance to agency components and personnel on the requirements of this section for matching programs;

(G) shall review agency recordkeeping and disposal policies and practices for matching programs to assure compliance with this section; and

(H) may review and report on any agency matching activities that are not matching programs.

(4) (A) Except as provided in subparagraphs (B) and (C), a Data Integrity Board shall not approve any written agreement for a matching program unless the agency has completed and submitted to such Board a cost-benefit analysis of the proposed program and such analysis demonstrates that the program is likely to be cost effective. [FN3]

(B) The Board may waive the requirements of subparagraph (A) of this paragraph if it determines in writing, in accordance with guidelines prescribed by the Director of the Office of Management and Budget, that a cost-benefit analysis is not required.

(C) A cost-benefit analysis shall not be required under subparagraph (A) prior to the initial approval of a written agreement for a matching program that is specifically required by statute. Any subsequent written agreement for such a program shall not be approved by the Data Integrity Board unless the agency has submitted a cost-benefit analysis of the program as conducted under the preceding approval of such agreement.

(5) (A) If a matching agreement is disapproved by a Data Integrity Board, any party to such agreement may appeal the disapproval to the Director of the Office of Management and Budget. Timely notice of the filing of such an appeal shall be provided by the Director of the Office of Management and Budget to the Committee on Governmental Affairs of the Senate and the Committee on Government Operations of the House of Representatives.

(B) The Director of the Office of Management and Budget may approve a matching agreement notwithstanding the disapproval of a Data Integrity Board if the Director determines that—

(i) the matching program will be consistent with all applicable legal, regulatory, and policy requirements;

(ii) there is adequate evidence that the matching agreement will be cost-effective; and

(iii) the matching program is in the public interest.

(C) The decision of the Director to approve a matching agreement shall not take effect until 30 days after it is reported to committees described in subparagraph (A).

(D) If the Data Integrity Board and the Director of the Office of Management and Budget disapprove a matching program proposed by the inspector general of an agency, the inspector general may report the disapproval to the head of the agency and to the Congress.

(6) In the reports required by paragraph (3)(D), agency matching activities that are not matching programs may be reported on an aggregate basis, if and to the extent necessary to protect ongoing law enforcement or counterintelligence investigations.

(v) Office of Management and Budget responsibilities.–The Director of the Office of Management and Budget shall–

(1) develop and, after notice and opportunity for public comment, prescribe guidelines and regulations for the use of agencies in implementing the provisions of this section; and

(2) provide continuing assistance to and oversight of the implementation of this section by agencies.

§ 552b.   Open meetings

(a) For purposes of this section–

(1) the term "agency" means any agency, as defined in section 552(e) of this title, headed by a collegial body composed of two or more individual members, a majority of whom are appointed to such position by the President with the advice and consent of the Senate, and any subdivision thereof authorized to act on behalf of the agency;

(2) the term "meeting" means the deliberations of at least the number of individual agency members required to take action on behalf of the agency where such deliberations determine or result in the joint conduct or disposition of official agency business, but does not include deliberations required or permitted by subsection (d) or (e); and

(3) the term "member" means an individual who belongs to a collegial body heading an agency.

(b) Members shall not jointly conduct or dispose of agency business other than in accordance with this section. Except as provided in subsection (c), every portion of every meeting of an agency shall be open to public observation.

(c) Except in a case where the agency finds that the public interest requires otherwise, the second sentence of subsection (b) shall not apply to any portion of an agency meeting, and the requirements of subsections (d) and (e) shall not apply to any information pertaining to such meeting otherwise required by this section to be disclosed to the public, where the agency properly determines that such portion or portions of its meeting or the disclosure of such information is likely to–

(1) disclose matters that are (A) specifically authorized under criteria established by an Executive order to be kept secret in the interests of national defense or foreign policy and (B) in fact properly classified pursuant to such Executive order;

(2) relate solely to the internal personnel rules and practices of an agency;

(3) disclose matters specifically exempted from disclosure by statute (other than section 552 of this title), provided that

such statute (A) requires that the matters be withheld from the public in such a manner as to leave no discretion on the issue, or (B) establishes particular criteria for withholding or refers to particular types of matters to be withheld;

(4) disclose trade secrets and commercial or financial information obtained from a person and privileged or confidential;

(5) involve accusing any person of a crime, or formally censuring any person;

(6) disclose information of a personal nature where disclosure would constitute a clearly unwarranted invasion of personal privacy;

(7) disclose investigatory records compiled for law enforcement purposes, or information which if written would be contained in such records, but only to the extent that the production of such records or information would (A) interfere with enforcement proceedings, (B) deprive a person of a right to a fair trial or an impartial adjudication, (C) constitute an unwarranted invasion of personal privacy, (D) disclose the identity of a confidential source and, in the case of a record compiled by a criminal law enforcement authority in the course of a criminal investigation, or by an agency conducting a lawful national security intelligence investigation, confidential information furnished only by the confidential source, (E) disclose investigative techniques and procedures, or (F) endanger the life or physical safety of law enforcement personnel;

(8) disclose information contained in or related to examination, operating, or condition reports prepared by, on behalf of, or for the use of an agency responsible for the regulation or supervision of financial institutions;

(9) disclose information the premature disclosure of which would–

(A) in the case of an agency which regulates currencies, securities, commodities, or financial institutions, be likely to (i) lead to significant financial speculation in currencies, securities, or commodities, or (ii) significantly endanger the stability of any financial institution; or

(B) in the case of any agency, be likely to significantly frustrate implementation of a proposed agency action, except that subparagraph (B) shall not apply in any instance where the agency has already disclosed to the public the content or nature of its proposed action, or where the agency is required by law to make such disclosure on its own initiative prior to taking final agency action on such proposal; or

(10) specifically concern the agency's issuance of a subpena, or the agency's participation in a civil action or proceeding, an action in a foreign court or international tribunal, or an arbitration, or the initiation, conduct, or disposition by the agency of a particular case of formal agency adjudication pursuant to the procedures in section 554 of this title or otherwise involving a determination on the record after opportunity for a hearing.

(d)(1) Action under subsection (c) shall be taken only when a majority of the entire membership of the agency (as defined in subsection (a)(1)) votes to take such action. A separate vote of the agency members shall be taken with respect to each agency meeting a portion or portions of which are proposed to be closed to the public pursuant to subsection (c), or with respect to any information which is proposed to be withheld under subsection (c). A single vote may be taken with respect to a series of meetings, a portion or portions of which are proposed to be closed to the public, or with respect to any information concerning such series of meetings, so long as each meeting in such series involves the same particular matters and is scheduled to be held no more than thirty days after the initial meeting in such series. The vote of each agency member participating in such vote shall be recorded and no proxies shall be allowed.

(2) Whenever any person whose interests may be directly affected by a portion of a meeting requests that the agency close such portion to the public for any of the reasons referred to in paragraph (5), (6), or (7) of subsection (c), the agency, upon request of any one of its members, shall vote by recorded vote whether to close such meeting.

(3) Within one day of any vote taken pursuant to paragraph (1) or (2), the agency shall make publicly available a written copy of such vote reflecting the vote of each member on the question. If a portion of a meeting is to be closed to the public, the agency shall, within one day of the vote taken pursuant to paragraph (1) or (2) of this subsection, make publicly available a full written explanation of its action closing the portion together with a list of all persons expected to attend the meeting and their affiliation.

(4) Any agency, a majority of whose meetings may properly be closed to the public pursuant to paragraph (4), (8), (9)(A), or (10) of subsection (c), or any combination thereof, may provide by regulation for the closing of such meetings or

portions thereof in the event that a majority of the members of the agency votes by recorded vote at the beginning of such meeting, or portion thereof, to close the exempt portion or portions of the meeting, and a copy of such vote, reflecting the vote of each member on the question, is made available to the public. The provisions of paragraphs (1), (2), and (3) of this subsection and subsection (e) shall not apply to any portion of a meeting to which such regulations apply: *Provided,* That the agency shall, except to the extent that such information is exempt from disclosure under the provisions of subsection (c), provide the public with public announcement of the time, place, and subject matter of the meeting and of each portion thereof at the earliest practicable time.

(e)(1) In the case of each meeting, the agency shall make public announcement, at least one week before the meeting, of the time, place, and subject matter of the meeting, whether it is to be open or closed to the public, and the name and phone number of the official designated by the agency to respond to requests for information about the meeting. Such announcement shall be made unless a majority of the members of the agency determines by a recorded vote that agency business requires that such meeting be called at an earlier date, in which case the agency shall make public announcement of the time, place, and subject matter of such meeting, and whether open or closed to the public, at the earliest practicable time.

(2) The time or place of a meeting may be changed following the public announcement required by paragraph (1) only if the agency publicly announces such change at the earliest practicable time. The subject matter of a meeting, or the determination of the agency to open or close a meeting, or portion of a meeting, to the public, may be changed following the public announcement required by this subsection only if (A) a majority of the entire membership of the agency determines by a recorded vote that agency business so requires and that no earlier announcement of the change was possible, and (B) the agency publicly announces such change and the vote of each member upon such change at the earliest practicable time.

(3) Immediately following each public announcement required by this subsection, notice of the time, place, and subject matter of a meeting, whether the meeting is open or closed, any change in one of the preceding, and the name and phone number of the official designated by the agency to respond to

requests for information about the meeting, shall also be submitted for publication in the Federal Register.

(f)(1) For every meeting closed pursuant to paragraphs (1) through (10) of subsection (c), the General Counsel or chief legal officer of the agency shall publicly certify that, in his or her opinion, the meeting may be closed to the public and shall state each relevant exemptive provision. A copy of such certification, together with a statement from the presiding officer of the meeting setting forth the time and place of the meeting, and the persons present, shall be retained by the agency. The agency shall maintain a complete transcript or electronic recording adequate to record fully the proceedings of each meeting, or portion of a meeting, closed to the public, except that in the case of a meeting, or portion of a meeting, closed to the public pursuant to paragraph (8), (9)(A), or (10) of subsection (c), the agency shall maintain either such a transcript or recording, or a set of minutes. Such minutes shall fully and clearly describe all matters discussed and shall provide a full and accurate summary of any actions taken, and the reasons therefor, including a description of each of the views expressed on any item and the record of any rollcall vote (reflecting the vote of each member on the question). All documents considered in connection with any action shall be identified in such minutes.

(2) The agency shall make promptly available to the public, in a place easily accessible to the public, the transcript, electronic recording, or minutes (as required by paragraph (1)) of the discussion of any item on the agenda, or of any item of the testimony of any witness received at the meeting, except for such item or items of such discussion or testimony as the agency determines to contain information which may be withheld under subsection (c). Copies of such transcript, or minutes, or a transcription of such recording disclosing the identity of each speaker, shall be furnished to any person at the actual cost of duplication or transcription. The agency shall maintain a complete verbatim copy of the transcript, a complete copy of the minutes, or a complete electronic recording of each meeting, or portion of a meeting, closed to the public, for a period of at least two years after such meeting, or until one year after the conclusion of any agency proceeding with respect to which the meeting or portion was held, whichever occurs later.

(g) Each agency subject to the requirements of this section shall, within 180 days after the date of enactment of this section, following consultation with the Office of the Chairman of the Administrative Conference of the United States and published notice in the Federal Register of at least thirty days and opportunity for written comment by any person, promulgate regulations to implement the requirements of subsections (b) through (f) of this section. Any person may bring a proceeding in the United States District Court for the District of Columbia to require an agency to promulgate such regulations if such agency has not promulgated such regulations within the time period specified herein. Subject to any limitations of time provided by law, any person may bring a proceeding in the United States Court of Appeals for the District of Columbia to set aside agency regulations issued pursuant to this subsection that are not in accord with the requirements of subsections (b) through (f) of this section and to require the promulgation of regulations that are in accord with such subsections.

(h)(1) The district courts of the United States shall have jurisdiction to enforce the requirements of subsections (b) through (f) of this section by declaratory judgment, injunctive relief, or other relief as may be appropriate. Such actions may be brought by any person against an agency prior to, or within sixty days after, the meeting out of which the violation of this section arises, except that if public announcement of such meeting is not initially provided by the agency in accordance with the requirements of this section, such action may be instituted pursuant to this section at any time prior to sixty days after any public announcement of such meeting. Such actions may be brought in the district court of the United States for the district in which the agency meeting is held or in which the agency in question has its headquarters, or in the District Court for the District of Columbia. In such actions a defendant shall serve his answer within thirty days after the service of the complaint. The burden is on the defendant to sustain his action. In deciding such cases the court may examine in camera any portion of the transcript, electronic recording, or minutes of a meeting closed to the public, and may take such additional evidence as it deems necessary. The court, having due regard for orderly administration and the public interest, as well as the interests of the parties, may grant such equitable relief as it deems appropriate, including granting an injunction against future violations of this section or ordering the agency to make available to the public such portion of the transcript, recording, or minutes of a meeting as is not authorized to be withheld under subsection (c) of this section.

(2) Any Federal court otherwise authorized by law to review agency action may, at the application of any person properly participating in the proceeding pursuant to other applicable law, inquire into violations by the agency of the requirements of this section and afford such relief as it deems appropriate. Nothing in this section authorizes any Federal court having jurisdiction solely on the basis of paragraph (1) to set aside, enjoin, or invalidate any agency action (other than an action to close a meeting or to withhold information under this section) taken or discussed at any agency meeting out of which the violation of this section arose.

(i) The court may assess against any party reasonable attorney fees and other litigation costs reasonably incurred by any other party who substantially prevails in any action brought in accordance with the provisions of subsection (g) or (h) of this section, except that costs may be assessed against the plaintiff only where the court finds that the suit was initiated by the plaintiff primarily for frivolous or dilatory purposes. In the case of assessment of costs against an agency, the costs may be assessed by the court against the United States.

(j) Each agency subject to the requirements of this section shall annually report to the Congress regarding the following:

(1) The changes in the policies and procedures of the agency under this section that have occurred during the preceding 1-year period.

(2) A tabulation of the number of meetings held, the exemptions applied to close meetings, and the days of public notice provided to close meetings.

(3) A brief description of litigation or formal complaints concerning the implementation of this section by the agency.

(4) A brief explanation of any changes in law that have affected the responsibilities of the agency under this section.

(k) Nothing herein expands or limits the present rights of any person under section 552 of this title, except that the exemptions set forth in subsection (c) of this section shall govern in the case of any request made pursuant to section 552 to copy or inspect the transcripts, recordings, or minutes described in subsection (f) of this section. The requirements of chapter 33 of title 44, United States Code, shall not apply to the transcripts, recordings, and minutes described in subsection (f) of this section.

(l) This section does not constitute authority to withhold any information from Congress, and does not authorize the closing of any agency meeting or portion thereof required by any other provision of law to be open.

(m) Nothing in this section authorizes any agency to withhold from any individual any record, including transcripts, recordings, or minutes required by this section, which is otherwise accessible to such individual under section 552a of this title.

§ 553. **Rule making**

(a) This section applies, according to the provisions thereof, except to the extent that there is involved–

(1) a military or foreign affairs function of the United States; or

(2) a matter relating to agency management or personnel or to public property, loans, grants, benefits, or contracts.

(b) General notice of proposed rule making shall be published in the Federal Register, unless persons subject thereto are named and either personally served or otherwise have actual notice thereof in accordance with law. The notice shall include–

(1) a statement of the time, place, and nature of public rule making proceedings;

(2) reference to the legal authority under which the rule is proposed; and

(3) either the terms or substance of the proposed rule or a description of the subjects and issues involved.

Except when notice or hearing is required by statute, this subsection does not apply–

(A) to interpretative rules, general statements of policy, or rules of agency organization, procedure, or practice; or

(B) when the agency for good cause finds (and incorporates the finding and a brief statement of reasons therefor in the rules issued) that notice and public procedure thereon are impracticable, unnecessary, or contrary to the public interest.

(c) After notice required by this section, the agency shall give interested persons an opportunity to participate in the rule making through submission of written data, views, or arguments with or without opportunity for oral presentation. After consideration of the relevant matter presented, the agency shall incorporate in the rules adopted a concise general statement of their basis and purpose. When rules are required by statute to be made on the record after opportunity for an agency hearing, sections 556 and 557 of this title apply instead of this subsection.

(d) The required publication or service of a substantive rule shall be made not less than 30 days before its effective date, except–

(1) a substantive rule which grants or recognizes an exemption or relieves a restriction;

(2) interpretative rules and statements of policy; or

(3) as otherwise provided by the agency for good cause found and published with the rule.

(e) Each agency shall give an interested person the right to petition for the issuance, amendment, or repeal of a rule.

§ 554. Adjudications

(a) This section applies, according to the provisions thereof, in every case of adjudication required by statute to be determined on the record after opportunity for an agency hearing, except to the extent that there is involved–

(1) a matter subject to a subsequent trial of the law and the facts de novo in a court;

(2) the selection or tenure of an employee, except a [FN1] administrative law judge appointed under section 3105 of this title;

(3) proceedings in which decisions rest solely on inspections, tests, or elections;

(4) the conduct of military or foreign affairs functions;

(5) cases in which an agency is acting as an agent for a court; or

(6) the certification of worker representatives.

(b) Persons entitled to notice of an agency hearing shall be timely informed of–

(1) the time, place, and nature of the hearing;

(2) the legal authority and jurisdiction under which the hearing is to be held; and

(3) the matters of fact and law asserted.

When private persons are the moving parties, other parties to the proceeding shall give prompt notice of issues controverted in fact or law; and in other instances agencies may by rule require responsive pleading. In fixing the time and place for hearings, due regard shall be had for the convenience and necessity of the parties or their representatives.

(c) The agency shall give all interested parties opportunity for–

(1) the submission and consideration of facts, arguments, offers of settlement, or proposals of adjustment when time, the nature of the proceeding, and the public interest permit; and

(2) to the extent that the parties are unable so to determine a controversy by consent, hearing and decision on notice and in accordance with sections 556 and 557 of this title.

(d) The employee who presides at the reception of evidence pursuant to section 556 of this title shall make the recommended decision or initial decision required by section 557 of this title, unless he becomes unavailable to the agency. Except to the extent required for the disposition of ex parte matters as authorized by law, such an employee may not–

(1) consult a person or party on a fact in issue, unless on notice and opportunity for all parties to participate; or

(2) be responsible to or subject to the supervision or direction of an employee or agent engaged in the performance of investigative or prosecuting functions for an agency.

An employee or agent engaged in the performance of investigative or prosecuting functions for an agency in a case may not, in that or a factually related case, participate or advise in the decision, recommended decision, or agency review pursuant to section 557 of this title, except as witness or counsel in public proceedings. This subsection does not apply–

(A) in determining applications for initial licenses;

(B) to proceedings involving the validity or application of rates, facilities, or practices of public utilities or carriers; or

(C) to the agency or a member or members of the body comprising the agency.

(e) The agency, with like effect as in the case of other orders, and in its sound discretion, may issue a declaratory order to terminate a controversy or remove uncertainty.

§ 555. Ancillary matters

(a) This section applies, according to the provisions thereof, except as otherwise provided by this subchapter.

(b) A person compelled to appear in person before an agency or representative thereof is entitled to be accompanied, represented, and advised by counsel or, if permitted by the agency, by other qualified representative. A party is entitled to appear in person or by or with counsel or other duly qualified representative in an agency proceeding. So far as the orderly conduct of public business permits, an interested person may appear before an agency or its responsible employees for the presentation, adjustment, or determination of an issue, request, or controversy in a proceeding, whether interlocutory, summary, or otherwise, or in connection with an agency function. With due regard for the convenience and necessity of the parties or their representatives and within a reasonable time, each agency shall proceed to conclude a matter presented to it. This subsection does not grant or deny a person who is not a lawyer the right to appear for or represent others before an agency or in an agency proceeding.

(c) Process, requirement of a report, inspection, or other investigative act or demand may not be issued, made, or enforced except as authorized by law. A person compelled to submit data or evidence is entitled to retain or, on payment of lawfully prescribed costs, procure a copy or transcript thereof, except that in a nonpublic investigatory proceeding the witness may for good cause be limited to inspection of the official transcript of his testimony.

(d) Agency subpoenas authorized by law shall be issued to a party on request and, when required by rules of procedure, on a statement or showing of general relevance and reasonable scope of the evidence sought. On contest, the court shall sustain the subpoena or similar process or demand to the extent that it is found to be in accordance with law. In a proceeding for enforcement, the court shall issue an order requiring the appearance of the witness or the production of the evidence or data within a reasonable time under penalty of punishment for contempt in case of contumacious failure to comply.

(e) Prompt notice shall be given of the denial in whole or in part of a written application, petition, or other request of an interested person made in connection with any agency proceeding. Except in affirming a prior denial or when the denial is self-explanatory, the notice shall be accompanied by a brief statement of the grounds for denial.

§ 556. Hearings; presiding employees; powers and duties; burden of proof; evidence; record as basis of decision

(a) This section applies, according to the provisions thereof, to hearings required by section 553 or 554 of this title to be conducted in accordance with this section.

(b) There shall preside at the taking of evidence–

(1) the agency;

(2) one or more members of the body which comprises the agency; or

(3) one or more administrative law judges appointed under section 3105 of this title.

This subchapter does not supersede the conduct of specified classes of proceedings, in whole or in part, by or before boards or other employees specially provided for by or designated under statute. The functions of presiding employees and of employees participating in decisions in accordance with section 557 of this title shall be conducted in an impartial manner. A presiding or participating employee may at any time disqualify himself. On the filing in good faith of a timely and sufficient affidavit of personal bias or other disqualification of a presiding or participating employee, the agency shall determine the matter as a part of the record and decision in the case.

  (c) Subject to published rules of the agency and within its powers, employees presiding at hearings may–

(1) administer oaths and affirmations;

(2) issue subpoenas authorized by law;

(3) rule on offers of proof and receive relevant evidence;

(4) take depositions or have depositions taken when the ends of justice would be served;

(5) regulate the course of the hearing;

(6) hold conferences for the settlement or simplification of the issues by consent of the parties or by the use of alternative means of dispute resolution as provided in subchapter IV of this chapter;

(7) inform the parties as to the availability of one or more alternative means of dispute resolution, and encourage use of such methods;

(8) require the attendance at any conference held pursuant to paragraph (6) of at least one representative of each party who has authority to negotiate concerning resolution of issues in controversy;

(9) dispose of procedural requests or similar matters;

(10) make or recommend decisions in accordance with section 557 of this title; and

(11) take other action authorized by agency rule consistent with this subchapter.

  (d) Except as otherwise provided by statute, the proponent of a rule or order has the burden of proof. Any oral or documentary evidence may be received, but the agency as a matter of policy shall provide for the exclusion of irrelevant, immaterial, or unduly repetitious evidence. A sanction may not be imposed or rule or order issued except on consideration of the whole record or those parts thereof cited by a party and supported by and in accordance with the reliable, probative, and substantial evidence. The agency may, to the extent consistent with the interests of justice and the policy of the underlying statutes administered by the agency, consider a violation of section 557(d) of this title sufficient grounds for a decision adverse to a party who has knowingly committed such violation or knowingly caused such violation to occur. A party is entitled to present his case or defense by oral or documentary evidence, to submit rebuttal evidence, and to conduct such cross-examination as may be required for a full and true disclosure of the facts. In rule making or determining claims for money or benefits or applications for initial licenses an agency may, when a party will not be prejudiced thereby, adopt procedures for the submission of all or part of the evidence in written form.

(e) The transcript of testimony and exhibits, together with all papers and requests filed in the proceeding, constitutes the exclusive record for decision in accordance with section 557 of this title and, on payment of lawfully prescribed costs, shall be made available to the parties. When an agency decision rests on official notice of a material fact not appearing in the evidence in the record, a party is entitled, on timely request, to an opportunity to show the contrary.

§ 557. Initial decisions; conclusiveness; review by agency; submissions by parties; contents of decisions; record

(a) This section applies, according to the provisions thereof, when a hearing is required to be conducted in accordance with section 556 of this title.

(b) When the agency did not preside at the reception of the evidence, the presiding employee or, in cases not subject to section 554(d) of this title, an employee qualified to preside at hearings pursuant to section 556 of this title, shall initially decide the case unless the agency requires, either in specific cases or by general rule, the entire record to be certified to it for decision. When the presiding employee makes an initial decision, that decision then becomes the decision of the agency without further proceedings unless there is an appeal to, or review on motion of, the agency within time provided by rule. On appeal from or review of the initial decision, the agency has all the powers which it would have in making the initial decision except as it may limit the issues on notice or by rule. When the agency makes the decision without having presided at the reception of the evidence, the presiding employee or an employee qualified to preside at hearings pursuant to section 556 of this title shall first recommend a decision, except that in rule making or determining applications for initial licenses—

(1)　instead thereof the agency may issue a tentative decision or one of its responsible employees may recommend a decision; or

(2)　this procedure may be omitted in a case in which the agency finds on the record that due and timely execution of its functions imperatively and unavoidably so requires.

    (c)　Before a recommended, initial, or tentative decision, or a decision on agency review of the decision of subordinate employees, the parties are entitled to a reasonable opportunity to submit for the consideration of the employees participating in the decisions–

(1)　proposed findings and conclusions; or

(2)　exceptions to the decisions or recommended decisions of subordinate employees or to tentative agency decisions; and

(3)　supporting reasons for the exceptions or proposed findings or conclusions.

The record shall show the ruling on each finding, conclusion, or exception presented. All decisions, including initial, recommended, and tentative decisions, are a part of the record and shall include a statement of–

    (A)　findings and conclusions, and the reasons or basis therefor, on all the material issues of fact, law, or discretion presented on the record; and

    (B)　the appropriate rule, order, sanction, relief, or denial thereof.

(d)(1)　In any agency proceeding which is subject to subsection (a) of this section, except to the extent required for the disposition of ex parte matters as authorized by law–

    (A)　no interested person outside the agency shall make or knowingly cause to be made to any member of the body comprising the agency, administrative law judge, or other employee who is or may reasonably be expected to be involved in the decisional process of the proceeding, an ex parte communication relevant to the merits of the proceeding;

    (B)　no member of the body comprising the agency, administrative law judge, or other employee who is or may reasonably be expected to be involved in the decisional process of the proceeding, shall make or knowingly cause to be made to any interested person outside the agency an ex parte communication relevant to the merits of the proceeding;

    (C)　a member of the body comprising the agency, administrative law judge, or other employee who is or may reasonably be expected to be involved in the decisional process of such proceeding who receives, or who makes or knowingly causes to be made, a communication prohibited by this subsection shall place on the public record of the proceeding:

(i) all such written communications;

(ii) memoranda stating the substance of all such oral communications; and

(iii) all written responses, and memoranda stating the substance of all oral responses, to the materials described in clauses (i) and (ii) of this subparagraph;

(D) upon receipt of a communication knowingly made or knowingly caused to be made by a party in violation of this subsection, the agency, administrative law judge, or other employee presiding at the hearing may, to the extent consistent with the interests of justice and the policy of the underlying statutes, require the party to show cause why his claim or interest in the proceeding should not be dismissed, denied, disregarded, or otherwise adversely affected on account of such violation; and

(E) the prohibitions of this subsection shall apply beginning at such time as the agency may designate, but in no case shall they begin to apply later than the time at which a proceeding is noticed for hearing unless the person responsible for the communication has knowledge that it will be noticed, in which case the prohibitions shall apply beginning at the time of his acquisition of such knowledge.

(2) This subsection does not constitute authority to withhold information from Congress.

§ 558.   Imposition of sanctions; determination of applications for licenses; suspension, revocation, and expiration of licenses

(a) This section applies, according to the provisions thereof, to the exercise of a power or authority.

(b) A sanction may not be imposed or a substantive rule or order issued except within jurisdiction delegated to the agency and as authorized by law.

(c) When application is made for a license required by law, the agency, with due regard for the rights and privileges of all the interested parties or adversely affected persons and within a reasonable time, shall set and complete proceedings required to be conducted in accordance with sections 556 and 557 of this title or other proceedings required by law and shall make its decision. Except in cases of willfulness or those in which public health, interest, or safety requires otherwise, the withdrawal, suspension, revocation, or annulment of a license is lawful only if, before the institution of agency proceedings therefor, the licensee has been given–

(1) notice by the agency in writing of the facts or conduct which may warrant the action; and

(2) opportunity to demonstrate or achieve compliance with all lawful requirements.

When the licensee has made timely and sufficient application for a renewal or a new license in accordance with agency rules, a license with reference to an activity of a continuing nature does not expire until the application has been finally determined by the agency.

§ 559.   **Effect on other laws; effect of subsequent statute**

This subchapter, chapter 7, and sections 1305, 3105, 3344, 4301(2)(E), 5372, and 7521 of this title, and the provisions of section 5335(a)(B) of this title that relate to administrative law judges, do not limit or repeal additional requirements imposed by statute or otherwise recognized by law. Except as otherwise required by law, requirements or privileges relating to evidence or procedure apply equally to agencies and persons. Each agency is granted the authority necessary to comply with the requirements of this subchapter through the issuance of rules or otherwise. Subsequent statute may not be held to supersede or modify this subchapter, chapter 7, sections 1305, 3105, 3344, 4301(2)(E), 5372, or 7521 of this title, or the provisions of section 5335(a)(B) of this title that relate to administrative law judges, except to the extent that it does so expressly.

§ 701.   **Application; definitions**

    (a) This chapter applies, according to the provisions thereof, except to the extent that–

(1) statutes preclude judicial review; or

(2) agency action is committed to agency discretion by law.

    (b) For the purpose of this chapter–

(1) "agency" means each authority of the Government of the United States, whether or not it is within or subject to review by another agency, but does not include–

(A) the Congress;

(B) the courts of the United States;

(C) the governments of the territories or possessions of the United States;

(D) the government of the District of Columbia;

(E) agencies composed of representatives of the parties or of representatives of organizations of the parties to the disputes determined by them;

(F)   courts martial and military commissions;

(G)   military authority exercised in the field in time of war or in occupied territory; or

(H)   functions conferred by sections 1738, 1739, 1743, and 1744 of title 12; chapter 2 of title 41; subchapter II of chapter 471 of title 49; or sections 1884, 1891-1902, and former section 1641(b)(2), of title 50, appendix; and

(2)   "person", "rule", "order", "license", "sanction", "relief", and "agency action" have the meanings given them by section 551 of this title.

§ 702.   **Right of review**

A person suffering legal wrong because of agency action, or adversely affected or aggrieved by agency action within the meaning of a relevant statute, is entitled to judicial review thereof. An action in a court of the United States seeking relief other than money damages and stating a claim that an agency or an officer or employee thereof acted or failed to act in an official capacity or under color of legal authority shall not be dismissed nor relief therein be denied on the ground that it is against the United States or that the United States is an indispensable party. The United States may be named as a defendant in any such action, and a judgment or decree may be entered against the United States: *Provided,* That any mandatory or injunctive decree shall specify the Federal officer or officers (by name or by title), and their successors in office, personally responsible for compliance. Nothing herein (1) affects other limitations on judicial review or the power or duty of the court to dismiss any action or deny relief on any other appropriate legal or equitable ground; or (2) confers authority to grant relief if any other statute that grants consent to suit expressly or impliedly forbids the relief which is sought.

§ 703.   **Form and venue of proceeding**

The form of proceeding for judicial review is the special statutory review proceeding relevant to the subject matter in a court specified by statute or, in the absence or inadequacy thereof, any applicable form of legal action, including actions for declaratory judgments or writs of prohibitory or mandatory injunction or habeas corpus, in a court of competent jurisdiction. If no special statutory review proceeding is applicable, the action for judicial review may be brought against the United States, the agency by its official title, or the appropriate officer. Except to the extent that prior, adequate, and exclusive opportunity for judicial review is provided by law, agency action is subject to judicial review in civil or criminal proceedings for judicial enforcement.

§ 704. **Actions reviewable**

Agency action made reviewable by statute and final agency action for which there is no other adequate remedy in a court are subject to judicial review. A preliminary, procedural, or intermediate agency action or ruling not directly reviewable is subject to review on the review of the final agency action. Except as otherwise expressly required by statute, agency action otherwise final is final for the purposes of this section whether or not there has been presented or determined an application for a declaratory order, for any form of reconsideration, or, unless the agency otherwise requires by rule and provides that the action meanwhile is inoperative, for an appeal to superior agency authority.

§ 705. **Relief pending review**

When an agency finds that justice so requires, it may postpone the effective date of action taken by it, pending judicial review. On such conditions as may be required and to the extent necessary to prevent irreparable injury, the reviewing court, including the court to which a case may be taken on appeal from or on application for certiorari or other writ to a reviewing court, may issue all necessary and appropriate process to postpone the effective date of an agency action or to preserve status or rights pending conclusion of the review proceedings.

§ 706. **Scope of review**

To the extent necessary to decision and when presented, the reviewing court shall decide all relevant questions of law, interpret constitutional and statutory provisions, and determine the meaning or applicability of the terms of an agency action. The reviewing court shall–

(1) compel agency action unlawfully withheld or unreasonably delayed; and

(2) hold unlawful and set aside agency action, findings, and conclusions found to be–

    (A) arbitrary, capricious, an abuse of discretion, or otherwise not in accordance with law;

    (B) contrary to constitutional right, power, privilege, or immunity;

    (C) in excess of statutory jurisdiction, authority, or limitations, or short of statutory right;

    (D) without observance of procedure required by law;

    (E) unsupported by substantial evidence in a case subject to sections 556 and 557 of this title or otherwise reviewed on the record of an agency hearing provided by statute; or

    (F) unwarranted by the facts to the extent that the facts are subject to trial de novo by the reviewing court.

In making the foregoing determinations, the court shall review the whole record or those parts of it cited by a party, and due account shall be taken of the rule of prejudicial error.

§ 1305.   Administrative law judges

For the purpose of sections 3105, 3344, 4301(2)(D), and 5372 of this title and the provisions of section 5335(a)(B) of this title that relate to administrative law judges, the Office of Personnel Management may, and for the purpose of section 7521 of this title, the Merit Systems Protection Board may investigate, prescribe regulations, appoint advisory committees as necessary, recommend legislation, subpena witnesses and records, and pay witness fees as established for the courts of the United States.

§ 3105.   Appointment of administrative law judges

Each agency shall appoint as many administrative law judges as are necessary for proceedings required to be conducted in accordance with sections 556 and 557 of this title. Administrative law judges shall be assigned to cases in rotation so far as practicable, and may not perform duties inconsistent with their duties and responsibilities as administrative law judges.

§ 3344.   Details; administrative law judges

An agency as defined by section 551 of this title which occasionally or temporarily is insufficiently staffed with administrative law judges appointed under section 3105 of this title may use administrative law judges selected by the Office of Personnel Management from and with the consent of other agencies.

§ 5372.   Administrative law judges

(a)   For the purposes of this section, the term "administrative law judge" means an administrative law judge appointed under section 3105.

(b)(1)(A) There shall be 3 levels of basic pay for administrative law judges (designated as AL-1, 2, and 3, respectively), and each such judge shall be paid at 1 of those levels, in accordance with the provisions of this section.

(B)   Within level AL-3, there shall be 6 rates of basic pay, designated as AL-3, rates A through F, respectively. Level AL-2 and level AL-1 shall each have 1 rate of basic pay.

(C)   The rate of basic pay for AL-3, rate A, may not be less than 65 percent of the rate of basic pay for level IV of the Executive Schedule, and the rate of basic pay for AL-1 may not exceed the rate for level IV of the Executive Schedule.

(2)   The Office of Personnel Management shall determine, in accordance with procedures which the Office shall by

regulation prescribe, the level in which each administrative-law-judge position shall be placed and the qualifications to be required for appointment to each level.

(3) (A) Upon appointment to a position in AL-3, an administrative law judge shall be paid at rate A of AL-3, and shall be advanced successively to rates B, C, and D of that level at the beginning of the next pay period following completion of 52 weeks of service in the next lower rate, and to rates E and F of that level at the beginning of the next pay period following completion of 104 weeks of service in the next lower rate.

(B) The Office of Personnel Management may provide for appointment of an administrative law judge in AL-3 at an advanced rate under such circumstances as the Office may determine appropriate.

(4) Subject to paragraph (1), effective at the beginning of the first applicable pay period commencing on or after the first day of the month in which an adjustment takes effect under section 5303 in the rates of basic pay under the General Schedule, each rate of basic pay for administrative law judges shall be adjusted by an amount determined by the President to be appropriate.

(c) The Office of Personnel Management shall prescribe regulations necessary to administer this section.

§ 7521. Actions against administrative law judges

(a) An action may be taken against an administrative law judge appointed under section 3105 of this title by the agency in which the administrative law judge is employed only for good cause established and determined by the Merit Systems Protection Board on the record after opportunity for hearing before the Board.

(b) The actions covered by this section are–

(1) a removal;

(2) a suspension;

(3) a reduction in grade;

(4) a reduction in pay; and

(5) a furlough of 30 days or less;

but do not include–

(A) a suspension or removal under section 7532 of this title;

(B) a reduction-in-force action under section 3502 of this title; or

(C) any action initiated under section 1215 of this title.

EXEC. ORDER NO. 12,866
(PRES. EXEC. ORDER), 58 FR 51735

Executive Order 12,866
Regulatory Planning and Review
September 30, 1993
The American people deserve a regulatory system that works for them, not against them: a regulatory system that protects and improves their health, safety, environment, and well-being and improves the performance of the economy without imposing unacceptable or unreasonable costs on society; regulatory policies that recognize that the private sector and private markets are the best engine for economic growth; regulatory approaches that respect the role of State, local, and tribal governments; and regulations that are effective, consistent, sensible, and understandable. We do not have such a regulatory system today.

With this Executive order, the Federal Government begins a program to reform and make more efficient the regulatory process. The objectives of this Executive order are to enhance planning and coordination with respect to both new and existing regulations; to reaffirm the primacy of Federal agencies in the regulatory decision-making process; to restore the integrity and legitimacy of regulatory review and oversight; and to make the process more accessible and open to the public. In pursuing these objectives, the regulatory process shall be conducted so as to meet applicable statutory requirements and with due regard to the discretion that has been entrusted to the Federal agencies.

Accordingly, by the authority vested in me as President by the Constitution and the laws of the United States of America, it is hereby ordered as follows:

Section 1. Statement of Regulatory Philosophy and Principles.

(a) The Regulatory Philosophy. Federal agencies should promulgate only such regulations as are required by law, are necessary to interpret the law, or are made necessary by compelling public need, such as material failures of private markets to protect or improve the health and safety of the public, the environment, or the well-being of the American people. In deciding whether and how to regulate, agencies should assess all costs and benefits of available regulatory alternatives, including the alternative of not regulating.

Costs and benefits shall be understood to include both quantifiable measures (to the fullest extent that these can be usefully estimated) and qualitative measures of costs and benefits that are difficult to quantify, but nevertheless essential to consider. Further, in choosing among alternative regulatory approaches, agencies should select those approaches that maximize net benefits (including potential economic, environmental, public health and safety, and other advantages; distributive impacts; and equity), unless a statute requires another regulatory approach.

(b) The Principles of Regulation. To ensure that the agencies' regulatory programs are consistent with the philosophy set forth above, agencies should adhere to the following principles, to the extent permitted by law and where applicable:

(1) Each agency shall identify the problem that it intends to address (including, where applicable, the failures of private markets or public institutions that warrant new agency action) as well as assess the significance of that problem.

(2) Each agency shall examine whether existing regulations (or other law) have created, or contributed to, the problem that a new regulation is intended to correct and whether those regulations (or other law) should be modified to achieve the intended goal of regulation more effectively.

(3) Each agency shall identify and assess available alternatives to direct regulation, including providing economic incentives to encourage the desired behavior, such as user fees or marketable permits, or providing information upon which choices can be made by the public.

(4) In setting regulatory priorities, each agency shall consider, to the extent reasonable, the degree and nature of the risks posed by various substances or activities within its jurisdiction.

(5) When an agency determines that a regulation is the best available method of achieving the regulatory objective, it

shall design its regulations in the most cost-effective manner to achieve the regulatory objective. In doing so, each agency shall consider incentives for innovation, consistency, predictability, the costs of enforcement and compliance (to the government, regulated entities, and the public), flexibility, distributive impacts, and equity.

(6) Each agency shall assess both the costs and the benefits of the intended regulation and, recognizing that some costs and benefits are difficult to quantify, propose or adopt a regulation only upon a reasoned determination that the benefits of the intended regulation justify its costs.

(7) Each agency shall base its decisions on the best reasonably obtainable scientific, technical, economic, and other information concerning the need for, and consequences of, the intended regulation.

(8) Each agency shall identify and assess alternative forms of regulation and shall, to the extent feasible, specify performance objectives, rather than specifying the behavior or manner of compliance that regulated entities must adopt.

(9) Wherever feasible, agencies shall seek views of appropriate State, local, and tribal officials before imposing regulatory requirements that might significantly or uniquely affect those governmental entities. Each agency shall assess the effects of Federal regulations on State, local, and tribal governments, including specifically the availability of resources to carry out those mandates, and seek to minimize those burdens that uniquely or significantly affect such governmental entities, consistent with achieving regulatory objectives. In addition, as appropriate, agencies shall seek to harmonize Federal regulatory actions with related State, local, and tribal regulatory and other governmental functions.

(10) Each agency shall avoid regulations that are inconsistent, incompatible, or duplicative with its other regulations or those of other Federal agencies.

(11) Each agency shall tailor its regulations to impose the least burden on society, including individuals, businesses of differing sizes, and other entities (including small communities and governmental entities), consistent with obtaining the regulatory objectives, taking into account, among other things, and to the extent practicable, the costs of cumulative regulations.

(12) Each agency shall draft its regulations to be simple and easy to understand, with the goal of minimizing the potential for uncertainty and litigation arising from such uncertainty.

Sec. 2. Organization. An efficient regulatory planning and review process is vital to ensure that the Federal Government's regulatory system best serves the American people.

(a) The Agencies. Because Federal agencies are the repositories of significant substantive expertise and experience, they are responsible for developing regulations and assuring that the regulations are consistent with applicable law, the President's priorities, and the principles set forth in this Executive order.

(b) The Office of Management and Budget. Coordinated review of agency rulemaking is necessary to ensure that regulations are consistent with applicable law, the President's priorities, and the principles set forth in this Executive order, and that decisions made by one agency do not conflict with the policies or actions taken or planned by another agency. The Office of Management and Budget (OMB) shall carry out that review function. Within OMB, the Office of Information and Regulatory Affairs (OIRA) is the repository of expertise concerning regulatory issues, including methodologies and procedures that affect more than one agency, this Executive order, and the President's regulatory policies. To the extent permitted by law, OMB shall provide guidance to agencies and assist the President, the Vice President, and other regulatory policy advisors to the President in regulatory planning and shall be the entity that reviews individual regulations, as provided by this Executive order.

(c) The Vice President. The Vice President is the principal advisor to the President on, and shall coordinate the development and presentation of recommendations concerning, regulatory policy, planning, and review, as set forth in this Executive order. In fulfilling their responsibilities under this Executive order, the President and the Vice President shall be assisted by the regulatory policy advisors within the Executive Office of the President and by such agency officials and personnel as the President and the Vice President may, from time to time, consult.

Sec. 3. Definitions. For purposes of this Executive order:
(a) "Advisors" refers to such regulatory policy advisors to the President as the President and Vice President may from time to time consult, including, among others: (1) the Director of OMB; (2) the Chair (or another member) of the Council of Economic Advisers; (3) the Assistant to the President for Economic Policy;

(4) the Assistant to the President for Domestic Policy; (5) the Assistant to the President for National Security Affairs; (6) the Assistant to the President for Science and Technology; (7) the Assistant to the President for Intergovernmental Affairs; (8) the Assistant to the President and Staff Secretary; (9) the Assistant to the President and Chief of Staff to the Vice President; (10) the Assistant to the President and Counsel to the President; (11) the Deputy Assistant to the President and Director of the White House Office on Environmental Policy; and (12) the Administrator of OIRA, who also shall coordinate communications relating to this Executive order among the agencies, OMB, the other Advisors, and the Office of the Vice President.

   (b) "Agency," unless otherwise indicated, means any
       authority of the United States that is an "agency" under
       44 U.S.C. 3502(1), other than those considered to be
       independent regulatory agencies, as defined in 44
       U.S.C. 3502(10).

   (c) "Director" means the Director of OMB.

   (d) "Regulation" or "rule" means an agency statement of
       general applicability and future effect, which the agency
       intends to have the force and effect of law, that is
       designed to implement, interpret, or prescribe law or
       policy or to describe the procedure or practice
       requirements of an agency. It does not, however, include:

(1) Regulations or rules issued in accordance with the formal
    rulemaking provisions of 5 U.S.C. 556, 557;

(2) Regulations or rules that pertain to a military or foreign
    affairs function of the United States, other than procurement
    regulations and regulations involving the import or export of
    non-defense articles and services;

(3) Regulations or rules that are limited to agency organization,
    management, or personnel matters; or

(4) Any other category of regulations exempted by the
    Administrator of OIRA.

   (e) "Regulatory action" means any substantive action by an
       agency (normally published in the Federal Register) that
       promulgates or is expected to lead to the promulgation
       of a final rule or regulation, including notices of inquiry,
       advance notices of proposed rulemaking, and notices of
       proposed rulemaking.

   (f) "Significant regulatory action" means any regulatory
       action that is likely to result in a rule that may:

(1) Have an annual effect on the economy of $100 million or
    more or adversely affect in a material way the economy, a

sector of the economy, productivity, competition, jobs, the environment, public health or safety, or State, local, or tribal governments or communities;

(2) Create a serious inconsistency or otherwise interfere with an action taken or planned by another agency;

(3) Materially alter the budgetary impact of entitlements, grants, user fees, or loan programs or the rights and obligations of recipients thereof; or

(4) Raise novel legal or policy issues arising out of legal mandates, the President's priorities, or the principles set forth in this Executive order.

Sec. 4. Planning Mechanism. In order to have an effective regulatory program, to provide for coordination of regulations, to maximize consultation and the resolution of potential conflicts at an early stage, to involve the public and its State, local, and tribal officials in regulatory planning, and to ensure that new or revised regulations promote the President's priorities and the principles set forth in this Executive order, these procedures shall be followed, to the extent permitted by law:

(a) Agencies' Policy Meeting. Early in each year's planning cycle, the Vice President shall convene a meeting of the Advisors and the heads of agencies to seek a common understanding of priorities and to coordinate regulatory efforts to be accomplished in the upcoming year.

(b) Unified Regulatory Agenda. For purposes of this subsection, the term "agency" or "agencies" shall also include those considered to be independent regulatory agencies, as defined in 44 U.S.C. 3502(10). Each agency shall prepare an agenda of all regulations under development or review, at a time and in a manner specified by the Administrator of OIRA. The description of each regulatory action shall contain, at a minimum, a regulation identifier number, a brief summary of the action, the legal authority for the action, any legal deadline for the action, and the name and telephone number of a knowledgeable agency official. Agencies may incorporate the information required under 5 U.S.C. 602 and 41 U.S.C. 402 into these agendas.

(c) The Regulatory Plan. For purposes of this subsection, the term "agency" or "agencies" shall also include those considered to be independent regulatory agencies, as defined in 44 U.S.C. 3502(10). (1) As part of the Unified Regulatory Agenda, beginning in 1994, each agency shall prepare a Regulatory Plan (Plan) of the most important significant regulatory actions that the agency reasonably expects to issue in proposed or final form in that fiscal year or thereafter. The

Plan shall be approved personally by the agency head and shall contain at a minimum:

(A) A statement of the agency's regulatory objectives and priorities and how they relate to the President's priorities;

(B) A summary of each planned significant regulatory action including, to the extent possible, alternatives to be considered and preliminary estimates of the anticipated costs and benefits;

(C) A summary of the legal basis for each such action, including whether any aspect of the action is required by statute or court order;

(D) A statement of the need for each such action and, if applicable, how the action will reduce risks to public health, safety, or the environment, as well as how the magnitude of the risk addressed by the action relates to other risks within the jurisdiction of the agency;

(E) The agency's schedule for action, including a statement of any applicable statutory or judicial deadlines; and

(F) The name, address, and telephone number of a person the public may contact for additional information about the planned regulatory action.

(2) Each agency shall forward its Plan to OIRA by June 1st of each year.

(3) Within 10 calendar days after OIRA has received an agency's Plan, OIRA shall circulate it to other affected agencies, the Advisors, and the Vice President.

(4) An agency head who believes that a planned regulatory action of another agency may conflict with its own policy or action taken or planned shall promptly notify, in writing, the Administrator of OIRA, who shall forward that communication to the issuing agency, the Advisors, and the Vice President.

(5) If the Administrator of OIRA believes that a planned regulatory action of an agency may be inconsistent with the President's priorities or the principles set forth in this Executive order or may be in conflict with any policy or action taken or planned by another agency, the Administrator of OIRA shall promptly notify, in writing, the affected agencies, the Advisors, and the Vice President.

(6) The Vice President, with the Advisors' assistance, may consult with the heads of agencies with respect to their Plans and, in appropriate instances, request further consideration or inter-agency coordination.

(7)   The Plans developed by the issuing agency shall be published annually in the October publication of the Unified Regulatory Agenda. This publication shall be made available to the Congress; State, local, and tribal governments; and the public. Any views on any aspect of any agency Plan, including whether any planned regulatory action might conflict with any other planned or existing regulation, impose any unintended consequences on the public, or confer any unclaimed benefits on the public, should be directed to the issuing agency, with a copy to OIRA.

(d)   Regulatory Working Group. Within 30 days of the date of this Executive order, the Administrator of OIRA shall convene a Regulatory Working Group ("Working Group"), which shall consist of representatives of the heads of each agency that the Administrator determines to have significant domestic regulatory responsibility, the Advisors, and the Vice President. The Administrator of OIRA shall chair the Working Group and shall periodically advise the Vice President on the activities of the Working Group. The Working Group shall serve as a forum to assist agencies in identifying and analyzing important regulatory issues (including, among others (1) the development of innovative regulatory techniques, (2) the methods, efficacy, and utility of comparative risk assessment in regulatory decision-making, and (3) the development of short forms and other streamlined regulatory approaches for small businesses and other entities). The Working Group shall meet at least quarterly and may meet as a whole or in subgroups of agencies with an interest in particular issues or subject areas. To inform its discussions, the Working Group may commission analytical studies and reports by OIRA, the Administrative Conference of the United States, or any other agency.

(e)   Conferences. The Administrator of OIRA shall meet quarterly with representatives of State, local, and tribal governments to identify both existing and proposed regulations that may uniquely or significantly affect those governmental entities. The Administrator of OIRA shall also convene, from time to time, conferences with representatives of businesses, nongovernmental organizations, and the public to discuss regulatory issues of common concern.

Sec. 5. Existing Regulations. In order to reduce the regulatory burden on the American people, their families, their communities, their State, local, and tribal governments, and their industries; to determine whether regulations promulgated by the executive branch of the Federal Government have become unjustified or unnecessary as a result of changed circumstances; to confirm that regulations are both compatible with each other and not duplicative or inappropriately burdensome in the aggregate; to ensure that all regulations are consistent with the President's priorities and the principles set forth in this Executive order, within applicable law; and to otherwise improve the effectiveness of existing regulations:

(a) Within 90 days of the date of this Executive order, each agency shall submit to OIRA a program, consistent with its resources and regulatory priorities, under which the agency will periodically review its existing significant regulations to determine whether any such regulations should be modified or eliminated so as to make the agency's regulatory program more effective in achieving the regulatory objectives, less burdensome, or in greater alignment with the President's priorities and the principles set forth in this Executive order. Any significant regulations selected for review shall be included in the agency's annual Plan. The agency shall also identify any legislative mandates that require the agency to promulgate or continue to impose regulations that the agency believes are unnecessary or outdated by reason of changed circumstances.

(b) The Administrator of OIRA shall work with the Regulatory Working Group and other interested entities to pursue the objectives of this section. State, local, and tribal governments are specifically encouraged to assist in the identification of regulations that impose significant or unique burdens on those governmental entities and that appear to have outlived their justification or be otherwise inconsistent with the public interest.

(c) The Vice President, in consultation with the Advisors, may identify for review by the appropriate agency or agencies other existing regulations of an agency or groups of regulations of more than one agency that affect a particular group, industry, or sector of the economy, or may identify legislative mandates that may be appropriate for reconsideration by the Congress.

Sec. 6. Centralized Review of Regulations. The guidelines set forth below shall apply to all regulatory actions, for both new and existing regulations, by agencies other than those agencies specifically exempted by the Administrator of OIRA:

(a) Agency Responsibilities. (1) Each agency shall (consistent with its own rules, regulations, or procedures) provide the public with meaningful participation in the regulatory process. In particular, before issuing a notice of proposed rulemaking, each agency should, where appropriate, seek the involvement of those who are intended to benefit from and those expected to be burdened by any regulation (including, specifically, State, local, and tribal officials). In addition, each agency should afford the public a meaningful opportunity to comment on any proposed regulation, which in most cases should include a comment period of not less than 60 days. Each agency also is directed to explore and, where appropriate, use consensual mechanisms for developing regulations, including negotiated rulemaking.

(2) Within 60 days of the date of this Executive order, each agency head shall designate a Regulatory Policy Officer who shall report to the agency head. The Regulatory Policy Officer shall be involved at each stage of the regulatory process to foster the development of effective, innovative, and least burdensome regulations and to further the principles set forth in this Executive order.

(3) In addition to adhering to its own rules and procedures and to the requirements of the Administrative Procedure Act, the Regulatory Flexibility Act, the Paperwork Reduction Act, and other applicable law, each agency shall develop its regulatory actions in a timely fashion and adhere to the following procedures with respect to a regulatory action:

(A) Each agency shall provide OIRA, at such times and in the manner specified by the Administrator of OIRA, with a list of its planned regulatory actions, indicating those which the agency believes are significant regulatory actions within the meaning of this Executive order. Absent a material change in the development of the planned regulatory action, those not designated as significant will not be subject to review under this section unless, within 10 working days of receipt of the list, the Administrator of OIRA notifies the agency that OIRA has determined that a planned regulation is a significant regulatory action within the meaning of this Executive order. The Administrator of OIRA may waive review of any planned regulatory action designated by the agency as significant, in which case the agency need not further comply with subsection (a)(3)(B) or subsection (a)(3)(C) of this section.

(B) For each matter identified as, or determined by the Administrator of OIRA to be, a significant regulatory action, the issuing agency shall provide to OIRA:

(i) The text of the draft regulatory action, together with a reasonably detailed description of the need for the regulatory action and an explanation of how the regulatory action will meet that need; and

(ii) An assessment of the potential costs and benefits of the regulatory action, including an explanation of the manner in which the regulatory action is consistent with a statutory mandate and, to the extent permitted by law, promotes the President's priorities and avoids undue interference with State, local, and tribal governments in the exercise of their governmental functions.

(C) For those matters identified as, or determined by the Administrator of OIRA to be, a significant regulatory action within the scope of section 3(f)(1), the agency shall also provide to OIRA the following additional information developed as part of the agency's decision-making process (unless prohibited by law):

(i) An assessment, including the underlying analysis, of benefits anticipated from the regulatory action (such as, but not limited to, the promotion of the efficient functioning of the economy and private markets, the enhancement of health and safety, the protection of the natural environment, and the elimination or reduction of discrimination or bias) together with, to the extent feasible, a quantification of those benefits;

(ii) An assessment, including the underlying analysis, of costs anticipated from the regulatory action (such as, but not limited to, the direct cost both to the government in administering the regulation and to businesses and others in complying with the regulation, and any adverse effects on the efficient functioning of the economy, private markets (including productivity, employment, and competitiveness), health, safety, and the natural environment), together with, to the extent feasible, a quantification of those costs; and

(iii) An assessment, including the underlying analysis, of costs and benefits of potentially effective and reasonably feasible alternatives to the planned regulation, identified by the agencies or the public (including improving the current regulation and reasonably viable nonregulatory actions), and an explanation why the planned regulatory action is preferable to the identified potential alternatives.

(D) In emergency situations or when an agency is obligated by law to act more quickly than normal review procedures allow, the agency shall notify OIRA as soon as possible and, to the extent practicable, comply with subsections (a)(3)(B) and (C) of this section. For those regulatory actions that are governed by a statutory or court-imposed deadline, the agency shall, to the extent practicable, schedule rulemaking proceedings so as to permit sufficient time for OIRA to conduct its review, as set forth below in subsection (b)(2) through (4) of this section.

(E) After the regulatory action has been published in the Federal Register or otherwise issued to the public, the agency shall:

(i) Make available to the public the information set forth in subsections (a)(3)(B) and (C);

(ii) Identify for the public, in a complete, clear, and simple manner, the substantive changes between the draft submitted to OIRA for review and the action subsequently announced; and

(iii) Identify for the public those changes in the regulatory action that were made at the suggestion or recommendation of OIRA.

(F) All information provided to the public by the agency shall be in plain, understandable language.

(b) OIRA Responsibilities. The Administrator of OIRA shall provide meaningful guidance and oversight so that each agency's regulatory actions are consistent with applicable law, the President's priorities, and the principles set forth in this Executive order and do not conflict with the policies or actions of another agency. OIRA shall, to the extent permitted by law, adhere to the following guidelines:

(1) OIRA may review only actions identified by the agency or by OIRA as significant regulatory actions under subsection (a)(3)(A) of this section.

(2) OIRA shall waive review or notify the agency in writing of the results of its review within the following time periods:

(A) For any notices of inquiry, advance notices of proposed rulemaking, or other preliminary regulatory actions prior to a Notice of Proposed Rulemaking, within 10 working days after the date of submission of the draft action to OIRA;

(B) For all other regulatory actions, within 90 calendar days after the date of submission of the information set forth in subsections (a)(3)(B) and (C) of this section, unless

OIRA has previously reviewed this information and, since that review, there has been no material change in the facts and circumstances upon which the regulatory action is based, in which case, OIRA shall complete its review within 45 days; and

(C) The review process may be extended (1) once by no more than 30 calendar days upon the written approval of the Director and (2) at the request of the agency head.

(3) For each regulatory action that the Administrator of OIRA returns to an agency for further consideration of some or all of its provisions, the Administrator of OIRA shall provide the issuing agency a written explanation for such return, setting forth the pertinent provision of this Executive order on which OIRA is relying. If the agency head disagrees with some or all of the bases for the return, the agency head shall so inform the Administrator of OIRA in writing.

(4) Except as otherwise provided by law or required by a Court, in order to ensure greater openness, accessibility, and accountability in the regulatory review process, OIRA shall be governed by the following disclosure requirements:

(A) Only the Administrator of OIRA (or a particular designee) shall receive oral communications initiated by persons not employed by the executive branch of the Federal Government regarding the substance of a regulatory action under OIRA review;

(B) All substantive communications between OIRA personnel and persons not employed by the executive branch of the Federal Government regarding a regulatory action under review shall be governed by the following guidelines:

(i) A representative from the issuing agency shall be invited to any meeting between OIRA personnel and such person(s);

(ii) OIRA shall forward to the issuing agency, within 10 working days of receipt of the communication(s), all written communications, regardless of format, between OIRA personnel and any person who is not employed by the executive branch of the Federal Government, and the dates and names of individuals involved in all substantive oral communications (including meetings to which an agency representative was invited, but did not attend, and telephone conversations between OIRA personnel and any such persons); and

(iii) OIRA shall publicly disclose relevant information about such communication(s), as set forth below in subsection (b)(4)(C) of this section.

(C) OIRA shall maintain a publicly available log that shall contain, at a minimum, the following information pertinent to regulatory actions under review:

(i) The status of all regulatory actions, including if (and if so, when and by whom) Vice Presidential and Presidential consideration was requested;

(ii) A notation of all written communications forwarded to an issuing agency under subsection (b)(4)(B)(ii) of this section; and

(iii) The dates and names of individuals involved in all substantive oral communications, including meetings and telephone conversations, between OIRA personnel and any person not employed by the executive branch of the Federal Government, and the subject matter discussed during such communications.

(D) After the regulatory action has been published in the Federal Register or otherwise issued to the public, or after the agency has announced its decision not to publish or issue the regulatory action, OIRA shall make available to the public all documents exchanged between OIRA and the agency during the review by OIRA under this section.

(5) All information provided to the public by OIRA shall be in plain, understandable language.

Sec. 7. Resolution of Conflicts. To the extent permitted by law, disagreements or conflicts between or among agency heads or between OMB and any agency that cannot be resolved by the Administrator of OIRA shall be resolved by the President, or by the Vice President acting at the request of the President, with the relevant agency head (and, as appropriate, other interested government officials). Vice Presidential and Presidential consideration of such disagreements may be initiated only by the Director, by the head of the issuing agency, or by the head of an agency that has a significant interest in the regulatory action at issue. Such review will not be undertaken at the request of other persons, entities, or their agents.

Resolution of such conflicts shall be informed by recommendations developed by the Vice President, after consultation with the Advisors (and other executive branch officials or personnel whose responsibilities to the President include the subject matter at issue). The development of these recommendations shall be concluded within 60 days after review has been requested.

During the Vice Presidential and Presidential review period, communications with any person not employed by the Federal

Government relating to the substance of the regulatory action under review and directed to the Advisors or their staffs or to the staff of the Vice President shall be in writing and shall be forwarded by the recipient to the affected agency(ies) for inclusion in the public docket(s). When the communication is not in writing, such Advisors or staff members shall inform the outside party that the matter is under review and that any comments should be submitted in writing.

At the end of this review process, the President, or the Vice President acting at the request of the President, shall notify the affected agency and the Administrator of OIRA of the President's decision with respect to the matter.

Sec. 8. Publication. Except to the extent required by law, an agency shall not publish in the Federal Register or otherwise issue to the public any regulatory action that is subject to review under section 6 of this Executive order until (1) the Administrator of OIRA notifies the agency that OIRA has waived its review of the action or has completed its review without any requests for further consideration, or (2) the applicable time period in section 6(b)(2) expires without OIRA having notified the agency that it is returning the regulatory action for further consideration under section 6(b)(3), whichever occurs first. If the terms of the preceding sentence have not been satisfied and an agency wants to publish or otherwise issue a regulatory action, the head of that agency may request Presidential consideration through the Vice President, as provided under section 7 of this order. Upon receipt of this request, the Vice President shall notify OIRA and the Advisors. The guidelines and time period set forth in section 7 shall apply to the publication of regulatory actions for which Presidential consideration has been sought.

Sec. 9. Agency Authority. Nothing in this order shall be construed as displacing the agencies' authority or responsibilities, as authorized by law.

Sec. 10. Judicial Review. Nothing in this Executive order shall affect any otherwise available judicial review of agency action. This Executive order is intended only to improve the internal management of the Federal Government and does not create any right or benefit, substantive or procedural, enforceable at law or equity by a party against the United States, its agencies or instrumentalities, its officers or employees, or any other person.

Sec. 11. Revocations. Executive Orders Nos. 12,291 and 12,498; all amendments to those Executive orders; all guidelines issued under those orders; and any exemptions from those orders heretofore granted for any category of rule are revoked.

APPENDIX D "PUTTING IT ALL TOGETHER"

Global warming: Is it real? Will it cause the polar ice caps to melt and cities to be flooded? How do the gases that come out of our cars impact global warming? The relevant administrative agency, the Environmental Protection Agency (EPA), took the position that it did not have the power to regulate new motor vehicle emissions of greenhouse gases. The EPA further stated that even if it has such a power it would not use its discretion to do so. Various environmental organizations and states sued to get the EPA to issue regulations under the Clean Air Act. The United States Supreme Court issued an opinion that covers these issues and more. The case, *Massachusetts v. EPA*, gives us a great chance to review and put together many of the varied concepts that we have studied in the text. Read the case and then work through the questions that follow the case.

Massachusetts v. EPA, 127 S. Ct. 1438 (2007).

Justice STEVENS delivered the opinion of the Court.
A well-documented rise in global temperatures has coincided with a significant increase in the concentration of carbon dioxide in the atmosphere. Respected scientists believe the two trends are related. For when carbon dioxide is released into the atmosphere, it acts like the ceiling of a greenhouse, trapping solar energy and retarding the escape of reflected heat. It is therefore a species—the most important species—of a "greenhouse gas."

Calling global warming "the most pressing environmental challenge of our time," FN1 a group of States, FN2 local governments, FN3 and private organizations, FN4 alleged in a petition for certiorari that the Environmental Protection Agency (EPA) has abdicated its responsibility under the Clean Air Act to regulate the emissions of four greenhouse gases, including carbon dioxide. Specifically, petitioners asked us to answer two questions concerning the meaning of § 202(a)(1) of the Act: whether EPA has the statutory authority to regulate greenhouse gas emissions from new motor vehicles; and if so, whether its stated reasons for refusing to do so are consistent with the statute.

FN1. Pet. for Cert. 22.

FN2. California, Connecticut, Illinois, Maine, Massachusetts, New Jersey, New Mexico, New York, Oregon, Rhode Island, Vermont, and Washington.

FN3. District of Columbia, American Samoa, New York City, and Baltimore.

FN4. Center for Biological Diversity, Center for Food Safety, Conservation Law Foundation, Environmental Advocates, Environmental Defense, Friends of the Earth, Greenpeace, International Center for Technology Assessment, National Environmental Trust, Natural Resources Defense Council, Sierra Club, Union of Concerned Scientists, and U.S. Public Interest Research Group.

In response, EPA, supported by 10 intervening States FN5 and six trade associations, FN6 correctly argued that we may not address those two questions unless at least one petitioner has standing to invoke our jurisdiction under *1447 Article III of the Constitution. Notwithstanding the serious character of that jurisdictional argument and the absence of any conflicting decisions construing § 202(a)(1), the unusual importance of the underlying issue persuaded us to grant the writ. 548 U.S. —, 126 S. Ct. 2960, 165 L. Ed. 2d 949 (2006).

FN5. Alaska, Idaho, Kansas, Michigan, Nebraska, North Dakota, Ohio, South Dakota, Texas, and Utah.

FN6. Alliance of Automobile Manufacturers, National Automobile Dealers Association, Engine Manufacturers Association, Truck Manufacturers Association, CO2 Litigation Group, and Utility Air Regulatory Group.

I

Section 202(a)(1) of the Clean Air Act, as added by Pub. L. 89-272, § 101(8), 79 Stat. 992, and as amended by, inter alia, 84 Stat. 1690 and 91 Stat. 791, 42 U.S.C. § 7521(a)(1), provides:

"The [EPA] Administrator shall by regulation prescribe (and from time to time revise) in accordance with the provisions of this section, standards applicable to the emission of any air pollutant from any class or classes of new motor vehicles or new motor vehicle engines, which in his judgment cause, or contribute to, air pollution which may reasonably be anticipated to endanger public health or welfare . . . ." FN7

FN7. The 1970 version of § 202(a)(1) used the phrase "which endangers the public health or welfare" rather than the more-protective "which may reasonably be anticipated to endanger public health or welfare." See § 6(a) of the Clean Air Amendments of 1970, 84 Stat. 1690. Congress amended § 202(a)(1) in 1977 to give its approval to the decision in Ethyl Corp. v. EPA, 541 F.2d 1, 25 (C.A.D.C. 1976) (en banc), which held that the Clean Air Act "and common sense . . . demand regulatory action to prevent harm, even if the regulator is less than certain that harm is otherwise inevitable." See § 401(d)(1) of the Clean Air Act Amendments of 1977, 91 Stat. 791; see also H.R.Rep. No. 95-294, p. 49 (1977), U.S. Code Cong. & Admin. News 1977, p. 1077.

The Act defines "air pollutant" to include "any air pollution agent or combination of such agents, including any physical, chemical, biological, radioactive . . . substance or matter which is emitted into or otherwise enters the ambient air." § 7602(g). "Welfare" is also defined broadly: among other things, it includes "effects on . . . weather . . . and climate." § 7602(h).

When Congress enacted these provisions, the study of climate change was in its infancy. FN8 In 1959, shortly after the U.S. Weather Bureau began monitoring atmospheric carbon dioxide levels, an observatory in Mauna Loa, Hawaii, recorded a mean level of 316 parts per million. This was well above the highest carbon dioxide concentration—no more than 300 parts per million—revealed in the 420,000-year-old ice-core record. FN9 By the time Congress drafted § 202(a)(1) in 1970, carbon dioxide levels had reached 325 parts per million. FN10

FN8. The Council on Environmental Quality had issued a report in 1970 concluding that "[m]an may be changing his weather." Environmental Quality: The First Annual Report 93. Considerable uncertainty remained in those early years, and the issue went largely unmentioned in the congressional debate over the enactment of the Clean Air Act. But see 116 Cong. Rec. 32914 (1970) (statement of Sen. Boggs referring to Council's conclusion that "[a]ir pollution alters the climate and may produce global changes in temperature").

FN9. See Intergovernmental Panel on Climate Change, Climate Change 2001: Synthesis Report, pp. 202–203 (2001). By drilling through thick Antarctic ice sheets and extracting "cores," scientists can examine ice from long ago and extract small samples of ancient air. That air can then be analyzed, yielding estimates of carbon dioxide levels. Ibid.

FN10. A more dramatic rise was yet to come: In 2006, carbon dioxide levels reached 382 parts per million, see Dept. of Commerce, National Oceanic & Atmospheric Administration, Mauna Loa CO2 Monthly Mean Data, www.esrl.noaa.gov/gmd/ccgg/trends/co2_mm_mlo.dat (all Internet materials as visited Mar. 29, 2007, and available in Clerk of Court's case file), a level thought to exceed the concentration of carbon dioxide in the atmosphere at any point over the past 20-million years. See Intergovernmental Panel on Climate Change, Technical Summary of Working Group I Report 39 (2001).

*1448 In the late 1970's, the Federal Government began devoting serious attention to the possibility that carbon dioxide emissions associated with human activity could provoke climate change. In 1978, Congress enacted the National Climate Program Act, 92 Stat. 601, which required the President to establish a program to "assist the Nation and the world to understand and respond to natural and man-induced climate processes and their implications," id., § 3. President Carter, in turn, asked the National Research Council, the working arm of the National Academy of Sciences, to investigate the subject. The Council's response was unequivocal: "If carbon dioxide continues to increase, the study group finds no reason to doubt that climate changes will result and no reason to believe that these changes will be negligible . . . . A wait-and-see policy may mean waiting until it is too late." FN11

FN11. Climate Research Board, Carbon Dioxide and Climate: A Scientific Assessment, p. vii (1979).

Congress next addressed the issue in 1987, when it enacted the Global Climate Protection Act, Title XI of Pub. L. 100-204, 101 Stat. 1407, note following 15 U.S.C. § 2901. Finding that "manmade pollution—the release of carbon dioxide, chlorofluorocarbons, methane, and other trace gases into the atmosphere—may be producing a long-term and substantial increase in the average temperature on Earth," § 1102(1), 101 Stat. 1408, Congress directed EPA to propose to Congress a "coordinated national policy on global climate change," § 1103(b), and ordered the Secretary of State to work "through the channels of multilateral diplomacy" and coordinate diplomatic efforts to combat global warming, § 1103(c). Congress emphasized that "ongoing pollution and deforestation may be contributing now to an irreversible process" and that "[n]ecessary actions must be identified and implemented in time to protect the climate." § 1102(4).

Meanwhile, the scientific understanding of climate change progressed. In 1990, the Intergovernmental Panel on Climate

Change (IPCC), a multinational scientific body organized under the auspices of the United Nations, published its first comprehensive report on the topic. Drawing on expert opinions from across the globe, the IPCC concluded that "emissions resulting from human activities are substantially increasing the atmospheric concentrations of . . . greenhouse gases [which] will enhance the greenhouse effect, resulting on average in an additional warming of the Earth's surface." FN12

FN12. IPCC, Climate Change: The IPCC Scientific Assessment, p. xi (J. Houghton, G. Jenkins, & J. Ephraums eds. 1991).

Responding to the IPCC report, the United Nations convened the "Earth Summit" in 1992 in Rio de Janeiro. The first President Bush attended and signed the United Nations Framework Convention on Climate Change (UNFCCC), a nonbinding agreement among 154 nations to reduce atmospheric concentrations of carbon dioxide and other greenhouse gases for the purpose of "prevent[ing] dangerous anthropogenic [i.e., human-induced] interference with the [Earth's] climate system." FN13 S. Treaty Doc. No. 102-38, Art. 2, p. 5 (1992). The Senate unanimously ratified the treaty.

FN13. The industrialized countries listed in Annex I to the UNFCCC undertook to reduce their emissions of greenhouse gases to 1990 levels by the year 2000. No immediate restrictions were imposed on developing countries, including China and India. They could choose to become Annex I countries when sufficiently developed.

*1449 Some five years later—after the IPCC issued a second comprehensive report in 1995 concluding that "[t]he balance of evidence suggests there is a discernible human influence on global climate" FN14 —the UNFCCC signatories met in Kyoto, Japan, and adopted a protocol that assigned mandatory targets for industrialized nations to reduce greenhouse gas emissions. Because those targets did not apply to developing and heavily polluting nations such as China and India, the Senate unanimously passed a resolution expressing its sense that the United States should not enter into the Kyoto Protocol. See S. Res. 98, 105th Cong., 1st Sess. (July 25, 1997) (as passed). President Clinton did not submit the protocol to the Senate for ratification.

FN14. IPCC, Climate Change 1995, The Science of Climate Change, p. 4.

II

On October 20, 1999, a group of 19 private organizations FN15 filed a rulemaking petition asking EPA to regulate "greenhouse gas emissions from new motor vehicles under § 202 of the Clean Air Act." App. 5. Petitioners maintained that 1998 was the "warmest year on record"; that carbon dioxide, methane, nitrous oxide, and hydrofluorocarbons are "heat trapping greenhouse gases"; that greenhouse gas emissions have significantly accelerated climate change; and that the IPCC's 1995 report warned that "carbon dioxide remains the most important contributor to [man-made] forcing of climate change." Id., at 13 (internal quotation marks omitted). The petition further alleged that climate change will have serious adverse effects on human health and the environment. Id., at 22–35. As to EPA's statutory authority, the petition observed that the agency itself had already confirmed that it had the power to regulate carbon dioxide. See id., at 18, n. 21. In 1998, Jonathan Z. Cannon, then EPA's General Counsel, prepared a legal opinion concluding that "CO2 emissions are within the scope of EPA's authority to regulate," even as he recognized that EPA had so far declined to exercise that authority. Id., at 54 (memorandum to Carol M. Browner, Administrator (Apr. 10, 1998) (hereinafter Cannon memorandum)). Cannon's successor, Gary S. Guzy, reiterated that opinion before a congressional committee just two weeks before the rulemaking petition was filed. See id., at 61.

FN15. Alliance for Sustainable Communities; Applied Power Technologies, Inc.; Bio Fuels America; The California Solar Energy Industries Assn.; Clements Environmental Corp.; Environmental Advocates; Environmental and Energy Study Institute; Friends of the Earth; Full Circle Energy Project, Inc.; The Green Party of Rhode Island; Greenpeace USA; International Center for Technology Assessment; Network for Environmental and Economic Responsibility of the United Church of Christ; New Jersey Environmental Watch; New Mexico Solar Energy Assn.; Oregon Environmental Council; Public Citizen; Solar Energy Industries Assn.; The SUN DAY Campaign. See App. 7–11.

Fifteen months after the petition's submission, EPA requested public comment on "all the issues raised in [the] petition," adding a "particular" request for comments on "any scientific, technical, legal, economic or other aspect of these issues that may be relevant to EPA's consideration of this petition." 66 Fed. Reg. 7486, 7487 (2001). EPA received more than 50,000 comments over the next five months. See 68 Fed. Reg. 52924 (2003).

Before the close of the comment period, the White House sought "assistance in identifying the areas in the science of climate change where there are the greatest certainties and uncertainties" from the National Research Council, asking for a response "as soon as possible." App. 213. *1450 The result was a 2001 report titled Climate Change: An Analysis of Some Key Questions (NRC Report), which, drawing heavily on the 1995 IPCC report, concluded that "[g]reenhouse gases are accumulating in Earth's atmosphere as a result of human activities, causing surface air temperatures and subsurface ocean temperatures to rise. Temperatures are, in fact, rising." NRC Report 1.

On September 8, 2003, EPA entered an order denying the rulemaking petition. 68 Fed. Reg. 52922. The agency gave two reasons for its decision: (1) that contrary to the opinions of its former general counsels, the Clean Air Act does not authorize EPA to issue mandatory regulations to address global climate change, see id., at 52925–52929; and (2) that even if the agency had the authority to set greenhouse gas emission standards, it would be unwise to do so at this time, id., at 52929–52931.

In concluding that it lacked statutory authority over greenhouse gases, EPA observed that Congress "was well aware of the global climate change issue when it last comprehensively amended the [Clean Air Act] in 1990," yet it declined to adopt a proposed amendment establishing binding emissions limitations. Id., at 52926. Congress instead chose to authorize further investigation into climate change. Ibid. (citing §§ 103(g) and 602(e) of the Clean Air Act Amendments of 1990, 104 Stat. 2652, 2703, 42 U.S.C. §§ 7403(g)(1) and 7671a(e)). EPA further reasoned that Congress' "specially tailored solutions to global atmospheric issues," 68 Fed. Reg. 52926—in particular, its 1990 enactment of a comprehensive scheme to regulate pollutants that depleted the ozone layer, see Title VI, 104 Stat. 2649, 42 U.S.C. §§ 7671–7671q—counseled against reading the general authorization of § 202(a)(1) to confer regulatory authority over greenhouse gases.

EPA stated that it was "urged on in this view" by this Court's decision in FDA v. Brown & Williamson Tobacco Corp., 529 U.S. 120, 120 S. Ct. 1291, 146 L. Ed. 2d 121 (2000). In that case, relying on "tobacco['s] unique political history," id., at 159, 120 S. Ct. 1291, we invalidated the Food and Drug Administration's reliance on its general authority to regulate drugs as a basis for asserting jurisdiction over an "industry constituting a significant portion of the American economy," ibid.

EPA reasoned that climate change had its own "political history": Congress designed the original Clean Air Act to address local air pollutants rather than a substance that "is fairly consistent in its concentration throughout the world's atmosphere," 68 Fed. Reg. 52927 (emphasis added); declined in 1990 to enact proposed amendments to force EPA to set carbon dioxide emission standards for motor vehicles, ibid. (citing H.R. 5966, 101st Cong., 2d Sess. (1990)); and addressed global climate change in other legislation, 68 Fed. Reg. 52927. Because of this political history, and because imposing emission limitations on greenhouse gases would have even greater economic and political repercussions than regulating tobacco, EPA was persuaded that it lacked the power to do so. Id., at 52928. In essence, EPA concluded that climate change was so important that unless Congress spoke with exacting specificity, it could not have meant the agency to address it.

Having reached that conclusion, EPA believed it followed that greenhouse gases cannot be "air pollutants" within the meaning of the Act. See ibid. ("It follows from this conclusion, that [greenhouse gases], as such, are not air pollutants under the [Clean Air Act's] regulatory provisions . . ."). The agency bolstered this conclusion '1451 by explaining that if carbon dioxide were an air pollutant, the only feasible method of reducing tailpipe emissions would be to improve fuel economy. But because Congress has already created detailed mandatory fuel economy standards subject to Department of Transportation (DOT) administration, the agency concluded that EPA regulation would either conflict with those standards or be superfluous. Id., at 52929.

Even assuming that it had authority over greenhouse gases, EPA explained in detail why it would refuse to exercise that authority. The agency began by recognizing that the concentration of greenhouse gases has dramatically increased as a result of human activities, and acknowledged the attendant increase in global surface air temperatures. Id., at 52930. EPA nevertheless gave controlling importance to the NRC Report's statement that a causal link between the two "'cannot be unequivocally established.'" Ibid. (quoting NRC Report 17). Given that residual uncertainty, EPA concluded that regulating greenhouse gas emissions would be unwise. 68 Fed. Reg. 52930.

The agency furthermore characterized any EPA regulation of motor-vehicle emissions as a "piecemeal approach" to climate change, id., at 52931, and stated that such regulation would conflict with the President's "comprehensive approach" to the problem, id., at 52932. That approach involves additional support for technological innovation, the creation of nonregulatory programs to encourage voluntary private-sector reductions in greenhouse gas emissions, and further research on climate change—not actual regulation. Id., at 52932–52933. According to EPA, unilateral EPA regulation of motor-vehicle greenhouse gas emissions might also hamper the President's ability to persuade key developing countries to reduce greenhouse gas emissions. Id., at 52931.

III

Petitioners, now joined by intervenor States and local governments, sought review of EPA's order in the United States

Court of Appeals for the District of Columbia Circuit. FN16 Although each of the three judges on the panel wrote a separate opinion, two judges agreed "that the EPA Administrator properly exercised his discretion under § 202(a)(1) in denying the petition for rule making." 415 F.3d 50, 58 (2005). The court therefore denied the petition for review.

FN16. See 42 U.S.C. § 7607(b)(1) ("A petition for review of action of the Administrator in promulgating any . . . standard under section 7521 of this title . . . or final action taken, by the Administrator under this chapter may be filed only in the United States Court of Appeals for the District of Columbia").

In his opinion announcing the court's judgment, Judge Randolph avoided a definitive ruling as to petitioners' standing, id., at 56, reasoning that it was permissible to proceed to the merits because the standing and the merits inquiries "overlap[ped]," ibid. Assuming without deciding that the statute authorized the EPA Administrator to regulate greenhouse gas emissions that "in his judgment" may "reasonably be anticipated to endanger public health or welfare," 42 U.S.C. § 7521(a)(1), Judge Randolph concluded that the exercise of that judgment need not be based solely on scientific evidence, but may also be informed by the sort of policy judgments that motivate congressional action. 415 F.3d, at 58. Given that framework, it was reasonable for EPA to base its decision on scientific uncertainty as well as on other factors, including the concern that unilateral regulation of U.S. motor-vehicle emissions could weaken efforts to reduce *1452 greenhouse gas emissions from other countries. Ibid.

Judge Sentelle wrote separately because he believed petitioners failed to "demonstrat[e] the element of injury necessary to establish standing under Article III." Id., at 59 (opinion dissenting in part and concurring in judgment). In his view, they had alleged that global warming is "harmful to humanity at large," but could not allege "particularized injuries" to themselves. Id., at 60 (citing Lujan v. Defenders of Wildlife, 504 U.S. 555, 562, 112 S. Ct. 2130, 119 L. Ed. 2d 351 (1992)). While he dissented on standing, however, he accepted the contrary view as the law of the case and joined Judge Randolph's judgment on the merits as the closest to that which he preferred. 415 F.3d, at 60–61.

Judge Tatel dissented. Emphasizing that EPA nowhere challenged the factual basis of petitioners' affidavits, id., at 66, he concluded that at least Massachusetts had "satisfied each element of Article III standing—injury, causation, and redressability," id., at 64. In Judge Tatel's view, the "'substantial probability,'" id., at 66, that projected rises in sea level would lead to serious loss of coastal property was a "far cry" from the kind of generalized harm insufficient to ground Article III jurisdiction. Id., at 65. He found that petitioners' affidavits more than adequately supported the conclusion that EPA's failure to curb greenhouse gas emissions contributed to the sea level changes that threatened Massachusetts' coastal property. Ibid. As to redressability, he observed that one of petitioners' experts, a former EPA climatologist, stated that "'[a]chievable reductions in emissions of CO2 and other [greenhouse gases] from U.S. motor vehicles would . . . delay and moderate many of the adverse impacts of global warming.'" Ibid. (quoting declaration of Michael MacCracken, former Executive Director, U.S. Global Change Research Program ¶ 5(e) (hereinafter MacCracken Decl.), available in 2 Petitioners' Standing Appendix in No. 03-1361, etc., (CADC), p. 209 (Stdg. App.)). He further noted that the one-time director of EPA's motor-vehicle pollution control efforts stated in an affidavit that enforceable emission standards would lead to the development of new technologies that "'would gradually be mandated by other countries around the world.'" 415 F.3d, at 66 (quoting declaration of Michael Walsh ¶¶ 7–8, 10, Stdg. App. 309–310, 311). On the merits, Judge Tatel explained at length why he believed the text of the statute provided EPA with authority to regulate greenhouse gas emissions, and why its policy concerns did not justify its refusal to exercise that authority. 415 F.3d, at 67–82.

IV

Article III of the Constitution limits federal-court jurisdiction to "Cases" and "Controversies." Those two words confine "the business of federal courts to questions presented in an adversary context and in a form historically viewed as capable of resolution through the judicial process." Flast v. Cohen, 392 U.S. 83, 95, 88 S. Ct. 1942, 20 L. Ed. 2d 947 (1968). It is therefore familiar learning that no justiciable "controversy" exists when parties seek adjudication of a political question, Luther v. Borden, 7 How. 1, 12 L. Ed. 581 (1849), when they ask for an advisory opinion, Hayburn's Case, 2 Dall. 409, 1 L. Ed. 436 (1792), see also Clinton v. Jones, 520 U.S. 681, 700, n. 33, 117 S. Ct. 1636, 137 L. Ed. 2d 945 (1997), or when the question sought to be adjudicated has been mooted by subsequent developments, California v. San Pablo & Tulare R. Co., 149 U.S. 308, 13 S. Ct. 876, 37 L. Ed. 747 (1893). This case suffers from none of these defects.

*1453 The parties' dispute turns on the proper construction of a congressional statute, a question eminently suitable to resolution in federal court. Congress has moreover authorized this type of challenge to EPA action. See 42 U.S.C. § 7607(b)(1). That authorization is of critical importance to the standing inquiry: "Congress has the power to define injuries and articulate chains of causation that will give rise to a case or controversy where none existed before." Lujan, 504 U.S., at 580, 112 S. Ct. 2130 (KENNEDY, J., concurring in part and concurring in judgment). "In exercising this power, however, Congress must at the very least identify the injury it seeks to vindicate and relate the injury to the class of persons entitled to bring suit." Ibid. We will not, therefore, "entertain citizen suits to vindicate the public's nonconcrete interest in the proper administration of the laws." Id., at 581, 112 S. Ct. 2130.

[1] EPA maintains that because greenhouse gas emissions inflict widespread harm, the doctrine of standing presents an insuperable jurisdictional obstacle. We do not agree. At bottom, "the gist of the question of standing" is whether petitioners have "such a personal stake in the outcome of the controversy as to assure that concrete adverseness which sharpens the presentation of issues upon which the court so largely depends for illumination." Baker v. Carr, 369 U.S. 186, 204, 82 S. Ct. 691, 7 L. Ed. 2d 663 (1962). As Justice KENNEDY explained in his Lujan concurrence:

"While it does not matter how many persons have been injured by the challenged action, the party bringing suit must show that the action injures him in a concrete and personal way. This requirement is not just an empty formality. It preserves the vitality of the adversarial process by assuring both that the parties before the court have an actual, as opposed to professed, stake in the outcome, and that the legal questions presented . . . will be resolved, not in the rarified atmosphere of a debating society, but in a concrete factual context conducive to a realistic appreciation of the consequences of judicial action." 504 U.S., at 581, 112 S. Ct. 2130 (internal quotation marks omitted).

[2] To ensure the proper adversarial presentation, Lujan holds that a litigant must demonstrate that it has suffered a concrete and particularized injury that is either actual or imminent, that the injury is fairly traceable to the defendant, and that it is likely that a favorable decision will redress that injury. See id., at 560–561, 112 S. Ct. 2130. However, a litigant to whom Congress has "accorded a procedural right to protect his concrete interests," id., at 572, n. 7, 112 S. Ct. 2130—here, the right to challenge agency action unlawfully withheld, § 7607(b)(1)—"can assert that right without meeting all the normal standards for redressability and immediacy," ibid. When a litigant is vested with a procedural right, that litigant has standing if there is some possibility that the requested relief will prompt the injury-causing party to reconsider the decision that allegedly harmed the litigant. Ibid.; see also Sugar Cane Growers Cooperative of Fla. v. Veneman, 289 F.3d 89, 94–95 (C.A.D.C. 2002) ("A [litigant] who alleges a deprivation of

a procedural protection to which he is entitled never has to prove that if he had received the procedure the substantive result would have been altered. All that is necessary is to show that the procedural step was connected to the substantive result").

[3] Only one of the petitioners needs to have standing to permit us to consider the petition for review. See *1454 Rumsfeld v. Forum for Academic and Institutional Rights, Inc., 547 U.S. 47, 52, n. 2, 126 S. Ct. 1297, 164 L. Ed. 2d 156 (2006). We stress here, as did Judge Tatel below, the special position and interest of Massachusetts. It is of considerable relevance that the party seeking review here is a sovereign State and not, as it was in Lujan, a private individual.

[4] Well before the creation of the modern administrative state, we recognized that States are not normal litigants for the purposes of invoking federal jurisdiction. As Justice Holmes explained in Georgia v. Tennessee Copper Co., 206 U.S. 230, 237, 27 S. Ct. 618, 51 L. Ed. 1038 (1907), a case in which Georgia sought to protect its citizens from air pollution originating outside its borders:

"The case has been argued largely as if it were one between two private parties; but it is not. The very elements that would be relied upon in a suit between fellow-citizens as a ground for equitable relief are wanting here. The State owns very little of the territory alleged to be affected, and the damage to it capable of estimate in money, possibly, at least, is small. This is a suit by a State for an injury to it in its capacity of quasi-sovereign. In that capacity the State has an interest independent of and behind the titles of its citizens, in all the earth and air within its domain. It has the last word as to whether its mountains shall be stripped of their forests and its inhabitants shall breathe pure air."

Just as Georgia's "independent interest . . . in all the earth and air within its domain" supported federal jurisdiction a century ago, so too does Massachusetts' well-founded desire to preserve its sovereign territory today. Cf. Alden v. Maine, 527 U.S. 706, 715, 119 S. Ct. 2240, 144 L. Ed. 2d 636 (1999) (observing that in the federal system, the States "are not relegated to the role of mere provinces or political corporations, but retain the dignity, though not the full authority, of sovereignty"). That Massachusetts does in fact own a great deal of the "territory alleged to be affected" only reinforces the conclusion that its stake in the outcome of this case is sufficiently concrete to warrant the exercise of federal judicial power.

When a State enters the Union, it surrenders certain sovereign prerogatives. Massachusetts cannot invade Rhode Island to force reductions in greenhouse gas emissions, it cannot negotiate an emissions treaty with China or India, and in some circumstances the exercise of its police powers to reduce in-state motor-vehicle emissions might well be pre-empted. See Alfred L. Snapp & Son, Inc. v. Puerto Rico ex rel. Barez, 458 U.S. 592, 607, 102 S. Ct. 3260, 73 L. Ed. 2d 995 (1982) ("One helpful indication in determining whether an alleged injury to the health and welfare of its citizens suffices to give the State standing to sue parens patriae is whether the injury is one that the State, if it could, would likely attempt to address through its sovereign lawmaking powers").

These sovereign prerogatives are now lodged in the Federal Government, and Congress has ordered EPA to protect Massachusetts (among others) by prescribing standards applicable to the "emission of any air pollutant from any class or classes of new motor vehicle engines, which in [the Administrator's] judgment cause, or contribute to, air pollution which may reasonably be anticipated to endanger public health or welfare." 42 U.S.C. § 7521(a)(1). Congress has moreover recognized a concomitant procedural right to challenge the rejection of its rulemaking petition as arbitrary and capricious. § 7607(b)(1). Given that procedural right and Massachusetts' stake in protecting its quasi-sovereign interests, the Commonwealth *1455 is entitled to special solicitude in our standing analysis. FN17

FN17. THE CHIEF JUSTICE accuses the Court of misreading Georgia v. Tennessee Copper Co., 206 U.S. 230, 27 S. Ct. 618, 51 L. Ed. 1038 (1907), see post, at 1464–1465 (dissenting opinion), and "devis[ing] a new doctrine of state standing," id., at 1454–1455. But no less an authority than Hart & Wechsler's The Federal Courts and the Federal System understands Tennessee Copper as a standing decision. R. Fallon, D. Meltzer, & D. Shapiro, Hart & Wechsler's The Federal Courts and the Federal System 290 (5th ed. 2003). Indeed, it devotes an entire section to chronicling the long development of cases permitting States "to litigate as parens patriae to protect quasi-sovereign interests—i.e., public or governmental interests that concern the state as a whole." Id., at 289; see, e.g., Missouri v. Illinois, 180 U.S. 208, 240–241, 21 S. Ct. 331, 45 L. Ed. 497 (1901) (finding federal jurisdiction appropriate not only "in cases involving boundaries and jurisdiction over lands and their inhabitants, and in cases directly affecting the property rights and interests of a state," but also when the "substantial impairment of the health and prosperity of the towns and cities of the state" are at stake).

Drawing on Massachusetts v. Mellon, 262 U.S. 447, 43 S. Ct. 597, 67 L. Ed. 1078 (1923), and Alfred L. Snapp & Son, Inc. v. Puerto Rico ex rel. Barez, 458 U.S. 592, 102 S. Ct. 3260, 73 L. Ed. 2d 995 (1982) (citing Missouri v. Illinois, 180 U.S. 208, 21

S. Ct. 331, 45 L. Ed. 497 (1901)), THE CHIEF JUSTICE claims that we "overloo[k] the fact that our cases cast significant doubt on a State's standing to assert a quasi-sovereign interest . . . against the Federal Government." Post, at 1466. Not so. Mellon itself disavowed any such broad reading when it noted that the Court had been "called upon to adjudicate, not rights of person or property, not rights of dominion over physical domain, [and] not quasi sovereign rights actually invaded or threatened." 262 U.S., at 484–485, 43 S. Ct. 597 (emphasis added). In any event, we held in Georgia v. Pennsylvania R. Co., 324 U.S. 439, 447, 65 S. Ct. 716, 89 L. Ed. 1051 (1945), that there is a critical difference between allowing a State "to protect her citizens from the operation of federal statutes" (which is what Mellon prohibits) and allowing a State to assert its rights under federal law (which it has standing to do). Massachusetts does not here dispute that the Clean Air Act applies to its citizens; it rather seeks to assert its rights under the Act. See also Nebraska v. Wyoming, 515 U.S. 1, 20, 115 S. Ct. 1933, 132 L. Ed. 2d 1 (1995) (holding that Wyoming had standing to bring a cross-claim against the United States to vindicate its "'quasi-sovereign' interests which are 'independent of and behind the titles of its citizens, in all the earth and air within its domain'" (quoting Tennessee Copper, 206 U.S., at 237, 27 S. Ct. 618)).

With that in mind, it is clear that petitioners' submissions as they pertain to Massachusetts have satisfied the most demanding standards of the adversarial process. EPA's steadfast refusal to regulate greenhouse gas emissions presents a risk of harm to Massachusetts that is both "actual" and "imminent." Lujan, 504 U.S., at 560, 112 S. Ct. 2130 (internal quotation marks omitted). There is, moreover, a "substantial likelihood that the judicial relief requested" will prompt EPA to take steps to reduce that risk. Duke Power Co. v. Carolina Environmental Study Group, Inc., 438 U.S. 59, 79, 98 S. Ct. 2620, 57 L. Ed. 2d 595 (1978).

The Injury

The harms associated with climate change are serious and well recognized. Indeed, the NRC Report itself—which EPA regards as an "objective and independent assessment of the relevant science," 68 Fed. Reg. 52930 —identifies a number of environmental changes that have already inflicted significant harms, including "the global retreat of mountain glaciers, reduction in snow-cover extent, the earlier spring melting of rivers and lakes, [and] the accelerated rate of rise of sea levels during the 20th century relative to the past few thousand years . . . ." NRC Report 16.

Petitioners allege that this only hints at the environmental damage yet to come. According to the climate scientist Michael

*1456 MacCracken, "qualified scientific experts involved in climate change research" have reached a "strong consensus" that global warming threatens (among other things) a precipitate rise in sea levels by the end of the century, MacCracken Decl. ¶ 15, Stdg. App. 207, "severe and irreversible changes to natural ecosystems," id., ¶ 5(d), at 209, a "significant reduction in water storage in winter snowpack in mountainous regions with direct and important economic consequences," ibid., and an increase in the spread of disease, id., ¶ 28, at 218–219. He also observes that rising ocean temperatures may contribute to the ferocity of hurricanes. Id., ¶¶ 23–25, at 216–217. FN18

FN18. In this regard, MacCracken's 2004 affidavit—drafted more than a year in advance of Hurricane Katrina—was eerily prescient. Immediately after discussing the "particular concern" that climate change might cause an "increase in the wind speed and peak rate of precipitation of major tropical cyclones (i.e., hurricanes and typhoons)," MacCracken noted that "[s]oil compaction, sea level rise and recurrent storms are destroying approximately 20–30 square miles of Louisiana wetlands each year. These wetlands serve as a 'shock absorber' for storm surges that could inundate New Orleans, significantly enhancing the risk to a major urban population." ¶¶ 24–25, Stdg. App. 217.

That these climate-change risks are "widely shared" does not minimize Massachusetts' interest in the outcome of this litigation. See Federal Election Comm'n v. Akins, 524 U.S. 11, 24, 118 S. Ct. 1777, 141 L. Ed. 2d 10 (1998) ("[W]here a harm is concrete, though widely shared, the Court has found 'injury in fact'"). According to petitioners' unchallenged affidavits, global sea levels rose somewhere between 10 and 20 centimeters over the 20th century as a result of global warming. MacCracken Decl. ¶ 5(c), Stdg. App. 208. These rising seas have already begun to swallow Massachusetts' coastal land. Id., at 196 (declaration of Paul H. Kirshen ¶ 5), 216 (MacCracken Decl. ¶ 23). Because the Commonwealth "owns a substantial portion of the state's coastal property," id., at 171 (declaration of Karst R. Hoogeboom ¶ 4), FN19 it has alleged a particularized injury in its capacity as a landowner. The severity of that injury will only increase over the course of the next century: If sea levels continue to rise as predicted, one Massachusetts official believes that a significant fraction of coastal property will be "either permanently lost through inundation or temporarily lost through periodic storm surge and flooding events." Id., ¶ 6, at 172. FN20 Remediation costs alone, petitioners allege, could run well into the hundreds of millions of dollars. Id., ¶ 7, at 172; see also Kirshen Decl. ¶ 12, at 198. FN21

FN19. "For example, the [Massachusetts Department of Conservation and Recreation] owns, operates and maintains approximately 53 coastal state parks, beaches, reservations, and wildlife sanctuaries. [It] also owns, operates and maintains sporting and recreational facilities in coastal areas, including numerous pools, skating rinks, playgrounds, playing fields, former coastal fortifications, public stages, museums, bike trails, tennis courts, boathouses and boat ramps and landings. Associated with these coastal properties and facilities is a significant amount of infrastructure, which the Commonwealth also owns, operates and maintains, including roads, parkways, stormwater pump stations, pier[s], sea wal[l] revetments and dams." Hoogeboom Decl. ¶ 4, at 171.

FN20. See also id., at 179 (declaration of Christian Jacqz) (discussing possible loss of roughly 14 acres of land per miles of coastline by 2100); Kirshen Decl. ¶ 10, at 198 (alleging that "[w]hen such a rise in sea level occurs, a 10-year flood will have the magnitude of the present 100-year flood and a 100-year flood will have the magnitude of the present 500-year flood").

FN21. In dissent, THE CHIEF JUSTICE dismisses petitioners' submissions as "conclusory," presumably because they do not quantify Massachusetts' land loss with the exactitude he would prefer. Post, at 1467–1468. He therefore asserts that the Commonwealth's injury is "conjectur[al]." See ibid. Yet the likelihood that Massachusetts' coastline will recede has nothing to do with whether petitioners have determined the precise metes and bounds of their soon-to-be-flooded land. Petitioners maintain that the seas are rising and will continue to rise, and have alleged that such a rise will lead to the loss of Massachusetts' sovereign territory. No one, save perhaps the dissenters, disputes those allegations. Our cases require nothing more.

*1457 Causation

EPA does not dispute the existence of a causal connection between man-made greenhouse gas emissions and global warming. At a minimum, therefore, EPA's refusal to regulate such emissions "contributes" to Massachusetts' injuries.

EPA nevertheless maintains that its decision not to regulate greenhouse gas emissions from new motor vehicles contributes so insignificantly to petitioners' injuries that the agency cannot be haled into federal court to answer for them. For the same reason, EPA does not believe that any realistic possibility exists that the relief petitioners seek would mitigate global climate change and remedy their injuries. That is especially so because predicted increases in greenhouse gas emissions from developing nations, particularly China and India, are likely to offset any marginal domestic decrease.

But EPA overstates its case. Its argument rests on the erroneous assumption that a small incremental step, because it is incremental, can never be attacked in a federal judicial forum. Yet accepting that premise would doom most challenges to regulatory action. Agencies, like legislatures, do not generally resolve massive problems in one fell regulatory swoop. See Williamson v. Lee Optical of Okla., Inc., 348 U.S. 483, 489, 75 S. Ct. 461, 99 L. Ed. 563 (1955) ("[A] reform may take one step at a time, addressing itself to the phase of the problem which seems most acute to the legislative mind"). They instead whittle away at them over time, refining their preferred approach as circumstances change and as they develop a more-nuanced understanding of how best to proceed. Cf. SEC v. Chenery Corp., 332 U.S. 194, 202, 67 S. Ct. 1575, 91 L. Ed. 1995 (1947) ("Some principles must await their own development, while others must be adjusted to meet particular, unforeseeable situations"). That a first step might be tentative does not by itself support the notion that federal courts lack jurisdiction to determine whether that step conforms to law.

And reducing domestic automobile emissions is hardly a tentative step. Even leaving aside the other greenhouse gases, the United States transportation sector emits an enormous quantity of carbon dioxide into the atmosphere—according to the MacCracken affidavit, more than 1.7 billion metric tons in 1999 alone. ¶ 30, Stdg. App. 219. That accounts for more than 6% of worldwide carbon dioxide emissions. Id., at 232 (Oppenheimer Decl. ¶ 3); see also MacCracken Decl. ¶ 31, at 220. To put this in perspective: Considering just emissions from the transportation sector, which represent less than one-third of this country's total carbon dioxide emissions, the United States would still rank as the third-largest emitter of carbon dioxide in the world, outpaced only by the European Union and China. FN22 Judged by any *1458 standard, U.S. motor-vehicle emissions make a meaningful contribution to greenhouse gas concentrations and hence, according to petitioners, to global warming.

FN22. See UNFCCC, National Greenhouse Gas Inventory Data for the Period 1990–2004 and Status of Reporting 14 (2006) (hereinafter Inventory Data) (reflecting emissions from Annex I countries); UNFCCC, Sixth Compilation and Synthesis of Initial National Communications from Parties not Included in Annex I to the Convention 7–8 (2005) (reflecting emissions from non-Annex I countries); see also Dept. of Energy, Energy Information Admin., International Energy Annual 2004, H.1co2 World Carbon Dioxide Emissions from the Consumption and Flaring of Fossil Fuels, 1980–2004 (Table), http://www.eia.doe.gov/pub/international/iealf/tableh1co2.xls.

The Remedy

While it may be true that regulating motor-vehicle emissions will not by itself reverse global warming, it by no means follows that we lack jurisdiction to decide whether EPA has a duty to take steps to slow or reduce it. See also Larson v. Valente, 456 U.S. 228, 244, n. 15, 102 S. Ct. 1673, 72 L. Ed. 2d 33 (1982) ("[A] plaintiff satisfies the redressability requirement when he shows that a favorable decision will relieve a discrete injury to himself. He need not show that a favorable decision will relieve his every injury"). Because of the enormity of the potential consequences associated with man-made climate change, the fact that the effectiveness of a remedy might be delayed during the (relatively short) time it takes for a new motor-vehicle fleet to replace an older one is essentially irrelevant. FN23 Nor is it dispositive that developing countries such as China and India are poised to increase greenhouse gas emissions substantially over the next century: A reduction in domestic emissions would slow the pace of global emissions increases, no matter what happens elsewhere.

FN23. See also Mountain States Legal Foundation v. Glickman, 92 F.3d 1228, 1234 (C.A.D.C. 1996) ("The more drastic the injury that government action makes more likely, the lesser the increment in probability to establish standing"); Village of Elk Grove Village v. Evans, 997 F.2d 328, 329 (C.A. 7 1993) ("[E]ven a small probability of injury is sufficient to create a case or controversy—to take a suit out of the category of the hypothetical—provided of course that the relief sought would, if granted, reduce the probability").

We moreover attach considerable significance to EPA's "agree[ment] with the President that 'we must address the issue of global climate change,'" 68 Fed. Reg. 52929 (quoting remarks announcing Clear Skies and Global Climate Initiatives, 2002 Public Papers of George W. Bush, Vol. 1, Feb. 14, p. 227 (2004)), and to EPA's ardent support for various voluntary emission-reduction programs, 68 Fed. Reg. 52932. As Judge Tatel observed in dissent below, "EPA would presumably not bother with such efforts if it thought emissions reductions would have no discernable impact on future global warming." 415 F.3d, at 66.

In sum—at least according to petitioners' uncontested affidavits—the rise in sea levels associated with global warming has already harmed and will continue to harm Massachusetts. The risk of catastrophic harm, though remote, is nevertheless real. That risk would be reduced to some extent if petitioners received the relief they seek. We therefore hold that petitioners have standing to challenge the EPA's denial of their rulemaking petition. FN24

FN24. In his dissent, THE CHIEF JUSTICE expresses disagreement with the Court's holding in United States v. Students Challenging Regulatory Agency Procedures (SCRAP), 412 U.S. 669, 687–688, 93 S. Ct. 2405, 37 L. Ed. 2d 254 (1973). He does not, however, disavow this portion of Justice Stewart's opinion for the Court:

"Unlike the specific and geographically limited federal action of which the petitioner complained in Sierra Club [v. Morton, 405 U.S. 727, 92 S. Ct. 1361, 31 L. Ed. 2d 636 (1972)], the challenged agency action in this case is applicable to substantially all of the Nation's railroads, and thus allegedly has an adverse environmental impact on all the natural resources of the country. Rather than a limited group of persons who used a picturesque valley in California, all persons who utilize the scenic resources of the country, and indeed all who breathe its air, could claim harm similar to that alleged by the environmental groups here. But we have already made it clear that standing is not to be denied simply because many people suffer the same injury. Indeed some of the cases on which we relied in Sierra Club demonstrated the patent fact that persons across the Nation could be adversely affected by major governmental actions. To deny standing to persons who are in fact injured simply because many others are also injured, would mean that the most injurious and widespread Government actions could be questioned by nobody. We cannot accept that conclusion." Ibid. (citations omitted and emphasis added).

It is moreover quite wrong to analogize the legal claim advanced by Massachusetts and the other public and private entities who challenge EPA's parsimonious construction of the Clean Air Act to a mere "lawyer's game." See post, at 1471.

*1459 V

[5] [6] The scope of our review of the merits of the statutory issues is narrow. As we have repeated time and again, an agency has broad discretion to choose how best to marshal its limited resources and personnel to carry out its delegated responsibilities. See Chevron U.S.A. Inc. v. Natural Resources Defense Council, Inc., 467 U.S. 837, 842–845, 104 S. Ct. 2778, 81 L. Ed. 2d 694 (1984). That discretion is at its height when the agency decides not to bring an enforcement action. Therefore, in Heckler v. Chaney, 470 U.S. 821, 105 S. Ct. 1649, 84 L. Ed. 2d 714 (1985), we held that an agency's refusal to initiate enforcement proceedings is not ordinarily subject to judicial review. Some debate remains, however, as to the rigor with which we review an agency's denial of a petition for rulemaking.

[7] There are key differences between a denial of a petition for rulemaking and an agency's decision not to initiate an enforcement

action. See American Horse Protection Assn., Inc. v. Lyng, 812 F.2d 1, 3–4 (C.A.D.C. 1987). In contrast to nonenforcement decisions, agency refusals to initiate rulemaking "are less frequent, more apt to involve legal as opposed to factual analysis, and subject to special formalities, including a public explanation." Id., at 4; see also 5 U.S.C. § 555(e). They moreover arise out of denials of petitions for rulemaking which (at least in the circumstances here) the affected party had an undoubted procedural right to file in the first instance. Refusals to promulgate rules are thus susceptible to judicial review, though such review is "extremely limited" and "highly deferential." National Customs Brokers & Forwarders Assn. of America, Inc. v. United States, 883 F.2d 93, 96 (C.A.D.C. 1989).

EPA concluded in its denial of the petition for rulemaking that it lacked authority under 42 U.S.C. § 7521(a)(1) to regulate new vehicle emissions because carbon dioxide is not an "air pollutant" as that term is defined in § 7602. In the alternative, it concluded that even if it possessed authority, it would decline to do so because regulation would conflict with other administration priorities. As discussed earlier, the Clean Air Act expressly permits review of such an action. § 7607(b)(1). We therefore "may reverse any such action found to be . . . arbitrary, capricious, an abuse of discretion, or otherwise not in accordance with law." § 7607(d)(9).

VI

[8] On the merits, the first question is whether § 202(a)(1) of the Clean Air Act authorizes EPA to regulate greenhouse gas emissions from new motor vehicles in the event that it forms a "judgment" that such emissions contribute to climate change. We have little trouble concluding that it does. In relevant part, § 202(a)(1) provides that EPA "shall by regulation *1460 prescribe . . . standards applicable to the emission of any air pollutant from any class or classes of new motor vehicles or new motor vehicle engines, which in [the Administrator's] judgment cause, or contribute to, air pollution which may reasonably be anticipated to endanger public health or welfare." 42 U.S.C. § 7521(a)(1). Because EPA believes that Congress did not intend it to regulate substances that contribute to climate change, the agency maintains that carbon dioxide is not an "air pollutant" within the meaning of the provision.

The statutory text forecloses EPA's reading. The Clean Air Act's sweeping definition of "air pollutant" includes "any air pollution agent or combination of such agents, including any physical, chemical . . . substance or matter which is emitted into or otherwise enters the ambient air . . . ." § 7602(g) (emphasis added). On its face, the definition embraces all airborne compounds of whatever stripe,

and underscores that intent through the repeated use of the word
"any." FN25 Carbon dioxide, methane, nitrous oxide, and
hydrofluorocarbons are without a doubt "physical [and] chemical . . .
substance[s] which [are] emitted into . . . the ambient air." The
statute is unambiguous. FN26

FN25. See Department of Housing and Urban Development v.
Rucker, 535 U.S. 125, 131, 122 S. Ct. 1230, 152 L. Ed. 2d 258
(2002) (observing that "'any' . . . has an expansive meaning, that is,
one or some indiscriminately of whatever kind" (some internal
quotation marks omitted)).

FN26. In dissent, Justice SCALIA maintains that because
greenhouse gases permeate the world's atmosphere rather than a
limited area near the earth's surface, EPA's exclusion of greenhouse
gases from the category of air pollution "agent[s]" is entitled to
deference under Chevron U.S.A. Inc. v. Natural Resources Defense
Council, Inc., 467 U.S. 837, 104 S. Ct. 2778, 81 L. Ed. 2d 694
(1984). See post, at 1469–1470. EPA's distinction, however, finds
no support in the text of the statute, which uses the phrase "the
ambient air" without distinguishing between atmospheric layers.
Moreover, it is a plainly unreasonable reading of a sweeping
statutory provision designed to capture "any physical, chemical . . .
substance or matter which is emitted into or otherwise enters the
ambient air." 42 U.S.C. § 7602(g). Justice SCALIA does not (and
cannot) explain why Congress would define "air pollutant" so
carefully and so broadly, yet confer on EPA the authority to
narrow that definition whenever expedient by asserting that a
particular substance is not an "agent." At any rate, no party to this
dispute contests that greenhouse gases both "ente[r] the ambient
air" and tend to warm the atmosphere. They are therefore
unquestionably "agent[s]" of air pollution.

Rather than relying on statutory text, EPA invokes
postenactment congressional actions and deliberations it views as
tantamount to a congressional command to refrain from regulating
greenhouse gas emissions. Even if such postenactment legislative
history could shed light on the meaning of an otherwise-
unambiguous statute, EPA never identifies any action remotely
suggesting that Congress meant to curtail its power to treat
greenhouse gases as air pollutants. That subsequent Congresses
have eschewed enacting binding emissions limitations to combat
global warming tells us nothing about what Congress meant when
it amended § 202(a)(1) in 1970 and 1977. FN27 And unlike EPA,
we have no difficulty reconciling Congress' various efforts to
promote interagency collaboration and research to better
understand *1461 climate change FN28 with the agency's pre-
existing mandate to regulate "any air pollutant" that may endanger

the public welfare. See 42 U.S.C. § 7601(a)(1). Collaboration and research do not conflict with any thoughtful regulatory effort; they complement it. FN29

FN27. See United States v. Price, 361 U.S. 304, 313, 80 S. Ct. 326, 4 L. Ed. 2d 334 (1960) (holding that "the views of a subsequent Congress form a hazardous basis for inferring the intent of an earlier one"); see also Cobell v. Norton, 428 F.3d 1070, 1075 (C.A.D.C. 2005) ("[P]ost-enactment legislative history is not only oxymoronic but inherently entitled to little weight").

FN28. See, e.g., National Climate Program Act, § 5, 92 Stat. 601, 15 U.S.C. § 2901 et seq. (calling for the establishment of a National Climate Program and for additional climate change research); Global Climate Protection Act of 1987, § 1103, 101 Stat. 1408–1409 (directing EPA and the Secretary of State to "jointly" develop a "coordinated national policy on global climate change" and report to Congress); Global Change Research Act of 1990, Tit. I, 104 Stat. 3097, 15 U.S.C. §§ 2921–2938 (establishing for the "development and coordination of a comprehensive and integrated United States research program" to aid in "understand[ing] . . . human-induced and natural processes of climate change"); Global Climate Change Prevention Act of 1990, 104 Stat. 4058, 7 U.S.C. § 6701 et seq. (directing the Dept. of Agriculture to study the effects of climate change on forestry and agriculture); Energy Policy Act of 1992, §§ 1601–1609, 106 Stat. 2999, 42 U.S.C. §§ 13381–13388 (requiring the Secretary of Energy to report on information pertaining to climate change).

FN29. We are moreover puzzled by EPA's roundabout argument that because later Congresses chose to address stratospheric ozone pollution in a specific legislative provision, it somehow follows that greenhouse gases cannot be air pollutants within the meaning of the Clean Air Act.

EPA's reliance on Brown & Williamson Tobacco Corp., 529 U.S. 120, 120 S. Ct. 1291, 146 L. Ed. 2d 121, is similarly misplaced. In holding that tobacco products are not "drugs" or "devices" subject to Food and Drug Administration (FDA) regulation pursuant to the Food, Drug and Cosmetic Act (FDCA), see 529 U.S., at 133, 120 S. Ct. 1291, we found critical at least two considerations that have no counterpart in this case.

First, we thought it unlikely that Congress meant to ban tobacco products, which the FDCA would have required had such products been classified as "drugs" or "devices." Id., at 135–137, 120 S. Ct. 1291. Here, in contrast, EPA jurisdiction would lead to no such extreme measures. EPA would only regulate emissions, and even then, it would have to delay any action "to permit the development and application of the requisite technology, giving appropriate consideration to the cost of compliance," § 7521(a)(2). However much a ban on tobacco products clashed with the "common sense" intuition that Congress never meant to remove those products from circulation, Brown & Williamson, 529 U.S., at 133, 120 S. Ct. 1291, there is nothing counterintuitive to the notion that EPA can curtail the emission of substances that are putting the global climate out of kilter.

Second, in Brown & Williamson we pointed to an unbroken series of congressional enactments that made sense only if adopted "against the backdrop of the FDA's consistent and repeated statements that it lacked authority under the FDCA to regulate tobacco." Id., at 144, 120 S. Ct. 1291. We can point to no such enactments here: EPA has not identified any congressional action that conflicts in any way with the regulation of greenhouse gases from new motor vehicles. Even if it had, Congress could not have acted against a regulatory "backdrop" of disclaimers of regulatory authority. Prior to the order that provoked this litigation, EPA had never disavowed the authority to regulate greenhouse gases, and in 1998 it in fact affirmed that it had such authority. See App. 54 (Cannon memorandum). There is no reason, much less a compelling reason, to accept EPA's invitation to read ambiguity into a clear statute.
[9] EPA finally argues that it cannot regulate carbon dioxide emissions from *1462 motor vehicles because doing so would require it to tighten mileage standards, a job (according to EPA) that Congress has assigned to DOT. See 68 Fed. Reg. 52929. But that DOT sets mileage standards in no way licenses EPA to shirk its environmental responsibilities. EPA has been charged with protecting the public's "health" and "welfare," 42 U.S.C. § 7521(a)(1), a statutory obligation wholly independent of DOT's mandate to promote energy efficiency. See Energy Policy and Conservation Act, § 2(5), 89 Stat. 874, 42 U.S.C. § 6201(5). The two obligations may overlap, but there is no reason to think the two agencies cannot both administer their obligations and yet avoid inconsistency.

While the Congresses that drafted § 202(a)(1) might not have appreciated the possibility that burning fossil fuels could lead to global warming, they did understand that without regulatory flexibility, changing circumstances and scientific developments would soon render the Clean Air Act obsolete. The broad language of § 202(a)(1) reflects an intentional effort to confer the flexibility necessary to forestall such obsolescence. See Pennsylvania Dept. of Corrections v. Yeskey, 524 U.S. 206, 212, 118 S. Ct. 1952, 141 L. Ed. 2d 215 (1998) ("[T]he fact that a statute can be applied in situations not expressly anticipated by Congress does not demonstrate ambiguity. It demonstrates breadth" (internal quotation marks omitted)). Because greenhouse gases fit well within the Clean Air Act's capacious definition of "air pollutant," we hold that EPA has the statutory authority to regulate the emission of such gases from new motor vehicles.

VII

The alternative basis for EPA's decision—that even if it does have statutory authority to regulate greenhouse gases, it would be unwise to do so at this time—rests on reasoning divorced from the statutory text. While the statute does condition the exercise of EPA's authority on its formation of a "judgment," 42 U.S.C. § 7521(a)(1), that judgment must relate to whether an air pollutant "cause[s], or contribute[s] to, air pollution which may reasonably be anticipated to endanger public health or welfare," ibid. Put another way, the use of the word "judgment" is not a roving license to ignore the statutory text. It is but a direction to exercise discretion within defined statutory limits.

[10] If EPA makes a finding of endangerment, the Clean Air Act requires the agency to regulate emissions of the deleterious pollutant from new motor vehicles. Ibid. (stating that "[EPA] shall by regulation prescribe . . . standards applicable to the emission of any air pollutant from any class of new motor vehicles"). EPA no doubt has significant latitude as to the manner, timing, content, and coordination of its regulations with those of other agencies. But once EPA has responded to a petition for rulemaking, its reasons for action or inaction must conform to the authorizing statute. Under the clear terms of the Clean Air Act, EPA can avoid taking further action only if it determines that greenhouse gases do not contribute to climate change or if it provides some reasonable explanation as to why it cannot or will not exercise its discretion to determine whether they do. Ibid. To the extent that this constrains agency discretion to pursue other priorities of the Administrator or the President, this is the congressional design.

[11] EPA has refused to comply with this clear statutory command. Instead, it has offered a laundry list of reasons not to regulate. For example, EPA said that a number of voluntary executive branch programs already provide an effective response to the threat of global warming, *1463 68 Fed. Reg. 52932, that regulating greenhouse gases might impair the President's ability to negotiate with "key developing nations" to reduce emissions, id., at 52931, and that curtailing motor-vehicle emissions would reflect "an inefficient, piecemeal approach to address the climate change issue," ibid.

Although we have neither the expertise nor the authority to evaluate these policy judgments, it is evident they have nothing to do with whether greenhouse gas emissions contribute to climate change. Still less do they amount to a reasoned justification for declining to form a scientific judgment. In particular, while the President has broad authority in foreign affairs, that authority does not extend to the refusal to execute domestic laws. In the Global Climate Protection Act of 1987, Congress authorized the State Department—not EPA—to formulate United States foreign policy with reference to environmental matters relating to climate. See § 1103(c), 101 Stat. 1409. EPA has made no showing that it issued the ruling in question here after consultation with the State Department. Congress did direct EPA to consult with other agencies in the formulation of its policies and rules, but the State Department is absent from that list. § 1103(b).

[12] Nor can EPA avoid its statutory obligation by noting the uncertainty surrounding various features of climate change and concluding that it would therefore be better not to regulate at this time. See 68 Fed. Reg. 52930–52931. If the scientific uncertainty is so profound that it precludes EPA from making a reasoned judgment as to whether greenhouse gases contribute to global warming, EPA must say so. That EPA would prefer not to regulate greenhouse gases because of some residual uncertainty—which, contrary to Justice SCALIA's apparent belief, post, at 1466–1468, is in fact all that it said, see 68 Fed. Reg. 52929 ("We do not believe . . . that it would be either effective or appropriate for EPA to establish [greenhouse gas] standards for motor vehicles at this time" (emphasis added))—is irrelevant. The statutory question is whether sufficient information exists to make an endangerment finding.

In short, EPA has offered no reasoned explanation for its refusal to decide whether greenhouse gases cause or contribute to climate change. Its action was therefore "arbitrary, capricious, . . . or otherwise not in accordance with law." 42 U.S.C. § 7607(d)(9)(A). We need not and do not reach the question whether on remand EPA must make an endangerment finding, or whether policy concerns can inform EPA's actions in the event that it makes such a finding. Cf. Chevron U.S.A. Inc. v. Natural Resources Defense Council, Inc., 467 U.S. 837, 843–844, 104 S. Ct. 2778, 81 L. Ed. 2d 694 (1984). We hold only that EPA must ground its reasons for action or inaction in the statute.

VIII

The judgment of the Court of Appeals is reversed, and the case is remanded for further proceedings consistent with this opinion. It is so ordered.

Chief Justice ROBERTS, with whom Justice SCALIA, Justice THOMAS, and Justice ALITO join, dissenting.

Global warming may be a "crisis," even "the most pressing environmental problem of our time." Pet. for Cert. 26, 22. Indeed, it may ultimately affect nearly everyone on the planet in some potentially adverse way, and it may be that governments have done too little to address it. It is not a problem, however, that has escaped the attention of policymakers in the Executive *1464 and Legislative Branches of our Government, who continue to consider regulatory, legislative, and treaty-based means of addressing global climate change.

Apparently dissatisfied with the pace of progress on this issue in the elected branches, petitioners have come to the courts claiming broad-ranging injury, and attempting to tie that injury to the Government's alleged failure to comply with a rather narrow statutory provision. I would reject these challenges as nonjusticiable. Such a conclusion involves no judgment on whether global warming exists, what causes it, or the extent of the problem. Nor does it render petitioners without recourse. This Court's standing jurisprudence simply recognizes that redress of grievances of the sort at issue here "is the function of Congress and the Chief Executive," not the federal courts. Lujan v. Defenders of Wildlife, 504 U.S. 555, 576, 112 S. Ct. 2130, 119 L. Ed. 2d 351 (1992). I would vacate the judgment below and remand for dismissal of the petitions for review.

I

Article III, § 2, of the Constitution limits the federal judicial power to the adjudication of "Cases" and "Controversies." "If a dispute is not a proper case or controversy, the courts have no business deciding it, or expounding the law in the course of doing so." DaimlerChrysler Corp. v. Cuno, 547 U.S. —, —, 126 S. Ct. 1854, 1860–1861, 164 L. Ed. 2d 589 (2006). "Standing to sue is part of the common understanding of what it takes to make a justiciable case," Steel Co. v. Citizens for Better Environment, 523 U.S. 83, 102, 118 S. Ct. 1003, 140 L. Ed. 2d 210 (1998), and has been described as "an essential and unchanging part of the case-or-controversy requirement of Article III," Defenders of Wildlife, supra, at 560, 112 S. Ct. 2130.

Our modern framework for addressing standing is familiar: "A plaintiff must allege personal injury fairly traceable to the defendant's allegedly unlawful conduct and likely to be redressed by the requested relief." DaimlerChrysler, supra, at —, 126 S. Ct., at 1861 (quoting Allen v. Wright, 468 U.S. 737, 751, 104 S. Ct. 3315, 82 L. Ed. 2d 556 (1984) (internal quotation marks omitted)). Applying that standard here, petitioners bear the burden of alleging an injury that is fairly traceable to the Environmental Protection Agency's failure to promulgate new motor vehicle greenhouse gas emission standards, and that is likely to be redressed by the prospective issuance of such standards.

Before determining whether petitioners can meet this familiar test, however, the Court changes the rules. It asserts that "States are not normal litigants for the purposes of invoking federal jurisdiction," and that given "Massachusetts' stake in protecting its quasi-sovereign interests, the Commonwealth is entitled to special solicitude in our standing analysis." Ante, at 1454, 1455 (emphasis added).

Relaxing Article III standing requirements because asserted injuries are pressed by a State, however, has no basis in our jurisprudence, and support for any such "special solicitude" is conspicuously absent from the Court's opinion. The general judicial review provision cited by the Court, 42 U.S.C. § 7607(b)(1), affords States no special rights or status. The Court states that "Congress has ordered EPA to protect Massachusetts (among others)" through the statutory provision at issue, § 7521(a)(1), and that "Congress has . . . recognized a concomitant procedural right to challenge the rejection of its rulemaking petition as arbitrary and capricious." Ante, at 1454. The reader might think from this unfortunate phrasing that Congress said something about the rights *1465 of States in this particular provision of the statute. Congress knows how to do that when it wants to, see, e.g., § 7426(b) (affording States the right to petition EPA to directly regulate certain sources of pollution), but it has done nothing of the sort here. Under the law on which petitioners rely, Congress treated public and private litigants exactly the same.

Nor does the case law cited by the Court provide any support for the notion that Article III somehow implicitly treats public and private litigants differently. The Court has to go back a full century in an attempt to justify its novel standing rule, but even there it comes up short. The Court's analysis hinges on Georgia v. Tennessee Copper Co., 206 U.S. 230, 27 S. Ct. 618, 51 L. Ed. 1038 (1907)—a case that did indeed draw a distinction between a State and private litigants, but solely with respect to available remedies. The case had nothing to do with Article III standing.

In Tennessee Copper, the State of Georgia sought to enjoin copper companies in neighboring Tennessee from discharging pollutants that were inflicting "a wholesale destruction of forests, orchards and crops" in bordering Georgia counties. Id., at 236, 27 S. Ct. 618. Although the State owned very little of the territory allegedly affected, the Court reasoned that Georgia—in its capacity as a "quasi-sovereign"—"has an interest independent of and behind the titles of its citizens, in all the earth and air within its domain."

Id., at 237, 27 S. Ct. 618. The Court explained that while "[t]he very elements that would be relied upon in a suit between fellow-citizens as a ground for equitable relief [were] wanting," a State "is not lightly to be required to give up quasi-sovereign rights for pay." Ibid. Thus while a complaining private litigant would have to make do with a legal remedy—one "for pay"—the State was entitled to equitable relief. See id., at 237–238, 27 S. Ct. 618.

In contrast to the present case, there was no question in Tennessee Copper about Article III injury. See id., at 238–239, 27 S. Ct. 618. There was certainly no suggestion that the State could show standing where the private parties could not; there was no dispute, after all, that the private landowners had "an action at law." Id., at 238, 27 S. Ct. 618. Tennessee Copper has since stood for nothing more than a State's right, in an original jurisdiction action, to sue in a representative capacity as parens patriae. See, e.g., Maryland v. Louisiana, 451 U.S. 725, 737, 101 S. Ct. 2114, 68 L. Ed. 2d 576 (1981). Nothing about a State's ability to sue in that capacity dilutes the bedrock requirement of showing injury, causation, and redressability to satisfy Article III.

A claim of parens patriae standing is distinct from an allegation of direct injury. See Wyoming v. Oklahoma, 502 U.S. 437, 448–449, 451, 112 S. Ct. 789, 117 L. Ed. 2d 1 (1992). Far from being a substitute for Article III injury, parens patriae actions raise an additional hurdle for a state litigant: the articulation of a "quasi-sovereign interest" "apart from the interests of particular private parties." Alfred L. Snapp & Son, Inc. v. Puerto Rico ex rel. Barez, 458 U.S. 592, 607, 102 S. Ct. 3260, 73 L. Ed. 2d 995 (1982) (emphasis added) (cited ante, at 1454). Just as an association suing on behalf of its members must show not only that it represents the members but that at least one satisfies Article III requirements, so too a State asserting quasi-sovereign interests as parens patriae must still show that its citizens satisfy Article III. Focusing on Massachusetts's interests as quasi-sovereign makes the required showing here harder, not easier. The Court, in effect, takes what has always been regarded as a necessary condition for *1466 parens patriae standing—a quasi-sovereign interest—and converts it into a sufficient showing for purposes of Article III.

What is more, the Court's reasoning falters on its own terms. The Court asserts that Massachusetts is entitled to "special solicitude" due to its "quasi-sovereign interests," ante, at 1455, but then applies our Article III standing test to the asserted injury of the State's loss of coastal property. See ante, at 1456 (concluding that Massachusetts "has alleged a particularized injury in its capacity as a landowner" (emphasis added)). In the context of parens patriae standing, however, we have characterized state ownership of land as a "nonsovereign interes[t]" because a State "is likely to have the same interests as other similarly situated proprietors." Alfred L. Snapp & Son, supra, at 601, 102 S. Ct. 3260.

On top of everything else, the Court overlooks the fact that our cases cast significant doubt on a State's standing to assert a quasi-sovereign interest—as opposed to a direct injury—against the Federal Government. As a general rule, we have held that while a State might assert a quasi-sovereign right as parens patriae "for the protection of its citizens, it is no part of its duty or power to enforce their rights in respect of their relations with the Federal Government. In that field it is the United States, and not the State, which represents them." Massachusetts v. Mellon, 262 U.S. 447, 485–486, 43 S. Ct. 597, 67 L. Ed. 1078 (1923) (citation omitted); see also Alfred L. Snapp & Son, supra, at 610, n. 16, 102 S. Ct. 3260.

All of this presumably explains why petitioners never cited Tennessee Copper in their briefs before this Court or the D.C. Circuit. It presumably explains why not one of the legion of amici supporting petitioners ever cited the case. And it presumably explains why not one of the three judges writing below ever cited the case either. Given that one purpose of the standing requirement is "'to assure that concrete adverseness which sharpens the presentation of issues upon which the court so largely depends for illumination,'" ante, at 1452–1453 (quoting Baker v. Carr, 369 U.S. 186, 204, 82 S. Ct. 691, 7 L. Ed. 2d 663 (1962)), it is ironic that the Court today adopts a new theory of Article III standing for States without the benefit of briefing or argument on the point. FN1

FN1. The Court seems to think we do not recognize that Tennessee Copper is a case about parens patriae standing, ante, at 1455, n. 17, but we have no doubt about that. The point is that nothing in our cases (or Hart & Wechsler) suggests that the prudential requirements for parens patriae standing, see Republic of Venezuela v. Philip Morris Inc., 287 F.3d 192, 199, n. (CADC 2002) (observing that " parens patriae is merely a species of prudential standing" (internal quotation marks omitted)), can somehow substitute for, or alter the content of, the "irreducible constitutional minimum" requirements of injury in fact, causation, and redressability under Article III. Lujan v. Defenders of Wildlife, 504 U.S. 555, 560, 112 S. Ct. 2130, 119 L. Ed. 2d 351 (1992). Georgia v. Pennsylvania R. Co., 324 U.S. 439, 65 S. Ct. 716, 89 L. Ed. 1051 (1945), is not to the contrary. As the caption makes clear enough, the fact that a State may assert rights under a federal statute as parens patriae in no way refutes our clear ruling that "[a] State does not have standing as parens patriae to bring an action against the Federal Government." Alfred L. Snapp & Son, Inc. v. Puerto Rico ex rel. Barez, 458 U.S. 592, 610, n. 16, 102 S. Ct. 3260, 73 L. Ed. 2d 995 (1982).

II

It is not at all clear how the Court's "special solicitude" for Massachusetts plays out in the standing analysis, except as an implicit concession that petitioners cannot establish standing on traditional terms. But the status of Massachusetts as *1467 a State cannot compensate for petitioners' failure to demonstrate injury in fact, causation, and redressability.

When the Court actually applies the three-part test, it focuses, as did the dissent below, see 415 F.3d 50, 64 (C.A.D.C. 2005) (opinion of Tatel, J.), on the State's asserted loss of coastal land as the injury in fact. If petitioners rely on loss of land as the Article III injury, however, they must ground the rest of the standing analysis in that specific injury. That alleged injury must be "concrete and particularized," Defenders of Wildlife, 504 U.S., at 560, 112 S. Ct. 2130, and "distinct and palpable," Allen, 468 U.S., at 751, 104 S. Ct. 3315 (internal quotation marks omitted). Central to this concept of "particularized" injury is the requirement that a plaintiff be affected in a "personal and individual way," Defenders of Wildlife, 504 U.S., at 560, n. 1, 112 S. Ct. 2130, and seek relief that "directly and tangibly benefits him" in a manner distinct from its impact on "the public at large," id., at 573–574, 112 S. Ct. 2130. Without "particularized injury, there can be no confidence of 'a real need to exercise the power of judicial review' or that relief can be framed 'no broader than required by the precise facts to which the court's ruling would be applied.'" Warth v. Seldin, 422 U.S. 490, 508, 95 S. Ct. 2197, 45 L. Ed. 2d 343 (1975) (quoting Schlesinger v. Reservists Comm. to Stop the War, 418 U.S. 208, 221–222, 94 S. Ct. 2925, 41 L. Ed. 2d 706 (1974)).

The very concept of global warming seems inconsistent with this particularization requirement. Global warming is a phenomenon "harmful to humanity at large," 415 F.3d, at 60 (Sentelle, J., dissenting in part and concurring in judgment), and the redress petitioners seek is focused no more on them than on the public generally—it is literally to change the atmosphere around the world.

If petitioners' particularized injury is loss of coastal land, it is also that injury that must be "actual or imminent, not conjectural or hypothetical," Defenders of Wildlife, supra, at 560, 112 S. Ct. 2130 (internal quotation marks omitted), "real and immediate," Los Angeles v. Lyons, 461 U.S. 95, 102, 103 S. Ct. 1660, 75

L. Ed. 2d 675 (1983) (internal quotation marks omitted), and "certainly impending," Whitmore v. Arkansas, 495 U.S. 149, 158, 110 S. Ct. 1717, 109 L. Ed. 2d 135 (1990) (internal quotation marks omitted).

As to "actual" injury, the Court observes that "global sea levels rose somewhere between 10 and 20 centimeters over the 20th century as a result of global warming" and that "[t]hese rising seas have already begun to swallow Massachusetts' coastal land." Ante, at 1456. But none of petitioners' declarations supports that connection. One declaration states that "a rise in sea level due to climate change is occurring on the coast of Massachusetts, in the metropolitan Boston area," but there is no elaboration. Petitioners' Standing Appendix in No. 03-1361, etc. (CADC), p. 196 (Stdg. App.). And the declarant goes on to identify a "significan[t]" non-global-warming cause of Boston's rising sea level: land subsidence. Id., at 197; see also id., at 216. Thus, aside from a single conclusory statement, there is nothing in petitioners' 43 standing declarations and accompanying exhibits to support an inference of actual loss of Massachusetts coastal land from 20th century global sea level increases. It is pure conjecture.

The Court's attempts to identify "imminent" or "certainly impending" loss of Massachusetts coastal land fares no better. See ante, at 1456–1457. One of petitioners' declarants predicts global warming will cause sea level to rise by 20 to 70 centimeters by the year 2100. Stdg. App. 216. Another uses a computer modeling *1468 program to map the Commonwealth's coastal land and its current elevation, and calculates that the high-end estimate of sea level rise would result in the loss of significant state-owned coastal land. Id., at 179. But the computer modeling program has a conceded average error of about 30 centimeters and a maximum observed error of 70 centimeters. Id., at 177–178. As an initial matter, if it is possible that the model underrepresents the elevation of coastal land to an extent equal to or in excess of the projected sea level rise, it is difficult to put much stock in the predicted loss of land. But even placing that problem to the side, accepting a century-long time horizon and a series of compounded estimates renders requirements of imminence and immediacy utterly toothless. See Defenders of Wildlife, supra, at 565, n. 2, 112 S. Ct. 2130 (while the concept of "'imminence'" in standing doctrine is "somewhat elastic," it can be "stretched beyond the breaking point"). "Allegations of possible future injury do not satisfy the requirements of Art. III. A threatened injury must be certainly impending to constitute injury in fact." Whitmore, supra, at 158, 110 S. Ct. 1717. (internal quotation marks omitted; emphasis added).

III

Petitioners' reliance on Massachusetts's loss of coastal land as their injury in fact for standing purposes creates insurmountable problems for them with respect to causation and redressability. To establish standing, petitioners must show a causal connection between that specific injury and the lack of new motor vehicle greenhouse gas emission standards, and that the promulgation of such standards would likely redress that injury. As is often the case, the questions of causation and redressability overlap. See Allen, 468 U.S., at 753, n. 19, 104 S. Ct. 3315 (observing that the two requirements were "initially articulated by this Court as two facets of a single causation requirement" (internal quotation marks omitted)). And importantly, when a party is challenging the Government's allegedly unlawful regulation, or lack of regulation, of a third party, satisfying the causation and redressability requirements becomes "substantially more difficult." Defenders of Wildlife, supra, at 562, 112 S. Ct. 2130 (internal quotation marks omitted); see also Warth, supra, at 504–505, 95 S. Ct. 2197.

Petitioners view the relationship between their injuries and EPA's failure to promulgate new motor vehicle greenhouse gas emission standards as simple and direct: Domestic motor vehicles emit carbon dioxide and other greenhouse gases. Worldwide emissions of greenhouse gases contribute to global warming and therefore also to petitioners' alleged injuries. Without the new vehicle standards, greenhouse gas emissions—and therefore global warming and its attendant harms—have been higher than they otherwise would have been; once EPA changes course, the trend will be reversed.

The Court ignores the complexities of global warming, and does so by now disregarding the "particularized" injury it relied on in step one, and using the dire nature of global warming itself as a bootstrap for finding causation and redressability. First, it is important to recognize the extent of the emissions at issue here. Because local greenhouse gas emissions disperse throughout the atmosphere and remain there for anywhere from 50 to 200 years, it is global emissions data that are relevant. See App. to Pet. for Cert. A-73. According to one of petitioners' declarations, domestic motor vehicles contribute about 6 percent of global carbon dioxide emissions and 4 percent of global greenhouse gas emissions. Stdg. App. 232. The amount of global emissions at issue here is *1469 smaller still; § 202(a)(1) of the Clean Air Act covers only new motor vehicles and new motor vehicle engines, so petitioners' desired emission standards might reduce only a fraction of 4 percent of global emissions.

This gets us only to the relevant greenhouse gas emissions; linking them to global warming and ultimately to petitioners' alleged injuries next requires consideration of further complexities. As EPA explained in its denial of petitioners' request for rulemaking,

"predicting future climate change necessarily involves a complex web of economic and physical factors including: our ability to predict future global anthropogenic emissions of [greenhouse gases] and aerosols; the fate of these emissions once they enter the atmosphere (e.g., what percentage are absorbed by vegetation or are taken up by the oceans); the impact of those emissions that remain in the atmosphere on the radiative properties of the atmosphere; changes in critically important climate feedbacks (e.g., changes in cloud cover and ocean circulation); changes in temperature characteristics (e.g., average temperatures, shifts in daytime and evening temperatures); changes in other climatic parameters (e.g., shifts in precipitation, storms); and ultimately the impact of such changes on human health and welfare (e.g., increases or decreases in agricultural productivity, human health impacts)." App. to Pet. for Cert. A-83 through A-84.

Petitioners are never able to trace their alleged injuries back through this complex web to the fractional amount of global emissions that might have been limited with EPA standards. In light of the bit-part domestic new motor vehicle greenhouse gas emissions have played in what petitioners describe as a 150-year global phenomenon, and the myriad additional factors bearing on petitioners' alleged injury—the loss of Massachusetts coastal land—the connection is far too speculative to establish causation.

IV

Redressability is even more problematic. To the tenuous link between petitioners' alleged injury and the indeterminate fractional domestic emissions at issue here, add the fact that petitioners cannot meaningfully predict what will come of the 80 percent of global greenhouse gas emissions that originate outside the United States. As the Court acknowledges, "developing countries such as China and India are poised to increase greenhouse gas emissions substantially over the next century," ante, at 1458, so the domestic emissions at issue here may become an increasingly marginal portion of global emissions, and any decreases produced by petitioners' desired standards are likely to be overwhelmed many times over by emissions increases elsewhere in the world.

Petitioners offer declarations attempting to address this uncertainty, contending that "[i]f the U.S. takes steps to reduce motor vehicle emissions, other countries are very likely to take similar actions regarding their own motor vehicles using technology developed in response to the U.S. program." Stdg. App. 220; see also id., at 311–312. In other words, do not worry that other countries will contribute far more to global warming than will U.S. automobile emissions; someone is bound to invent something, and places like the People's Republic of China or India will surely require use of the new technology, regardless of cost. The Court previously has explained that when the existence of an element of standing "depends on the unfettered choices made by independent actors not before the courts and whose *1470 exercise of broad and legitimate discretion the courts cannot presume either to control or to predict," a party must present facts supporting an assertion that the actor will proceed in such a manner. Defenders of Wildlife, 504 U.S., at 562, 112 S. Ct. 2130 (quoting ASARCO Inc. v. Kadish, 490 U.S. 605, 615, 109 S. Ct. 2037, 104 L. Ed. 2d 696 (1989) (opinion of KENNEDY, J.); internal quotation marks omitted). The declarations' conclusory (not to say fanciful) statements do not even come close.

No matter, the Court reasons, because any decrease in domestic emissions will "slow the pace of global emissions increases, no matter what happens elsewhere." Ante, at 1458. Every little bit helps, so Massachusetts can sue over any little bit.

The Court's sleight-of-hand is in failing to link up the different elements of the three-part standing test. What must be likely to be redressed is the particular injury in fact. The injury the Court looks to is the asserted loss of land. The Court contends that regulating domestic motor vehicle emissions will reduce carbon dioxide in the atmosphere, and therefore redress Massachusetts's injury. But even if regulation does reduce emissions—to some indeterminate degree, given events elsewhere in the world—the Court never explains why that makes it likely that the injury in fact—the loss of land—will be redressed. Schoolchildren know that a kingdom might be lost "all for the want of a horseshoe nail," but "likely" redressability is a different matter. The realities make it pure conjecture to suppose that EPA regulation of new automobile emissions will likely prevent the loss of Massachusetts coastal land.

V

Petitioners' difficulty in demonstrating causation and redressability is not surprising given the evident mismatch between the source of their alleged injury—catastrophic global warming—and the narrow subject matter of the Clean Air Act provision at issue in this suit. The mismatch suggests that petitioners' true goal for this litigation may be more symbolic than anything else. The constitutional role of the courts, however, is to decide concrete cases—not to serve as a convenient forum for policy debates. See Valley Forge Christian College v. Americans United for Separation of Church and State,

Inc., 454 U.S. 464, 472, 102 S. Ct. 752, 70 L. Ed. 2d 700 (1982) ("[Standing] tends to assure that the legal questions presented to the court will be resolved, not in the rarified atmosphere of a debating society, but in a concrete factual context conducive to a realistic appreciation of the consequences of judicial action").

When dealing with legal doctrine phrased in terms of what is "fairly" traceable or "likely" to be redressed, it is perhaps not surprising that the matter is subject to some debate. But in considering how loosely or rigorously to define those adverbs, it is vital to keep in mind the purpose of the inquiry. The limitation of the judicial power to cases and controversies "is crucial in maintaining the tripartite allocation of power set forth in the Constitution." DaimlerChrysler, 547 U.S., at —, 126 S. Ct., at 1860–1861 (internal quotation marks omitted). In my view, the Court today—addressing Article III's "core component of standing," Defenders of Wildlife, supra, at 560, 112 S. Ct. 2130— fails to take this limitation seriously.

To be fair, it is not the first time the Court has done so. Today's decision recalls the previous high-water mark of diluted standing requirements, United States v. Students Challenging Regulatory Agency Procedures (SCRAP), 412 U.S. 669, 93 S. Ct. 2405, 37 L. Ed. 2d 254 (1973). *1471 SCRAP involved "[p]robably the most attenuated injury conferring Art. III standing" and "surely went to the very outer limit of the law"—until today. Whitmore, 495 U.S., at 158–159, 110 S. Ct. 1717; see also Lujan v. National Wildlife Federation, 497 U.S. 871, 889, 110 S. Ct. 3177, 111 L. Ed. 2d 695 (1990) (SCRAP "has never since been emulated by this Court"). In SCRAP, the Court based an environmental group's standing to challenge a railroad freight rate surcharge on the group's allegation that increases in railroad rates would cause an increase in the use of nonrecyclable goods, resulting in the increased need for natural resources to produce such goods. According to the group, some of these resources might be taken from the Washington area, resulting in increased refuse that might find its way into area parks, harming the group's members. 412 U.S., at 688, 93 S. Ct. 2405.

Over time, SCRAP became emblematic not of the looseness of Article III standing requirements, but of how utterly manipulable they are if not taken seriously as a matter of judicial self-restraint. SCRAP made standing seem a lawyer's game, rather than a fundamental limitation ensuring that courts function as courts and not intrude on the politically accountable branches. Today's decision is SCRAP for a new generation. FN2

FN2. The difficulty with SCRAP, and the reason it has not been followed, is not the portion cited by the Court. See ante, at

1458–1459, n. 24. Rather, it is the attenuated nature of the injury there, and here, that is so troubling. Even in SCRAP, the Court noted that what was required was "something more than an ingenious academic exercise in the conceivable," 412 U.S., at 688, 93 S. Ct. 2405, and we have since understood the allegation there to have been "that the string of occurrences alleged would happen immediately," Whitmore v. Arkansas, 495 U.S. 149, 159, 110 S. Ct. 1717, 109 L. Ed. 2d 135 (1990) (emphasis added). That is hardly the case here.

The Court says it is "quite wrong" to compare petitioners' challenging "EPA's parsimonious construction of the Clean Air Act to a mere 'lawyer's game.'" Ante, at 1458–1459, n. 24. Of course it is not the legal challenge that is merely "an ingenious academic exercise in the conceivable," SCRAP, supra, at 688, 93 S. Ct. 2405, but the assertions made in support of standing.

Perhaps the Court recognizes as much. How else to explain its need to devise a new doctrine of state standing to support its result? The good news is that the Court's "special solicitude" for Massachusetts limits the future applicability of the diluted standing requirements applied in this case. The bad news is that the Court's self-professed relaxation of those Article III requirements has caused us to transgress "the proper—and properly limited—role of the courts in a democratic society." Allen, 468 U.S., at 750, 104 S. Ct. 3315 (internal quotation marks omitted).

I respectfully dissent.

Justice SCALIA, with whom THE CHIEF JUSTICE, Justice THOMAS, and Justice ALITO join, dissenting.

I join THE CHIEF JUSTICE's opinion in full, and would hold that this Court has no jurisdiction to decide this case because petitioners lack standing. The Court having decided otherwise, it is appropriate for me to note my dissent on the merits.

I

A

The provision of law at the heart of this case is § 202(a)(1) of the Clean Air Act (CAA), which provides that the Administrator of the Environmental Protection Agency (EPA) "shall by regulation prescribe . . . standards applicable to the emission of any air pollutant from any class or classes of new motor vehicles or new motor vehicle engines, which in his *1472 judgment cause, or contribute to, air pollution which may reasonably be anticipated to endanger public health or welfare." 42 U.S.C. § 7521(a)(1) (emphasis added). As the Court recognizes, the statute "condition[s] the exercise of EPA's authority on its formation of a 'judgment.'" Ante, at 1462. There is no dispute that the Administrator has made no such judgment in this case. See ante, at 1463 ("We need not and do not reach the question whether on remand EPA must make an endangerment finding"); 68 Fed. 52929 (2003) ("[N]o Administrator has made a finding under any of the CAA's regulatory provisions that CO2 meets the applicable statutory criteria for regulation").

The question thus arises: Does anything require the Administrator to make a "judgment" whenever a petition for rulemaking is filed? Without citation of the statute or any other authority, the Court says yes. Why is that so? When Congress wishes to make private action force an agency's hand, it knows how to do so. See, e.g., Brock v. Pierce County, 476 U.S. 253, 254–255, 106 S. Ct. 1834, 90 L. Ed. 2d 248 (1986) (discussing the Comprehensive Employment and Training Act (CETA), 92 Stat. 1926, 29 U.S.C. § 816(b) (1976 ed., Supp. V), which "provide[d] that the Secretary of Labor 'shall' issue a final determination as to the misuse of CETA funds by a grant recipient within 120 days after receiving a complaint alleging such misuse"). Where does the CAA say that the EPA Administrator is required to come to a decision on this question whenever a rulemaking petition is filed? The Court points to no such provision because none exists.

Instead, the Court invents a multiple-choice question that the EPA Administrator must answer when a petition for rulemaking is filed. The Administrator must exercise his judgment in one of three ways: (a) by concluding that the pollutant does cause, or contribute to, air pollution that endangers public welfare (in which case EPA is required to regulate); (b) by concluding that the pollutant does not cause, or contribute to, air pollution that endangers public welfare (in which case EPA is not required to regulate); or (c) by "provid[ing] some reasonable explanation as to why it cannot or will not exercise its discretion to determine whether" greenhouse gases endanger public welfare, ante, at 1462, (in which case EPA is not required to regulate).

I am willing to assume, for the sake of argument, that the Administrator's discretion in this regard is not entirely unbounded—that if he has no reasonable basis for deferring judgment he must grasp the nettle at once. The Court, however, with no basis in text or precedent, rejects all of EPA's stated "policy judgments" as not "amount[ing] to a reasoned justification," ante, at 1463, effectively narrowing the universe of potential reasonable bases to a single one: Judgment can be delayed only if the Administrator concludes that "the scientific uncertainty is [too] profound." Ibid. The Administrator is precluded from concluding for other reasons "that it would . . . be better not to regulate at this time." Ibid. FN1 Such other reasons—perfectly valid reasons— were set forth in the agency's statement.

FN1. The Court's way of putting it is, of course, not quite accurate. The issue is whether it would be better to defer the decision about whether to exercise judgment. This has the effect of deferring regulation but is quite a different determination.

"We do not believe . . . that it would be either effective or appropriate for EPA to establish [greenhouse gas] standards for motor vehicles at this time. As described in detail below, the President has laid out a comprehensive approach *1473 to climate change that calls for near-term voluntary actions and incentives along with programs aimed at reducing scientific uncertainties and encouraging technological development so that the government may effectively and efficiently address the climate change issue over the long term.

. . . . .

"[E]stablishing [greenhouse gas] emission standards for U.S. motor vehicles at this time would . . . result in an inefficient, piecemeal approach to addressing the climate change issue. The U.S. motor vehicle fleet is one of many sources of [greenhouse gas] emissions both here and abroad, and different [greenhouse gas] emission sources face different technological and financial challenges in reducing emissions. A sensible regulatory scheme would require that all significant sources and sinks of [greenhouse gas] emissions be considered in deciding how best to achieve any needed emission reductions.

"Unilateral EPA regulation of motor vehicle [greenhouse gas] emissions could also weaken U.S. efforts to persuade developing countries to reduce the [greenhouse gas] intensity of their economies. Considering the large populations and growing economies of some developing countries, increases in their [greenhouse gas] emissions could quickly overwhelm the effects of [greenhouse gas] reduction measures in developed countries. Any potential benefit of EPA regulation could be lost to the extent other nations decided to let their emissions significantly increase in view of U.S. emissions reductions. Unavoidably, climate change raises important foreign policy issues, and it is the President's prerogative to address them." 68 Fed. Reg. 52929–52931 (footnote omitted).

The Court dismisses this analysis as "rest[ing] on reasoning divorced from the statutory text." Ante, at 1462. "While the statute does condition the exercise of EPA's authority on its formation of a 'judgment,' . . . that judgment must relate to whether an air pollutant 'cause[s], or contribute[s] to, air pollution which may reasonably be anticipated to endanger public health or welfare.'" Ibid. True but irrelevant. When the Administrator makes a judgment whether to regulate greenhouse gases, that judgment must relate to whether they are air pollutants that "cause, or contribute to, air pollution which may reasonably be anticipated to endanger public health or welfare." 42 U.S.C. § 7521(a)(1). But the statute says nothing at all about the reasons for which the Administrator may defer making a judgment—the permissible reasons for deciding not to grapple with the issue at the present time. Thus, the various "policy" rationales, ante, at 1463, that the Court criticizes are not "divorced from the statutory text," ante, at 1462, except in the sense that the statutory text is silent, as texts are often silent about permissible reasons for the exercise of agency discretion. The reasons the EPA gave are surely considerations executive agencies regularly take into account (and ought to take into account) when deciding whether to consider entering a new field: the impact such entry would have on other Executive Branch programs and on foreign policy. There is no basis in law for the Court's imposed limitation.

EPA's interpretation of the discretion conferred by the statutory reference to "its judgment" is not only reasonable, it is the most natural reading of the text. The Court nowhere explains why this interpretation is incorrect, let alone why it is not entitled to deference under *1474 Chevron U.S.A. Inc. v. Natural Resources Defense Council, Inc., 467 U.S. 837, 104 S. Ct. 2778, 81 L. Ed. 2d 694 (1984). As the Administrator acted within the law in declining to make a "judgment" for the policy reasons above set forth, I would uphold the decision to deny the rulemaking petition on that ground alone.

B

Even on the Court's own terms, however, the same conclusion follows. As mentioned above, the Court gives EPA the option of determining that the science is too uncertain to allow it to form a "judgment" as to whether greenhouse gases endanger public welfare. Attached to this option (on what basis is unclear) is an essay requirement: "If," the Court says, "the scientific uncertainty is so profound that it precludes EPA from making a reasoned judgment as to whether greenhouse gases contribute to global warming, EPA must say so." Ante, at 1463. But EPA has said precisely that—and at great length, based on information contained in a 2001 report by the National Research Council (NRC) entitled Climate Change Science: An Analysis of Some Key Questions:

"As the NRC noted in its report, concentrations of [greenhouse gases (GHGs)] are increasing in the atmosphere as a result of human activities (pp. 9–12). It also noted that '[a] diverse array of evidence points to a warming of global surface air temperatures' (p. 16). The report goes on to state, however, that '[b]ecause of the large and still uncertain level of natural variability inherent in the climate record and the uncertainties in the time histories of the various forcing agents (and particularly aerosols), a [causal] linkage between the buildup of greenhouse gases in the atmosphere and the observed climate changes during the 20th century cannot be unequivocally established. The fact that the magnitude of the observed warming is large in comparison to natural variability as simulated in climate models is suggestive of such a linkage, but it does not constitute proof of one because the model simulations could be deficient in natural variability on the decadal to century time scale' (p. 17).

"The NRC also observed that 'there is considerable uncertainty in current understanding of how the climate system varies naturally and reacts to emissions of [GHGs] and aerosols' (p. 1). As a result of that uncertainty, the NRC cautioned that 'current estimate of the magnitude of future warming should be regarded as tentative and subject to future adjustments (either upward or downward).' Id. It further advised that '[r]educing the wide range of uncertainty inherent in current model predictions of global climate change will require major advances in understanding and modeling of both (1) the factors that determine atmospheric concentrations of [GHGs] and aerosols and (2) the so-called "feedbacks" that determine the sensitivity of the climate system to a prescribed increase in [GHGs].' Id.

"The science of climate change is extraordinarily complex and still evolving. Although there have been substantial advances in climate change science, there continue to be important uncertainties in our understanding of the factors that may affect future climate change and how it should be addressed. As the NRC explained, predicting future climate change necessarily involves a complex web of economic and physical factors including: Our ability to predict future global anthropogenic emissions of GHGs and aerosols; the fate of these emissions once they enter the atmosphere (e.g., what percentage are absorbed *1475 by vegetation or are taken up by the oceans); the impact of those emissions that remain in the atmosphere on the radiative properties of the atmosphere; changes in critically important climate feedbacks (e.g., changes in cloud cover and ocean circulation); changes in temperature characteristics (e.g., average temperatures, shifts in daytime and evening temperatures); changes in other climatic parameters (e.g., shifts in precipitation, storms); and ultimately the impact of such changes on human health and welfare (e.g., increases or decreases in agricultural productivity, human health impacts). The NRC noted, in particular, that '[t]he understanding of the relationships between weather/climate and human health is in its infancy and therefore the health consequences of climate change are poorly understood' (p. 20). Substantial scientific uncertainties limit our ability to assess each of these factors and to separate out those changes resulting from natural variability from those that are directly the result of increases in anthropogenic GHGs.

"Reducing the wide range of uncertainty inherent in current model predictions will require major advances in understanding and modeling of the factors that determine atmospheric concentrations of greenhouse gases and aerosols, and the processes that determine the sensitivity of the climate system." 68 Fed. Reg. 52930.

I simply cannot conceive of what else the Court would like EPA to say.

II

A

Even before reaching its discussion of the word "judgment," the Court makes another significant error when it concludes that "§ 202(a)(1) of the Clean Air Act authorizes EPA to regulate greenhouse gas emissions from new motor vehicles in the event that it forms a 'judgment' that such emissions contribute to climate change." Ante, at 1459 (emphasis added). For such authorization, the Court relies on what it calls "the Clean Air Act's capacious definition of 'air pollutant.'" Ante, at 1460.

"Air pollutant" is defined by the Act as "any air pollution agent or combination of such agents, including any physical, chemical, . . . substance or matter which is emitted into or otherwise enters the ambient air." 42 U.S.C. § 7602(g). The Court is correct that "[c]arbon dioxide, methane, nitrous oxide, and hydrofluorocarbons," ante, at 1462, fit within the second half of that definition: They are "physical, chemical, . . . substance[s] or matter which [are] emitted into or otherwise ente[r] the ambient air." But the Court mistakenly believes this to be the end of the analysis. In order to be an "air pollutant" under the Act's definition, the "substance or matter [being] emitted into . . . the ambient air" must also meet the first half of the definition—namely, it must be an "air pollution agent or combination of such agents." The Court simply pretends this half of the definition does not exist.

The Court's analysis faithfully follows the argument advanced by petitioners, which focuses on the word "including" in the statutory definition of "air pollutant." See Brief for Petitioners 13–14. As that argument goes, anything that follows the word "including" must necessarily be a subset of whatever precedes it. Thus, if greenhouse gases qualify under the phrase following the word "including," they must qualify under the phrase preceding it. Since greenhouse gases come within the capacious phrase "any physical, chemical, . . . substance or matter which is emitted into or otherwise enters the ambient air," *1476 they must also be "air pollution agent[s] or combination[s] of such agents," and therefore meet the definition of "air pollutant[s]."

That is certainly one possible interpretation of the statutory definition. The word "including" can indeed indicate that what follows will be an "illustrative" sampling of the general category that precedes the word. Federal Land Bank of St. Paul v. Bismarck Lumber Co., 314 U.S. 95, 100, 62 S. Ct. 1, 86 L. Ed. 65 (1941). Often, however, the examples standing alone are broader than the general category, and must be viewed as limited in light of that category. The Government provides a helpful (and unanswered) example: "The phrase 'any American automobile, including any truck or minivan,' would not naturally be construed to encompass a foreign-manufactured [truck or] minivan." Brief for Federal Respondent 34. The general principle enunciated—that the speaker is talking about American automobiles—carries forward to the illustrative examples (trucks and minivans), and limits them accordingly, even though in isolation they are broader. Congress often uses the word "including" in this manner. In 28 U.S.C. § 1782(a), for example, it refers to "a proceeding in a foreign or international tribunal, including criminal investigations conducted before formal accusation." Certainly this provision would not encompass criminal investigations underway in a domestic tribunal. See also, e.g., 2 U.S.C. § 54(a) ("The Clerk of the House of Representatives shall, at the request of a Member of the House of Representatives, furnish to the Member, for official use only, one set of a privately published annotated version of the United States Code, including supplements and pocket parts"); 22 U.S.C. § 2304(b)(1) ("the relevant findings of appropriate international organizations, including nongovernmental organizations").

In short, the word "including" does not require the Court's (or the petitioners') result. It is perfectly reasonable to view the definition of "air pollutant" in its entirety: An air pollutant can be "any physical, chemical, . . . substance or matter which is emitted into or otherwise enters the ambient air," but only if it retains the general characteristic of being an "air pollution agent or combination of such agents." This is precisely the conclusion EPA reached: "[A] substance does not meet the CAA definition of 'air pollutant' simply because it is a 'physical, chemical, . . . substance or matter which is emitted into or otherwise enters the ambient air.' It must also be an 'air pollution agent.'" 68 Fed. Reg. 52929, n. 3. See also id., at 52928 ("The root of the definition indicates that for a substance to be an 'air pollutant,' it must be an 'agent' of 'air pollution'"). Once again, in the face of textual ambiguity, the Court's application of Chevron deference to EPA's interpretation of the word "including" is nowhere to be found. FN2 Evidently, the Court defers only to those reasonable interpretations that it favors.

FN2. Not only is EPA's interpretation reasonable, it is far more plausible than the Court's alternative. As the Court correctly points out, "all airborne compounds of whatever stripe," ante, at 1460, would qualify as "physical, chemical, . . . substance[s] or matter which [are] emitted into or otherwise ente[r] the ambient air," 42 U.S.C. § 7602(g). It follows that everything airborne, from Frisbees to flatulence, qualifies as an "air pollutant." This reading of the statute defies common sense.

B

Using (as we ought to) EPA's interpretation of the definition of "air pollutant," we must next determine whether greenhouse gases are "agent[s]" of "air pollution." If so, the statute would authorize *1477 regulation; if not, EPA would lack authority.

Unlike "air pollutants," the term "air pollution" is not itself defined by the CAA; thus, once again we must accept EPA's interpretation of that ambiguous term, provided its interpretation is a "permissible construction of the statute." Chevron, 467 U.S., at 843, 104 S. Ct. 2778. In this case, the petition for rulemaking asked EPA for "regulation of [greenhouse gas] emissions from motor vehicles to reduce the risk of global climate change." 68 Fed. Reg. 52925. Thus, in deciding whether it had authority to regulate, EPA had to determine whether the concentration of greenhouse gases assertedly responsible for "global climate change" qualifies as "air pollution." EPA began with the commonsense observation that the "[p]roblems associated with atmospheric concentrations of CO_2," id., at 52927, bear little resemblance to what would naturally be termed "air pollution":

"EPA's prior use of the CAA's general regulatory provisions provides an important context. Since the inception of the Act, EPA has used these provisions to address air pollution problems that occur primarily at ground level or near the surface of the earth. For example, national ambient air quality standards (NAAQS) established under CAA section 109 address concentrations of substances in the ambient air and the related public health and welfare problems. This has meant setting NAAQS for concentrations of ozone, carbon monoxide, particulate matter and other substances in the air near the surface of the earth, not higher in the atmosphere . . . . CO2, by contrast, is fairly consistent in concentration throughout the world's atmosphere up to approximately the lower stratosphere." Id., at 52926–52927.

In other words, regulating the buildup of CO2 and other greenhouse gases in the upper reaches of the atmosphere, which is alleged to be causing global climate change, is not akin to regulating the concentration of some substance that is polluting the air.

We need look no further than the dictionary for confirmation that this interpretation of "air pollution" is eminently reasonable. The definition of "pollute," of course, is "[t]o make or render impure or unclean." Webster's New International Dictionary 1910 (2d ed. 1949). And the first three definitions of "air" are as follows: (1) "[t]he invisible, odorless, and tasteless mixture of gases which surrounds the earth"; (2) "[t]he body of the earth's atmosphere; esp., the part of it near the earth, as distinguished from the upper rarefied part"; (3) "[a] portion of air or of the air considered with respect to physical characteristics or as affecting the senses." Id., at 54. EPA's conception of "air pollution"—focusing on impurities in the "ambient air" "at ground level or near the surface of the earth"—is perfectly consistent with the natural meaning of that term.

In the end, EPA concluded that since "CAA authorization to regulate is generally based on a finding that an air pollutant causes or contributes to air pollution," 68 Fed. Reg. 52928, the concentrations of CO2 and other greenhouse gases allegedly affecting the global climate are beyond the scope of CAA's authorization to regulate. "[T]he term 'air pollution' as used in the regulatory provisions cannot be interpreted to encompass global climate change." Ibid. Once again, the Court utterly fails to explain why this interpretation is incorrect, let alone so unreasonable as to be unworthy of Chevron deference.

. . .

The Court's alarm over global warming may or may not be justified, but it ought *1478 not distort the outcome of this litigation. This is a straightforward administrative-law case, in which Congress has passed a malleable statute giving broad discretion, not to us but to an executive agency. No matter how important the underlying policy issues at stake, this Court has no business substituting its own desired outcome for the reasoned judgment of the responsible agency.

Questions
1. What agency is involved with this case?
2. What federal statute is under review?

3. Nineteen organizations and several states, including Massachusetts, filed suit to force the agency to do something. What is that something?

4. The Environmental Protection Agency (EPA) refused to do this and gave two reasons why it would not. State those two reasons.

5. The Court discusses the standing issue and concludes that the Petitioners (the nineteen organizations and states) have standing. Those three elements of standing are:
   A. That a litigant must demonstrate that it has suffered a concrete and particularized injury that is either actual or imminent. (Injury)
   B. That the injury is fairly traceable to the defendant and that it is likely that a favorable decision will result. (Causation)
   C. That a court has the ability to redress that injury. (Redressibility—the Remedy)

Summarize what the Court stated on each of these three parts of standing.

6. The Court is exercising judicial review as it decides this case. What is the scope of review of the Supreme Court in this case?

7. The Court discusses the fact that the sovereign state of Massachusetts is one of the parties and therefore has a unique place with respect to the standing issue.

Discuss this statement with respect to issues of federalism.

8. The preceding questions center on procedural issues and standing. When the Court turns to the underlying case, it is addressing *the merits* of the case. What is the first question on the merits, and how does the Court answer it?

9. A. Give the reasons the EPA says it cannot regulate greenhouse gases.
   B. Explain how these reasons fit into the concept of congressional delegation of power to administrative agencies such as the EPA.
   C. Explain how these reasons fit into the concept of presidential control of administrative agencies.

10. Even if the EPA has the authority to regulate greenhouse gases, it says it would not anyway.
    A. State why.
    B. How does this fit into the concept of agency discretion?

11. How does the Court answer the EPA concerning the answers to questions 9 and 10?

12. The Court's ruling gives specific instructions on how the EPA was to proceed with respect to the regulation of

greenhouse gases. State what the Court said the EPA must do.

13. Chief Justice Roberts, in dissent, disagrees with the Court that there is standing in the case. What are the Chief Justice's main arguments?

A P P E N D I X   E

ADMINISTRATIVE LAW SUMMARY

Creation
Created by the enabling act when Congress or a state legislature delegates power to an administrative agency.
   • Delegation requires an intelligible principle.

History
Early Years of the Country—1789–1870s
Populist Era—1870s–1890s
Progressive Era—1890s–1920s
Depression and New Deal—1920s–1930s
Post New Deal and Adoption of Administrative Procedure
   Act (APA)—1946
Modern Era—1960–Present

Sources of Administrative Law
The Constitution
Statutes
Federal and State Administrative Procedure Acts
Common Law
Executive Orders
Rules or Regulations

POWER POSSESSED BY MANY AGENCIES THROUGH DELEGATION

Legislative—agencies issue regulations
Executive—agencies investigate and enforce their regulations
Judicial—agencies adjudicate disputes

MULTITUDE OF NAMES OF AN AGENCY

Agency
Bureau
Commission
Board
Department
Center
Office
Authority

OVERVIEW OF AGENCY ACTIVITY

Legislative Power
Rules/Regulation
Informal Rulemaking
Formal Rulemaking
Hybrid Rulemaking
Exempted Rulemaking
Negotiated Rulemaking
Federal Regulations Published in the Federal Register and Code of
    Federal Regulations

Executive Power
Enforcement of Regulations
Record Keeping and Reporting
Investigations/Inspections
Search Warrants and the Fourth Amendment
Subpoenas and the Fourth Amendment
Agency Enforcement by Filling a Complaint
Fifth Amendment Rights
Fifth Amendment and State Agencies
Issues of Immunity

Judicial Power
Formal Adjudications
Informal Adjudications

Overview of Agency Activity
Applications and Claims
Licensing
Negotiations, Settlement, and Alternative Dispute Resolution
    Agency Advice Testing and Inspections Recalls, Seizures,
    Suspensions and Quarantines Agency Disclosure of Information
    Freedom of Information Act Privacy Act

Adjudication and Rulemaking Compared

Adjudication	Judicial function	Involves specified individuals	Looks backward	Resolves conflicts	An administrative law judge can issue an order granting social Security benefits.
Rulemaking	Legislative function	Involves large groups	Looks forward	Implements law by filling gaps	Social Security Administration issues a rule defining disability and the criteria to be met to obtain benefits.

CONTROL OF ADMINISTRATIVE AGENCIES

Judicial Control
Judicial Review
Procedural Due Process
Substantive Due Process
Other Fundamental Rights
Strict Scrutiny and Rational Basis
Equal Protection
Classifications Under Equal Protection
Equal Protection—Race—Strict Scrutiny
Equal Protection—Fundamental Rights—Strict Scrutiny
Equal Protection—Gender—Middle Level
Equal Protection—Illegitimacy—Middle Level
Equal Protection—Economic and Social Classifications—Rational Basis
Equal Protection—Alienage—Strict Scrutiny and Rational Basis
Equal Protection—Other Classifications—Rational Basis
Equal Protection and Affirmative Action
Delegated Power and Judicial Control
Judicial Control and Agency Discretion
How Much Judicial Review? Scope of Review
Judicial Review of Agency Inaction
Barriers to Judicial Review
The Statute Precludes Review
The Decision Is Committed to Agency Discretion
Exhaustion of Administrative Remedies and Ripeness
Final Agency Action and Deadlines to Appeal
Standing
Primary Jurisdiction
Other Methods of Judicial Control—Lawsuits

Legislative Control

Control by the Enabling Act
Control by Abolition and Sunset
Control by New Legislation
Control by Funding
Control by Approval of Agency Officials
Control by Oversight
Control by Direct Contact
Control by Sunshine Provisions
Control by Legislative Veto
Control by the Congressional Review Act
Paperwork Reduction Act
Regulatory Flexibility Act and Unfunded Mandates Act
Agencies to Oversee Other Agencies
Advisory Committees

Executive Control

Appointment/Removal Power and Separation of Powers
Power over the Budget
Executive Orders
Control by Policy Setting
Power to Veto
Power over Litigation
Reorganization
Power to Pardon

Glossary

A

adjudicate—power of courts to hold hearings and settle disputes delegation.

administrative agency—a subbranch of the government set up by a legislature to carry out laws by wielding legislative, executive, and judicial power.

administrative law—the study of how agencies are created, how agencies do their work in exercising their delegated powers, and how agencies are controlled.

administrative law judge—the official who is the presiding officer at administrative hearings. Depending on the applicable agency, this person can also be called a hearings examiner, hearings officer, referee, or claims examiner.

Administrative Procedure Act (APA)—a federal law that describes how federal agencies must do business (such as rulemaking, holding hearings, and other procedures) and how disputes go from the federal agencies into a court. Some states also have administrative procedure acts.

affirmative action—programs designed to include disfavored minorities into areas where they have been excluded because of past discrimination.

Alternative Dispute Resolution (ADR)—the term used for the various methods to quickly and efficiently resolve matters before an agency.

Appointments Clause—a provision in the U.S. Constitution, Article II, Section 2 that vests power to the president to appoint officials to the federal government.

B

bicameralism—the principle that requires both houses of Congress to pass a bill before the bill can be presented to the president.

C

Code of Federal Regulations—the compilation of all the rules and regulations issued by federal agencies. It is updated each year and divided into subject areas.

Commerce Clause—the provision of the U.S. Constitution, Article I, Section 8, Clause 3 that gives Congress power to control interstate commerce; also known as commerce power.

Common Law—legal principles created by judges in the absence of a statute.

compelling interest—a strong enough reason for a state that justifies and makes Constitutional the use of race.

concurrent power—power that is possessed by both the federal and state governments.

consent decree—the settlement of an administrative adjudication in which a person or business agrees to take certain actions without admitting fault.

D

de novo—trying a case as if no decision had been made.

delegation—the transfer of power from Congress to an executive agency.

delegation doctrine—when Congress creates an agency by passing a law (an enabling act) and transferring power to the agency. The transfer of legislative, executive, and judicial power is delegation that gives life to the agency and enables the agency to do its work.

department—the major administrative division headed by an officer of cabinet rank who is known as a secretary.

discretion—the ability of an agency to make choices concerning how the agency will do its work.

due process clause of the Fifth Amendment—prohibits the federal government from depriving persons of life, liberty, or property without due process of law.

due process clause of the Fourteenth Amendment—prohibits the states from depriving persons of life, liberty, or property without due process of law.

E

enabling act—a statute which creates and empowers an administrative agency.

entitlements—various forms of government benefits that cannot be taken away without due process.

enumerated powers—the powers granted to Congress and listed specifically in Article I of the U.S. Constitution.

Equal Protection Clause—the Fourteenth Amendment requirement that states not set up illegal categories to justify treating people unfairly.

estoppel—an equitable doctrine invoked to avoid injustice when one person makes a misrepresentation of fact to another person and that other person reasonably relies on the misrepresentation to his detriment.

executive order—a directive issued by the president or governor to agencies or officials the purpose of which is to implement a statute or an administrative policy.

executive power—power to investigate and carry out rules and regulations.

exempted rules—rules that are not implemented by formal or informal methods and which generally do not have the force of law.

exhaustion of administrative remedies—the principle that a court will not exercise judicial review before the review procedures inside the agency are completed.

F

Federal Register—the first place where federal rules and regulations are published.

federalism—the division of power into one federal government and the government of the 50 states.

formal agency activity—actions taken by an agency with a formal hearing that is on the record.

formal rulemaking—when an agency uses a hearing on the record to establish a rule.

Freedom of Information Act (FOIA)—a law that requires federal agencies to disclose records or information upon written request.

fundamental rights—basic or crucial rights that are most strongly protected by the U.S. Constitution.

H

hearing—also called an adjudication; the process in which facts and evidence are presented before an agency official for a decision.

hearing on the record—an enabling act provision which requires an agency to perform formal rulemaking and formal adjudication.

hybrid rule—a rule with some characteristics of both formal and informal rulemaking.

I

immunity—the freedom from prosecution based on anything the witnesses says that is given by the government to a witness who is forced to testify.

independent agency—an agency not under the direct control of the president which can be headed by a single person or be composed of multiple members in the form of a board or commission.

informal agency activity—actions taken by an agency that are not on the record and without a formal hearing.

informal rulemaking—rulemaking done with the notice and comment procedure.

intelligible principle—the principle that when Congress delegates power to an agency, the delegation includes enough guidelines and standards for the agency to exercise that power in a Constitutional manner.

interstate commerce—things, people, and commercial activities that cross state lines.

J

judicial review—1. when a court looks at a decision of an administrative agency to see if the decision of the agency is in conformity with Constitutional and statutory requirements. The decision reviewed by the court can be rulemaking or adjudication. 2. The power to declare acts of Congress, actions of the president, and acts of the states unconstitutional when those acts conflict with the U.S. Constitution. Judicial review in the context of administrative law also means when a court looks at a decision of an administrative agency to see if the decision of the agency is in conformity with Constitutional and statutory requirements. The decision reviewed by the court can be rulemaking or adjudication.

L

leak—an unauthorized release of information by an anonymous agency employee.

legislative rule—a rule that has the force of law and carries out the intent of the statute, the most familiar of which are formal and informal.

legislative veto—the power of the legislative branch to cancel or veto a decision of an agency. The Congressional legislative veto was declared to be unconstitutional in the case of *INS v. Chadha*, 462 U.S. 919 (1983).

liberty—a Constitutional right that not only includes freedom from bodily restraint, but also the fundamental right of individuals to procreate, to use contraceptives, to have an abortion, to travel, to refuse medical attention, to live as a family, to marry (heterosexual), and to make decisions regarding child rearing.

line item veto—a law that gives authority to the president or a governor to cancel individual items of spending. The presidential line item veto was declared unconstitutional in the case of *Clinton v. New York*, 524 U.S. 417 (1998).

M

middle level scrutiny—the test used when a law classifies on the basis of gender or illegitimacy. The law must be substantially related to important governmental interests to be Constitutional under the Equal Protection Clause.

N

narrowly tailored—a requirement that is designed to ensure that the use of race furthers a compelling state interest.

Necessary and Proper Clause—the provision of the U.S. Constitution (Article I, Section 8, Clause 18) that gives Congress the power to pass all laws appropriate to carry out its functions; also called the elastic clause.

nondelegation doctrine—the limits and requirements for a Constitutionally valid transfer of power to an agency as established by the Supreme Court.

O

official notice—when an agency decisionmaker recognizes the existence of certain facts without proof.

open fields doctrine—the principle that a search warrant is not usually required for search of an open area far from an occupied building.

order—the final disposition of an administrative adjudication. The order can compel an action or provide a penalty for violation of a regulation.

P

plain view—the rule that if police officers see or come across something while acting lawfully, that item may be used as evidence in a trial even if the police did not have a search warrant.

police power—power possessed by states to pass laws for the health, safety, and welfare of its citizens.

political appointees—heads of the cabinet who serve at the pleasure of the president and who can be removed by the president at any time and for any reason.

preempted—when Congress takes over an entire field of law by passing laws under the Supremacy Clause, with the nullifying of conflicting state law.

preponderance of the evidence—the standard of proof required in most administrative hearings, just enough evidence to make it more likely than not that the claimant should win; or being convinced by about 51 percent.

primary jurisdiction—the principle that even if a court has the power to hear a case, if the case involves issues that are better decided by an administrative agency, the court will give the agency the first opportunity to resolve the issue.

Privacy Act—federal statute that sets out agency procedures for maintaining records on individuals and which gives the right of an individual to have access to his or her records and correct any errors.

privilege—the right to prevent disclosure, or duty to refrain from disclosing information communicated within a specially recognized confidential relationship.

procedural due process—requires the government to provide a fair procedure before life, liberty, or property can be taken away.

R

rational basis—the test used to assess all laws that do not implicate a fundamental right; the law only needs to be rationally related to a legitimate state interest.

record—the information the agency actually uses in reaching its decisions.

regulatory agency—an agency that issues rules and regulations that must be obeyed by individuals and businesses; for example, the Environmental Protection Agency (EPA) is a regulatory agency.

removal for cause—the principle that an official does not serve at the pleasure of the president and can only be removed for misconduct or incapacity.

ripeness—the doctrine whose basic rationale is to prevent the courts, through avoidance of premature adjudication, from entangling themselves in abstract disagreements over administrative policies and also to protect the agencies from judicial interference until an administrative decision has been formalized and its effects felt in a concrete way.

rule or regulation—a statement of policy issued by an agency to implement a statute and which has the force of law. Rules and regulations represent the legislative power of agencies.

S

search warrant—a court order directing that a search and seizure can occur. In criminal law, it is issued on a showing of probable cause.

social welfare agency—an agency that dispenses social services such as Social Security.

standing—a person's right to bring a claim because he or she is directly affected by the issues raised.

state action—the principle that only the federal, state, or local governments can violate Constitutional rights.

statutes—laws enacted by a legislature.

strict scrutiny—the test used to assess a law that implicates a fundamental right; the law must be necessary to further a compelling state interest.

subcabinet—an agency that is located inside a cabinet department; for example, the Centers for Disease Control (CDC) is located inside the Department of Health and Human Services.

subpoena—a court's order to a person that he or she appears in court to testify in a case. Some administrative agencies may also issue subpoenas.

subpoena duces tecum—a subpoena by which a person is commanded to bring documents to court or to an administrative agency.

substantive due process—the principle stemming from "liberty" of the due process clause which bars arbitrary government actions regardless of the fairness of the procedures used to implement them.

substantive law—the area of law that establishes rights, responsibilities, and duties.

sunset provision—a provision of an enabling act that calls for the termination of an agency in a fixed time period.

sunshine laws—a law requiring open meetings of government agencies.

Supremacy Clause—Article VI, Clause 2 of the U.S. Constitution which makes the Constitution and federal law superior to conflicting state law.

suspect class—a group such as racial or ethnic minorities that has suffered historic, intentional discrimination and thus requires extraordinary protection by the courts.

T

Tenth Amendment—the Amendment that states that all powers not given to the federal government are reserved to the states and the people.

W

whistle-blower statute—a law that provides legal protection to a government employee when the employee releases information that exposes government wrongdoing.

Index

Dow Chemical Co. v. United States, 476 U.S. 227, 239 (1986), 86
drug testing, 88
due process clause, 174, 182t, 216
    procedural, 174–179, 179t
    substantive, 179–181
    violations of, 214
Dunlop v. Bachowski, 421 U.S. 560 (1975), 239
Dye, David G., 276

E

"Earth Summit," 427
economic classifications, 189–190, 191
EDF. *See* Environmental Defense Fund
education
    classification, 191
    Department of, 29t
EEOC. *See* Equal Employment Opportunity Commission
enabling act, 12, 264–266
Endangered Species
    Act, 215
    list, 270
Energy
    Department of, 29t
    Policy Act of 1992, 444
    Policy and Conservation Act, 445
entitlement, 177
enumerated powers, 8
Environmental Defense Center v. Babbitt, 73 F.3d 867 (9th Cir. 1995), 270
Environmental Defense Fund (EDF), 158
Environmental Protection Agency (EPA), 8, 9, 144, 423
    creation of, 314
    failure of, 448
    hazardous waste laws implemented by, 158
    obligations of, 197–198
    pollutant standards set by, 18
    regulation of motor vehicle emissions, 460
Environmental Quality: The First Annual Report 93, 425
EPA. *See* Environmental Protection Agency
Equal Employment Opportunity Commission (EEOC), 8, 64, 266
    enforcement procedures, 92–93
equal protection clause, 184–185, 187–188
    affirmative action and, 191, 193–195
    alienage and, 190–191

classifications under, 185, 192t
economic classifications and, 189–190
gender and, 188–189
illegitimacy and, 189
social classifications and, 189–190
ergonomics, 271, 279
    OSHA on, 270
    rejection of rule on, 280t
estoppel, 144, 145
Ethyl Corp. v. EPA, 541 F.2d 1, 25 (C.A.D.C. 1976), 425
evidence, preponderance of, 113
executive control, 300
Executive department, 26–27, 28t–31t
    list of, 265
executive orders, 23, 303–308
    congressional hearing on use of, 329
    list of, 308, 329
    10,340, 318
    13,281, 304
    12,866, 306, 407–421
executive power, 9, 80

F

FAA. *See* Federal Aviation Administration
FCC. *See* Federal Communications Commission
FCC v. League of Women Voters of Cal. 468 U.S. 364 (1984), 326
FDA. *See* Food and Drug Administration
FDA v. Brown and Williamson, 529 U.S. 120 (2000), 66, 173
FDIC. *See* Federal Deposit Insurance Corporation
Federal Advisory Committees Act, 282
Federal Aviation Administration (FAA), 142, 272
Federal Communications Commission (FCC), 142, 264
Federal Deposit Insurance Corporation (FDIC), 98, 100
    Professional Liability Section of, 99
Federal Election Commission (FEC), 301
Federal Election Comm'n v. Akins, 524 U.S. 11, 24, 118 S. Ct. 1777, 141 L.Ed.2d 10 (1998), 437
Federal Energy Regulatory Commission, 34
Federal Home Loan Bank Board (FHLBB), 278
federalism, 7, 181